Diffidence and Ambition

The Intellectual Sources
of U.S. Foreign Policy

New Approaches to Peace and Security
Richard Ned Lebow, Series Editor

Anxiety about conventional and nuclear war has triggered a corresponding interest in books that treat these themes. This burgeoning literature is largely descriptive and narrowly technical and often reflects a prodefense bias. This series, by contrast, will address broader theoretical and policy questions associated with conflict and conflict management. On the whole, its perspective is critical of conventional wisdom in the realm of both policy and theory. The overarching goal of the series is to help lay the intellectual foundations for alternative approaches to thinking about security.

Titles in This Series

This publication was made possible
through the cooperation of Biblioteca Italia,
a Giovanni Agnelli Foundation program
for the diffusion of Italian culture.

Diffidence and Ambition

The Intellectual Sources of U.S. Foreign Policy

Carlo Maria Santoro

Westview Press

BOULDER • SAN FRANCISCO • OXFORD

E
806
S28613
1991

New Approaches to Peace and Security

Table 1 is reprinted from Wilfred Hardy Callcott, *The Western Hemisphere* (Austin: University of Texas Press, 1968), p. 384; used by permission of the University of Texas Press. Table 2 is reprinted from Samuel Eliot Morison, *History of the United States Naval Operations in World War II, Volume I, The Battle of the Atlantic, 1939–1943* (Boston: Little, Brown, 1947), p. lxi, copyright © 1947 by Samuel Eliot Morison; used by permission of Little, Brown and Company.

English-language edition copyright © 1992 by Westview Press, Inc. Translated by Andrew Ellis and Leslie Gunn. This translation has been revised and updated from the Italian original.

English-language edition published in 1992 in the United States of America by Westview Press, Inc., 5500 Central Avenue, Boulder, Colorado 80301-2847, and in the United Kingdom by Westview Press, 36 Lonsdale Road, Summertown, Oxford OX2 7EW

First published in 1987 in Italy as *La perla e l'ostrica: Alle origini della politica globale Americana* by Franco Angeli, Milan

Library of Congress Cataloging-in-Publication Data
Santoro, Carlo Maria, 1935–
  [Perla e l'ostrica. English]
  Diffidence and ambition : the intellectual sources of U.S. foreign
policy / Carlo Maria Santoro ; translated by Andrew Ellis
and Leslie Gunn.
    p. cm. — (New approaches to peace and security)
  Translation of: La perla e l'ostrica.
  Includes bibliographical references and index.
  ISBN 0-8133-7710-2
  1. United States—Foreign relations—1933–1945. 2. World War,
1939–1945—Diplomatic history. 3. World War, 1939–1945—United
States. 4. Council on Foreign Relations—History. I. Title.
II. Series.
E806.S28613 1992
327.73—dc20   91-21126
                                                                         CIP

FLORIDA STATE
UNIVERSITY LIBRARIES

NOV 2

TALLAHASSEE, FLORIDA

Printed and bound in the United States of America

The paper used in this publication meets the requirements
of the American National Standard for Permanence of Paper
for Printed Library Materials Z39.48-1984.

10   9   8   7   6   5   4   3   2   1

Why, then the world's mine oyster,
which I with sword will open.

—William Shakespeare

I consider the world as made for me, not me for the world. It is my maxim
therefore to enjoy it while I can, and let futurity shift for itself.

—Tobias G. Smollet

An American is a complex of occasions themselves a geometry of spatial nature.

—Charles Olson Maximus

Contents

Acknowledgments

The idea for this book came to me in June 1977 as I was crossing the threshold of the Council on Foreign Relations (CFR) building, at the intersection of Park Avenue and 68th Street in New York, about to hold a conference on Eurocommunism. The austere temple of American internationalism I was entering had over the past sixty years been honored by great thinkers, statesmen and prime ministers, and scholars and specialists of every race and country and in 1922 had inaugurated the publication *Foreign Affairs*, one of the world leaders in its field. The establishment suddenly struck me as a singular workshop of intellectual creativity that successfully produced and developed information and ideas, receiving and transmitting information on international politics, a temple kept permanently up to date by a highly trained staff, a tight web of collaborators, and a constant flow of diverse guests.

The building's basement housed a treasury, only partially explored, of half-finished or never-operationalized projects, which would prove a richer source of information on American political culture than the diplomatic records and official paperwork. What particularly attracted me was the special documentation on the War and Peace Studies (WPS) project carried out over the period 1939–1945; given the specific nature of that documentation, it was a highly appetizing quarry. The WPS records included memoranda written by people belonging to the internationalist milieu, which found its voice when the war in Europe finally coaxed the United States out of the confines of its isolationist lake and into the open sea of globalism. I was not disappointed, even though it took many years to piece together this book from the wealth of analytical writings I found there.

Several institutions allowed me to work in comfort, putting all their facilities at my disposal: their archives, libraries, and work areas. First and foremost, the council allowed me to plunder its archives on several occasions, starting in 1979. Then at the Center for International Affairs at Harvard I spent a most fecund period of research as a fellow in 1981. And finally, I worked also at the U.S. National Archives in Washington, D.C., and Suitland, Maryland; the New York Public Library; the Franklin D. Roosevelt Library in Hyde Park, New York; the Library of Congress in Washington; the Sterling Library at Yale; the Princeton University Library (Woodrow Wilson Institute); the Columbia Oral History Collections at Columbia University, New York; and the Hoover Institution on War, Revolution and Peace at Stanford University, where I was able to compare the CFR records with available diplomatic and personal accounts, some of governmental origin, some from other study centers, and with secondary literature, either contemporary or written later. The Italian Ministry of Education also assisted me in my work by partially financing this research project.

Throughout this "odyssey" through the realm of American internationalism I received help and advice from a great many people in both Italy and the United States. I would like to be able to mention them all, but no doubt the list would still be incomplete. So I shall only mention those with a special contribution to the production of this book.

First and foremost, my thanks go to William Diebold, former senior research fellow at the CFR in New York, who helped me through the labyrinth of archives and names at the council, virtually guiding me by the hand. He also kept a close and thoughtful watch on the gradual development of the book, patiently reading numerous early drafts of the various chapters as I reworked them, clarifying and integrating the new information I had gathered, enhancing the text with facts, and putting at my disposal the rich, annotated bibliography he himself had compiled between 1941 and 1945 for the Economic and Financial Group of the CFR. I would also like to thank those members of the CFR who during the ensuing years have kept me in constant touch with the council. These include Winston Lord, John Temple Swing, Zygmunt Nagorski, Edward Morse, Margaret Osmer, Rolland Bushner, Grace Darling Griffin, Janet Rigney, and the librarians and archivists.

I am also very grateful to those kind friends and colleagues who spared the time to read sections or whole chapters of the work in preparation or who helped me in my search for source material. Those who helped me in the United States include Robert D. Putnam, Ernest R. May, Charles S. Maier, Stanley Hoffmann, Samuel P. Huntington, Joseph La Palombara, and Eric Foner. In Italy they include Luigi Bonanate, David W. Ellwood, Maurizio Vaudagna, Douglas Stuart (who suggested the original Italian title), Richard Ned Lebow, Andrew Ellis (who translated the book), Leslie Gunn (who revised the English translation), Luisa Cucchi, and Sandro Perini (who assisted me in compiling the Notes and the Bibliography).

While carrying out my research, I received firsthand information and knowledgeable advice through interviews with and letters from a wide number of specialists, people who were witnesses and survivors of the processes and events described in these pages. Special mention must go to William T.R. Fox, Gaddis Smith, John K. Galbraith, Fritz Stern, Harry Magdoff, Paul M. Sweezy, Alger Hiss, Laurence Shoup, William Minter, Anton W. DePorte, Arthur Upgren, Lauchlin Currie, and Eugene Staley. I owe special thanks to John Keller, Gisa Pedani, and Margherita Uras, from the United States Information Service (USIS) in Milan, for their kind help on many occasions.

A separate word of thanks must go to Lorenzo Attolico and Enzo Viscusi, faithful friends in New York, and Eric Nordlinger of Cambridge, Massachusetts, who were party to my enterprise from the very outset, giving me invaluable support. Without them this research would never have reached completion.

Naturally, I accept all responsibility for the text and for whatever errors and omissions the reader may find.

Carlo Maria Santoro

Introduction

In a famous verse in *The Merry Wives of Windsor*, Shakespeare wrote, "Why, then the world's mine oyster, which I with sword will open" (2.2.2). Paraphrased in different ways, this verse became popular in the United States in the 1950s and 1960s and was frequently cited to represent the recent definitive "internationalization" of the U.S. political role.

Shakespeare's verse was translated into modern terms to read, "The world is our oyster." But it is a complex metaphor that hides as much as it reveals. If the world is the oyster, the shell, the crust, then the United States can only be the pearl, a "City of the Sun," which a Manifest Destiny has consigned to all humankind. In that case the oyster would provide nourishment to the pearl, linked in a differentiated and asymmetrical relationship of interdependence. But the oyster is also a hard shell, a tight refuge that both protects and imprisons, safeguarding the pearl, a container that, in the words of Shakespeare, "I with sword will open." The semantic ambivalence of the saying is self-evident. It reflects the profound contradictions of a country in the throes of a genetic mutation, a radical upheaval brought about by its globalization on an international political level.

There is another equally enlightening quote that bestows further meaning on the metaphor of the "pearl and the oyster," this time from *Roderick Random*, by Tobias Smollett, an eighteenth-century novelist reintroduced by critic Harold Bloom to contemporary literary circles in the United States. Smollett wrote, "I consider the world as made for me, not me for the world. It is my maxim therefore to enjoy it while I can, and let futurity shift for itself." Two quotes, two distinct, even contrasting, outlooks. On the one hand, there is the conviction of being at the center of the world, of controlling its mechanisms, even of turning them to one's own advantage by breaking the chains that had impeded the United States from fulfilling its destiny. On the other hand, there are the unshakable traces of a philosophy that "every man is an island," of a nation essentially alienated from and suspicious of all things beyond its own continent, but nonetheless infused with an optimistic self-confidence and belief in its own strength. This is the United States that emerged to face the new bipolar international system, which it so

1

decidedly contributed to creating. The rules of that system, however, in those early years, had yet to be written. Our task is to assess the degree of Americanization of the world and, in particular, the links of interdependence binding the leading superpower with the global system.

Let us imagine the international political system, especially the one in force during the "Thirty Years' War, 1914–1945,"[1] as a kind of complex work of architecture, composed of pillars and columns, arches and cupolas, stairs and false projections, mirrors and glass, little shacks and imposing cathedrals, all interlocking, as intricate as the awesome natural architecture of the tropical rain forests. The ecology of this labyrinthine structure cannot be classified, once and for all, by applying some kind of grammar to each of its "units,"[2] or "actors." We would need an external viewpoint, a tree high above all the others or, even better, a telescopic view from another planet to enable us to contemplate the dynamics and revolutions of the international system, to distinguish and classify the types of actors involved and determine its structure. But we would also need to follow the inner workings of its interactive mechanisms, so as to define its functions and trends.

Since, however, it is quite obvious that the international system cannot be thus scrutinized from afar, we are obliged to fix our sights on specific angles and vistas, each one different, to gain a set of distinct perspectives and images of the situation, according to quality and dimension and whether the viewer is an actor observing for political purposes or an analyst trying to fathom the hidden laws of motion. This multiplicity of viewpoints, this anomalous and "a-centric" condition,[3] this continuous reciprocal scrutiny between nations and other actors, from above, from below, sideways, and the bizarre and sometimes misleading perspectives that emerge represent far more than a straightforward hierarchy of power or role or function, the geometrical differences between the axes and therefore the position of the various points on the international time-space continuum.[4]

What frequently happens is that certain medium powers (such as Italy), or "minor" ones (e.g., Honduras), observe their giant neighbors, the Soviet Union, China, the United States, and see only what they can distinguish and not the overall design of the latter's actions or the image these giants wish to project to the outside world. This dilemma manifests itself in the form of the political initiatives of giants and minor actors alike and engenders cases of critical misperception[5] or even conflict.[6] In each case, the multiplicity of perspectives and the differences of each horizon are immediately felt in the performance of the actors in the system, impairing general efficiency and functioning.[7]

In other words, Honduras, basing its understanding on its own horizon and international viewpoint, as well as its historical experience, might well claim that since the United States has tended to be heavy-handed in Central America, Honduras has no means of international communication other than political and economic violence.[8] To extend the metaphor, it might likewise be suggested that from its own position (marginal and subordinate within the dynamics of the Caribbean), Honduras, which gets nothing but the "boot" from its colossal neighbor, reasonably assumes that this all-pervading presence is an integral part of U.S. foreign policy, a policy in which any form of subtlety or more sophisticated diplomacy is utterly outlawed.

Thus, the "authoritarian," "revolutionary," or "rebel" paths to independence and sovereignty become quite natural. Likewise, putsch mentalities are equally natural, in the name of maintaining the domestic and/or regional status quo. The larger national actors can fall into the same error. Their viewing angle is similarly distorted by their height and breadth, and by the intellectual and cultural distance between them and the reality of those with whom they are trying to communicate.

Frequently the United States has presented itself as a massive political, economic, and ethical monolith equipped with a formidable concentration of real power and persuasive ability and hence adept at commanding (and controlling) other countries. Yet its initiatives toward outsiders are much more filtered and diluted than those of other countries, owing to the dense jungle of domestic politics impeding the way to the ocean of international politics.

This centrifugal course required of U.S. policy has undoubtedly drained and benumbed the vast concentration of power that, theoretically, the U.S. government has had at its disposal. As a result, its initiatives have been seriously impaired, inconsistent, and ineffectual. This brand of "bilateral nearsightedness" afflicts both large and small objects and actors in the international system (though in different ways and for different reasons) and is accompanied by a marked astigmatism in focusing problems and situations, which as a result appear bloated and distorted.

For these reasons, when I embarked on my study of U.S. foreign relations during and after World War II, focusing specifically on the formation of the key concepts of foreign policy, I was inevitably apprehensive, not only about the obvious scientific and technical difficulties, but also about trespassing on land that was only half-explored. I was entering a realm dotted with allusive "fixtures" and symbolic relics of the U.S. domestic political system written in a practically unknown—and, for a European, often untranslatable—language. This was the realm (or jealous reserve?) of shrewd and knowledgeable U.S. historians of World War II and the cold war.[9]

I decided to advance, albeit tentatively, with wholly inadequate means and utmost prudence, guided by a difference of viewpoint that perhaps only European scholars could allow themselves, though at their own risk. It seemed that this quest was worth the effort. I took it for granted that it would be impossible to achieve a complete, firsthand idea of the geographical and cultural "context" of this particularly fecund moment in U.S. political history. I therefore did not expect to acquire a scientific understanding of the history of the United States over the 1930s and 1940s. Instead, I limited my inquiry to gathering an extensive bibliography of secondary sources and plowed my way through every detail of a debate that had engaged all the various schools of historiography— orthodox, revisionist, and postrevisionist alike—creating a kind of conceptual safety net that permitted me to indulge in some acrobatic interpretations, some of which I imagine will perplex historians but may, I hope, be received with greater understanding by political scientists.

Thus forewarned, I had no pretensions to being able to decode the established schemes of interpretation and analytical models that filled the literature on the contemporary international system. Instead I thought I might confirm their validity with the help of a special case study, namely, the War and Peace Studies, piloted by the Council on Foreign Relations of New York. My inquiry was thus focused on the formation of certain sets of symbolic concepts that could be loosely grouped into two formulas, "interdependence" and "national security," which seemed to provide an invaluable key to interpreting U.S. foreign policy in the decades since the last war. From my vantage point in Europe, these two concepts and their respective sets of underpinning ideas seemed (somewhat emblematically perhaps) to embody the two basic "rationales" of U.S. political philosophy toward the rest of the world.

Despite the great complexity and internal differentiation of the bipolar international system, its evolution in the decades following 1945 was driven by two counterpoised forces, moving in parallel, which in the United States went by the name of "interdependence" and "national security." Even the current crisis in the bipolar system—more strictly a crisis of performance than of identity—brought on by the steady diffusion of power and the implosion of the Communist world,[10] can be traced back to the very first step, namely, the war itself.[11]

In the past twenty years, American and European authors have often pored over the bipolar system, in the hope of forecasting its future behavior; alternatively they have sketched blueprints to explain how it "normally" functions.[12] Often, however, such analysts have forgotten the original geopolitical coordinates, namely, the division of the globe into two subsystems governed by wholly different laws and forms of management, subsystems that to this day largely embody the tactical positions reached at the close of World War II, especially in the Old and New Worlds.

1

The American Theorem

The Premise

The "time" of history and the "time" of politics do not usually coincide, and rarely do they merge into a single process of social action. When they do, it is a magical moment in which the equilibriums, especially international ones, disintegrate, and new actors come onstage, replacing existing hegemonies and leaders, as the latter decline or expire.[1] The pattern of events suddenly becomes more complex, and the tension reaches such a pitch that the only escape valve is war, that great generator and restorer of order and of international, regional, and global structures.[2]

World War II was one such exceptional moment, when the timeworn international balance of power—still buckling under the awesome weight of the events of World War I—was inexorably shattered by the blitz the Germans unleashed on the western front in May–June 1940. Between 1940 and 1945 international society lived through the dramatic experience of this singular fusion of history and politics as it sought a new order to give cohesion to an approaching postwar world. Every option was possible, including an "imperial" system of Axis powers, a polyarchy of the smaller powers,[3] schemes of "restoration" involving the ex-"godfathers" of the old Eurocentric system, and the Comintern's messianic expectations of world revolution.

The bipolar international system that actually did emerge after the events of the war had not been among the options considered feasible at the time. It was certainly not part of the plans of the United States, which, at the outbreak of war in 1939, was still busy deciding how to relate to the rest of the world.[4] Nonetheless, this fusion of history and politics, which had become all too clear by the summer of 1940, drove the United States into a long period of questioning and self-analysis, and the issue of the U.S. role in the world has not been entirely resolved even today.[5]

This issue is one of the central concerns of U.S. political tradition: Questions are asked about the form such a relationship could or should

5

take; the degree of the world's permeability to American culture, and vice versa; and the usefulness or risk (or the cost-efficiency) that this contact entails. One might even go as far as to say that these have been persistent issues since colonial times.[6] The controversial nature and sheer complexity of the interpretations adopted are the very fabric of the "American theorem." The solution seems to be different each time and yet remains unchanged, as if the definitive answer is being perpetually postponed because of the controversial dynamic of the U.S. role in the world.

As it had been at least twice before (in 1898 and, more important, in 1914), the United States in 1940 was obliged to inquire into the real nature and structure of its relationship with the international framework, both as a compendium of separate states with which Washington maintained more or less positive diplomatic, commercial, and financial relations and as an overall system of interactions, that is, a functional machine that influenced, and was in turn affected by, the behavior of each of its component parts.[7]

The sudden power vacuum created by the fall of France was in danger of being filled by a continental, Germanized Europe that was ready to swallow up Great Britain and from there reach out across the Atlantic.[8] The United States and the American continent (North and South America) suddenly risked becoming the front line in a head-on confrontation with the new European tyranny. The immunity the Americans had enjoyed for 170 years had quite unexpectedly been put in jeopardy.

Hence the search for international power formulas and scenarios that might effectively halt such a nightmare from becoming a reality—or delay it as long as possible. And hence the growing U.S. awareness of the need for the nation to assume a more decisive role in the European conflict, and perhaps later in the postwar world, to bail out a Eurocentric international system that had begun to list badly.

After the negative experiences of the interwar years, the "American theorem" became more complex. From the start, the scenarios analyzed were less naïve than Woodrow Wilson's earlier hypotheses of the League of Nations.[9] The institutional machinery envisaged for the "new world" (the United Nations) was not restricted to legalistic norms and procedural rules alone, as the League of Nations had been, but involved international policing carried out by the four Great Powers—especially by the strongest of the four, the United States.[10] There could be the deployment of armed forces to safeguard the international order, to patrol and supervise the entire planet. The Americans had learned from the problematic economic relations between the wars and from the harmful drift of political and strategic matters, which had begun to deteriorate drastically in 1931 with the Japanese invasion of Manchuria. They were considering the remaining options for relations with the rest of the world, should Roosevelt's dream of the United Nations prove too ambitious. The gradual and almost "natural" subjection of nearly all the Great Powers (with the partial exception of the Soviet Union) to U.S. military, political, and economic hegemony and guardianship—largely envisaged from the beginning of the hostilities[11] and subsequently dictated by the developments and outcome of the war—provoked considerable speculation throughout the country as to what form the "American theorem" would eventually take. There were various alternatives offered. First, there was the hierarchical, and therefore semi-imperial, model (in the style of Liska rather than LaFeber), but this clashed with U.S. political tradition and with the last lingering rays of U.S. isolationism.[12]

Second, a more functional and publicly acceptable intervention was considered, a scheme that was more limited both temporally and spatially, aimed at reconstructing a war-torn world. It put the United States in the Bismarckian role of the "honest broker" of world affairs, who, from his superior moral and material standpoint (and, of course, geographical isolation) was in a position to placate tensions and defuse hostilities in Europe and the Far East before they escalated into full-blown conflict. Third, there was an argument for a structural (albeit discreet) presence based on U.S. economic, monetary, and commercial interdependence with the rest of the international economic system, to guarantee the expansion of the pattern of production and consumption promoted by the United States even before the 1929–1932 crisis—a model with enormous export potential.[13]

However, what World War II and cold war analysts generally overlook is the U.S. "strategic-military"[14] scheme for the postwar world, a program that received scant support, at least until 1945. Basically, during the war years, the issue of security had a marginal place among the various schemes constituting the "American theorem," though it acquired greater weight after 1946 and, with the Truman Doctrine and the North Atlantic Treaty Organization (NATO), became a central feature of U.S. foreign policy. However, the true importance of security emerged only as the international postwar system began to settle and the coalition of the victorious powers crystallized into a dyadic and bipolar structure with an inherent "dueling" tendency, making it therefore a "war system."[15]

But once more, history and politics branched off in different directions. This time it was the new international system, rising from the ashes of conflict, that determined the maneuvers of the principal actors—including the Americans, who suddenly found themselves having to cope with the terse diplomacy of "bipolarism," which they did with concerted pragmatism and without the aid of schemes or models.[16] The new situation signaled the end of a long and fruitful phase of foreign-policy planning in which nearly all the parties to World War II had been engaged on one level or another, the United States in particular.[17] The sweeping schemes the Americans sketched out for Europe (such as the European Recovery Plan and NATO) and for East Asia (plans thwarted, however, by the "loss of China" in 1949) were nearly always the product of an "action-reaction" style of foreign policy,[18] far different from the somewhat utopian approach that had characterized the heroic years of postwar foreign-policy planning, between 1939 and 1945.[19]

But a closer look at the logic behind U.S. foreign policy in the early postwar years shows that many decisions were influenced by earlier deliberations: Ideas were remolded to suit the new circumstances.[20] This is patently true of the philosophy behind the ambitious projects mentioned above: the reconstruction programs for Europe and East Asia, and the blueprint for the U.S. policy of security in the framework of the new bipolar situation (NATO and the 1951 treaty with Japan).[21]

If postwar official documents were compared with those preceding the war,[22] their inherent concepts would probably be marked by similarities and perhaps even close linguistic and textual affinities.[23] But what is most important is that the "perverse" mutation of Roosevelt's original prospect of international bipolar relations not only impeded the U.S. programs but also prevented the cardinal concepts of foreign policy pieced together during the conflict in those intellectual "laboratories" of postwar planning (which will be discussed in greater depth in Chapter 4) from being organized in a hierarchy of compatible priorities. In fact, U.S. foreign policy was forced to improvise in the first years after the war, and both the administration and the politicians were prompted to make use of nearly all the material drafted in the course of the war. This marked the start of a dense web of contradictions and parallelisms in U.S. policy decisions, eroding the credibility of U.S. foreign policy both at home and abroad.

The outcome was that the scenarios and options, procedures and methods, of U.S. action toward the outside world, together with the nation's main criteria for action, were frequently contradictory, distorted, or overturned—provoking serious flaws in operational effectiveness, bureaucratic conflicts within the decision-making apparatus, and harmful misperceptions of the outside world.[24] As a consequence, U.S. conduct was either inconsistent or diverging and at times hamstrung by overly legalistic, institutionalized conduct (such as the handling of the General Assembly of the United Nations in the first years of the Korean War and the "United for Peace Resolution" in December 1950); in other instances, it was markedly "economicistic" (such as in the management of the General Agreement on Tariffs and Trade [GATT] and in the politics of the International Monetary Fund [IMF] and the World Bank) or even unabashedly "imperialist" (as in Guatemala in 1954, Santo Domingo in 1965, or Grenada in 1984).[25]

In certain instances (the war in Vietnam is a macroscopic example), an attempt was made to reconcile the various components of U.S. foreign policy, but such attempts did not succeed in tempering the components' conceptual anomalies or in making them work reciprocally. Instead what virtues they did have were eclipsed by misguided management—resulting in political and diplomatic stalemate, military defeat, and an utter waste of economic and financial resources.[26]

The key to understanding the motives and behavior of an international actor of such towering political stature as the United States, from its debut on the international stage until the present day, should be sought further back in time: One must study how the pivotal concepts emerged and how the basic thematic issues—the sources of later lines of action—developed. If instead we look at the literature, we can see that the entrance of the United States into world politics and the upheaval this provoked in the international political system have preoccupied a great many historians and political scientists inquiring into the nagging question of the origins of the cold war.[27] Consequently, the strategies developed by the United States after World War II (particularly the doctrine of containment[28]) and their historical origins were presented as products of the war and of the events that ensued rather than as the consequence of the years that immediately preceded the conflict. The war and its disruption of the international order have thus been widely interpreted as a kind of watershed between two distinct periods. Indeed, the course of events before 1939 has become the conventional area of inquiry into the "causes" of the world conflict, and the years and events after 1941 have merely become study material for determining the "consequences" of that conflict.[29]

As a result, historians have neglected to investigate the political trajectories and cultural paths on which the action of the postwar administrations was based. Furthermore, there has been no thoroughgoing analysis of the critical years during which the ideas that underlay all U.S. foreign policy throughout the successive decades actually germinated. The aim of this book is to show that the crucial formative period for the set of concepts and scenarios upon which U.S. foreign policy is based was neither the period leading up to the war nor the years immediately following it, but the two years of U.S. neutrality, namely, 1940 and 1941.

The Key Concepts

In this book we will be taking a close look at some of the ways that the generation of new ideas during those years affected the international system and the forms that U.S. foreign policy could have assumed at the close of the war in Europe.[30] I have set the options and programs in an interpretative framework to illustrate, explain, and validate the historical case study.

This book is the fruit of extensive research carried out in 1979 in the United States, England, and Italy and is based on archival material (mostly unpublished), interviews, firsthand accounts, and papers. I have followed four basic paths of inquiry into U.S. foreign policy in the decades following World War II in order to identify its context, its key concepts and its historical origins and to construct an informal explanatory model.

An examination of the international "context" of the political and intellectual debate that spawned the key concepts of U.S. foreign policy and security during and after World War II[31] involves first defining the situation that led to the extinction of the Eurocentric balance-of-power system (in its "intermediate" version of 1919–1939) and the emergence of the new bipolar international system from its ashes. Special attention has been given to the dynamic aspects of the model of international relations prevailing at the end of the 1930s (the second phase of the "intermediate system"), its evolution between 1940 and 1941 during the conflict in Europe, and also the structural changes that occurred at the war's end with the emergence and entrenchment of Soviet-American bipolarity.

In this analysis I seek to identify a set of "constants" in U.S. foreign policy in the period in which the United States was transforming itself from a continental power (with aspirations in the Pacific) to a superpower of global stature. These constants developed in the course of interaction among (1) the internal political system, (2) the government's foreign-policy activities, and (3) the international context. It is commonly accepted that this shift in the U.S. role between 1940 and 1945 depended greatly on the reorganization taking place in the international system as a whole. In fact, to some extent the preeminence achieved by the United States was the heart and the engine of the entire phase of transition of the international system after the collapse of the interwar system.

Basically, the Americanization of the international system (which until 1940 had been essentially Eurocentric) would determine the forms and rules of the new interaction model that emerged from the war, especially in its initial phase (1945–1955).[32] That was true despite the apparently bipolar structure that the situation had acquired since the beginnings of the cold war.[33] Consequently, any study of the essential components of the contemporary international system in its bipolar form requires some understanding of the gestation process[34] and subsequent rapid transition of the United States from a continental power to world superpower between 1898 and 1945.[35] This understanding is vital for appreciating the structural and operational mutations of the international system as a whole. My approach is rather atypical, as studies of international relations generally focus on the structure of interaction within the system, without paying too much attention to the reasons behind the individual actors' behavior and decisions; likewise, studies of foreign policy tend to analyze it as an autonomous facet of domestic political activity.[36]

This interweaving of the evolution of the political system of the United States and the dynamics of the international system has had important consequences. The globalization of the United States, the voluntary assumption of responsibility for the whole world—at times as a substitute for the declining European powers—was the prerequisite for the radical transformation of U.S. political action both during and after the war. However, the new world role of the United States also became the principal agent of the structural and functional transformation of the international system as a whole.

Historical studies of this particular period often show a divergence between those who consider this change of "rules" as the fault of the United States and those who consider it as a virtue of U.S. political farsightedness. Most literature on the origins of the cold war quite rightly tends to consider the role of the United States to be absolutely fundamental in determining the outcome of World War II. At the same time, however, it has also been said that Washington did nothing but react to the actions of others, curbing excesses and limiting possible damage, almost as if the postwar world had been organized independently from the United States, which had merely stepped in to prevent others (notably the Soviets) from distorting the new status quo. Although it seemed as if the United States had entered World War II with the single intention of preserving the international system and its rules of conduct, in fact the very process of U.S. globalization laid the groundwork for the definitive transformation of international relations from being Eurocentric to global, and thence from polycentric to bipolar.

Ever since the years of neutrality, the United States has assumed an essentially dual role. On the one hand, the official policy of the government was that of a strict neutrality. However, on the other hand, the administration adopted an increasingly interventionist view, almost priming the situation for the government's subsequent reactive behavior.[37] By the same token, one of the effects of globalization was to pressure the United States into assuming some of the obligations and restrictions that, in other circumstances, would have been the responsibility of the major European countries, equally involved and capable of intervening. This is clearly by no means a minor factor—between 1940 and the present, the United States has intervened more than once in areas and geopolitical contexts where, had this "globalization" not taken place, it would never have ventured.[38]

This process of a state becoming an empire, and an international system constructing itself upon this premise, transformed both the United States and the world. It dramatically altered the interactive logic between the actors and the system, creating a "system-archetype" (of imperial stamp, in Liska's sense) crossed with what Krasner and others have defined as a "regime-archetype."[39] "The set of principles, rules, norms, and procedures of decision making"[40] that distinguished the "international regime" in the West (i.e., the implicit "handbook"[41] of conduct defining the responsibilities of the "empire-archetype" as against the "eccentric-archetype,"[42]) by definition entailed a series of far-reaching consequences that affected the very structure of the system and the behavior code of the actors involved, even if this code was only provisional, created for a unique international context.

In the first place, a partial "de-internationalization" of the international system took place, in the sense that certain fundamental structural rules of the game among nation-states disappeared. Hence, in some respects, the resulting system (whether "imperial" or "regime") tended to work as if it were a domestic political system with a hierarchical and centralized order. Such an order functions under the aegis of a recognized actor-object, which is in a position (even if with a low level of centralized control) to impose a set of "authoritative allocations" of values, i.e., of political decisions.[43] However, there are always two different motives behind the transformation of a pluralistic structure into an imperial or semi-imperial one. "A preimperial community's concerns with irreducible security and sustenance," wrote Liska, "are the original motives which initiate expansion."[44]

But this kind of internal-international (split-level) regime or empire maintains all the forms of the preceding polyarchy (as in the classical balance of power), even though it basically acts as if the medium-sized and minor nations were for various reasons merely quasi actors with limited international legal clout. This encroachment on the sovereignty of the majority of nations involved is also evident in the bipolar system, which for fifty years, until 1989, was, simply put, little more than a bilateral empire-archetype: that is, two imperial forms, the two sub-systems, separated by a war frontier, the Iron Curtain.[45]

In the context of this new historical event, World War II (whose outcome transformed the international system), the assumption of global responsibilities by a superpower such as the United States would not have come about had this phenomenon hinged on traditional principles, that is, if—as in the era of the balance of power—the employment of a certain sense of "balance" and a realistic use of "power" had been sufficient to justify national egoism, both domestically and abroad.[46] Instead, the assumption of an "imperial" role, i.e., the creation of a "regime" structure, involved formulating a set of conceptual and methodological principles onto which a credible foreign policy could be grafted. The United States was obliged to draw the key concepts for its foreign policy from its own intellectual heritage, choosing them according to criteria that would later have wider application—principles that would be viable for the outside, non-American world, but that would safeguard the country's most vital interests.[47]

The Historical Context

Let us assume that the two principal criteria that served as the theoretical basis of U.S. foreign policy from the outbreak of war were *growth* and *power*.[48] The first of these concepts provided a backdrop for most U.S. political images and metaphors from the 1940s on. It received the support of all those who wanted to explain the continued presence of the United States in Europe (and East Asia) after the war's end in terms of assistance, aid for reconstruction, raising the standard of living, and so forth. However, leaving aside the literature about this era (e.g., Feis, Gaddis, Yergin), the concept of growth seems to conceal a structural interpretation that runs far deeper.[49] Neither the lavish aid nor the imperialist expansionism were ends in themselves. There was no special philanthropy involved, nor a diabolical plot to overrun the world. The issue was probably much more objective and at the same time more far-reaching.[50]

The second concept, power, like some historical coda tacked onto the previous concept, seems to have derived from European-style imperialist and naval experience of the period from 1890 to 1914[51] during the clash between foreign and domestic politics, between the proponents of what was termed the Age of Reform and those urging the country into war. In those years, the United States fought two full-blown wars (with Spain and Germany) and a quasi war (with Mexico), conducted a war of colonial repression (in the Philippines), came just short of armed conflict with Chile and Great Britain, and intervened dozens of times in Latin America.[52] During this period, the concept of power was formed and tested; it was subsequently employed during and after World War II.[53]

At the beginning the meaning of the concept of power was quite generic—and not immediately reducible into rules of conduct. It was experimented with in the course of World War II, as in some kind of laboratory test, in the Allied Military Governments (AMGs), first in Italy and then in Austria, Germany, Japan, and the other occupied countries.[54] This kind of administration of conquered or liberated countries was to some extent also a functional and provisional structure, somewhere between the classical military government of occupied territories for purely military ends and a special trusteeship geared to assist in the countries' rehabilitation and form the basis for postwar reconstruction.[55] In some cases, these provisional administrations enabled Washington to test out the appropriate balances between growth and power, between political and military control and a rise in the population's living standards, in close economic and financial interaction with the economy and security of the United States.

In this book I shall show why and to what extent the guiding criteria of growth and power, as employed through the AMGs and the complex machinery of economic, military, ideological, and political mobilization of U.S. public opinion,[56] were gradually transformed into the two key principles of action and doctrine, becoming a yardstick for gauging policies to adopt both at home and abroad. These two principles are neatly summed up as *interdependence* and *national security*.

My aim is to verify if, and to what extent, the single global model—political and economic, hierarchical, and substantially homogeneous[57] (unaffected by the partial "heterogeneousness" of the Soviet Union, China, and other socialist countries[58])—that had governed the international situation in both the North and the South in the postwar era,[59] was not simply a package of analogies and functional affinities or rules common to the fields of economy, science, and technology, a package of cultural models and models of socialization. Perhaps the single global model was also a true conceptual and programmatic heart, a framework endowed with its own specific methodology and based on the permanent interaction between economic and financial interdependence and national or collective security. A further question to be answered is the extent to which this constant trade-off between the two principles characterizing U.S. foreign policy from the 1940s on, together with the globalization of the nation's role, has become a central mode of conduct in international bipolar relations as a whole.

The Model

The two principles of action—interdependence on one hand and national security on the other—which determine the functional structures of the bipolar model of international relations, are also the two major parameters of an analysis of the logic of postwar U.S. foreign policy. Owing to the role the United States has played in the formation of the system and its continued importance, the language of U.S. international policy has become the language of the international bipolar system in its Western version. This conceptual and semantic premise has often hindered U.S. understanding of other nations, which have insisted on using idiom of a different cultural matrix—as has happened on occasion with the French and the British, with the Soviets and the Chinese, and with many Third World countries for that matter. The arguments of the Realpolitik of the nineteenth century,[60] of British and continental inspiration (from Metternich to Bismarck and Gladstone), have always had a lesser part in the vocabulary of the superpowers (and likewise in that of the new actors of the Third World), who often cloak the language of politics and reality in ideology.[61]

This non–mutually intelligible idiom, or "newspeak,"[62] is much more dangerous for the stability of the international system than is generally imagined, especially where the system is largely governed by the two superpowers. The process of interpretation becomes complex. First, each power is obliged to "translate" the idiom of the other into its own language; second, this translation has to be retranslated for the use of the allied nations, with an ever-greater risk of becoming unintelligible or of being misinterpreted at some stage in the process. In the case of the United States, the consistent use of the two clear-cut concepts of interdependence and national security has in some ways facilitated things, as the "rate of intensity" with which one or the other concept is utilized has gradually become the criterion for assessing the validity of U.S. political action abroad, even when that action has turned out to be harmful or counterproductive.

In other words, an increase in either interdependence or national security was always considered a good thing, and a decrease almost always undesirable. Therefore, when Washington found itself forced to reduce either one or the other (as in economic or monetary relations after 1971 or in the contradictory initiatives in the Middle East), it had to find a scapegoat, a cause outside that scheme, so as not to jeopardize its basic interpretative model. Thus the model itself is based on inconstant balance between interdependence and national security, which is used as a kind of functional grid, or methodological skeleton, upon which the entire system of U.S. foreign policy is organized.[63]

For all its vast size, the United States was nonetheless parochial in character when it entered the war in 1941. In a famous book on U.S. collective habits and behavior during World War II, John Martin Blum wrote that "during the war, the political openings were limited by the cultural limits" of the American people.[64] The war brought not only victory to the United States but also a remodeling of its political culture. It is no coincidence that entire academic disciplines (and particularly certain social sciences) were created from scratch in the closing years of the war, and these were successively consolidated during the golden decade of U.S. hegemony (1945–1955).

The formation of the concepts of interdependence and national security was a lengthy process, however, and a proper balance between them was hard to achieve. If we focus on the history of these concepts, we can see how difficult it was to find a scientific, coherent definition of the concepts that could withstand the inflow of political acts affecting the United States from outside and on the basis of which the Americans could conduct their relations with the world.[65]

As far as interdependence was concerned, it was imperative to break out of the limited field of assistance-related policies and strictly monetary and financial relations with Europe. With regard to national security, it was necessary to unify the military infrastructures and acquire a more precise "geopolitical awareness,"[66] to champion a peacetime military alliance—the first in world history—while pinpointing the potential "enemy."[67] And this enemy had to be described in terms of the existing conceptual framework, avoiding an excess of wartime negativity, but making sure not to succumb to the illusion of prewar appeasement.[68] The model that materialized had no fixed rules and, like a gyroscope, adjusted its angle to suit each occasion, providing a flexible and reusable scheme of reference.

The Case Study

For this research, I analyzed the concepts and the texts of the documents on U.S. postwar foreign-policy planning, sifting through a great quantity of material stored in some of the major public and private archives. On occasion, I compared records to match semantic and lexical details. But more often, I looked for the intellectual starting point of the various themes of U.S. policy and their evolution over time, tracing wherever possible the cultural links and cross-pollination of ideas as well as the synergic interaction that frequently derived from such exchanges.

In addition, I took into account clusters and "families" of concepts, along with the gradual transformation of their semantic contents. The impact of these concepts on public opinion and on the country's political culture I assessed by examining opinion polls and newspapers and magazines of the period. I have been careful to use the least disputed definitions for terms such as "isolationism," "internationalism," "neutralism," "cooperation," "integration," "national interest," "interventionism," "globalism," "geopolitics," "idealism," "societal legalism," and so forth, up to the definition of the two key concepts of interdependence and national security.[69]

Finally, among the many official documents on U.S. postwar foreign-policy planning[70] collected by private bodies or the various academic research centers, I was drawn to the archives of the Council on Foreign

Relations (CFR) of New York.[71] My examination of the CFR documents—which cover a broad spectrum of themes and also represent an early example (if not the first) of postwar foreign-policy planning—substantiated my hypothesis that the conceptual principles of U.S. foreign policy originally stem from the period of neutrality, 1940–1941, prior to the Japanese bombing of Pearl Harbor.

2

The International Context and the Analytical Categories

The Balance of Power and the "Intermediate System"

By the end of World War I, the international balance-of-power system, Eurocentric by definition,[1] had begun to list badly. The disappearance of certain essential actors, such as the Austro-Hungarian and Ottoman empires, and the marginalization of others, such as Russia and Germany, had conspired to make the system highly precarious and to upset its inner mechanisms. This instability was aggravated by the isolationist withdrawal of the major non-European nation, the United States, and by the regional basis of Japan's power. The lack of a stabilizing force and the reduction of the number of essential actors from six to four (Great Britain, France, Italy—and after 1925, Germany) triggered ominous realignments of power, along lines similar to those that had presaged the 1914 war.

Despite preserving some of the features of its predecessor (i.e., Eurocentrism and polycentrism), the system that emerged from Versailles was basically a weak imitation of its predecessor. According to some scholars, the post-Versailles system demonstrated certain original characteristics that could have—or should have—made it, conceptually and chronologically, an autonomous "intermediate system."[2]

Briefly, it differed from the classical balance-of-power system in the following ways. First, although this "intermediate system" was indeed largely Eurocentric, it was affected by issues of global importance that could not be settled within the erstwhile union of the European powers of the 1800s. This impotence could be seen in the handling of the situation in the Pacific and Far East between 1919 and 1937, in which the European powers, which had prevailed in the area until 1918, vacated the field to the United States, the Soviet Union, and Japan.[3]

Second, the drop in number of essential actors had wrought changes to certain fundamental rules of the model (as developed by Morton A. Kaplan in 1957). These were either rendered ineffective or distorted, which impaired the working of the entire institutional machinery.[4]

Third, there was a new ingredient, the League of Nations. Although this institution completely lacked executive power, its inherent anomalies with respect to the traditions of international relations had undermined the ideological and political credibility of the old system of consultation between the European chancelleries. The new system was made even less plausible by the disintegration of the traditional diplomatic cadres, which had enjoyed a common language and caste solidarity that often transcended national borders and that had sparked and dissolved international tensions.

Fourth, despite their being merely "latent" powers, the very existence of other major nations (Japan, the United States, and the Soviet Union), as yet without direct influence on European relations, had thrown the system off center. This asymmetry undermined the classical balance of forces.[5]

Thus conditioned, the "intermediate system" passed through two basic phases during the twenty years between the wars: The first phase (1919–1929) was one of consolidation and stabilization, as the preeminence of the victorious European powers was acknowledged and as those defeated were gradually reabsorbed into the system; the second phase (1929–1939) witnessed widespread dismemberment and conflict, triggered the discontent and later violent "revisionist" movement of the defeated powers against the 1919 territorial settlements of Versailles. With the economic crisis of 1929–1932, these nations finally found the means for toppling this precarious international order.[6]

Even by the end of the 1930s, the "intermediate system" already appeared to be a flawed and doomed device, lacking the necessary self-regulating mechanisms. It was already atoning for its original sin—namely the ambiguities it had engendered by claiming to be what it was not: a system of international relations that had radically modified Europe and the form of domestic political regimes, with the objective of stemming conflict and friction. In truth, however, it had failed to supplant the worn-out mechanisms with any new institutional or functional system able to give the structure cohesion.[7]

The End of the "Intermediate System"

The established international order, based on four essential actors guaranteeing the collective security of the European continent (the "spirit of Locarno" of 1925), was swept aside in a single blow by the fall of

France in June 1940. The more attentive observers (particularly those in the United States), who as early as the 1920s had been well aware of the instability of the postwar system, soon realized the novelty of the structure that was emerging. Few Europeans, except perhaps Adolf Hitler, had even begun to take stock of the events taking place. In 1940 the centuries-old system of self-governing international relations was scuttled—a system that had been inaugurated in 1648 by the Peace of Westphalia and consolidated at the Congress of Vienna of 1815, living its last, brief season at Versailles in 1919.[8]

During the summer of 1940 a long phase of transition and structural reorganization began, based on a new reality and quite unlike anything else during the entire twentieth century. Europe's primacy in international relations, which the Axis (Hitler in particular) was so dramatically trying to curtail, seemed to be nearing its end. Whatever the outcome of the war, the Eurocentric system was doomed. This sudden systemic crisis posed a great many questions for the Americans, who for their part still clung to the illusion that the United States was a *zona franca* (invulnerable in terms of security).[9]

During the months immediately following the fall of France, a variety of alternative options and scenarios for reordering the society of states was debated in certain internationalist spheres. Although today some of the outlooks presented at that time may appear utopian or unrealistic, most of the participants in those debates carefully took into account the situation at hand. Considering the prevailing mentality and attitudes of the era, the various alternatives were explored fairly realistically. Six main scenarios were sketched out, and the more plausible schemes had additional variants; others were open options that depended directly on the eventual outcome of the war.

1. One possible development was that continental Europe, instead of retaining its pre-1940 configuration, would be more consolidated under the German stranglehold, becoming a provisional "international war system." There would be a forced grouping of the conquered nations or vassal states, depending on the progress of the war. Among the possible variants of this model of "Germanic Europe," one included the British Isles, if London were to surrender or be occupied; other possible configurations included North and Central Africa or the Middle East and the Gulf (as a reservoir of resources) or a combination of both. In the German conquest scenario, both Japan and the Soviet Union could have remained neutral, though not without sacrificing claims on the colonial empires of France, England, and Holland. That neutrality would clearly have isolated the United States, resulting in a rigid bipolar arrangement[10] (in Kaplan's sense) between the United States and Nazi Germany (a kind of Anglo-Teutonic Atlanticism) representing the role

of the new international system and leaving the Bolshevik Soviet Union and militarist Japan on the fringes.[11] Yet other hypotheses could be formulated based on past history and war events.

2. Alternatively, the preexisting balance could have been gradually enlarged—though not as a Eurocentric system (given the disappearance of certain essential players, such as France)—and could assume a more global configuration. This enlargement could have led to a world pentarchy of powers (or tetrarchy, depending on Britain's position) based on the interaction of the United States (with Great Britain either independent or incorporated), Germany, the Soviet Union, and Japan. The rules of the balance of power would be more or less respected through the subdivision of the spoils of the European colonial empires, together with the regional management of the spheres of influence: the "sphere of co-prosperity" for Japan; the "island of the world" centered on Asia for the Soviet Union; the "Atlantic System" for the United States and Great Britain; and continental Europe, Central and North Africa, and the Middle East for Hitler's Axis.[12]

3. Another outcome explored was the possible formation of a "Eurasiatic" military bloc (Germany, the Soviet Union, and Japan), allied against the Anglo-Saxons (the United States and Great Britain). That would assuredly have been a "war system" and, as such, would have engendered constant friction between two wholly irreconcilable political and ideological outlooks—totalitarianism and democratic liberalism. In 1940 this hypothesis was a source of great concern to many observers in both Washington and London. It was a very plausible outcome and would have fueled Germany's old designs on the Orient. It implied that Hitler himself, who intended to continue his Lebensraum policy through steady expansion eastward, realized that war was not the only means for pursuing his ends.

4. The scenario that did eventually materialize during the war, in mid-1940, was one of the least imaginable. The idea of a massive alliance among the United States, Great Britain, and the Soviet Union had never been even remotely contemplated. Until the middle of 1940, the German-Soviet alliance of the preceding August still held together and even enabled the two powers to redefine the frontiers of the Balkan states and Eastern Europe, to mutual advantage. However things might have developed, the fall of France raised the question of the fate of the international system as a whole. The hypothesis that prevailed—the formation of a Grand Alliance against the Axis Powers—by no means eased the task at hand. It still meant that at the end of the war, there would almost certainly be a vast power vacuum in Europe, should the Allies win the war.

5. In fact, at the end of the war, Europe was made up of a group of defeated and crippled nations. The political decline of France and Italy (the first two countries to be defeated), and then of Germany, which had been at the core of the entire system, was compounded by the irreversible weakening of Great Britain. In the Far East, the situation was equally bleak: The Japanese had been crushed, and there was a burgeoning civil war in China. The implosion of both great powers in Asia created another vast power vacuum—inducing serious problems of stability in the other actors. At the start of the war, however, the possibility of such a vacuum—later the principal geopolitical cause of the creation of the bipolar arrangement between the United States and the Soviet Union—had not been foreseen.[13] In fact, to some extent the United States had feared an excessive buildup of power through the relentless aggrandizement of the German empire, as it ate through continental Europe. Equally perturbing were the ramifications of Japanese control throughout the Pacific.[14]

6. Completing the panorama, there was also a lobby of thinkers of Wilsonian persuasion that, as early as 1940, pressed to resuscitate an earlier experiment in international organization that had met with failure—the League of Nations. After the isolationist disappointments of the 1920s and 1930s, the institutional and multilateral notion of "collective security" guaranteed through treaty, a product of progressive and internationalist American political thought, resurfaced in the catastrophe of the extremist Realpolitik that had prevailed between the wars.[15] This conceptual line, which was to make much headway from the Atlantic Charter to the Charter of the United Nations, had the advantage of addressing the structural problem caused by the utter collapse of the balance of power in all its forms. The United Nations attempted, at least theoretically, to fill the postwar power vacuum in Europe, supplying a code of behavior and penalties for all those who violated the norms.

U.S. Foreign Policy and the Fall of France

The impact on the U.S. public of the defeat of France has been described and studied in depth by historians and analysts of all countries.[16] No one seems to challenge the opinion that it helped change the detached and noncommittal attitude toward the war in Europe. The "phony war" of the autumn and winter of 1939–1940 had reinforced the expectation of a negotiated (and in any case relatively undamaging) solution to the war under way. With an unpleasant jolt, the U.S. public became suddenly and acutely aware of the fact that their continent, apparently screened from either Asian or European fronts, was no longer impervious to attack, and that the last veil of protection for the United States lay with the British fleet.

June 1940 was therefore a watershed in the two-year period of U.S. wartime neutrality. However, the twenty-seven months in which the United States merely "looked on," as it were, can be subdivided into four distinct phases, each of which marked one step further toward American intervention. The first phase ran from the German and Russian assaults on Poland in September 1939 to the fall of France in June 1940.

The second phase, from June to December 1940, was a period in which the U.S. public and the president himself were most uncertain as to how to act. Various ideas were tentatively explored, including the possibility of "peaceful coexistence" with a Germanized continental Europe. All hopes were focused on Britain's ability to withstand the terrible air strike that was presumed to harbinger the invasion of the British Isles. When the Germans seemed to abandon the idea of invasion, President Franklin D. Roosevelt, in a revision of policy, promised the British war effort full U.S. backing, at whatever cost.[17] Thus, the period of U.S. ambivalence ended at the year's close with the formulation of a political process that led to the Lend-Lease Act of the following March.[18]

The third phase can be divided into two parts. The first began in December 1940 and terminated in August 1941 with the Roosevelt-Churchill meeting in Placentia Bay. This meeting generated the Atlantic Charter, a full-fledged programmatic and political manifesto for the postwar world. The period saw the escalation of the U.S. defense effort, which complemented (and sometimes conflicted with) the exportation of arms and war matériel of all kinds to Great Britain in a bid to sustain the military effort and boost civil morale in that country. In the wake of Hitler's attack on Russia on June 22, 1941, the Americans also embarked on a complex system of aid to the Soviets.[19]

The second part of the third phase ran from August to the fateful "day of infamy,"[20] December 7, 1941, when the Japanese bombed Pearl Harbor. This phase was essentially a prelude to direct military confrontation, as naval incidents between the U.S. and German fleets continued to escalate and were on occasion even provoked. Talks with the Japanese proved fruitless and U.S. delegates came away empty-handed. With some reluctance, the U.S. public accepted the idea that war was inevitable.[21]

However, in practice the transition from isolationism to internationalism in the United States was a more complex and drawn-out affair. It did not actually begin on September 1, 1939, nor did it end on December 7, 1941. In-depth studies into this aspect of U.S. politics can be found in the works of Selig Adler and Leroy N. Rieselbach. Likewise, the highly detailed studies of Wayne S. Cole[22] provide broad outlines of the historical, geographical, sociological, and cultural background of this laborious transition.

During the years of neutrality, a real genetic mutation took place in traditional U.S. policy regarding the Monroe Doctrine and the concept of Manifest Destiny, a destiny to which the Americans seemed to be called, or so they believed.[23] The main cause for this profound and perhaps irreversible change was not simply the American response to the appeals of peoples suffering under Fascist and militarist yokes or a desire to halt the tide of capitalist fascism bent on conquering the markets and resources of the entire planet (especially those of Europe and the colonial empires) through ruthless means. The metamorphosis of Homo americanus from 1939 to 1941 was more radical.

The transition from isolation (if not from "isolationism") to globalism meant above all coming to terms with a new commitment, a geopolitical and systemic responsibility that the Americans would not have been able to ignore, even had they wanted to. Under the circumstances, they tackled the matter with the relatively limited conceptual and cultural tools at their disposal. They were also somewhat short of experience, but they demonstrated imagination and organizational skill.[24]

The "Vichy gamble," based on the ambiguous relations between the U.S. government and Marshal Pétain's government from mid-1940 to the end of 1941, testifies to the air of uncertainty that reigned in U.S. foreign-policy circles, even in the State Department, among the internationalist elites. William C. Bullitt, ambassador to Paul Reynaud's Third Republic government, was recalled after the fall of Paris (June 16), and there was a brief interregnum for the latter half of the year, while the government reassembled in Bordeaux; it was then transformed into Marshal Pétain's Etat Français in Vichy. During this period of confusion, which was also the most bleak of those being discussed, Bullitt's successor, Anthony D. Biddle, had no precise role at all, nor was he particularly active. However, as soon as the marshal's government began to settle in, Roosevelt sent a new ambassador to Vichy, Admiral William D. Leahy, and thereby initiated a highly complex diplomatic interchange between the United States and Pétain's regime—an association that has been subject to many interpretations over the decades, the first of which began to appear toward the end of the war.[25]

Leahy's mission was subjected to heavy censure. From the exchange of letters with Cordell Hull and Roosevelt,[26] it would appear that the framework of the relations between the United States and Germany and its allies and satellites was far from clear, even to the president or secretary of state—at least in the spring of 1941. The mission was later accused of being a kind of "parallel diplomacy," in conflict with the country's stock pro-English line, but it was in fact an understandable attempt at not breaking with the old international "order," which represented the only frame of reference in this crucial phase of radical transformation in international relations.[27]

There is a certain correlation between the changing forms assumed by the war in Europe in 1939–1941 and the phases of U.S. neutrality sketched out here. This link was responsible for the evolution of U.S. legislation on neutrality (between 1935 and 1941), which, especially from 1939 on, proceeded in leaps and bounds.[28] The first phase coincided with the "phony war"; the second with the German blitz on England and the Italian defeats in Greece, Libya, and Taranto; the third phase coincided with the resumed German advance in the East (the Balkans, the Soviet Union), an area that quickly became the key theater of war;[29] the second part of the third phase ties in with the Battle of the Atlantic and with Japan's entry into the war, ushering the spread of armed conflict to almost the entire planet.

This correlation between forms of war and the phases of U.S. neutrality, without any further specification of terms, is perhaps rather crude, but it does provide insights into the underlying mechanisms of U.S. diplomacy and the evolution of attitudes among the intellectual elites and the U.S. public. The question becomes clearer if we start with the assumption that the collapse of the "intermediate system" hinged on the parallel emergence of an international "war system" that was both provisional and regional (in that only Europe and part of North Africa were directly involved in the conflict). The international "war system" added a new strategic variable to the workings of the international "peace system," subordinating the war system's functioning to the dynamics of military operations. Thus, unlike in the diplomacy of earlier years, the strictly tactical component now worked as an independent variable. Moreover, to this independent variable (provided by operational tactics) was added the dependent variable of the strategic component, i.e., the general political ends that the belligerents hoped to achieve through war.

These two variables provided a new ingredient and demonstrated the conceptual and functional diversity between a war system inaugurated in September 1939 and the earlier peace system. In other words, the existence of hostilities, in any corner of the world, also rendered the diplomatic tools of the neutral actors dependent on the outcome of that conflict. Indeed, the war system moved between two forms of logic at once alternative and complementary—the logic of force and the logic of diplomacy, both at work in the same milieu and at the same time.[30]

An analysis of war systems, therefore, must take into consideration the existence of a dual linguistic code, a code that tends to transform the conduct of the nations involved by means of a "defensive" model (the code of diplomacy) that is in constant interaction and/or contrast with an "offensive" model (the code of force). Furthermore, the actors' behavior during the various phases—for example, U.S. foreign policy over the neutral period 1939–1941[31]—was undoubtedly influenced as much by the rapid unfolding of military events as by the evolution of domestic conditions.

The war in Europe, its impact on the media (press, radio, and cinema), and the dynamics of military operations had a far more immediate effect on the U.S. public and government than peacetime foreign-policy decisions could ever have achieved. In this sense, the correlation between the phases of U.S. policy and the actual pace of the war is quite tenable, despite the country's being so far from the main theater of war in 1940–1941.[32]

The War Aims of the Great Powers

Perhaps the most significant link between force and diplomacy during a war is contained in what may be termed as the "war aims" of each national actor, which embody the working philosophy of the nation. War aims form a kind of idealistic bridge between the prewar peace system—which determines the initial reaction to and the claims of each state upon the outbreak of war—and the eventual postwar peace system. They tend to ignore the war system created at the outbreak of hostilities, focusing instead on a set of maximalist or minimalist objectives that are assumed will provide the basis for the postwar order.

These aims can be grouped according to type and level of definition. Some are directed toward transforming the system in force before the war; others are geared to preserving it. Whatever the case, the provisional war system generated when war breaks out is unlikely to outlive the conflict. It is equally rare that the original prewar peace system is resurrected once hostilities cease. Consequently, war aims are an implicit form of advance planning for postwar foreign policy, in accordance with the objectives of each of the nations involved.

Such aims are rarely realized in full, and their effects cannot be forecast. Even the aims of the victorious nations undergo extensive modification because the interaction between force and diplomacy typical to war systems in effect while hostilities last often causes the revision or even renunciation of many projects for institutional or territorial organization. In such cases they are supplanted by pragmatic improvisations, mediation, or compromise.

A full study of the war aims of World War II, their comparison and their dynamics, would be a useful means of plotting the tactical course followed by the political and military elites during the war. For reasons of space, they will not be analyzed in detail here, but I will be referring closely to the studies, research papers, and collections of documents that testify to the postwar planning efforts that, to greater or lesser extent, all the major powers embarked on during the war.

The only powers to nurture truly global war aims (compared with strictly regional or at most "continental" ones) were the United States and Nazi Germany. Studies carried out on Nazi war aims on historiographical and political levels (both in Germany and elsewhere) amply confirm this. A.J.P. Taylor[33] argued (along lines similar to those of Gustav Stresemann) that Hitler was a "political revisionist," a leader who was cautious in his own designs of conquest but quick to exploit each situation pragmatically as it arose. Here I will adopt the competing view, namely, that the Nazi war was based on premeditated expansionist aims.[34]

There is not a great deal of difference between Hugh Trevor-Roper's thesis of 1960[35] on the essential importance of the *Drang nach Osten* and the notion of Lebensraum in Russia, and Andreas Hillgruber's model for the "gradual conquest" of the world. The Reich's expansionist strategy soon turned into a program of successive conquests aimed at carrying the Nazi flag to all corners of the world, fueled (as Norman Rich maintained) by the "reciprocal causal link between the conquest of living space and racial supremacy."[36]

Basically, the war aims of Nazi Germany correspond to the historiographic interpretation that depicts them as "continental" in nature. But they also match with the later analysis[37] that judged them "global." The first stage of the Nazi program envisaged the acquisition of a European continental empire, with its stronghold in Russia; this is the geopolitical theory put forward by Mackinder and substantiated by Haushofer. The second stage was supposedly a phase of colonial expansion, which was to include Central Africa, the Indian Ocean, and the eastern Atlantic. The third stage would have precipitated the isolation of the United States through an alliance with Japan and even one with Britain. The fourth and last stage was to be left for the post-Hitler generation and would have involved an intercontinental struggle against the United States for a single, world hegemony, a total "Germanic Reich of German nationality."[38] Clearly, the plan was somewhat abstract and to some extent utopian. The use of Britain as a stepping-stone to German domination was certainly out of the question. However, although many unexpected events drew Hitler away from his projects, the military operations between 1939 and 1943 are a clear testament to Germany's attempt to realize at least the first two stages of this program. Fantastic as this vision may seem, the urge to conquer the world had strong foundations in German tradition, originating long before World War I.[39]

Many scholars agree with the assertion that Hitler's program represented the "apex of all the political questions that had emerged in the Reich since 1866–1871: the demand for an economic empire in Europe; Central Africa as an area for expansion; a policy of rearmament as a means of stimulating the economy; and the use of these arms for auspicious blitz campaigns."[40] The global nature of the scheme is evident in diplomatic and military records. Of particular interest is a brief of February 17, 1941 (predating Operation Barbarossa against the Soviet Union), which outlined a plan to assemble forces in Afghanistan for a foray against British India, part of the third stage of the Reich's global expansion program.

The war aims of the other members of the Tripartite Pact, namely, Italy and Japan, are quite another matter. In Italy's case, apart from certain references in Ciano's diaries[41] and the memoirs of a few leading figures, the Fascist war aims are much harder to determine.[42] To all intents and purposes, even the more farfetched objectives dreamed up by Rome were basically regional in nature. The Italians had always considered the Atlantic as virtually beyond their reach.

The Japanese war aims were more organic, both before and during the war. Nevertheless, the creation of a "Greater East Asia Co-Prosperity Sphere" clearly shows the territorial perimeter of Japan's ambitions for expansion to be largely regional.[43] The Japanese area of expansion was to include India and foresaw also the addition of Australia and New Zealand and perhaps even part of Siberia and the Hawaiian Islands. Designs on California and Latin America were excluded. Meanwhile, Europe was left entirely to the "New Order," to Nazi and Fascist hands.

The Soviets' war aims were even more modest, at least in the first part of the war, when their main aspiration was to retrieve territories they had lost at Brest Litovsk in 1918 and later in Warsaw in 1920. Their hope was to construct a complete system of security by forming a chain of allied buffer states (and, if possible, also vassal states) serving the Soviet Union.[44] We have to exclude the possibility that, technically, apart from the Comintern's aspirations for worldwide revolution, the Soviets intended to go farther than this defense-offensive perimeter (which became Eastern Europe after the war). But unlike Germany and Japan, the Soviet Union successfully coped with being spread out over two continents at the same time, i.e., in both Asia and Europe.

Moscow's claims on Asia were less clear, however. The Soviets' centrifugal "global" thrust mainly manifested itself in their ambitions in China, Korea, and other Japanese territories on the continent, though this did not include any specific naval aspirations. The continental structure of the Soviet Union was at that time absolutely unmodifiable. Despite the geopolitical theories of Mackinder, even in the event of a Nazi defeat, the Soviets could have never aspired to anything greater than a Eurasiatic supercontinent, its borders policed by an ever-watchful Anglo-Saxon navy.

Owing to its unparalleled naval and colonial strength, only Great Britain could have attempted to perform the role of the global guardian of the postwar order, once France no longer ranked among the Great Powers. Britain was fully aware that the war signaled the start of an implosion of its power and the inevitable reduction of its empire. Indeed, for most of the war, the war aims of the British government—including those mentioned variously by Winston Churchill or traceable in British diplomatic and military records—vacillated with the fluctuating successes of Allied war operations.[45] Throughout the covert dissension that grew up between Churchill and Roosevelt in the two years of U.S. neutrality,[46] this changeable attitude toward the war was a constant point of contention. During the first years of the alliance, Churchill insisted that Britain remain on an equal footing, at the very least, with the Americans in their operations. Later Churchill courted a closer entente with Joseph Stalin (as in his visit to Moscow in October 1944) in a bid to offset the growing prevalence of U.S. power in the Anglo-American "special relationship."[47]

As the war progressed, Britain's global control became increasingly precarious. The country's links with its empire weakened progressively and, with them, London's ability to hold the empire together while pursuing the war effort. The hopes of the British and their leader Churchill rested on the possibility of bringing the war to an end before British power was irreversibly depleted.

The path the Americans trod was altogether different. The United States was the only nation in which the formation of war aims had proceeded at the same pace as military operations and was in tune with the changing dynamics of the international upheavals provoked by the war and by the shifts of power between warring and neutral nations. For the Americans, it all began in mid-1940. The sudden involvement of the United States in the war in Europe upon the fall of France inspired the internationalists in the United States to take action. They promptly initiated a series of analytical studies from which it became clear that after the war, the role of the United States would be global, and definitively so. The forms this radical mutation of U.S. foreign policy would assume were as yet undetermined. The lack of any groundwork for the United States to draw on in the formulation of a global identity turned out to be a stimulus for new, futuristic ideas on the reorganization of the international system. The architects of the new thinking were the same individuals who had fostered internationalism throughout the dark years of U.S. isolationism.

War Aims and the War System

The model of international relations for the United States during the formulation of U.S. war aims between 1940 and 1941, and hence while plans were drawn up for postwar foreign policy, was composed of two separate structures. On the one hand, there was the depressing spectacle of the "intermediate system," built on the ruins of the noble balance-of-power system. On the other hand, a crude and simple mechanism of interaction was slowly forming a pragmatic and provisional international structure, based on force and astuteness and established by and sub-ordinated to the laws of war: the war system.

The failure of the "intermediate system" was all too apparent, par-ticularly to those Americans who had closely followed the events in Europe and Asia between 1931 and 1939; it was clearly not to be resuscitated. Its Eurocentricity not only contrasted with the patently global development of conflicts but also was the chief reason behind the contention. Equally unlikely was the chance of restoring the former balance of power that had been obliterated in 1914, a system the Americans blamed for the appalling carnage of World War I.[48]

Lacking other models for an international system, the American theoreticians had only the current war system, which, unlike the system of World War I, contained some highly original features of considerable importance—primarily its polycentric or a-centric structure (it spread through Europe and East Asia as well as North Africa) but also its planetary scope. Second, it constantly challenged the balance inside the two alliances, which was altered by each new development in the war, such as the occupation or loss of territories. Within the German-Italian relationship, this shifting balance was evident even before the United States entered the war. In fact, although the "parallel war" of Fascist Italy had begun later than the rest of the European war (not until June 1940), within six months it was virtually at an end. The Italian defeats in Greece and Albania, the disastrous retreat from Cyrenaica, and the British bombing attack on the Italian fleet in Taranto swiftly demolished any illusion of Italian military and political autonomy from its ally Germany. The war system brutally imposed its own rules. The coalition of the Axis had suddenly become asymmetrical, both politically and militarily, and the epicenter of power had shifted from the Alps directly to Berlin.[49]

The internal evolution of the respective alliances within the war system provided the Americans (and more generally, the future victors of the war) with a viable rationale for de-alignment and realignment[50] (i.e., the ways in which alliances are formed or dissolved) and supplied the conceptual foundations of a more functional and possibly more stable postwar international system. The escalation of events in the war system in 1940–1941 had in fact hastened changes that in a peace system could have been obtained only after a considerable span of time, if at all. A typical instance was the elimination in a few years of many national actors (Austria, Czechoslovakia, Albania, Poland, Latvia, Lithuania, Estonia, and Yugoslavia), the birth of new ones (Slovakia, Croatia, Montenegro), the modification of frontiers, the loss of sovereignty of the many states occupied by foreign armies, and the reduction of sovereignty of other allies or satellites—including France, some Balkan countries, and, finally, Italy. This unusual productivity of the war system intensified as the conflict spread. In 1940 and 1941, Washington quickly forgot about the "intermediate system," set up between the wars. What the Americans witnessed was a mechanism driven by a violence that was at once destructive and generative, a mechanism that if handled appropriately, could be used as an effective lathe for the new world order in a way never previously imagined.

This is probably the key to the great political and institutional battle waged by President Roosevelt, and before him by those groups of internationalists who tried to exploit the occasion history was offering the Americans to remedy the "misdeeds" of the Europeans.[51] Paradoxically, the "war system" presented the Americans a chance to realize an objective that they had promised themselves as far back as 1917, when they stepped into World War I—namely, to use "the war to end all wars."[52]

On that occasion too, there had been extensive political debate within the United States between those who sought to safeguard the country's neutrality and those who favored intervention.[53] President Wilson had been watchful then, as Roosevelt was to be twenty-three years later, choosing to move by degrees. "It was necessary for me," wrote Wilson to a friend, "by very slow stages indeed and with the most genuine purpose to avoid war to lead the country on to a single way of thinking."[54] Nonetheless, in addition to being Eurocentric, the 1914–1918 war system— until the Russian revolution of February–October 1917—retained the prewar balance of power (apart from a handful of frontier changes), a configuration in which the Americans played no part at all. Consequently, affinities between the two situations are more apparent than real. In addition to being global almost from the outbreak of hostilities, the war system of World War II provided the only international structure in existence. When they entered the war, the Americans had to reckon with the only truly working mechanism of the international context. They found themselves faced with an international situation quite unlike its predecessor, although its structure did not, and could not, have the consistency of a stable and permanent system.[55]

Therefore, as the conceptual framework of the new bipolar international order was being forged during and after the war, the only existing concrete point of reference was the war system that had been in force since the summer of 1940. The entire structure of the bipolar system is colored by this premise. The belligerent nature of the successive bipolar system of 1945 is probably a direct consequence of the fact that the power vacuum created in Europe at the end of World War II had also erased the traces of the polyarchic "intermediate system" that preceded it.

Thus, the norms, rules, decisional procedures, laws, and conformities that technically characterized the new bipolar system, based on the criteria of deterring and compelling, together with its warlike structure that qualified it as an atypical war system,[56] were not determined only by the existence of the atomic bomb, the "absolute weapon."[57] They also derived directly from the functional structure itself—the only one operating in wartime—which was almost automatically maintained until the advent of the postwar world. Indeed, many structural characteristics of today's bipolarity were borrowed en bloc from the 1939–1945 war system. Examples have been the administrative regimes of the European frontiers (particularly in Germany until 1990, with the antiquated conventions such as the Inter-Allied commissions constituted on the basis of the quadripartite agreements), or the limits to sovereignty decided by the rules of war and imposed on the constitutions of certain former enemy states (Germany and Japan) and maintained to this day—albeit only formally. Other examples include the abolition of the armed forces in Japan—established on the basis of a "constitution" imposed by the occupying forces—or the abolition of the Wehrmacht, and the permanently "provisional" conditions of armistice, which as of 1990 have not been followed up by a peace treaty between victors and vanquished. The architecture of the bipolar system basically contains a nagging initial flaw, i.e., that it derives from the war system in force during the conflict, which for years represented the only bridge linking prewar and postwar international orders and provided the only functional paradigm for all international interaction.

The Internationalism of
U.S. Political Culture, 1940–1941

In 1940, the war system framework was the only reality the United States had for assessing the international situation. In fact, since the Civil War, political attitudes toward the outside world had passed through three basic phases of development.

The first phase opened with what Charles S. Campbell defined as the "transformation of American politics"[58] between 1865 and 1900 and developed in parallel with the nation's transformation from an agricultural to an industrial society. The Americans, and in particular the East Coast elites, had their first taste of expansionism during these years.[59] This transformation was slow and really only took hold in the twenty years from 1898 to 1920. The so-called Reform Age[60] was in fact an era of assertive activism in U.S. foreign policy that concluded in 1920 with the Senate's refusal to ratify the Covenant of the League of Nations.[61]

The second phase was one of isolation, beginning under Warren Harding's presidency and extending uninterruptedly to 1940, though not without some variations in style. During those years the nation seemed to forget its imperial background and its glory in the trenches of St. Michel in 1918 and limited its movements until 1940 largely to the colonial policing of Central America.

The third phase was catalyzed by the fall of France in June 1940 and, combining the various strands of old American internationalism, wove a new brand of internationalism. After Pearl Harbor, this fresh awareness would be translated into bipartisanship, an unprecedented consensus of both political parties on foreign-policy issues, heartedly condoned by a popular majority. In 1940–1941, however, this ideological conversion was just beginning. Despite the abundance of study and research groups, schools of thought, books, conferences and lectures, newspaper articles and pamphlets, even announcements in the press paid for by those in favor of the rebirth of internationalism,[62] and of course, the appeal for aid by the Allies themselves, little could be done to rouse the sleepy and apprehensive isolationist public, a nation that was still catching its breath after a crippling economic crisis.[63]

Yet, during the preceding period of Republican and isolationist administrations,[64] certain core ideas of internationalism had been nurtured through a tenacious campaign of information, analysis, and documentation. A prime example was the series *American Foreign Relations*, initiated in 1928 with a volume edited by Charles P. Howland; in 1931 the series title was changed to *The United States in World Affairs*, an annual publication issued by the New York–based Council on Foreign Relations (and edited in the first years by Walter Lippmann).[65] Other publications include the studies on international relations, illustrated in detail in a volume edited in 1934 by Edith Ware, with an introduction by James T. Shotwell,[66] a name we will come across frequently. The material contained in these works is very revealing. As might be expected, studies in economy, international finance, and international law tend to outweigh those strictly on international politics. However, the list of agencies and research centers operating in the field of foreign affairs (in the mid-1930s) already included some of the institutions that would continue to raise awareness and further public knowledge on these themes in the postwar years—such as the Carnegie Endowment for Peace, the Rockefeller Foundation, the Social Science Research Council, the National Research Council, as well as organizations like the Foreign Policy Association, the World Peace Foundation, the Institute of Current World Affairs, and the Council on Foreign Relations.

In those years, relatively little attention was directed at Europe. In fact, in the list of geographical areas of interest to the U.S. internationalists cited by Ware, Europe was assigned a mere three pages, as compared to forty-three on the Pacific, sixteen on Latin America, and eighteen pages on relations with Canada.[67] This disregard for Europe was part of a deep-rooted U.S. tradition (signs of which have occasionally emerged in more recent times), which left little margin for the keener internationalists who, like Francis Miller and Clarence Streit, urged a closer U.S. alignment with Europe in the 1930s than had ever existed.[68]

Given this framework, it seems almost a miracle that only a few months after Pearl Harbor, by the beginning of 1942, the number of private and public organizations devoted to the study of postwar planning and Europe had multiplied. According to the *Bulletin of the Commission to Study the Organization of Peace* (edited in New York and directed by Shotwell), which listed the groups and research in progress regarding postwar foreign-policy planning in the United States and furnished bibliographies and suggestions for further reading,[69] there were a great many deeply committed organizations, private and otherwise. There existed a total of ninety-one private organizations, complemented by thirty-two universities and other so-called learned societies, seventeen religious groups, and twenty-eight government agencies. Foreign or international groups operating from outside (of less interest here) numbered no fewer than forty-one. Another list (preceding Shotwell's by a few months), found among the "Pasvolsky Papers" of the State Department, recorded thirty-six private and university organizations conducting highly advanced research projects, plus twelve public bodies of various levels also engaged in the study of solutions for the postwar world.

This almost obsessive interest in the future, in stark contrast with the behavior of nearly every other country, belligerent or neutral, testifies to an American predisposition for organizing reality (including on a technical level). It also indicates a kind of unconscious or premonitory sensation that the burden of decision regarding the future world order lay indeed with the United States itself.

3

Interdependence and National Security: The Two Pillars of U.S. Foreign Policy

Definitions:
Interdependence and National Security

What was still needed to confer an operative framework on the sweeping generalizations that had always served as the basis of U.S. foreign policy was an occasion supplied by history itself. That opportunity came between 1940 and 1941 in the revolution triggered by the definitive collapse of the "intermediate system," the post-1919 version of the balance of power. The seedbed had been amply prepared, and the historical context did the rest.

The transformation of the two rudimentary concepts of growth and power into the effective, sophisticated formulas of "interdependence" and "national security" was a unique historical event. Despite their cultural and genetic differences, these two pillars of future U.S. foreign policy were made to work in unison, at times prompting decisive synergies. They also offered an effective means of persuading the public at home and abroad.

Both concepts were fundamental and derived directly from their somewhat primitive and less serviceable forerunners, which supplied their theoretical and cultural justification. They gradually assumed the role of the philosophical and ideological premises for method and action and at the same time became honed-down analytical tools.

From the very outset, "interdependence" was a highly comprehensive idea, drawing on a peaceful approach to international politics based on bargaining theory and on the traditional mystique of the free market. One of the undisputed postulates of interdependence was the conviction that fostering economic and financial interaction between countries would of itself improve international relations, automatically creating reciprocal

35

advantages between partner nations that would benefit the entire world. Interdependence also implicitly envisaged the preservation of the international status quo, so as to avoid sparking off open conflict, while at the same time avoiding an international stalemate. Indeed, it was hoped that the application of the theory of interdependence would trigger a process of gradual and painless transformations that would in turn increase the U.S. role vis-à-vis the outside world.

The stabilizing effect of the Bretton Woods Conference on the international monetary system is a good example of such an approach to postwar international relations. In the same vein, the Marshall Plan influenced the revival of the European economy in general and was a boost to U.S. businesses.[1]

"National security" was a considerably more elusive concept, however. It was based on a complex analytical formula rooted in the strategic and geopolitical approach according to which the potentially anarchic order of international society could be safeguarded (or imposed) only through permanent military readiness. This readiness rests on a network of naval, air, and land bases, a certain balance of power in relation to the main international actors, and the capacity to intervene with force, "like a firm and wise policeman,"[2] in the face of dangerous or crisis situations, whether threatened or actually under way, in any corner of the world, should these situations seem to jeopardize the security of the United States. Examples of this particular conception of foreign policy came in the wake of the war. U.S. resolve to apply the Truman Doctrine of containment in 1947 as a yardstick for U.S. political activity and U.S. commitment (the first ever in peacetime) to a defensive military alliance with other Western European countries (NATO) were both decisions fueled by the awareness that the security of the nation had to be defended beyond the oceans and that the gradual extension of the concept of national security had become irreversible.

Neither of these two concepts was new to U.S. foreign policy, not even in the 1940s. But what made them so significant was their interaction and political usefulness during and after World War II. The formula proved so successful that both the leaders and the public were galvanized into a common vision of foreign policy: They saw the two concepts as being in harmony with the basic tone of U.S. political culture, referred to as the "American creed"[3] and the "American myth."[4] "In America," wrote Huntington, "political ideas may have been less sophisticated in theory but they have also been more important in impact than in most other societies." He added that "they have been a critical element in the definition of national identity and in the delimitation of political authority."[5]

The definition of the "American identity" had to be realized more in normative than in real terms, which is why ideas, in contrast to history and events, have had such a creative and binding force in the United States. What has been dubbed as the "I-v-I gap," i.e., the gap between "ideals" and "institutions" and hence between "promises" and "performance," could by analogy be applied to the specific section of the U.S. political system that regulates its relations with the outside world.⁶

The concepts of interdependence and national security straddle both ideals and institutions. But when they were originally formulated, and especially at the moment they passed from the fantasy realm of Manifest Destiny to being an effective part of global policy, they attained extraordinary political and cultural weight. They converted a country that had long fostered a bias for isolationism or, at best, a marked aversion to European politics into an active society, willing to assume burdensome global responsibilities. Furthermore, these two effective and interactive formulas, like a distillate of the country's entire political heritage, gave rise to political "bipartisanship," a wholly original two-party accord on foreign-policy issues that was to last without interruption from 1941 to 1968.⁷

For the first time, the United States was able to draw on a methodological and operative infrastructure, a mixture of idealism and realism, which, in the wake of the "Americanization" of the Western world, was soon transformed into an international working philosophy accepted by the other nations and by the metanational bodies (authorities and institutions) for a good four decades. In sum, one can say that interdependence was a mandatory functional twin of national security and vice versa.

In the course of this book, I will verify how and why this interactive dyad of concepts worked so well and for so long, especially in the creation of the Atlantic System, a delicate geopolitical-functional balance established between the United States and Western Europe after the war. The historical roots of the concepts lead back to the formation of the Atlantic area, which in the first years of World War II was destined to become a "mediterranean" basin of communication, of interdependence, and of reciprocal security, and to cease to be a barrier between the two continents.

Whereas the natural synergy between the developed nations of like culture around the Atlantic is aptly embodied in the concept of interdependence,⁸ the importance of the Atlantic in connection with national security is less easily pinned down. And yet, on closer inspection, national security too was molded by the course of events in and around the Atlantic. The concept of security developed and expanded in 1940–

1941 largely because of disputes about the Atlantic itself. The increasingly firm arguments the United States used in contesting the German right to navigate freely Atlantic waters and to retain bases in the Caribbean, Greenland, and Iceland provided the basis for justifications that were to be widely used later to sustain the idea of U.S. national security in the postwar era.[9]

If after the war, there was some functional unevenness in the employment of this conceptual dyad in U.S. foreign policy, it was due to Washington's failure to persuade other nations or regional areas to adopt this Atlantic or "Euro-American" model of interdependence and national security, with everything it implied.[10] As it happened, things did not always go smoothly when the paradigm was mechanically applied elsewhere. So far, it has worked reasonably well with Japan, although the forms assumed by interdependence with the Japanese have been far less simple and stable than they seem to have been in Europe. The United States has managed to maintain an easier footing with Tokyo on national security issues also—even though the interaction between the two concepts (and thereby their reciprocal substitution) in response to developments has too often been impeded from evolving with due flexibility and speed. On some occasions, instead of ensuring a positive and combined result, the two concepts have provoked a stalemate or induced negative political repercussions, as in the case of the long and belabored relationship between the United States and Indochina or the United States and the Middle East.

During the neutral and wartime years, the concept of security took priority. Later, during the reconstruction period, the economic and financial criteria of interdependence took the lead. In the 1960s and into the 1970s, the two generally balanced out. From the latter part of the 1970s until the late 1980s, new tensions and economic hardships in the Western system once again brought the issue of security—the military side of the structural transformation of the economic model—to the fore. In the late 1980s the pendulum shifted again, and the evolution of the Communist world gave a renewed role to the concept of interdependence.[11]

The Origins of Interdependence

The term "interdependence" has its origins in a broad family of closely related concepts and is essentially a merger of two different notions: integration and dependence.[12] Without going further into the semantic and Anglo-Saxon geographical origins of the concept,[13] I will note that Roosevelt himself, in his inaugural address of March 4, 1933, used the term "interdependence,"[14] but with a very different meaning from the one it was to acquire in due course. In any case, in studies from Rappard to R. Cooper, interdependence is implied to have been essentially an American "discovery."[15]

As can be seen from Roosevelt's "Quarantine Speech" of October 5, 1937,[16] the concept was originally adopted as a means to avoid the possible perils of an open internationalist commitment, rather than to provoke or seek a commitment.[17] It soon changed into a kind of conceptual skeleton key. In 1937 the concept of "interdependence" was employed to avoid a political broadside with Congress and its largely isolationist viewpoint. In 1941 it was used to secure durable ties with Great Britain. In 1947 it was transformed into a philosophy (for domestic use) to justify the U.S. presence in Europe during the era of the European Recovery Program and the Marshall Plan. Once the range of action for interdependence had been determined, the model went into active operation during the war years and after.[18]

Despite supposed parity on the normative level, interdependence actually implied a marked asymmetry in relations among nations (whether allied or adversary). The fact of acting in a situation of apparent neutrality (in which the real inequality of power between nations was subordinated to a theoretical statute of parity delineating them) depended exclusively on the basic premise of impartiality presumed by the Ricardian theory of comparative costs and advantages.[19]

Nor must we forget that the concept of interdependence stemmed from the "peaceful" facet of U.S. political culture. Unlike its twin concept (national security), interdependence immediately evokes an idea of affinities and communication, as opposed to clash and withdrawal. This occurs because the policy of interdependence aims to maintain quasi-objective ties between nations. That is, they are supposedly regulated by objective economic laws, accompanied by the automatic defense mechanism that Robert Keohane and Joseph N. Nye defined in terms of "sensitivity" and "vulnerability."[20] The "interdependent" spirit of U.S. foreign policy therefore helped bridle the narcissistic or neoisolationist undercurrents that frequently kindled bouts of hypernationalism focused almost exclusively on the question of security.

In the two-year buildup to the war, interdependence was still in embryonic form. Although no longer simply equated with the traditional free-trader outlook, it had not yet found the right path for becoming an organic component of American political action in the world. After some hesitation, it would orient itself toward restoring a neoliberal international economic order, piloted by the U.S. economy.[21]

The "institutionalist" path of trade accords, which generated whole bodies of entirely new technical norms and a set of permanent and multinational economic structures, later appeared to be the most viable course. It was to do away with some of the traditional nationalistic egoism, thus creating a safety net, a sort of economic first line of defense of the security of the postwar world, which, for various reasons, anticipated and compensated for the shortcomings of traditional politico-strategic-based national security.

The Origins of National Security

The origins of national security are altogether different, though the term itself, like interdependence, is the outcome of a kind of linguistic merger—again of two concepts: collective security and national interests.[22] The second expression, with its seemingly precise and solid appeal, is undoubtedly the more important. To some extent, "national interests" is a modern term expressing the concept of *raison d'Etat*, of French revolutionary times.[23] The notion of national interests did not become an operative analytical concept until the period during and after World War II.[24] Distinct from the "public interest," "national interests" embodied a concept that was potentially "able to describe, explain, and orient" the foreign policy of nations.[25]

There was one hurdle, however. In the political newspeak of postwar international relations, the formula of national security seemed too explicit and contrasted too much with the postwar "universalist" philosophy. It jarred with the earlier (and failed) experience of collective security, whose disintegration had precipitated World War II, but which remained one of the victors' guiding standards in 1945.[26] As with the concept of interdependence, which had ensured U.S. participation in international postwar economic relations without jeopardizing the total autonomy of the nation's basic choices in any way, the concept of national security also stemmed from a twofold and apparently contradictory need. On the one hand, it was crucial to overcome the selfish isolation implied by a restricted vision of national interests; on the other, there were several advantages to be gained from achieving collective security through the normative mechanisms of a multilateral alliance (like NATO) or through a bilateral nonaggression agreement (with the Soviet Union).

As a means of conducting power relations among nation-states through a partially centralized system of security agreements, collective security suggested greater openness and real international commitments. It also implied the creation of a new network of interactive communications based on regulations defined through treaties and international bodies. The potential risk of collective security was the need to delegate out portions of national sovereignty, i.e., to entrust supranational bodies and organisms with the safeguarding of national interests. But the utter failure of attempts to map out the areas of collective security in Europe and Asia between 1919 and 1939 dispelled all hope that such designs had anything concrete to offer.

The two faces of the emerging national security concept had already been well defined by the time the Eurocentric system collapsed, and the United States (and especially the internationalist public) was suddenly forced to adopt a definite position on the war—a war that threatened to spill out of Europe and engulf the rest of the world.[27] This linking of U.S. national interests with the notion of a future system of collective security marked the beginnings of a conviction that in the course of the war was first adopted by the elites and then spread throughout the entire country.

Such a linguistic and political conjugation could not come about until the events of the war (and hence the forceful dynamics of the "war system") led the United States to assume ever-greater responsibilities in the conduct of the conflict. Thus the two forms of security almost seemed to coincide, and the U.S. national interests were virtually equated or confused with the collective security of the world at large. This marked association of the two different formulas was neither entirely nor permanently accepted by the other nations involved—especially the Soviet Union and Great Britain, which equated the new setup with the end of international polyarchy and with the irremediable decline of national sovereignty, giving way to a universalist or even neoimperialist international framework.[28]

A more scientific definition of the term "national security" was not achieved until much later, upon the unification of the U.S. armed forces and the creation of the National Security Council. In substance, the new definition went back to the source of the arguments, stemming from the events and outcome of the war—i.e., the virtually total identification of national interests with collective security on both a regional and a global scale. However, the two concepts gained a theoretical framework and an implicit prescriptive nature when national security was described as "the ability of a nation to protect its internal values from external threats."[29] The protection of internal values obviously included the possibility of quantifying and classifying those values as well as the ability to defend them with "force" against external enemies.[30]

This "exportation" of concepts drawn from the domestic political culture, such as the notion of "internal values," is a recurrent feature of U.S. history. In the final analysis, these values are the paradigms for the U.S. collective identity. Their history and meaning can be traced in some detail to the texts of the Founders, in the formal Constitution and in the "material" constitution—the political literature produced by the Founders of the nation and assimilated by the masses since the first decades of the new republic, and successively transmitted to all those who flocked to the United States seeking their fortune.

Paradoxically, we can affirm that the conversion of certain internal values into values for export (i.e., into foreign-policy guidelines) has been a far longer and more laborious process than the task of adapting those internal values to survive in a hostile international context, where they were supposed to take effect. It took the Americans some time to realize that, to be successfully exported, the home values needed careful revising and their formulas likewise adjusting. By failing to adapt them adequately, the Americans were responsible for incidents of reciprocal misunderstanding that sorely tested U.S. relations with the rest of the world. Some otherwise incomprehensible political operations, such as the U.S. alternation between expansion and regression, visible from 1898 to the present day, were caused by this failure to master the differences in method and form between domestic and foreign policy.

The concept of national security therefore also suffered from this seesawing between internal motivations and outside requirements and has been subjected to a great many analytical revisions in the course of the century. Examples can be seen in the series of definitions made by the National Security League,[31] which predate the U.S. entry into World War I. Since 1916, this organization had been running a systematic information campaign on the concept of national security—first through the publication of a guidebook,[32] and then (toward the end of the 1920s and early 1930s) in a magazine entitled *National Security Quarterly*. The publication openly voiced the notion that a "war of defense was always practicable,"[33] an idea few shared at the time. The argument generated a great deal of discussion during World War II, and after the war, several countries altered the title "secretary of war" to the more toned-down "secretary of defense."[34]

Even in 1917, the concept of national "security" was interchangeable with that of national "defense"—as can be clearly inferred from the subtitle of a National Security League publication, "A National Defense Catechism for the Busy Man or Woman."[35] Another example is Eugene J. Young's book of 1936 in which he sketched a rather biased interpretation of international history between 1919 and 1935 and clearly exposed the concept of U.S. "security" as distinctly expansionist. Young's scenarios were in fact feasible. First of all, he maintained that the United States, faced with the decline of the European powers, would sooner or later have to assume the duty of "stabilizer" within a new power structure that would no longer be centered on Europe. According to Young, there were two options—either an imperial setup or a system of "world freedom."[36] Further on in the book, however, resurrecting themes dear to Francis Miller and Clarence Streit, Young also accorded the United States a military role and specific strategic tasks—responsibilities the Americans had not yet had or dreamed of assuming. The idea of a close collaboration between English-speaking countries (a sort of Atlantic System) and provisions for a "world peace power" (an idea that Roosevelt brought up frequently in his speeches during the war) were already themes that Young and certain contemporaries pursued, often very explicitly. Reviewing the situation as it stood, Young wrote that "we police the Caribbean Region, seeing to it that the surrounding nations do not misbehave too violently. We have asserted the right to intervene in dangerous situations in South America, having taken a leading part in the peace proceedings that ended the Chaco war. Our Asiatic fleet appears wherever there may be trouble on the coast of China; and our warships have a share in the patrol of the Yangtze River. Our government was once formally committed to the world policy by the formula laid down by Theodore Roosevelt in his corollary to the Monroe Doctrine; and has since been committed less directly by utterances of later Presidents who have held that trouble making anywhere in the world is a concern of ours."[37]

It was not until later, during World War II (and especially afterward), that the various components of the internationalist notion of security were examined and developed fully. Walter Lippmann's 1943 definition of security has become a classic: "A country has security when it does not have to sacrifice its legitimate interests to avoid war, and is able, if challenged, to maintain them by war."[38] The concept at stake here is more complex, however. Despite its proclaimed aspirations, Lippmann's definition was born in and remained specific to the war period, more as a method for action and as a national political philosophy upon the country's entering the war than as a result of the identification of U.S. war aims for the postwar world. Here too, there is no clear definition of the meaning of terms such as "legitimate interests," which represented the core of the problem. It was also unclear how far the United States could, or should, entangle itself.

The association of war aims with postwar planning had already conferred a permanent semantic ambivalence between the formulas drawn from traditional idealist culture and those of more realist extraction.[39] This equivocation was to dog U.S. foreign policy until the final disintegration of party consensus and bipartisanship in 1968.[40] This theoretical uncertainty has never been entirely overcome. Even in the normative laws relating to the security machinery, sanctioned and buttressed by the National Security Act of 1947, that inherent ambiguity is evident in the official texts and in subsequent interpretations.[41]

Limits to Research: The Atlantic System

The first concrete attempt to purge the national security issue of the ambiguities that inhibited the formulations of a generalized theory was the institution of a territorial and geopolitical subsystem, the actualization of such a theory. That subsystem, discussed above, was the Atlantic System, which was grounded in the special relationship between the United States and Great Britain. The Atlantic System supplied the operative core of the Grand Alliance and provided the heart of the entire structure of U.S. alliances both during and after the war. Around that system the United Nations would be formed. The Anglo-American coalition thus was the bedrock of the new postwar international system, and as such it had to reflect, at least in general, the method and the ultimate intentions of the Americans.

The new demands arising from the war situation, however, forced Washington to modify its initial approach, almost from the very outset. In the long run, the model the Americans eventually drew on, both ideologically and politically, was the one that had crystallized during the war, from the "destroyers for bases" deal of the summer of 1940 (when the United States gave fifty destroyers to the British in exchange for several naval bases in the Caribbean) until the announcement of the Atlantic Charter the following summer. None of the later subsystems of international interaction, whether set up voluntarily or in response to requirements arising in the decades after the war, could match the Atlantic System for theoretical soundness or functionality. Shortly after the war, the system was refined and extended to cover the whole of Western Europe.

For this reason, too, this book has precise limits of time and space, as I cannot hope to cover the (as yet largely unexplored) terrain of concepts formed in other countries both before and during the war relative to the other main territorial regions—Japan and East Asia, and then the Soviet Union and its sphere of influence, which had been steadily growing since 1939. My attention here is focused primarily on the relations in the Western Hemisphere, and on the Atlantic System, which began to take shape during the first months of neutrality as the conceptual embryo of a general "quasi theory" of international relations.

To complete the picture, one should also perhaps deal with the Pacific, which played a major role in determining war developments and their consequences. However, the process through which Washington and the internationalist elites in the United States constructed their schemes for postwar East Asia is perhaps not that different from the process of compiling the far more complex and sophisticated scheme for regulating relations within Europe.[42] One might even add that many U.S. policy miscarriages in Asia between the end of World War II and the 1970s were at least in part due to traces of prewar philosophy lingering in the U.S. attitude toward Asia.

Since the end of the nineteenth century the Americans had had a well-defined policy for Asia,[43] with a special body of rules of conduct (ranging from John Hay's notes on the Open Door Policy, to official policies for China, the Philippines, and Japan) and an entire generation of specialists in civil, academic, and military affairs for the Far East. Consequently, when the new bipolar international system effaced the existing power balance in the East, the Americans found themselves in serious operative straits. The need to bring the old Asian policy—which hinged on mediation with the European colonial powers rather than with the main on-site actors[44]—into line with the two-way partitioning of ideological, political, and geostrategic influences between the United States and the Soviet Union resulted in a great many miscalculations on Washington's part.[45]

In any case, Washington's inconsistency in trying to pin down a "rationale" for its Asian policy over three and one-half decades—until it resumed relations with China and the Indochina war was terminated— testified to a lack of planning: Even the papers of the CFR and other institutions involved in postwar policy planning showed a decided lack of innovation and articulation on Asian issues compared with the theoretical development of the Atlantic System. There was one exception perhaps, U.S. policy on China itself, which involved a clash between two schools of thought immediately after the war; the issue was brusquely resolved by the inquiries of Senator Joseph McCarthy.[46]

An analysis of U.S. relations with the Soviet Union and its system of influence in Eastern Europe would be equally complex and perhaps pointless, chiefly because U.S. and Soviet policy were so opposed that, for reasons intrinsic to the very nature of the bipolar international system, relations between the two superpowers were regulated by norms and behavior that differed considerably from those the United States employed with the rest of the world.[47] In some ways, U.S.-Soviet relations were the only part of U.S. foreign policy in which the outside world (the Soviet Union in this case) was "internalized" by the national political culture, through ideology, perceptions, Sovietology, and the arms race. The Eastern European subsystem was itself a residual product of the anomalous interaction between the United States and the Soviet Union. And as such, for decades it had no other autonomy than that of being a kind of unknown territory negatively defined as a "non-Europe" or "non-Atlantic" entity.[48] The implosion of the Soviet external empire in 1989 was necessary for the restoration, even in the West, of the feeling that East-Central Europe was truly Europe.

The evolution of the concept of national security was rather laborious and was subject to continuous refinement even after its conceptual and normative definition in the period 1947–1950.[49] Upon analysis, its structure reveals various factors at work—some constants and others variables—but nearly all from the American viewpoint with domestic or, rather, "national" references. The factors of context and interaction with the outside world, including the behavior of the Soviet Union, were therefore subordinated to the country's internal political factors.

There were thus really only two constants influencing the formation and evolution of the policy of national security: (1) internationalism, as a means of establishing those dangerous "entangling alliances," thereby getting around George Washington's legacy; and (2) the doctrine of containment, which after the war became the mainstay of the entire system of external U.S. values in the United States.[50] But these two constants catalyzed the formation of a great variety of key words, political formulas, and operative concepts, which, unlike the constants themselves, followed a very erratic path of evolution. The decision to stick by choices made during and after World War II, to respect the wartime alliances even in peacetime (the first constant), and to base U.S. foreign policy on the containment of Soviet and Communist expansion throughout the world (the second constant) was prompted from within. The set of variables, however, was dramatically influenced by other inputs, some of which stemmed from the domestic political system, some from the international context. Running parallel to internationalism and containment and providing a sort of operating code for those constants, there were two key issues: (1) the evolution of strategic doctrines underlying the question of security; and (2) the problem of domestic political support on security doctrines and needs, i.e., the level of consensus from the public and the elites toward government policy.[51]

However, all these issues fall outside this book's area of research, which is deliberately limited to the Western Hemisphere and the period 1939–1941 because of my conviction that U.S. postwar foreign policy has its roots in political developments that occurred before World War II and the nation's subsequent rise to world primacy. The origins lie in the country's cultural and political substratum, as the United States sought the operative formulas and historical occasions to create—as it indeed attempted to create—a world in its own image.[52]

4

The Case Study:
The Council on Foreign Relations

The War and Peace Studies Project

The grand strategies for the reorganization of the postwar world,[1] and particularly the guidelines for "asymmetric interdependence" between the United States and Europe,[2] were shaped gradually in a process determined by a multiplicity of sources, beyond the scope of any one group, even the specialists.[3] However, a set of ideas about the future began to be established within this belabored political process.[4]

After carefully sifting through much unpublished material, I traced some of these "special" (and informal) cultural and political sources generated by the internationalist group, which acted together in the formulation of strategies for relations between the United States and Europe.[5] Without attempting to gauge exactly what cultural influence or political weight these sources had, or to organize the various documents on a clearly defined scale of roles and functions within the framework of the foreign-policy decision-making process, I have picked out some of the more original themes of the debate about U.S. global responsibilities during the initial period of the war, when Washington was still neutral (1940–1941).[6]

Distinct conceptual and even linguistic leitmotivs running through all the records provide a sort of chronological catalogue of the rapid evolution of the concepts of U.S. foreign policy during that two-year period. Central to this evolution were the main world powers and their politics—particularly the Axis countries, which were potential enemies of the United States, and of course the most powerful of them, Nazi Germany.

Throughout this phase of uncertainty, U.S. policy was continually retuned to the changing options (whether real or imaginary) open to Germany and Japan (and, very marginally, Italy). Furthermore, there were interesting parallels of approach between the themes analyzed and scenarios imagined, which derived from the interaction between the "peace aims" officially broadcast throughout the United States and the "war aims" of Nazi Germany, constantly readjusted to the changing course of military operations in Europe and the evolution of public perceptions within the United States.

For my main source material, I have chosen a broad selection of records from the New York–based Council on Foreign Relations (CFR), coordinated in the War and Peace Studies project (WPS).[7] Most of these documents are either memoranda or discussion digests drafted by the study groups specially set up within the WPS according to specific areas of interest: Economic and Financial (EF); Security and Armaments (SA); Political (P); Territorial (T); and Peace Aims (PA).

Despite the WPS records' being the output of a private and nonpartisan organization (the Council on Foreign Relations), they are of particular interest for a variety of reasons: (1) They provide a distillate of ideas and international political culture within the East Coast Establishment, which for many decades informally held the reins of foreign affairs; (2) they express the interests and political options of the major groups of the U.S. business community, with their links to the international economy and finance; (3) they are "confidential" studies and papers designed to influence Washington—directly or indirectly, on short-term issues and more far-reaching matters alike—by providing original concepts and arguments; (4) they are the work of individuals in close, ongoing interaction (often personal) with the political system; (5) these documents were not merely CFR offerings to the State Department, but they were frequently requested by higher ranks of the administration and, as such, answered real and immediate needs of the State Department, feeding the flow of information and analysis that was being channeled toward Washington from various quarters; and finally, (6) they proved to be one of the first examples of systematic reflection and organic political proposals existing in the country from the beginning of the conflict.

For a clearer idea of the historical value of the WPS archives, one should look at some of the leading names of the CFR study groups, especially the members of the Steering Committee coordinating the work. These include Norman H. Davis (who was president of the entire WPS project from 1939 to 1944), Hanson W. Baldwin, Isaiah Bowman, Allen W. Dulles, Carter Goodrich, Alvin H. Hansen, Whitney H. Shepardson, Jacob Viner, Edward P. Warner, and Henry M. Wriston. Among the various study groups, one need only list the more noted figures: In the Security and Armaments Group there were Gen. Clayton Bissell, Adm. William F. Pratt, Harold Sprout, and Gen. George W. Strong. Besides the two famous economists, Hansen and Viner, the Economic and Financial Group included William Diebold, Percy W. Bidwell, Eugene

Staley, Arthur R. Upgren, Winfield W. Riefler. In the Political Group were Frank Altschul, Hamilton Fish Armstrong, John Foster Dulles, Maj. George F. Eliot, Thomas K. Finletter, William Langer, Owen Lattimore, Philip E. Mosely, James T. Shotwell, and Nicholas Roosevelt. The Territorial Group included John Gunther, Bruce C. Hopper, and others, including the famous geographer Isaiah Bowman. In the last group, studying Peace Aims, which was constituted in 1941, there were many of those already mentioned from other groups, plus William L. Shirer, James G. McDonald, Frank D. Graham, Oscar C. Stine, Tracy B. Kittredge, and others.

The participants in these groups had had direct experience with the preparatory work for the Paris Peace Conference (1919), and some had had even earlier experience—during World War I—such as J. F. Dulles and Shotwell, who had been members of the Inquiry, an organization of scholars and specialists serving as an advisory bureau to President Woodrow Wilson between 1917 and 1919.[8] All these men were leaders in the broadest sense, operating in the broad fields of economy, banking, and other liberal professions (lawyers in particular), at Ivy League universities, or in the civil and military administrations.[9] If one also bears in mind that during the war many of these men took on important positions in the government—A. W. Dulles, for example, left the WPS in 1943 to work in the Office of Strategic Services (OSS) in Europe—it is not hard to imagine the great importance of the discussions within the CFR in orienting the formation of concepts on U.S. foreign policy during and after the war.[10]

And we should not overlook the fact that the WPS was born as a complex research project before the State Department and other government units began any serious work on these themes. Harley Notter clearly pointed that out in his well-known book:

> The Council on Foreign Relations in New York, upon the initiative of Hamilton Fish Armstrong, Editor of *Foreign Affairs*, and Walter H. Mallory, Executive Director, had proposed to Assistant Secretary of State George S. Messersmith as early as September 12 [1939] to expand its studies on foreign relations and to make them available for the use of the Department. This offer was accepted after consideration by Secretary Hull and Under Secretary Welles.[11]

At the time however, the staff of the State Department was very small indeed. In October 1939, the entire professional and clerical corps amounted to only 900 people, only 200 of whom were at the executive level. It was therefore highly improbable that the Committee on Problems of Peace and Reconstruction, set up by Cordell Hull on December 27,

1939, with the specific task of surveying "the basic principles which should underlie a desirable world order to be evolved after the termination of present hostilities, with primary reference to the best interests of the United States," could reasonably carry out its duty. It was not until the end of May 1940, when the German victories in Europe began to rouse the ministries, that the State Department thought seriously about setting up the machinery for postwar planning, but at least until the end of 1941 there was hardly any.

Apart from the possible influence of the WPS on the administration's foreign-policy planning, my study focuses on the intellectual climate (and hence the forms of "perception"[12]) in internationalist circles in relation to the events taking place in Europe, and especially attitudes toward German actions. My hypothesis is that from the opening years of the war in Europe, even before the United States entered the fray, there had been a gradual buildup of a "globalist" theoretical infrastructure for the postwar world order. This scheme, though implicit and informal in nature, denoted the confluence of a series of internationalist sources, especially those that later identified themselves with the joint formula of interdependence and national security. It was not simply another imaginary role for the United States articulated through a somewhat prophetic though isolated proposal—as in the political "literature" of Archibald C. Coolidge at the start of the century (1908), or Miller and Hill in 1930, or Streit in 1938.[13]

The dawn of "globalist" awareness in the United States came in the difficult months of the spring and summer of 1940, with the growing crisis in the European balance of power, when the fall of France and the utter isolation of Great Britain heralded the start of an irreversible metamorphosis in international relations.[14] The problem American internationalists faced, under the mounting pressure of events, was not whether the United States should assume a role and function equal to those of other Great Powers in the international system, but whether to replace the prewar international balance of power with a new model, a scheme invented from scratch.[15]

These topics found an extraordinary laboratory of ideas and analysis in the work of the WPS. This does not mean that the postwar planning of the CFR or the later official work of the Interdepartmental Group to Consider Post-War International Economic Problems and Policies (with the participation of the State Department, the Treasury, the Department of Commerce, and the Department of Agriculture) or of other similar organizations was in fact the outcome of programmed, detailed planning. Furthermore, I do not believe that the work of other public research centers, i.e., those not coordinated with the Department of State, such as the Department of War, the Board of Economic Warfare (after 1942), or the Office of Strategic Services, really played the role of "invisible government," as claimed by some U.S. historians and political scientists.

It is now generally agreed that U.S. foreign policy, at the operational level during and after the war, was not the political transposition of planning theory and scenarios originated by the study centers but the product of events and many different factors. In part, that policy was the result of the interaction within the country between the interest groups and the ideas of certain statesmen, whereas in the international arena U.S. foreign policy was the outcome of "perceptions" and inter-actions among the main actors in the conflict. It should not be forgotten, however, that the large number of studies, analyses, and proposals produced by the many organizations operating in the area of U.S. postwar planning offer an extraordinary chronicle and a wealth of ideas for study. These cannot be compared with work done in this area by other nations, belligerent or neutral.[16]

Obviously, for the studies of certain U.S. historians (such as Divine, Kolko, Dallek, and Chadwin[17]) to shed light on the formation of foreign-policy decisions, they must be centered on the postwar planning carried out by the several groups set up by the State Department under the guidance of Cordell Hull and Sumner Welles (coordinated by Leo Pasvolsky) and similar activities run by the other departments and public bodies (including the Export-Import Bank, the Federal Security Agency, and the Tariff Commission). As we have seen, the vast amount of work turned out by the various government organizations and agencies was not entirely independent from the work being undertaken by other private "nonpartisan" study centers. For this reason, the output of the State Department was sometimes a product or a synthesis not only of the "official" political processes but also of the reading of papers and documents produced by private institutions. The working style of the CFR study groups, the absolute confidentiality of the texts distributed (in never more than twenty-five copies) to politicians and high-level functionaries of the State Department, the total absence of publicity on either the work sessions or the resulting documentation, and the frequency and systematic scheduling of the meetings held by each group—are all factors that imply (and in some cases prove[18]) that there was a kind of informal contract for the drafting of these memoranda, not only on the part of the main recipient (the administration and/or the president himself), but also by the internationalist lobby at large, which needed concrete schemes, structures, rules, institutions, and guidelines for man-aging the future U.S. hegemony, in order to direct it most effectively, according to their own interests as well as their own political and cultural convictions.

The years 1940–1941 saw the birth of the first conceptual structure (which would take on a definitive form only in 1945–1950) of what was later to be labeled "consensus diplomacy," which would last uninterruptedly until 1968.[19] Also developing were the beginnings of a closer political interaction among the academics, the administration, and the business community, a relationship that was to become a central factor during the first years of Harry Truman's presidency and later of John F. Kennedy's presidency.[20] A network of people was forming, a true structure or framework, at once conservative and liberal, imaginative and yet very elitist, a network confident of its own ability to develop as well as of its power. Although that network would not determine the major presidential decisions (which are always a product of a highly complex process), it would certainly influence most U.S. international political initiatives. This interactive framework engendered the set of concepts and opinions on the functional morphology that the postwar international system would assume in order for it to be consistent and compatible with the government of the future "empire" the United States was about to inherit. The structure also gave rise to an innovative and continuous stream of planning and channeling of cultural and political sources into the common interest of a "new" U.S. internationalism, which was later to become the ideology of the Atlantic System and of the "free world" as a whole.[21]

The Basis of Postwar Planning

Historical assessments of World War II, including American analyses (whether orthodox or revisionist), have concentrated almost exclusively on two main sets of issues whose development was greatly influenced by the work of the East Coast internationalist lobby. The first was the creation of the legalistic and institutional formulas for the "world order" of the United Nations, with the United States at its head. This markedly "legalistic and normative component," to quote R. G. Gardner,[22] was a constant throughout U.S. foreign policy, and its cultural origins went far back in time, merging with the constitutionalist tradition going back to the era of the Founders. However, the legalistic component transcended the customary limits of American tradition, leading to a new awareness of foreign policy at the turn of the century, and finally flourishing in the person of President Woodrow Wilson.[23]

The second block of issues concerned the reorganization of the economic and monetary system after the lacerating effects of the Great Depression and the war. The reorganization effort was aimed at restoring free trade and a system of international payments able to advance the export of the U.S. production and consumption model throughout the world. This line of international intervention also had distant origins: It can be traced back to Hay's notes on the Open Door Policy of 1889–1900. But more concretely, it was in the 1920s with the Dollar Diplomacy that the first signs of linking financial flows, national economic obligations (such as the payment of war debts and reparations), and foreign policy appeared in U.S. financial circles.[24] But that kind of political action, in its "precrisis" form, had also undergone gradual modification. Relations between the United States and Europe at the start of the 1940s were not, even potentially, the same as they had been during the era of Charles Evans Hughes and Herbert Hoover.[25] In the new postwar relationships the U.S. economy was seen as an overall model for Western economies, not only from the financial point of view (in the style of Thomas Lamont), nor even just from the point of view of free trade (according to the doctrine of Cordell Hull). The exportation of a "model" involved a massive structural transformation and the permanent mobilization of a complex system of forces (and not only of the economic-productive kind). This result could only come about through a war at the global level.[26] The forms of U.S. global intervention in Europe transcended both the juridical and the commercial-financial traditions, uniting them in a more complex machinery driven by a "political-military-diplomatic" force. It was of paramount importance to lay the foundations of that force and decide its structure without delay.

The intellectual history of the processes, scenarios, and models of this titanic operation (concentrated between 1940 and 1949) has not yet been written—not by historians, not by political scientists. Only passing attention has been paid to the general problem of retracing the internationalist sources that provided the backdrop for the assimilation of a globalist politico-institutional culture in U.S. foreign policy, enabling the transmission of the American model to Europe.[27] This complex operation required above all the "deprovincialization" of U.S. foreign policy. It needed to be purged of its regionalist outlook and required the construction of a solid technical and bureaucratic structure to support it, a structure imbued with internationalist culture rather than the pro-British snobbery and cosmopolitan inspirations displayed by the former generation of State Department diplomats.[28] Instead, foreign policy would have to be tied to the U.S. cultural tradition of being "first" and the businesslike organization of the state machinery, even in the image it projected of itself overseas.

Devising this foreign policy entailed creating an attitude less specific but also more complex than a readiness to construct international institutions of a universal nature, such as the United Nations, the International Monetary Fund, the World Bank, or the planned World Trade Organization. What was needed was a general analytical awareness and understanding of the international implications of concrete foreign-policy activity with respect to both the war allies (Great Britain and the Soviet Union, but also Vichy and Gaullist France) and the potential enemies (Germany, Italy, and Japan), in the light of the upcoming system of international relations, which had to be geopolitical and military, socioeconomic, and legal-institutional all at the same time.

The role played by organizations such as the CFR was to assist in and enrich this ambitious transformation process in U.S. foreign policy, the evolution of which seemed to take on aspects of Wilsonian idealism. The transformation process also drew on the "southern" liberalism à la Cordell Hull and tapped the burgeoning Europe-oriented balance-of-power realism of the civil servants in the State Department, as well as in the East Coast financial circles, whose international experience went back to the Paris Peace Conference of 1919 and especially to the Dawes and Young plans of 1924 and 1931 respectively. In the postwar years, this task of coordinating men and ideas witnessed the birth of important politicians and theoreticians from the so-called realist school—George Kennan, Hans Morgenthau, Arnold Wolfers, Walter Lippmann, Averell Harriman, Robert Strausz-Hupé, and Reinhold Niebuhr.[29] In some ways, the process can be described as a "New Deal" in U.S. foreign policy, just as important as the one for domestic policy during Roosevelt's first presidential term.[30]

The Study Groups

The memoranda of the Council on Foreign Relations regarding the implications of war developments in Europe for U.S. foreign policy, especially in the two-year period 1940–1941, betray traces of this new modernist and globalist mentality. It was something quite original and cannot be found in diplomatic records of the same period. The documents of certain study groups, especially the memoranda of the Economic and Financial Group and the Territorial Group, attest to a greater level of technical and cultural sophistication than others had. The EF Group's memoranda in particular show a considerable knowledge of the subjects involved, which doubtlessly stems from the political and economic (and above all financial) legacy of the Harding-Coolidge-Hoover administrations, when the "bankers" stood in for the administration in many areas of U.S. foreign policy.

But even in regard to doctrine (economic theory and policy), the analyses of trends and the laying out of options and proposals by the EF and the T groups are often more intriguing and advanced than those of the other groups. Their analyses reflected the grand debate under way between Keynesian economists, such as Alvin Hansen, and neoclassical economists, like Jacob Viner, cochairmen of the EF Group. The divergent views of the latter reveal how much room was left for the possible merger of the two lines of research into what was later called a "neoclassical synthesis."[31]

The EF Group, which was the most prolific, also managed to avoid lapsing into the detached technicism of quantitative formulas or a model-oriented utopianism based on flawless reconstructions of the international economy for the postwar world. The authors instead tried to come up with the possible scenarios (even the bleaker ones such as the utter defeat of Great Britain) in a bid to find the most lucid, innovative, and workable solutions to the problem.

Another key set of documents was produced by the Political Group. Although this material was certainly less complex, it was highly varied in its topics and showed an advanced level of exposition, skillfully summarizing the general ideas of the East Coast Establishment. These texts were often a political distillate of the original ideas of U.S. internationalism (from both the juridical and economistic versions), blended with the realist experimentalism of the European school.

Those documents were less interesting, however, regarding their long-term proposals, especially in the first two years (1940–1941). And yet, some of the P Group memoranda displayed considerable skill in developing the material—particularly when dealing with political questions. Prime examples are the documents drawn up in collaboration with the Territorial Group on the question of military bases in the Caribbean, Greenland, and Iceland in 1940 and 1941. The sudden inclusion of the latter within the Western Hemisphere, on the suggestion of the Political Group, blocked Germany from extending its dominion to the Atlantic and thence to other key strategic positions.[32]

The Territorial Group, whose name seemed to imply an approach to international relations anchored to the nineteenth-century belief that the main outcome of war was the delimitation (and change) of national frontiers, represented a cultural perspective that, albeit in a changed political and cultural climate, had prevailed until Versailles and that, after a period of eclipse, resurfaced with the onset of the war. It was above all the Territorial Group memoranda that catalyzed the formation of the concepts that in the space of a few years led to the definition of the analytical category of national security, which, together with interdependence, would provide the foundations for postwar foreign policy.

In fact, the T Group's memoranda reflected the underlying philosophy of many of its members, particularly of its chairman, the geographer Isaiah Bowman. Some participants, such as John Foster Dulles, had been present at the Paris Peace Conference as a legal consultant to the diplomatic specialists on border matters. All of them had felt that in those drawn-out negotiations, the United States had been tricked by the Europeans—particularly on territorial issues, which had not been debated enough: The U.S. delegation had shown open unwillingness to discuss the issues on the basis of geopolitical realism and insisted on following the broad ideal conceptions based on the principle of self-determination of nations and on the lines of ethnic separation.[33]

The members of the T Group maintained that the fixing of the borders in the peace treaties after World War I had been the source of infinite tension and explosive conflict. This led them to conclude that any planning of the coming postwar order needed special attention on the geopolitical problems at stake: In order to obviate the further unleashing of ambitions and expansionist appetites at the end of the war, workable optional solutions had to be settled beforehand.[34]

Such an approach differed greatly from the epistemological orientation of the Economic and Financial Group, which was bent on constructing scenarios of multilateral or even globalist international economic integration organized around issues, rather than by geographical areas. Nonetheless, the early documents produced by the EF Group reflected the climate of the period, which was affected by a conceptual orientation largely similar to those of the stauncher territorialists. The exercise of piecing together the schemes for economic and commercial self-sufficiency, grounded in the identification of integrated and closed areas of varying sizes and resources (the Western Hemisphere, the Pacific, the British Empire, the German-controlled area), as documented by Memorandum E-B10 and those that followed,[35] betrayed a somewhat protectionist streak. It was therefore to some extent also territorialist, and only the details of some economic analyses regarding the issue of raw material supplies showed signs of what in 1942–1943 became a full-blown conceptual and institutional reconstruction of the postwar economic order.[36]

In any case, the activities of the T Group bore significant fruit in the long term. Although the group was clearly in no position to compete with the universalist theme of an international order expressed by the United Nations formula from Placentia Bay (August 1941) on, the views of the T Group on territorialism were fully reinstated and taken seriously at the war's end, when the precarious Rooseveltian balance between idealism and realism encountered the early intransigence of the Truman administration.[37]

This respect for territorialism marked the return to a picture of international relations that successive Democratic administrations (from Wilson through Roosevelt) had always officially and ideologically disputed, namely, the European balance-of-power principle (albeit in a new bipolar version) and the zones of influence. This sudden revival of the geopolitical spheres of influence was certainly not the exclusive handiwork of the Territorial Group. It had resurfaced much earlier in the debate on the configuration of postwar Germany (a debate initiated at the administration level in 1943) and even before—in the Roosevelt administration's deliberations on the Good Neighbor Policy toward Latin America in the 1930s. Nevertheless, the WPS documents contained a peculiar singular foretaste of certain themes we shall be encountering in later chapters of this book regarding the concept of the Western Hemisphere and the future of Eastern and Central Europe—concepts that date from 1940 and 1942 respectively, i.e., to a phase of the war in which an Allied victory was far from certain.[38]

The output of the Security and Armaments Group is probably of least interest here. Most of the group's memoranda related directly to military events and developments, not to strategic options or long-term scenarios. The suggestions of the SA Group (and particularly those put forward by the group's military members) often reflected the mediation of interests and conflicts between the War and Navy departments, the war industry, and other branches of the administration.

Discussions in the SA Group tended to revolve around the application and/or revision of the Neutrality Acts, passed by Congress from 1935 on, culminating in the Lend-Lease Act of 1941; other major issues included the question of military aid to the Allies in Europe and the urgent rearmament of the United States. But many texts of the SA Group shed much light on the dynamics of public opinion, the administration, and Congress between 1939 and 1941 regarding military issues—something not even historians who have examined official documents on this particular subject have yet managed to clarify fully.[39] The SA Group's material offers valuable insight on the changing orientation of the military leaders as the war became ever more onerous, and as the logistic and organizational problems affecting the liberated territories made the politics of the military departments more and more complex and ambitious. Some sectors of the U.S. military and of the Army Air Force began to foster the idea of permanent military control over the occupied territories through a system of U.S. military presence and a worldwide network of fixed bases.[40]

Finally, the Peace Aims of the European Nations (PA) Group, set up some time after the others, in June 1941, is of vital interest because it examined the situation affecting each of the European countries in turn (except Germany, Great Britain, and the Soviet Union), analyzing their political systems, socioeconomic policies, and the state of their institutions, even occasionally considering hypothetical political and constitutional reorganizations to be effected after the war. Their chief interest was the fate of Europe. No groups were ever set up ad hoc to study viable solutions for East Asia, Africa, or the Pacific. Solutions for those areas were considered in relation to the reorganization of the European colonial empires.

The documents produced by the PA Group were generally of two types, which differed greatly in both content and methodology. The first was normally drafted by foreign specialists and consisted of an overview of the political, economic, and social conditions of a particular European country. The second type offered a summary of the study group minutes on discussions regarding the contributions of foreign guest speakers. The latter memoranda tended to be a compendium of the views of opposition leaders from Axis countries (or satellites) who had emigrated or the views of representatives of exiled governments from Fascist- or Nazi-occupied countries. As such, they were the means by which the WPS groups updated their knowledge of "other" countries.

In many cases, the documents were analytical and neutral. However, they were aimed at influencing the course of the debate, including the contributions of guest speakers (as in the case of Count Sforza and L. Pavia in the memorandum on Italy, and of Hedwig Wachenheim and Hans Simon in the German memorandum).[41] This influence was achieved by establishing beforehand a schedule of arguments in which the wording of the items on the agenda "steered" the discussion along predetermined lines. By documenting these discussions with foreign visitors, the PA Group also aimed to affect the "perceptions" of the State Department, which received copies of the memoranda and discussion minutes.

The way the material itself was structured is also worth noting here. The Peace Aims Group was in the habit of simplifying arguments by repeatedly abridging its material and consequently condensing (and altering) the message of earlier drafts. At times this process led to memoranda that were definitive digests of everything that had gone before. The most striking example is Memorandum EN-A17, of December 15, 1941, which presented a schematic summary of topics covering positions expressed in the course of various meetings with foreign speakers from more than twenty countries, for which ad hoc memoranda had been drafted beforehand.[42]

The way in which this mass of information, convictions, political stances, and ambiguities—in the case of some European contributors—was selected, grouped, and harshly pared down was very crude and at times verged on caricature. The very act of summarizing a text involved some kind of transformation. Revision was never evenly carried out and resulted in a weakening of content and loss of subtleties. Consequently, the subject matter could become elusive. Instead of capturing the specifics of the contributions made by foreign speakers, the specifics were "induced" from outside, depending on the persuasion of the person drafting the summary.

The main impression one has here (and elsewhere in U.S. foreign-policy documentation) is of being faced with a "collective perception," either regional or subregional (the Europe of the medium or smaller powers), for which common conceptual parameters (even paradigms) were being sought. There was an analytical slant similar to the one found earlier (since Monroe) in the style of U.S. foreign policy on Latin America and even in the more recent Good Neighbor Policy.[43]

Europe was seemingly unified (by analogy with Latin America) by the war spreading through it, by the forced cohabitation within the German-controlled area, and by the acute political marginalization of the foreign speakers—members of minority opposition groups or governments in exile. In a way these foreigners had also become representatives of cultural marginalization, locked into the old disputes and the attitudes of the day or year of their compulsory emigration, sharing the condition of being political refugees in the United States.

This oversimplification was not entirely the fault of the WPS members. The texts personally written by some of the foreign contributors (as well as their analyses and proposals for their own countries) displayed an astonishing degree of superficiality and contradiction, redolent of the "old Europe" of prewar days (especially noticeable in the speeches of representatives from the Danube Basin and elsewhere in the Balkans), and almost deserved the sometimes arbitrary abridging carried out by the meetings' secretaries.[44]

But let us take a closer look at Memorandum P-C3, on Nazi Germany's war aims, dated February 1941, which gave the clearest idea of the perception that the CFR had of German policy after two years of war in Europe, and which presented it certainly with greater symbolic cogency than the memorandum on the peace aims of anti- and post-Fascist Italy (EN-A10). The memorandum outlined the set of aims[45] that the Nazi government had set for itself during the war, as gathered from German political literature (which was essentially geopolitical and economic). This text therefore predated all other formulas for a new order in Europe (and the world) after the envisaged Allied victory.[46]

The document seems tailored to advise the Establishment and the administration of the inherent dangers of German international ideology, supplying arguments culled from some of the more authoritative Nazi publications. Although it was undoubtedly meant to persuade its readership, Memorandum P-C3 effectively exposed the ideological and cultural sources of Nazi expansionist principles and sketched out the main political and economic alternatives to the German ideology.

The document was also largely influenced by the climate prevailing in those years at the New School for Social Research (NSSR) in New York, a burgeoning center for European cultural affairs. The sizable gathering of intellectuals and politicians (especially Germans, German Jews, and anti-Fascists or non-Fascists of other countries), ensured that the NSSR had a lasting effect on the academic and liberal circles of the northeastern internationalist lobby.[47] This cultural enclave, which was mainly historicist and/or idealist in outlook, with a vein of Marxism and Weberism, enjoyed the esteem of the WPS, which was striving to enhance the cultural mold of American "idealistic" and "financial" nationalism with European influences.

Hence, with a few exceptions,[48] the memorandum viewed the Fascist regimes in Rome and Berlin as pathological phenomena of those political systems (both the "liberal" version and the Third International Marxist interpretation of fascism and nazism) or as an irrational parenthesis rather than a new form of political development. But that kind of political outlook on nazism and fascism was not shared by all members of the Council on Foreign Relations, where there was still a prevalently economic and financial approach to international relations—an approach that, in the 1920s, had viewed fascism as a stabilizing force curbing the perils of social unrest in Europe.[49] It took the depression and the crisis of political-economic formulas that swept through the United States to finally demolish such views, creating new and original ideas on the reorganization of the world system.[50]

In this respect, Memorandum P-C3 testified to a shift to the left on the part of traditional East Coast internationalism. It was a condensation of in-depth studies of recent German source material (cultural sources included) and of the blueprint of Hitler's geopolitical imperial expansion—an analysis that only a German could have undertaken. One of the central features of this memorandum was the theory of Lebensraum (as expounded by Carl Schmitt), which Franz Neumann (the German guest speaker) saw as a kind of "German Monroe Doctrine,"[51] and its corollary, the Grossraum theory, for reorienting international economic relations. The latter, decidedly geopolitical, philosophy had been translated directly into international law as a "principle" by Gerhard Jentsch and was supposed to draw on a dense network of political and social productive links, to consolidate and institutionalize the unification of continental Europe and perhaps even North Africa and the Near East.

5

Coexistence with Nazi Europe: One Scenario

The Philosophy of the Economic and Financial Group

Memorandum P-C3 of the Council on Foreign Relations was very important. As we have already seen, the postwar planning machine set in motion by the War and Peace Studies groups was created with the basically limited objective of determining the concepts and procedures necessary for the time when, at the war's end, the European powers (and only these) would negotiate for peace. Before May 10, 1940 (Hitler's attack on the Low Countries), although the Germans had stormed Poland and pushed northward into Denmark and Norway, it was still hoped in the United States that the European powers, including Germany, might eventually meet around the bargaining table and negotiate an end to the hostilities.

With France prostrate, however, the prospects soured. U.S. "internationalists," who until then had believed some advantage could be had from the war in Europe, though without direct U.S. involvement, suddenly found themselves faced with two crucial new developments. The first was the growing German stranglehold on continental Europe and the implications of that on political and economic relations; the second was the definitive collapse of the old European balance of power as it had been created at Versailles.[1]

The WPS memoranda showed this shift in the political horizon after May 1940; the Economic and Financial Group began to issue a series of papers analyzing the commercial and economic effects of the alternatives of "conflict" and "coexistence" with German areas in Europe. The authors took their cue from Germany's own scheme for a "New Economic Order" in Europe, which was an incarnation of the theory of *Grossraumwirtschaft*, summed up point by point on July 25, 1940, in a statement by the Reichsminister of Industry and Trade and by the governor of the Reich's bank, Walther Funk.[2] The projected German economic area, based on principles advanced as early as 1934 by Hijalmar Schacht in the *Neuer Plan,* and applied for the first time with the German-Hungarian currency-clearing agreement that same year, generated a compact and centralized economic unit of considerable strength.[3]

The EF Group documents written over the period 1940–1941 illustrated the undecided state in which the internationalists operated. That state of uncertainty had to be dispelled in order to forge a new international order compatible with their own ideals. On the one hand, it was necessary to prepare the country for the speedy transformation of the nation's production system into a war economy. This was to be done through a combination of technical programs and political persuasion, directed toward achieving the necessary consensus and decisions.[4] On the other hand, it was also important to begin the task of planning the economic order of the postwar world.[5]

The War and Peace Studies material can be grouped thematically into two main batches, corresponding to two separate phases. The two batches had substantially different aims. The first batch ran from the fall of France (May–June 1940) to the Japanese attack on Pearl Harbor. During those eighteen months it became obvious that sooner or later the United States would join the war. Hence it was of paramount importance to take advantage of the "quiet before the storm," not only to step up the nation's rearmament effort (which was at the mercy of a recalcitrant Congress), but also to determine the lines on which the war economy would be based after the United States entered the war.

The second batch of documents began at the end of 1941 and was concerned with planning for the readjustment of the economy and sociopolitical order after the war. This phase closed with the war's end and the disbanding of the study groups in the summer of 1945.

The CFR internationalists' goal was basically twofold. They aimed to foster the preparation of a "war economy" in peacetime (Phase 1) and to provide political strategies, complex scenarios, and alternative options to make the job easier for the administration, which was still hamstrung by public opinion and a fundamentally reluctant Congress. Once the United States had entered the war (Phase 2), the internationalists set about designing the future "peace economy," which would be generated during and by means of the "war economy," exploiting the growing climate of patriotic internationalism, the resource-controlling structures already in operation, and the political amenability of the other nations.

During Phase 1, the period that most interests us here, it was the fear of the formidable economic clout (and military prowess) that Germany would gain from Funk's *Grossraumwirtschaft* that prompted much of the WPS memoranda, especially those of the EF Group, and that justified their influence on the administration. The real paradox lies in the fact that the Germans—who had been the first to speak of an "economic rearmament" as early as 1934,[6] and whose *Grossraum* theory had led people to believe in a complete unification of Europe and the total militarization of the German economy from the very start of the war (in 1939)[7]—really did not begin to put into effect a full "war economy" until Albert Speer[8] replaced Fritz Todt as minister of armaments in 1942. In this they were far behind the British, already under economic pressure in 1940, and even behind the United States, which, though still neutral, already had many large-scale mobilization programs under way for both war and civil industries.[9] Although some historians continue to claim that "in accordance with the demands of the modern conduct of war, the [German] rearmament program was not limited to the manufacture of arms, but involved the entire state economy . . . and that Hitler's Germany was the first to introduce a war economy in peacetime, through state intervention,"[10] it was in fact the Allies who adopted drastic measures for centralizing and planning the economy around the war, long before the Germans.

Speer himself spoke of this in his memoirs: "Despite the technical and industrial progress, even during the height of our military successes in 1940 and 1941, we failed to achieve the same level of arms production reached in World War I." Further on he added, "The Americans and Russians knew how to set up more streamlined organizational systems, which enabled them to achieve better results; while we, with our old and rusty organizational formulas, failed to accomplish anything comparable."[11] Thus commented Speer in 1944, in the closing stages of the war, when German production was at its peak.

As Alan Milward wrote, quoting from the bombing survey, "Before the war, Germany was busy carrying out an 'extension rearmament' rather than an 'in-depth rearmament.' It had organized its economy so as to maintain a relatively high level of ready arms, but had not undertaken the investments and economic transformation necessary for producing a sufficient output to insure success in the war against countries equipped with greater production capacity."[12]

Trade Blocs and the Clearing Union

Whatever the validity of the views quoted above, it might be added that from the mid-1930s on the techniques of *Grossraumwirtschaft*, at least regarding "interarea" relations (with Danubian and Balkan countries), had created a trade bloc that worked better than the more-extensive trade blocs based largely on the transfer of currency, such as the British Empire or the Western Hemisphere. In 1940–1941, the *Grossraum* itself was a fairly compact region directly controlled from its center and almost self-sufficient both in raw materials and in food production. On the other hand, the ossification of the trade blocs, predicted in the *Grossraum* doctrine and in Funk's guidelines, was not only consistent with the visions of the Nazi political elites but also highlighted a tendency (on the rise in the 1930s) to increase protectionist restrictions and set up closed areas, trade barriers, tariffs, and quotas, a situation that was accentuated by the lack of a recognized financial system of fixed or flexible exchange rates.[13]

This led some U.S. and British observers in political and economic circles to overestimate (perhaps instrumentally in some cases) the viability of the German "model." The British, including Lord Keynes, voiced their concern and took the German trade bloc very seriously. Discussing the task of establishing a new international system of payments and arguing against the gold standard in use before 1914, on November 20, 1940, Keynes wrote: "If Funk's plan is taken at its face value, it is excellent and just what we ourselves ought to be thinking of doing. If it is to be attacked, the way to do it would be to cast doubt and suspicion on its bona fides. The point is, I should have thought, not that what Funk purports to do is objectionable, but what we will actually do." And he added further on: "To sum up, it is my opinion: a) that we should not pose as champions of the status quo; b) that we should not produce at this stage any post-war economic scheme of our own, if only on the ground that no one I have yet seen has the foggiest idea of what such a plan ought to be."

In a later note (dubbed the "Spanish Article" because it was intended for use as counterpropaganda by the British ambassador to Madrid), Keynes suggested a set of mixed technical and currency solutions lifted straight from Funk's theories and proposed the incorporation of Spain into the sterling area. Such a system would make the clearing schemes for the exchange of British and Spanish currency (until then regulated through bilateral agreements) identical to those in force among Eastern and Central European states dominated by the German Mark.[14] The clearing union Keynes championed at the end of 1940 was nothing more than an Anglicized version of the *Grossraum* philosophy and the WPS's U.S. trade bloc, advocated in Memorandum E-B12 and those that followed.[15] The debate was not so much over methodology as over the dimensions of the economic areas and on their self-sufficiency and potential reciprocal competitiveness.

Thus, in various documents drafted by the EF Group, based on ideas expressed by Keynesian economist Alvin H. Hansen,[16] the group as a whole decided to imitate the German idea and propose the creation of a full-fledged federal "corporation" to manage all U.S. overseas trade (and perhaps even the entire non-German trade bloc). This innovation was necessary in view of the expansion of international trade on a "clearing" basis between the two largest trade zones of the world, the German *Grossraum* and the would-be Grand Area, led by the United States.

The analyses of the *Grossraum* program in Memorandum P-C3 and in the E-B12 and P-B13 series focused chiefly on this problem (clearing and trade zones).[17] The idea of a corporation seemed so innovative at the time that it virtually provided a statute for a new economic system. Yet, ironically, that system was based on the concept of Lebensraum (with its core in Germany and periphery in the East, notably the Ukraine).[18] Had the *Grossraum* mechanism worked well, the two trade zones' noncommunicating "closed economies" (admittedly, only of regional dimensions) would have hampered commercial and financial flows and the supply of raw materials and food to the Anglo-Saxon powers.

The U.S. business community had few qualms about pragmatically probing into all the possible openings: It mattered little if the alternative schemes were drafted by the enemy, so long as they were functional.[19] Arguments of ultrademocratic origin were quickly adapted to fit the occasion—by analogy, the "inequality of people" became a kind of "inequality of nations," and consequently there was nothing objectionable in such an inequality emerging, as long as the poorer nations could rely on the protection of the stronger ones. This type of reasoning recurred from time to time during the formulation of Roosevelt's version of the United Nations.

According to this mixed idealist and realist doctrine (influenced by the unhappy experience of the League of Nations), the self-determination and hence sovereignty of the United States was somewhat impaired by the future international police that would have to be set up by the Great Powers alone (the two Anglo-Saxon powers in the first stage and then, after the Teheran Conference in 1943, the Soviet Union as well)—negative traces of which can still be seen in the voting system of the Security Council of the United Nations, with veto power accorded to the "Big Five" by the San Francisco charter.[20] The elite members of the CFR (concentrated in the WPS groups) could hardly have balked at this philosophy, knowing full well that the rules of the Open Door Policy had in the past generated an asymmetrical and hierarchical international division of labor among the various economies.[21] But deep down, this association of the principle of *Grossraum* with the idea of a self-sufficient (and hence closed) Anglo-Saxon economic system contrasted with the political philosophy of most CFR members, who were strongly in favor of liberalizing trade and reorganizing the monetary mechanisms along the lines of fixed exchange rates indexed to the dollar as the most efficient means of exporting the U.S. productive model to the entire world.[22]

Although the United States was still technically only an onlooker and the public still strongly opposed involvement (a fact confirmed by direct and indirect polling),[23] in this first phase the study groups vetted every possible alternative—"short of war"—for reorganizing the international economic system. Their analysis consisted of a subtle step-by-step examination of international trade, moving out in ever-increasing circles from its geographical core, the U.S. trading system.

The first hypothesis, immediately discarded, involved ascertaining whether the United States could survive on its own internal supply of raw materials and food products, should a global war break out. It was a purely academic exercise. Despite the crisis, U.S. interests were still spread out all over the world and, as such, could hardly be abandoned. Memorandum E-B10, of April 15, 1940, was the only one to contemplate this decidedly isolationist option,[24] which would have excluded the control of territories traditionally under the umbrella of the U.S. economy, such as Central America and Canada. The documents drafted in this first period analyzed trade methods and trends for clues as to what new commercial trends might emerge from the war in Europe.[25]

But the German invasion of Denmark and Norway and thereafter of Holland, Belgium, and France changed the picture dramatically. The study of trade options became more systematic, and entirely new ideas were examined. Setting aside its previous detached and quasi-neutral assessments of the repercussions that the war in distant Europe was having on the supply of raw materials, the Economic and Financial Group switched to a more specific inquiry into larger economic areas, including purely hypothetical ones (at least for the time being).

Owing to the insights of the specialists on the international economy and to their relative unfamiliarity with the complex themes of U.S. political participation in European questions, the first main arguments the group tackled were of an economic nature. As reported by Notter, whose official role is irrefutable: "By 1940 the general goals of our economy could be more clearly defined than could our objectives in the political and territorial fields. This government had already taken steps toward these goals through the Trade Agreement Act and through the various economic policies and arrangements agreed upon with the twenty other American republics."[26] However, elsewhere he added: "Many of those taking part in the Department's early preparatory work thought that public opinion in this country would go further in support of United States participation in international economic cooperation than in international political arrangements, which the national interest in peace seemed increasingly to require, and that the way might best be paved for the latter through the former."[27]

But this international economic cooperation (later chosen by the State Department for its postwar planning drive) took far longer to put into effect than had been foreseen in the studies of the CFR. In many ways, the work of the WPS predated that of the various government committees and subcommittees. The best example was the work of the Political Subcommittee of the Advisory Committee on Problems of Foreign Relations, set up by the State Department on May 31, 1940, with the specific task of working out "other foreseeable consequences of a possible German victory." This committee was supposed to establish what the German conquest of European countries with colonies in the Western Hemisphere would signify in terms of the possible transfer of the sovereignty of such territories to Nazi dominion.

The issue was settled by a resolution adopted by the Senate on June 17, 1940, and by the House of Representatives the following day, stating that the United States "would refuse to recognize or acquiesce in a transfer of territory in the hemisphere, regarded as including Greenland but not Iceland, from one non-American country to another non-American country."[28] But the Territorial Group of the CFR had already turned out two ad hoc memoranda on the same issues in March–April 1940, "The Strategic Importance of Greenland" and "The Strategic Importance of Iceland,"[29] expressing the group's fears and specifying solutions that two months later were submitted by the administration for Senate approval.

However broad this interpretation of the Monroe Doctrine was, it never really hazarded an openly "globalist" ideology regarding the U.S. role in the world. It was certainly stretching traditional ideas to consider Greenland, and later Iceland, as part of the American continent. But it was justified with traditional political and geographical arguments— such as the principle of the defense for the Western Hemisphere—and not in terms of U.S. intervention in areas outside the American continent.[30]

Attitudes were different when it came to economic and trade relations. While on the one hand the Economic and Financial Group was busy formulating economic and trade scenarios and options compatible with the average State Department bureaucrat's grasp of foreign-policy issues, on the other they were sponsoring markedly innovative solutions with far-reaching political consequences. The innovation was particularly noticeable in the way the concepts were laid out in the group's documents. In this first phase, the series of pilot studies into economic strategy tended to affect the work of the other groups, whose task within the CFR's economics-oriented outlook was to provide political and military conceptual backing for the security of the trade areas identified by the EF Group.[31]

The Evolution of Pan-Americanism

The growing contradiction between the continentalist political tradition of the United States and the need to expand its area of "direct interest" became gradually more evident in certain documents drafted by the Political, Territorial, and Economic and Financial groups—the three main CFR study groups.[32] The first revealing document was the EF Group's Memorandum E-B12, which defined the guidelines of a "Pan-American Trade Bloc," discussed on June 7, 1940. The two "supplements" accompanying the first draft of this text examined the Western Hemisphere's ability to supply itself with all the necessary kinds of merchandise. The memorandum not only gathered and processed the data but also suggested a vast range of means for defending that economic area.[33] However, beneath this objective presentation of data lay the authors' seeming desire to demonstrate the limits to the self-sufficiency of the American continent in manufacturing, food, and trade, should a regionally based trading policy come into force. The tactic suggested was to reduce gradually the dependence of Latin America (a traditional exporter of farm produce and raw materials) on continental Europe (dominated at the time by Germany) by instituting a series of trade-regulating devices, especially for the export of surplus produce, in order to yoke the subcontinent firmly to the United States.

There were indications that the authors meant to use their figures to support their claim that the political isolation of the American continent was far from practicable. The memorandum contained all the premises for an expansion of the trade bloc and, in the long run, hinted at the eventual abandonment of the key concept of "continental security."

A second, highly interesting document (written during approximately the same period), on the "Principles of United States Foreign Policy," was drawn up by the Territorial Study Group.[34] The underlying political philosophy was very ambiguous. It wavered between "continental geo-politicism" (called the "geographical principle"), the Wilsonian "morality principle," the "rationalist principle" (based on the idea that peace is the normal condition of international relations), and the "legalistic principle" (an integral part of the political culture of the American nation), before finally reconfirming the validity of the Monroe Doctrine in its most rigid version, which assigned the United States the task of guaranteeing the security of the entire American continent. This was not yet a return to the Roosevelt Corollary, i.e., the right to intervene in the subcontinent, a principle Theodore Roosevelt had championed at the beginning of the century, but neither was it the more moderate Good Neighbor Policy that excluded such intervention a priori. In fact, the text tread a comfortable middle ground. As when Secretary of State Charles Evans Hughes practiced the Good Neighbor Policy without disavowing the Roosevelt Corollary, so now, under the pressure of a war in Europe and the danger of German infiltration in Latin America, the memorandum invoked loyalty to the Lima Declaration of 1938 and at the same time asked Washington to "pressure" the twenty-one republics into "converting" their agricultural or industrial production to accommodate the new market conditions brought on by the war.[35] Altogether, however, this approach to the Western Hemisphere was basically quite conventional; it had undertones of turn-of-the-century imperialism, but its solutions never strayed outside the confines of the American continent.

The third key document, Memorandum P-B8,[36] came from the Political Group; it tackled the theme of "Western Hemisphere Affinities" with a series of arguments urging the administration to strengthen political ties with and buttress U.S. control of the twenty-one American republics as well as U.S. influence over the British Dominion of Canada. The document presented different options, tailored according to each geopolitical area. For relations with Canada, it suggested a "tactful negotiation and education of the public in both countries" to secure closer cooperation. For Central America and the northern strip of South America, it would "probably be necessary to combine political tact with economic temptation and military pressure."

The text explained that in a world in which "certain dictators" had generated conflicting ways of perceiving life, which could be summed up as "them or us," it would be "unwise to 'tread softly' for fear of hurting the sensibilities of temperamental but physically weak neighbors whose possessions form a military approach to our own borders."[37] The document stayed within the bounds of a verbally aggressive U.S. continentalism, without any plan of intervention outside this "direct interest" area. The potential political and economic burden was on the Latin American countries.

Of the three texts, the Economic and Financial Group's memorandum was far ahead of its time in its broad analysis of new operative scenarios for U.S. foreign policy for both the short and the long term. However, after the fall of France, the arguments changed. The EF Group, for instance, began to study many alternative scenarios to offset the formation of the German trade bloc on the European continent. Due to their quality, scope, and depth of research, the resulting documents probably exerted considerable influence on the conceptualizing of U.S. foreign policy during the period of U.S. neutrality.[38]

The Hansen Document

Sparking off the whole series of inquiries, the first memorandum was written and signed by Alvin H. Hansen, who was deeply shocked by the German blitz and the occupation of France. The document title was significant: "Alternative Outcomes of the War: American Interests and Re-Orientation."[39] Chronologically, this was the first WPS text to deal with the possible "global" expansion of the United States (at least from an economic point of view) and hence with the idea of a joint Anglo-American domination of the world.

Further evidence that the summer of 1940 was felt to be a turning point in U.S. neutrality (and not just by the specialists) came from public opinion polls carried out at the time. The U.S. public began to realize that the defeat of France opened the way for new power relationships catalyzed by the crisis in the international system. This situation posed a threat to the security of the United States itself. The polls revealed a broad awareness that Great Britain represented "an essential factor in American defense strategy."[40] The reasons behind the widespread feeling of affinity with Great Britain and France had changed. The United Kingdom, instead of as a linguistic and cultural cousin, was suddenly perceived as the front line of defense for the United States and the Western Hemisphere.

A poll carried out in early May 1940 revealed that 55 percent of the public was still convinced that the Allies (Britain and France) would win the war; only 17 percent were convinced of German victory; and 28 percent made no comment. Less than two months later, at the end of June, more than 35 percent of those questioned envisaged a German victory, while those who believed the Allies would win dropped to 32 percent, and those withholding judgment rose to 33 percent.[41] But in spite of such dramatic developments, the number of Americans who openly wished for U.S. involvement in the war remained conspicuously low.[42] The figure never rose more than 10 points above the 14 percent high of June 1940. On average, until war was declared in December 1941, it hovered around 20 percent. Meanwhile there was a growing number of people who realized that sooner or later the United States would be dragged into the war. The so-called coefficient of fatalism was steadily rising, passing from 51 percent in May 1940 to 59 percent in December that year and 82 percent by the following April.[43]

It was in this ambivalent climate and in the shadow of the imminent U.S. commitment that the memoranda of the EF Group were written, particularly the one drafted by Hansen. The objective of the memoranda was not to influence public opinion directly, as they were reserved for the eyes of a closed group of politicians and diplomats whose internationalist leanings were well known. Instead, the texts supplied a set of alternative solutions that were consonant with the official foreign-policy line of the period in which they were prepared. The members were drawing up scenarios that were essentially compatible (at least on the surface) with the neutral line of the administration, though by implication their proposals tended to stray outside the somewhat cautious sphere of government policy of the time.

It is quite clear from the texts that the majority of EF Group members were already entertaining the idea of more resolute worldwide intervention on the part of the United States. But the unofficial destination of the WPS memoranda—the State Department—formally limited their analytical horizons to scenarios that excluded a priori any direct U.S. involvement in the war, however possible this was theoretically. This seems to confirm that the memoranda were intrinsically "arguments for war," i.e., designed to present a case to the opinion leaders and the higher echelons of the administration, which, in turn, would have "persuaded" the public-at-large.

Hansen was therefore the first to explore the possible outcomes of the war already under way and advanced five hypotheses. First, he surveyed the possibility of (1) "a continental German victory involving the conquest of France." Then he tackled the chance of (2) "a sweeping German victory, involving the conquest of England." His next hypotheses were (3) "an Allied victory culminating in a postwar military regime" and (4) "a European social revolution," and the last was (5) "a 'liberal' Allied victory, and a world federation under Anglo-American leadership." The fifth hypothesis was made over a year before the Placentia Bay summit between Roosevelt and Churchill, during which the Atlantic Charter and the groundwork of all Anglo-American designs for the postwar world were drawn up; as such, Hansen's text envisaged something that until then had been quite unthinkable.[44]

But scenarios 3 and 4 were also prophetic, not because historically they came true, but because they testified to the potential attitude of the United States toward Europe, traces of which were to surface in the ensuing years. Scenario 3 envisaged a joint Anglo-French occupation of Germany and its satellites, and the constitution of military administrations, as was later to happen with the AMGs (Allied Military Governments) set up in the various liberated countries.[45] Scenario 4 exorcized the dangers of a "revolution" in Europe by exposing the potential differences of political approach that could emerge between Communist governments in Western Europe and Moscow; it also took the position that, even in such a case, the Soviet Union would not be able actually to extend its grip as far as the Atlantic through the support of left-wing parties in Europe.[46]

After weighing the first four hypotheses, Hansen then turned to the last one, which portrayed a world federation under Anglo-American leadership. He noted that such a federation would "doubtless appear fanciful" to many[47] but emphasized its innovative scope and rationale. In fact it presupposed that "a German continental victory might drive the United States into an Anglo-American military, political and economic union."

The concept hinged on an idea of the U.S. "internationalists" of the interwar period. They thought that the structure of international relations needed streamlining and that the entire system should change from being "multipolar," based on the Eurocentric model of balance, to a "bipolar" setup, arranged around two large subsystems interacting simultaneously through a balance of cooperation and conflict.[48]

In the initial phase, this early form of bipolarity was still envisaged as a kind of cautious coexistence of the German area on one side and the Anglo-Saxon area on the other. The two Great Powers least amenable to such an arrangement (Japan and the Soviet Union) were left out, but in later revisions of the WPS schemes, they were gradually phased in as potential partners, at times on the side of the Germans, then on the Anglo-Saxon side, depending on the kind of scenario being developed.[49]

This political orientation betrayed the inveterate hostility of many Americans toward Eurocentric structures and their deep conviction that the European balance of power was long outdated and would be definitively scuttled by the war. There were also echoes of Wilsonian universalist fantasies of an international order that the League of Nations had failed to secure. These echoes were coupled with the realization that the concept of self-determination, and hence the proliferation of smaller states in Eastern Europe and Asia Minor after the fall of the Austro-Hungarian and Ottoman empires, had engendered a great many more problems than had actually been solved, problems connected with the "nationality principle" and the "safeguarding of ethnic minorities."

Though only implicit for the time being, this attitude was at odds with the policies the British had been pursuing between the wars in their search for two unreconcilable objectives. The main objective had been to restore the pre-1914 European balance of power to Europe, both territorially and economically (such as making the British pound convertible into gold at a fixed exchange rate in 1925), thereby recovering Europe's global role (which had been irremediably damaged by World War I). The second was to stem Europe's declining power by erecting a barrier of "imperial preferences" (the system of trade relations instituted at the Ottawa Conference in 1932). In conclusion, though Great Britain was coming to terms with the sinister reality of Germany's victories throughout Europe and with the warming relations between Berlin and

Moscow, the possibility of a Nazi-Bolshevik war was never entirely ruled out.[50]

The incipient bipolarist undertone of this document also owed much to Hansen's view of the economic factors. The idea of close cooperation in both the economic and the military fields between the United States and the United Kingdom was considered necessary and irreplaceable. Far less importance was given to a possible "political union" between the two nations, as occurred after the project of an Anglo-French "federation" was proposed in extremis by Churchill to the Paris government on June 16, 1940: "The ends which it will seek to attain are so overwhelmingly important that even loose and quite informal arrangements are likely to work quite as effectively and perhaps more effectively, than ambitious, formalized schemes of political union."[51]

There was no sign in Hansen's document of the ideas broached in Streit's book *Union Now*.[52] Hansen's reasons for agreements with the British were quite different: "The United States, instead of being discriminated against as now by the British Imperial Preference System, would be an equal part of the Anglo-American bloc. Two thirds of the trade of the United States, both imports and exports, is with the British Empire."[53] The idea was to make immediate use of the "economic union" as a lever against British trade barriers, in the full knowledge that the war was draining British competitiveness.[54]

But Hansen, leader of the American Keynesian economists, was not only contemplating a free-trader blueprint or simply the idea of reactivating international financial flows. Given the burden of 10.5 million still unemployed in the United States,[55] Hansen was more and more convinced that generalized free trade was still a long way from being established, and that just the opposite was happening as valuable European markets were sealed off inside the swelling "Deutsche Reichsmark area." So he put forward a bold scheme for the economic development and integration (both internally and externally) of a vast area, embracing the entire Western Hemisphere plus Great Britain. The philosophy behind this project was borrowed from earlier domestic economic policy during the New Deal era.

According to Hansen's plan, the Anglo-American alliance would

> involve a far closer integration of the Western Hemisphere from both the military and the economic standpoint through a vast intra-hemisphere network of express highways. These in turn would feed into an extensive intra-hemisphere tourist traffic with the development of subsidiary and related service industries. Closer interaction of the Western Hemisphere would moreover involve large capital investments in Latin America in public utilities and in lighter manufacturing industries. The progressive

rise in the standard of living in Latin America would moreover represent a field for investments. Housing, particularly low-cost subsidized housing throughout the whole area, including the United Kingdom and the United States, both rural and urban, together with the armament industry and intra-hemisphere road building, probably represent the most likely feasible outlet for expansion.[56]

Hansen's was a full-blown program for launching and developing the entire area as a potent antidote to Funk's program. As with the latter, Hansen's scheme pivoted on public intervention in the economy (to be coordinated between London and Washington), as well as on the possible expansion of demand within the bloc rather than external demand between different areas.

But Hansen was not the only one to draw up a program for international trade in the New Deal tradition. Henry Wallace—who was chosen by Roosevelt as vice presidential candidate in the November 1940 election—also favored a broad program of international public works. Other experts (often speaking from individual and not always shared standpoints) were busy studying the technical feasibility of such schemes. Wallace had even tendered what he dubbed an "international" version of the 1933 Tennessee Valley Authority and proposed "a combination of highways and air routes running from the southernmost tip of South America, through the United States, Canada, and Alaska, and through to Siberia and Europe, with motorways linking with China, India and the Middle East."[57]

However, apart from these "developmentalist" fantasies, Hansen's text had a further key ingredient: Unlike its predecessors,[58] Memorandum E-B16, with its examination of "five scenarios," adopted a methodological approach to interaction, based on the "if-then" proposition. The possible outcomes were not assessed exclusively in relation to the effects they would have on the United States or the American continent as a whole, which would have betrayed an implicitly separatist approach toward Europe. U.S. moves were also analyzed in an interactive relationship to gauge the effects they would have on the Nazi economy and hence the reaction from Berlin.[59]

The study of different scenarios implies something more than simply identifying political proposals ready for application, like those then being tested by the government. Indeed, it presupposes an intellectual freedom that states and clarifies the entire logical process and cultural referents of the pronouncements, without falling into bureaucratic rhetoric (the difference in language and style between WPS and diplomatic documents is most revealing).

In one significant paragraph, Hansen wrote that "Western international collectivism would be so markedly different from the Soviet communism as to prevent integration of the West with the Russian system." And to further pacify the fearful, he added, "Thus it is not a foregone conclusion that a social revolution in Western Europe would involve the extension of Russian communism to the Atlantic and the amalgamation of radical Western social-philosophy with [the] communist ideology and social structures."[60] These phrases foreshadow at least one of the concerns that emerged during the war (and particularly afterward) regarding links between the Soviet Union and the formation of left-wing political movements in the West.

The Other Texts

The style of and methodology in Hansen's document became the working standard for the Economic and Financial Group, a standard that was used for the series of memoranda that gradually delineated the perimeter of the potential economic "Grand Area," whose ever-expanding domain eventually coincided with the entire world, except, for the time being, the Soviet Union and the German-controlled area.[61] The objective of this batch of texts was twofold. On the one hand they used statistical cross-referencing and the guiding criteria of self-sufficiency to demonstrate that U.S. expansion beyond the Western Hemisphere was a "natural" prerequisite of the U.S. economy. On the other hand they made a realistic assessment of the possibility of coexistence with the German economic area.[62]

These texts showed a marked conceptual change from their predecessors and a change in perception of the nature of the international system as a whole. The essential actors with whom the United States was forced to contend were reduced to two—the United Kingdom, in the Allied camp, and the German Reich, in the enemy camp. Both Japan and the Soviet Union were considered dependent variables in the equation of conflict between the Anglo-American bloc and the Euro-Germanic area.

Once again, these documents showed that the globalization of U.S. foreign policy was essentially entailed in the redefinition of U.S. relations with Europe. In 1940 Europe was provisionally in the hands of the Germans, whereas previously it had been under the British, and after 1945 it risked falling into Soviet hands. Europe was still the fulcrum of world order. Fluctuations of power or lack of power were to become the "currency" of international relations[63] and would determine the method, the limits, and the ambitions of U.S. intervention. This attitude about Europe on the part of the U.S. elites was most understandable, given that the "sources of legitimacy" for most of the rest of the world, then at the apogee of colonial expansion, were in Europe, and Europe itself was the largest potential market for U.S.-manufactured goods and food products, an essential factor for the export of the U.S. productive and organizational model, based on mass consumption, services, and technology.

It is also worth noting the differences in the attitude of the administration and President Roosevelt himself, during 1940–1941, toward Germany on the one hand and Japan on the other. Although the priority of Europe over East Asia was a foregone conclusion and Germany was considered the main enemy, the one to be crushed first, Roosevelt was very cautious in his handling of the "undeclared naval war" with Germany and showed much greater diplomacy in that affair than Wilson had in 1915 and 1917 during the submarine war that the Imperial German Navy had conducted in the Atlantic.[64]

U.S. involvement in Europe in World War II was a choice that would inevitably have far-reaching repercussions. It confirmed that the United States had finally embraced a role that in 1917 had been unthinkable. The power vacuum that would result in Central Europe upon Hitler's defeat could be filled only by the United States, either alone or jointly with the Soviet Union. There was no longer any question of reinstating the previous century's balance of power under British control. Washington and especially the internationalist groups soon realized that U.S. commitment against the Germans would catalyze a truly radical change in the country's foreign policy.

The U.S. relationship with Japan was much less clear, however. American arrogance and political clumsiness during 1940–1941 had raised many questions for historians and policymakers, both after Pearl Harbor and when the war was over. The blunders and diplomatic gaucheries of Roosevelt, Hull, and other U.S. leaders toward the Japanese approaches (when there were any) betrayed a lingering, subtle racism that led the United States to underrate Japan's readiness to pit itself against the U.S. giant on the opposite shore of the Pacific.[65]

The lack of sophistication in U.S. handling of relations with East Asia is emblematic of the "imperialist" traits of U.S. policy in the area. Even the war against Japan failed to catalyze changes in U.S. policy in the Pacific. This may easily be detected in one of the memoranda sent by the Political Group of the CFR to the State Department, perhaps upon the latter's request. The document posed the question of Japan's reaction to the barrage of economic sanctions inflicted by the United States and illustrated the rigid and superficial way in which even the most attentive sectors of the intellectual and political East Coast Establishment dealt with the highly delicate and risky question of cutting off essential supplies to Japan.[66]

However, the harsh line the United States took with Japan was long-standing. It had begun at the 1921–1922 naval conference in Washington, where, under the aegis of Secretary of State Hughes, Japan was cruelly humiliated in its ambitions and reduced to accepting "coprimacy" in the Western Pacific, while the United Kingdom was coerced into severing its alliance with Tokyo (dating from 1902), an arrangement that had provided a vital pivot for Japanese politics for twenty years.[67] It is worth mentioning that since as far back as the Spanish-American War of 1898 and the time of John Hay's notes on the Open Door Policy, Japan had been included in the U.S. orbit of action, whereas Europe, despite the brief interval with Wilson as president (1917–1920) and the Dollar Diplomacy of Calvin Coolidge and Herbert Hoover, remained essentially outside this orbit.[68]

However, there were other vital determinants that hindered U.S. intervention, in addition to the widespread isolationism of the public and the mystique of "nonentangling alliances." Some people already feared that the liquidation of the German hegemony in Europe would open the door to Soviet expansion toward the West. In 1940 this hardly seemed feasible, but Soviet aggression in Finland, the division of Poland, and the annexation of the Baltic states and Romanian Bessarabia had alerted many observers in the United States and elsewhere to the expansionist bent of the Soviet Union.[69] This fear was heightened by the fact that although in 1940 it was already possible to picture U.S. entry into the war on the side of Britain, it still seemed out of the question to station U.S. troops in Europe permanently or to construct a system of alliances and collective military and political security with Europe (or part of it). Such an arrangement did in fact come to pass after the war, with the NATO Treaty. At most, at this early stage, it was not impossible to imagine a universal international organization, albeit split up at first into regional areas and only later joined together on a global scale, in tune with the late Wilsonianism among elements of the administration, including Roosevelt himself.

The Coexistence Scenario: Armed Truce

The German victory in continental Europe had a twofold effect—on the one hand it caused an upheaval in power relations and unhinged the 1919–1939 "intermediate system," leaving the way clear for further German political expansion and hegemony—a possibility that deeply troubled the Americans. On the other hand, however, it erected a solid bastion against Soviet expansion toward the west and south—an expansion that would be difficult to halt if Germany fell.

This ambivalence toward Germany and the war's outcome, which was dissipating by mid-1941, figured even in the arguments of the WPS groups, especially in mid-1940, when internal contradictions were rife. Two different approaches to the problem were being developed at once, indicating a conceptual split between the CFR study groups—particularly noticeable between the Economic and Financial Group and part of the Political and Territorial groups; this rift was never in fact completely healed.

As shown by Hansen's Memorandum E-B16, the EF Group's economic analysis of the options at stake was not neutral. Some observers might discern the pressure of manufacturing and public utilities industries, which were anxious to break the impasse of the depression and the new bout of stagnation that had set in during 1937–1939; they hoped to accomplish this through public investment and a military budget. Such a program would have had the dual aim of helping the Allies in Europe and of reequipping the U.S. Armed Forces, thereby galvanizing domestic demand for civil consumer goods and consequently propagating new investments. But the more traditional internationalist sectors of the business community had other plans in mind, far more ambitious than those centered on galvanizing arms production and public works. The depression had left deep scars in capitalist circles and had evaporated some of the die-hard liberal self-confidence of the "southern" free-trader philosophy.

The depression had also prompted some reflection on the employment and investment advantages, and also hazards, that a war economy could offer for the U.S. system of production once demobilization was started. The possibility that a new economic slump might drag under not only the economic system but also the U.S. sociopolitical system was a permanent nightmare for the elites of the time, as has been amply shown by many historians.[70] A growing cadre began to feel that it was necessary to venture beyond the New Deal economic measures, which had been largely based on the expansion of effective demand through state intervention in the form of deficit spending or tax maneuvers.

The U.S. economic model developed in the 1920s and partially maintained throughout the 1930s was essentially based on the mass diffusion of consumer durables, services, private transport, private housing, and urban reconstruction, as well as on the leadership of certain sectors (automobiles, home appliances, refined chemicals). For this type of economy to survive, it had to spread beyond the U.S. frontier. Europe was the ideal market, indeed the only one in a position to match the rhythm of this strategic exportation of the U.S. model of production and consumption.[71]

But continental Europe was in the grip of the Germans and cordoned off to the outside. Hitler, Funk, and Todt (and his successor Speer) envisioned a state-controlled (mixed) economy with foreign trade and currency exchange governed by a rigid protectionism, laws of barter, and strict politico-military dependence.[72] As for the United Kingdom, it was a shrinking economic island, drained by the immense burden of war and isolated from the outside world by its own system of imperial preferences. Faced with this situation, during 1940–1941, both the United States and the CFR "planners" had been forced to come to terms with reality and hypothesize an extension of the area of U.S. economic intervention beyond the territories of the Western Hemisphere (which, though vast, were relatively unprofitable) to the more problematic areas in the Pacific (China and the Dutch colonies included) and, in the last analysis, to the varied areas and peoples of the British Empire.

In the literature on U.S. foreign policy between 1943 and 1954, G. Kolko, W. R. Louis, and others have highlighted the importance of the covert conflict with Great Britain over commercial and currency issues, a conflict that affected the relationship for the entire span of the war.[73] Drawing on personal experience and critical readings, other authors have directly examined certain key episodes of this intricate and cruel struggle, as well as the obstinate way that Washington imposed its own political line on the British in the course of the war (and after).[74] The first detailed analyses of any importance on the discord in Anglo-American relations were found in the EF Group's texts, together with the first official documents of the Advisory Group of the Division of Special Research, of the State Department, and in the work of the research staff of the Interdepartmental Advisory Group on Postwar Planning, of the federal administration.[75]

Even the title of Memorandum E-B19 ("Needs of Future United States Foreign Policy," of September 1940) plainly exposed the authors' objectives (not only economic), and the text delineated the basic reasons that, apart from the effects of the events of war, triggered a structural readjustment of U.S. international economic policy.[76] The memorandum's focus on the evolution of the trade flows with the extra-European economic areas and the assertion that the commercial importance of the Continent and the United Kingdom was increasingly less important to the United States seemed to imply that coexistence between the United States and German-dominated Europe was not only economically viable but even opportune.

The German domination of the continent, and its probable influence on the Middle East, North Africa, and perhaps even Central Africa, indicated the possible perimeter of the economic area under consideration. Moreover, Britain's tenacity during the Battle of Britain seemed to suggest that the German perimeter was unlikely to expand in that direction.

From these premises, it became clear that "it leaves a great residual area potentially available to us and upon the basis of which United States foreign policy may be framed. . . . Thus that large part of the world that is defended by Britain from German penetration—an area greatly in excess of that which is dependent for defense upon the United States—is an area with respect to which the United States at the present time has great freedom of action."

The analysis was carefully phrased. The next step was to analyze the consequences of the war on Europe, and the picture became even clearer:

> The blockade of Europe, sustained by British resistance in a sense may be considered actually as a double blockade.
>
> On the one hand it is a blockade of Germany and more recently has become a blockade of the Continent. It is however also a blockade of Britain and of the rest of the world, except the Continent of Europe. The latter aspect of the blockade is usually not considered important because of the presumption that the non-German world possesses such great independence in resources that a blockade of it from Europe is without significance.
>
> To the United States the continued existence of this blockade is of outstanding importance. True, maintenance of it deprives the United States of access of European market[s].[77]

And this was precisely the point. However, in this early phase, U.S. intentions were not to unblock the European market for U.S. products, technology, and its consumer model. This was to happen later with the Marshall Plan.[78] For the moment, there was a different problem. The European trade blockade was in truth a double-sided issue. Although it barred U.S. access to the European market, it left the Americans free to cultivate all other markets—they could simply bypass German and British competition by tapping the markets of Latin America, East Asia, and Africa directly.

But this was not the chief point of the memorandum. The potential for expansion of U.S. trade had to be justified by the more general interest of the rest of the world in cooperating with the United States in a vaster economic area. For the other American states it was even clearer: Because they were big exporters to Europe of food products (corn, meat, tropical products), the blockade in continental Europe was more damaging to them than to the United States. But even an association of the Pacific area (Southeast Asia and Oceania) with the Western

Hemisphere would not have been sufficient to offset the U.S. export deficit. The only solution was to link Great Britain (the world's leading importer of foodstuffs) with the Western Hemisphere. The Western Hemisphere and the Pacific alone would have been enough to guarantee the U.S. self-sufficiency, especially in terms of raw materials, but they would not have been able to absorb the food surplus of Central and South America. In light of this, an alliance with Great Britain could also prove highly desirable for the Latin American countries.

The only flaw in the memorandum was the fact that the technical data and statistics for E-B19 (and Supplement 1) detailed a situation that in 1940 had already been deeply altered. The figures dated from 1937 and referred to farm produce and industrial goods, which were prone to considerable fluctuation in those years. The figures no longer reflected the real relationship between the areas concerned, which had changed dramatically: Because of the war effort and the blockade, the composition and scope of the domestic demand of each country had been transformed.[79]

However, as an intellectual exercise, the scenario had some political significance. It reflected the aspirations of significant branches of the U.S. business community, which, in view of the broadening of its own sphere of influence, was set on obtaining a twofold aim: (1) to avoid formulating a hypothesis of war with the German area during the peak of German triumphs, and (2) to circulate the idea of an international economic order, led by the United States, for the entire non-German world.

The idea of building up a "Grand Area," composed of the Western Hemisphere, the Pacific, and the British Empire, ignored the political, institutional, and cultural factors of U.S. foreign policy. Its promoters claimed that such a huge trade zone could construct political alliances and ensure strategic supremacy almost exclusively through boosting trade and piloting the international financial system.[80] The memorandum openly stated that the "extremes of choice appear to be (1) a policy of isolation, or (2) a policy of militant and economic leadership in the present non-German world."[81] Obviously the authors' preferences lay with the second choice, which, owing to its implicit mercantilist outlook, entailed a bipolar system of relations for the two areas that could be described as a kind of "armed truce."[82]

The creation of a unified trade area (the Grand Area) would nonetheless have required establishing an adequate defense program for maintaining intra-area shipping routes and the security of its perimeter. But since one of the components of the hypothesized area, Great Britain (and the British Empire), was already at war with the opposing area, the creation of a Grand Area would have implied coordination and cooperation on a military and naval level among the countries adhering to this trade zone. Above all, it would have meant an extension of aid to Great Britain, plus the maintenance of the blockade until agreements for an "armed peace" were made. These agreements would have been followed by controlled and coordinated trade flows between the two areas.

There was even mention of a plan (successful later on, with the postwar multinational financial organizations) for aid to countries in difficulty in the non-German area: "This aid might be given through the device of a corporation possessing funds for intra-area investment and vested with the independent right to determine what investment should be made." Furthermore, "monetary arrangements might be directed toward the creation of a currency bloc and the maintenance of exchanges through the means of credit and trade flows."[83] As for trade with the German area, in the absence of a convertible currency system and free trade, the idea was to centralize everything "under clearing agreements a variant of which would be the Aski mark system" or "to centralize all trade with Germany in a single government corporation."

Even changes on political-institutional grounds were suggested, foreshadowing the debate over the United Nations, which was not set up until after the meeting at Placentia Bay and the drafting of the Atlantic Charter:

> The political requirements of the United States (as well as of the area as a whole) consist in a general way of modifications of national sovereignty necessary to achieve supremacy of this area that is made up of individual national sovereignty—a problem now not faced by Germany on the Continent. This suggests the equivalent of a constitution for the new international sovereignty—a constitution that probably should have its greatest emphasis upon functional arrangements rather than upon the police power to be vested in a super international sovereignty—an arrangement featuring many similar proposals in the past. . . . These arrangements would have to embrace the methods of negotiation between sovereignties and the relation to them of all colonies within the area. Here another type of trusteeship or administration is involved and the suggestion of "internationalization" of colonies within the area can be made.[84]

It is worth noting that this is perhaps the first time the term "trusteeship" is used with this particular meaning in reference to the possible future legal status of colonial territories after the war.[85] What is not specified is whether trusteeship would be applied just to the colonies of defeated countries (such as Italy) or also to those of the victorious allied nations (especially Great Britain).[86]

In conclusion, it may be said that the hypotheses contained in Memoranda E-B16 and E-B19, composed while Germany was enjoying sustained victories, focused on the possible construction of a bipolar structure of international relations ("rigid" in the German area and "flexible" in the non-German area),[87] headed by the United States and Germany, with Great Britain ranking second,[88] and with the rest of the world economically integrated around the two leading countries in a "core-periphery" pattern. This conceptual structure, with some variations (the Soviet Union in place of Germany), would in fact come to pass.

However, there were harsh objections to such a project, even within the Council on Foreign Relations. The Political Group spoke out against the ideas and proposals of the Economic and Financial Group—a rare occurrence in the history of the groups. The two schools of U.S. internationalism were finally coming out into the open.

The Criticisms of the Political Group

In a special memorandum (P-B13),[89] criticizing Memorandum E-B19, the Political Group expressed a competing "internationalist" approach. The ensuing debate looked at times like an all-out epistemological duel between the technocratic approach of the EF Group and the largely geopolitical line of the P Group.[90]

Memorandum P-B13 contested the very first concept underlying the entire economic-commercial machinery developed in Memorandum E-B19. The idea of strategic stalemate and economic coexistence (i.e., an "armed truce" resembling the postwar cold war) between German and non-German areas was openly criticized on national ethical grounds, as it was a case of "a deviation from much precedent in past great western wars when the fighting customarily was carried to the point of admitted defeat by one side or the other." The memorandum was also criticized for opportunism: "Such a 'stalemate' would in essence represent a defeat for the Germans because of the opportunity it would afford the London government to prepare for an eventual renewal of the armed combat under conditions potentially not less favorable to the British than to the Nazis; it has not been made clear why the Third Reich should be expected to acquiesce in what might well be regarded by Berlin as no new 'inequality.'"[91]

The second argument was the Political Group's expansionist and "imperialistic" interpretation of the Third Reich's foreign policy, in the belief that Memorandum E-B19 had largely underestimated the independence of Soviet and Japanese attitudes and behavior. Therefore, it was feared, the possible reaction of these two major powers, onlookers to the contest being played out between the Euro-German and Anglo-American blocs, may also have been underestimated. This is doubtlessly a more simplified (and perhaps more ideological) approach to international politics, but it would later turn out to be much more realistic than its technocratic and model-oriented counterpart put forward by the Economic and Financial Group.

The guiding idea behind the Political Group's analysis was the firm conviction that fascism, militarism, and communism all sprang from the same seed, "totalitarianism."[92] By their reckoning, the most likely development was an alliance among the three "totalitarian" countries (Germany, the Soviet Union, and Japan), creating a kind of "Eurasian Zone," which would have had the energy, the means, and the territorial continuity to oust the British from large areas of their empire (such as India, North Africa, the Middle East, and Southeast Asia), utterly compromising any hopes of establishing the Grand Area. Backing up their arguments with recent German geopolitical analyses that spoke in somewhat far-fetched tones of a coordinated political and military structure of the Eurasian landmass, those who participated in the discussions that led to Memorandum P-B13 (written by W. C. Langsam)[93] sought to demonstrate the political impossibility of the plan stressed in Memorandum E-B19 (written by A. R. Upgren) and suggested a more traditional play-off between "continentalism" and "navalism."

The two lines of approach, with their differing cultural matrices, were never to coincide completely, and the divergence reemerged after the war. On the one hand, the business-oriented convictions of the Economic and Financial Group ran deep: Its members believed that the only way to avoid an economic collapse after the war was to construct an "international economic order" run by the United States.[94] On the other hand, the prevailing logic was a combination of antitotalitarian ideology, political "realism," and the staunch anticommunism of the Political Group, which had seen in the Soviet-German nonaggression pact of August 23, 1939, a glimpse of a "natural" war alliance between Germany and the Soviet Union, an alliance that Japan may have felt tempted to join.[95] Both memoranda revealed a mixture of understandable opacity and singular insights that should be examined dialectically. P-B13 especially presaged a perception of international relations that later became a regular criterion for assessment in U.S. foreign-policy making: namely, the sense of the "good" or "bad" nature of the nations and the statesmen running them.

The basic notion was that Hitler's Germany was "by nature" an aggressive nation with unbridled expansionist aims. The conviction stemmed from Hitler's own declaration of his doctrine in *Mein Kampf*, later put into practice through Haushofer's ideas, which determined the political actions of Berlin.[96] This was a view of international politics that percolated, almost naturally, through into the U.S. analysis of Soviet foreign policy, especially after 1944. This superimposition of doctrine on action, mistaking the latter for a binding implementation of the former, is a characteristic that might well have remained within the output of the WPS; instead, since it had germinated from the very humus of U.S. political culture, it became a conceptual and unyielding paradigm of the cold war.[97]

But there are other original ideas in Memorandum P-B13. In their desire to criticize the bipolar economic order for the two areas, suggested in the Economic and Financial Group's memorandum, the Political Group members developed a strong argument against coexistence between the two trade blocs. They considered it impossible, not only for economic and trade reasons,[98] but also for technical-functional reasons pertaining to the very structure of that projected bipolar system.

This concept inaugurated a theoretical debate on the functioning and the physiology of political systems based on two poles, which is still a central topic of international studies.[99] Furthermore, even E-B19, although based on the idea of the predominantly economic and commercial reorganization of the various non-German regions of the world, by no means excluded a highly complex politico-military framework for safeguarding the economic intervention (both "intra-area" and "interarea"). Indeed, the memorandum presupposed it.

Memorandum P-B13, however, stressed that the political was far more important than the technical feasibility of the economic order laid out in E-B19. Drawing on German sources, P-B13 emphasized the absolute political nature of the Third Reich's program for political and military supremacy, which would clearly have given second place to the new economic order, including the development of the *Grossraumwirtschaft*. On the basis of this conceptual reversal of priorities, the memorandum maintained that coexistence between the German bloc and the Grand Area was out of the question. By the same token, it also stressed the structural instability of the bipolar system as a balanced model of competitive equivalence between two economic and geopolitical zones of such opposite natures.

It is worth quoting the arguments in full because of the great importance they have in this phase of transition of the system of international relations, of which at the time perhaps only H. C. Carr, Q. Wright, and later M. Wight were fully aware:[100]

> Under the system proposed in memorandum E-B19, there would be no balance of power (except possibly one held by the Soviet Union), for there would be only two outstanding rivals in the world; there could thus be only a preponderance of one side over the other.
> Hence, having once become the stronger of the two dominant powers in the world, it would be necessary for us to continue increasing our

economic and military might ad infinitum, lest the German area succeed in closing the war-potential gap so clearly outlined in the economic memorandum.

In other words, such an alignment doubtless would bring with it ceaseless effort, on the one side, to maintain this preponderance unchanged, and on the other, to reverse it completely.[101]

The nagging flaw in the bipolar system, including the system actually set up between the United States and the Soviet Union after the war, was lucidly described there. Though generated from notions of international relations largely borrowed from the old Eurocentric balance of power, this appraisal was valid for almost fifty years. Up to the end of the 1980s, bipolarity never eradicated the constant race for political, military, and economic supremacy—which, rather than remove, only exacerbated the risks of a clash between the two rivals. The sudden implosion of the Soviet bloc and empire in 1989 has changed radically such a political architecture, eliminating one of the two poles (the USSR) from the game.[102]

However, Memorandum P-B13 also displayed an awareness of the implicit asymmetry in the bipolar system. Despite the opinions of M. A. Kaplan, R. N. Rosecrance, and K. N. Waltz,[103] bipolarity does not postulate a real balance of the two forces; the system functions only if pole B continues to remain weaker than pole A, which has always been the stronger of the two. Pole B's aspiration to equality (i.e., "parity" and "essential equivalence") or to supremacy over A has led directly to the arms race and has multiplied the risk of war.[104]

These functional considerations anticipated the risk of preventive solutions, or at least drastically preemptive solutions, even before the bipolar system was established. "It were better to fight at once, than to face the prospect of such a prolonged and feverish armed truce."[105]

6

The Grand Area and
Self-sufficiency: Another Scenario

The Second Phase of Neutrality

The period referred to in Chapter 2 as the second phase of U.S. neutrality, lasting from June 1940 to the year's end, was a time of great conceptual innovation and lively political activity. While both the public and Congress continued to reject the possibility of war, the Gallup polls carried out in the course of those months revealed just how much the views of most Americans had changed on a broad range of foreign-policy issues and likewise their assessments of the international situation in general.[1]

To some extent, the administration itself had fostered this change through the activities of groups such as the "White Committees"[2] and, after war broke out in Europe, through the creation of federal agencies or new administrative bodies such as the Office of Emergency Management and the Council of National Defense (both set up in 1940 along the lines of the 1916 National Defense Act) or the Office of Government Reports (OGR), an ad hoc administrative department of the White House staff.[3] In June 1940, a group of private citizens, many of whom were members of the Council on Foreign Relations, published a declaration at their own expense in several national newspapers, stating that the United States, even if neither provoked nor directly attacked, would have to declare war on Germany.[4]

The various "isolationist" blocs and groups—particularly in the rural areas of the Midwest and in the Senate, where the old "irreconcilables" from the 1920s continued to hold out—began to take a more defensive position. Likewise, the business community, which until mid-1940 was split between interventionists and isolationists, each with its specialist press mouthpiece, readied itself to switch sides and rally in support of Great Britain and a greater defense commitment.[5]

The about-face of June 1940 was articulated in the declaration made by F. D. Roosevelt on June 10: "In our unity, in our American unity, we will pursue two obvious and simultaneous courses; we will extend to the opponents of force the material resources of this Nation and, at the same time, we will harness and speed up the use of those resources in order that we ourselves in the Americas may have equipment and training equal to the task of any emergency and every defense."[6] As such, the declaration revealed Washington's dual intention: On the one hand, it reaffirmed the U.S. desire to extend assistance to Great Britain, which implied accelerating the U.S. rearmament effort, while on the other hand it underscored the exclusively defensive nature of such action. The document is objectively highly explicit, but vague in regard to what commitments would be assumed—commitments that, if need be, could be promptly reversed.[7]

This highly charged climate saw the start of the third phase of U.S. neutrality, a period that witnessed an increase in the likelihood of a clash with the Axis powers and with Japan, accentuated by several irreversible government decisions. This period lasted for three-quarters of a year (from the fall of 1940 to August 1941), during which time the final touches were put on the U.S. foreign-policy blueprint for the conduct of the war and the major lines of the postwar reorganization of international relations gradually emerged.

The phase began at the close of the eventful summer of 1940 and was consolidated in March 1941 with the approval of the Lend-Lease Act, concluding with the meeting in Placentia Bay the following August. But already in the autumn of 1940, several key elements of the U.S. "gamble" in Europe had become clearer: The British had showed remarkable staying power in staving off the German air offensive, and the Italian effort had meanwhile proved to be a failure from the very outset.

The pattern of war events between the summer and winter of 1940 is mirrored in the fluctuating output of CFR memoranda, which provide useful indicators of the changing "perceptions" of contemporary opinion and the way political "concepts" were formed by the East Coast Establishment.[8] The daily and periodical press of the time gave ample confirmation of this correlation and revealed the close links between the U.S. and European press and the evolution of the international political issues debated in the Council on Foreign Relations.

In their constant and systematic sifting of the available chronicles, the study groups acquired a keen awareness of the main issues, which were organized according to subject matter and geographical areas, as well as chronologically, according to short- and long-term forecasts. But while WPS members kept a general vigil on the country's pulse, they were clearly biased toward issues that brought grist to the internationalist mill. By the same token, the groups had a clear tendency to overlook the positions and arguments of the isolationist camp, or supporters of the *Festung Amerika* (Fortress America).

The memoranda of the War and Peace Study groups are a kind of distillate of the thinking of experts who represented a very broad spectrum of economic and political interests, and who used the memoranda as a means of furthering the "globalist" reformulation of U.S. foreign policy. The Council on Foreign Relations also performed a promotional role for internationalist foreign policy among the country's opinion leaders, suggesting solutions through articles, commentaries, and critical essays in the daily, periodical, and scientific press. This activity was a kind of targeted dissemination of the council's ideas, carefully blended with material and contributions coming from the outside.[9]

The End of the "Coexistence" Scenario

The evolution of the debate within the War and Peace Studies groups on the potential creation of a Grand Area of free trade (or, more strictly speaking, "integrated" trade), controlled by the United States and aimed at counterbalancing the German-led "Paneuropa," revealed that even within a structurally internationalist organism like the Council on Foreign Relations, opinion was divided over the kind of relations to establish with Germany (which was seen as a trading partner of sorts) and over the role the United States should perform in such a European "order."[10] However, the initial differences did not persist, and by the end of 1940, members were largely in agreement.

The debate on and clarification of the first version of the concept of the Grand Area and the possible interaction with a Nazi Europe contributed to narrowing the divergences in outlook among the main study groups of the CFR. There was no grand merger between the two traditions or an annulment of the economist and technocratic preferences of the one camp (the Economic and Financial Group), and the geopolitical and realist preferences of the other (especially the Territorial and the Political groups); the radical differences in style and method were to remain unaltered. However, the two philosophies suddenly found common ground in their faith in internationalism (almost parallel to the burgeoning Democratic-Republican bipartisanship on foreign-policy issues, of which Wendell Willkie's candidacy in the presidential election was the first significant political sign).[11] The conceptual basis of the new harmony among group members lay in their awareness that the "European system" of international relations (the balance of power) was irreparably compromised, and that the world space was completely open to any power that wished or knew how to exploit the occasion.[12]

The prolonged debate over the Grand Area as a working concept (defined in Memorandum T-A14) was proof of the groups' concerted interests. A further series of documents was then drawn up and discussed in full by the Economic and Financial Group, based on the notes on the "Economic Trading Blocs."

However, from the outset, the EF Group was cool toward the observations of the Political and Territorial groups. In particular, it contested the other groups' criticism of part of Memorandum E-B19, which had not favored coexistence with the German economic bloc in Europe and instead advocated a broader trade bloc. In the presence of Walter Langsam (who defended Memorandum P-B13 in his role as its author), Hansen, Viner, Riefler, Diebold, and others all firmly endorsed the arguments contained in Memorandum E-B19.[13] The real controversy, which can be inferred from the discussion digest, did not hinge so much on whether there were real openings for trade areas big enough to bipolarize the world (at least on the level of trade), as on whether the forecasts expounded in the EF Group's text were tenable or not and on the viability of the concept of an "integrated economic area" (today better described as "interdependence").

The most radical criticism leveled against Memorandum E-B19 was a functional doubt based on the forecast that, in the medium term, Germany and Japan would not accept the speculated stalemate, or truce, contained in the document. It was argued that the physiological instability of this coexistence would rapidly be transformed "into an all-out arms race, and would then break out into conflict."[14] In response, certain members of the EF Group (headed by Hansen and Viner) spoke out, saying that even if a stalemate were a fleeting or even remote possibility, it was still clear that the studies on compatible trade blocs could be put to use immediately, to identify the "order" of the postwar international economy.[15]

The clash of opinions was therefore somewhat relative. Guided by the firm conviction of the need to create large regional trade areas based on the regulations of the clearing agreements drawn up by Arthur R. Upgren, the statistical studies and examinations of the various possible geoeconomic options were continued. From August 1940 on, the studies were directed by the new secretary of the Economic and Financial Group, William Diebold. As of February 1941, a succession of proposals and adjustments had been made, culminating in a brief but fundamental text, Memorandum E-B34 (July 24, 1941). The document was a milestone in the EF Group's assessments and presented an entirely new version of the Grand Area.[16]

The idea of a bipolar monopoly of the world economy under German-American control had lost credibility, even as a working hypothesis. But the notion of establishing regional trade areas was still viable—in fact it was enhanced, shedding its prior mercantilist tenor in favor of an increasingly politico-institutional connotation. The memorandum spelled out a far more complex scheme of international economic collaboration or cooperation, based on flexible criteria, including a customs union and the possibility of integration of an "imperial" nature.[17] As such, the memorandum foreshadowed postwar debates on the various options of regional, economic, and political integration and interdependence, such as those between Great Britain and India, and echoed the system of trade relations decided at the Ottawa Conference in 1932, which had instituted the "imperial preferences" of the British.

In the first half of 1941, the idea of a stalemate with Germany had become no more than an intellectual exercise and was soon abandoned altogether. However, two possible outcomes of considerable importance still had to be addressed: total victory for the Germans or total victory for the British.[18] The debate on the Grand Area took on new meaning.[19] By that time, certain opinions had begun to emerge that presaged the philosophy of the "New World Order," a new economic, political, and institutional order, at the heart of which would be the United States itself.[20]

Memorandum E-B34 (dated July 24, 1941, a few weeks prior to the Placentia Bay Conference between F. D. Roosevelt and British Prime Minister Winston Churchill) was in fact the fruit of collaboration between Upgren and a younger scholar, William Diebold. Whereas Upgren was an economist of traditional leanings, the latter was animated by new ideas on international economic relations, some of which he had picked up in England, at the London School of Economics and Political Science.[21] Moreover, the "supplement" prepared in June, describing the methods adopted for assessing the extent of self-sufficiency of the various trade blocs, was in fact the work of Diebold alone, who pointed out the weaknesses of the statistical techniques used in the preceding memoranda that had statistical appendixes.[22]

Diebold's supplement showed the first signs of the declining importance of self-sufficiency, the ideological mainstay of the protectionist politics of the 1930s, from the Smoot-Hawley Act on. This decline has been pointed out by many historians of both revisionist and orthodox bent, such as Lloyd Gardner, Charles Kindleberger, William Leuchtenburg, Arthur Schlesinger, Jr., Robert Dallek, and Wayne Cole.[23]

Just as the main warring countries were squeezing the most out of their domestic economic resources so as to depend as little as possible on outside sources,[24] the United States was toying with a new concept, interdependence,[25] which was later to become the basis of all postwar planning on economic and financial matters. In many respects, the Democratic administration was reversing its traditional preference for a closed and protectionist economy, redirecting it toward a "free traderist" philosophy.[26]

The Premises of the Grand Area

Thus, little by little, the very concept of neomercantilist trade blocs began to give way to a new philosophy of the future, turning on the idea (at once old and new) of an interdependent "world economy." The choice was clear at this point, as well as the possible options for international economic relations: "The Grand Area, then, is the amount of the world the United States can defend most economically, that is, with the least readjustment of the American economy," said Memorandum E-B34. It continued, "To maintain a maximum defense effort, the United States must avoid economic readjustment caused by the constriction of the trading area if the military cost of defending the area is not too great."[27]

The memorandum introduced two new, logically coupled concepts. The first was the vital importance of the "maximum defense effort." Although the planners had moved far beyond the absolute prudence of the previous year, at the same time they were still maneuvering inside a purely defense-oriented option that differed greatly from the one voiced by the "Warhawk" lobbyists or the concept of "total defense," developed by Henry Wallace and M. Ezekiel.[28]

Driven by the tide of events, which, after June 1940, speeded the strengthening of political and military bonds between the United States and Great Britain, consequently drawing the administration into an ever-finer mesh of obligations, in March 1941 Congress finally passed the Lend-Lease Act,[29] an agreement that signaled a decisive about-turn in the third phase of U.S. neutrality. After this, U.S. relations with both Germany and Japan were to plummet. It was fairly clear that although officially maintaining its intention to remain neutral at all costs, the United States would be forced sooner or later to enter the war.

The second innovative concept in Memorandum E-B34 was that the United States might as well set in motion the defense effort and focus on the Grand Area. This would enable Washington to avoid effecting drastic adjustments on the U.S. economy once the bottlenecks in labor and industrial capacity—the result of channeling manufacturing toward the production of substitutes for imported raw materials, many of which came from Southeast Asia (rubber, tin, jute, vegetable oils)—had passed.

The Grand Area was thus justified and even deemed essential for safeguarding the U.S. economic system "in times of war as in times of peace."[30] This was a curious argument: On the one hand, it seemed to be a provisional measure dictated by circumstances, implying that the Grand Area was not a permanent goal but merely a guarantee for the commodity markets necessary for ensuring internal U.S. economic growth through the war period. On the other hand, it suggested that this large-scale market might outlast the war. If it became impossible to maintain the stalemate between the Grand Area and the German area, then the United States would need to consider using arms to defend the Grand Area and prevent the Germans from taking hold of it, as well as to preempt defections from within its perimeter.

The newly emerging concept was that of containment, which was to play a leading role in postwar history: The adversary was to be "contained" by U.S. political and economic control over its own "area of influence."[31] Once the Grand Area had been identified and assessed in economic and trade terms and its geographical perimeter traced out, it was almost automatically seen as a somehow unified entity and as such as an "object" (and not an "actor") that required "defending." The fact that this area could include distant continents and regions, with differing peoples and governments, seemed in no way to detract from the sense of the area's unity. The unifying criterion was being determined, abstractly, by the dominant power, which represented the single center of interaction for the entire territory of the Grand Area.

Fundamentally, the Grand Area anticipated some of the features that would later figure in the international bipolar system. More specifically, it hypothesized the existence of what was to become the "Western subsystem," which, unlike Germanic Europe, was generated by a "passive" or defensive system of coming together, rather than by imperialist aggression. The Grand Area was born, therefore, as a countermeasure (primarily against Nazi Europe and German expansionism and secondarily against the Soviet Empire and international communism), rather than as an original institutional and/or organizational scheme or model. Consequently, the Grand Area assumed the connotations of a defensive alliance against an external threat. Its cohesion was directly proportional to the extent of the threat itself.[32]

To survive, the Grand Area needed the kind of cohesion that could come only from an increase in communication flows within its perimeter. At the same time, it required a central organizing device able to tap resources and rechannel them, creating the foundations for increasing commercial, political, and military integration. In 1940–1941, given the collapse of France and the steady bleeding of England, the United States was the only traditional international actor (excluding Germany, the Soviet Union, and Japan) capable of carrying out this enormous task.

Memorandum E-B34 did not contain such implications, nor could it at the time. However, the idea of a permanent Grand Area as the basis of the postwar political system, particularly for the Atlantic System, was foremost in the minds of the document's authors. It was a modified version of the "American Century" proclaimed by Henry R. Luce in the pages of *Life* magazine on February 17, 1941,[33] less epic perhaps, but decidedly more concrete.

The memorandum explained that in the case of an Anglo-American victory, much would have to be done to reform the world, especially Europe. The organization of the Grand Area could be directed toward these ends. During the period of transition, while readjustment and reconstruction effort was under way, the Grand Area could have a major stabilizing effect on the world economy. Most likely, thought the authors, the institutions created to integrate the area would provide useful experience in tackling European issues and, perhaps, it would even be possible to link the economies of European countries with that of the Grand Area.

In the simplest of terms, the document expressed the conviction that the institution of a Grand Area was in fact nothing more than a metaphor concealing the fact that the only area sufficiently large was the one equivalent to the world economy as a whole and driven by the United States. The coming to this awareness was gradual, proceeding through a series of thresholds: from continental defense to the defense of the United Kingdom as an outpost of the United States, to the hypothesis of a close alliance (a true embryo of bipolarism) with the British Empire. But as Luce had fully understood when he wrote that the United States had been at war since 1940 and that the idea that "we entered the war to save the English was completely off target," since the real task of the United States was to "establish American dominion across the globe," the problem was no longer to keep the (German) "tyranny" at bay, but to impose an (American) "new order."[34]

Unlike Luce, a Republican opponent of the president, who until a few months earlier had bitterly criticized his political actions, attacking Roosevelt daily through the publications of the Time/Life chain, the Council on Foreign Relations was not in a position to spell things out explicitly. In fact, the council's credibility with the administration came from the fact that its analyses drew directly on the same political directives as did the administration itself, reworking them, often reversing them conceptually, but always salvaging the formal framework.

Memorandum E-B34 was necessarily based on the absolute priority of egalitarian links with the British. Its preamble stated that "Anglo-

American collaboration is the key to the integration of the Grand Area, both as a wartime measure and in forging an enduring peace on the lines desired by the two countries."[35] The memorandum was deeply rooted in Anglo-Saxon orthodoxy, the very cornerstone of the internationalist philosophy of the East Coast Establishment. However, this document also pointed the way for a series of other texts devoted to the knotty question of Anglo-American relations.

On the political front, even the Political Group attempted to delimit the field of inquiry, the respective roles, and the possible course of relations between London and Washington both during the war and after.[36] But all these immediate or future problems of Anglo-American cooperation did not hide the U.S. ambition to steer the world's economy. At bottom, it concerned the more limited though not incompatible aim of transforming the supply agreement between the United States and Great Britain into a permanent bilateral interaction, which would subsequently manifest itself in the historic alliance.

The entire debate over the Grand Area therefore tended to assume a deeper and almost symbolic political meaning in the evolving foreign policy of the Eastern Establishment. Less than twelve months had passed since the "Summons to Speak Out" of June 1940 issued by the "Warhawks" (which swarmed with CFR members)[37] and the exacting definition of the possible kinds of alliance with Great Britain (advantageous to the United States).

During this relatively brief span, the move for closer relations with the British was no longer contested, not once the Land-Lease Act was passed and the president (on May 27, 1941) declared a state of "unlimited national emergency"—a decision based, not simply on the ethnic and linguistic affinities of the Anglo-Saxon Eastern Establishment and its British counterparts, but also on enduring historical links between the two nations. The more internationalist groups justified their staunch support for the British cause on far more realistic grounds, that is, the advantageous cost-benefit ratio the United States would derive from allying itself with the British.

The potential of such a relationship had already been outlined in Memorandum E-B34:

> The integration of the Grand Area is based on American-British collaboration. At the same time, American and British interests are neither identical nor entirely parallel. Not only will there be disagreements as to what policy is best, but also real clashes of interests which can be resolved only to the hurt of certain groups within one or the other country. In wartime the tendency is for such clashes of interest to be submerged and subordinated to the single goal of winning the war. At the peace and

after it, they tend to re-emerge, sometimes more sharply than ever. With the outside pressure of a common enemy removed, such conflicts of interest can easily destroy the whole program of continued international cooperation. One of the most important tasks of the Grand Area studies will be to detect present and prospective clashes of interests, define them so far as possible, and seek means of eliminating, alleviating, or compromising them.[38]

Indeed, friction with the British was long-standing, though it had always been kept within tolerable boundaries. But potential conflict was unpredictable. In all likelihood, further clashes would arise over the new global functions the United States was assuming, which included using the alliance with London as a springboard. It was clear that the emergence of any new conflicts could jeopardize a postwar alliance. Toward the end of the war, for example, there were various people (including some within the Council on Foreign Relations, the State Department, and the White House) who felt that the British, together with the Soviets, should perhaps be left to rule over Europe, while the United States should retire to the Western Hemisphere and confine its hegemony to the Pacific Basin.

But the U.S. partnership with Great Britain was more than a binding bilateral accord. It was a sort of management "consortium" for the Grand Area, which functioned as a feasible model for international postwar relations, since the time-worn European balance-of-power system had finally disintegrated. Furthermore, in the spring of 1941 there was real uncertainty regarding the next moves of the main actors (Japan and the Soviet Union).

A treaty of nonaggression signed on April 13 between the Soviets and the Japanese had further heightened the tension, causing the United States additional concern about the future involvement of the Soviet Union in the war under way. This problem, which was closely linked to the question of the contents and aims of the Anglo-American alliance, was studied by the Council on Foreign Relations. The Political Group delved into the "British question," while the Territorial Group developed an analysis of the implications of the five-year Soviet-Japanese neutrality agreement.[39]

7

Anglo-American Relations and the Atlantic System

The Beginning of the System

Not even the Anglo-American (or Atlantic) model was without its flaws. It worked because of the basic disproportion of forces between the Americans and the British, an imbalance that was growing more evident every day. It was rather like dealing with a company in which the major shareholders had done their best to outdo each other in order to seize the majority holding, while continuing to apportion the dividends equally.[1]

Above all, the alliance quickly showed itself to be the option for active U.S. intervention, first of all against Britain (only second against Germany) and its organizational logic, the protectionist mechanisms of its tariff preference system, and indeed against the very philosophy of the British Empire. For the Americans, safeguarding Britain, the "mother country," presupposed their having a free hand in the empire and the entire imperial system. Paradoxically, the alliance became a means of settling many old scores with the British, albeit in a peaceful and "cooperative" fashion.[2]

The plan is well delineated in Memorandum P-B19, presented by the Political Group on May 16, 1941, and carrying the unabashed title, "The Island of Great Britain as a Factor in the Strategy of American Defense." Because the war in Europe had shifted to retaliation against the German blitzkrieg, the document (written by Major George Eliot) stressed that "the United States is prepared to take the offensive with its naval and naval aviation forces," very realistically assigning a highly limited task area for the U.S. Army, given its size.[3] In order for the United States to prepare itself for the offensive, which had become a necessity at this point, it was "strategically of the first importance to the United States to maintain close military relations with Great Britain."[4] Britain was therefore to be supported for essentially strategic reasons. The memo-

randum explained that "lacking the British base, the United States will
not be able to use its present weapons offensively and may be compelled
to fall back on the defensive attitude which has been the inevitable
prelude to defeat."[5]

It was also underscored that Britain's function within the new alliance
would be to serve as an "advance base" for U.S. operations in Europe
and other places throughout the world. The "bases" theory (according
to the strategic criteria of sea power and air power, in that order),[6] was
composed of two essential principles that became the central axioms of
U.S. military doctrine for the rest of the twentieth century. These were
(1) to prevent the enemy from taking possession of any base that would
allow him to attack vital centers of the·country and (2) to try to obtain
further forward bases from which vital centers of the enemy could be
attacked.[7]

Many of the political and military events the countries of North and
South America found themselves involved in during the war and later
and also much diplomatic activity and international perceptions were
influenced by these cardinal concepts. Although their history goes far
back in time, they were not turned into a permanent model for ad-
ministering power on a world scale until World War II.[8] In the first
years of the conflict, when the early studies into the postwar setup were
initiated, the question of a network of military bases strung across the
globe became a realistic one, in order to guarantee the future "world
order" or, alternatively, to guarantee the Pax Americana.

The question of the "bases" was a conceptual landmark in U.S.
globalist thinking. For an oceanic, insular power, the control of the sea
and air was understood to be vital to national security.[9] Sea and air
control was also a key geostrategic issue to be debated in order to
determine the perimeter and eventual extension of the potential zone
of U.S. influence throughout the world.[10]

The issue is one of the most acute indicators of the evolution of
interventionist ideas during the three phases of U.S. neutrality. The
assumption of direct military responsibility was gradual. Troop assign-
ments were limited to small and remote areas (island and coastal bases),
but the patrolling of increasingly vast areas of ocean or stretches close
to foreign coastland was in blatant contrast to Washington's insistence
on the strictly defensive nature of its military and political activity.

The gradual buildup of U.S. military capability in the Atlantic, together
with growing restrictions imposed on Japanese movement in the Pacific,[11]
was repeatedly justified with the argument of safeguarding U.S. interests
in the Western Hemisphere. But as the perimeter of this web of defense
was gradually extended to territories and areas never before included

(or considered), the operation inevitably began to resemble an offensive and was indeed perceived as such by both Germans and Japanese.

The network of bases became progressively denser and more far-flung.[12] In the first of many formal and informal steps that were to continue after the war, the United States traded fifty torpedo boat destroyers to the British as "rent" for a set of British bases in the Caribbean (on ninety-nine-year leases). Roosevelt justified the operation by likening it to the Louisiana Purchase President Thomas Jefferson had transacted with Napoleon in 1803.

As Bailey and Ryan have pointed out,[13] while the two events may have political parallels, the comparison was quite inappropriate. Despite both events being justified in terms of national security against the encroaching perils of a European war, the defensive-offensive character of the operations was self-evident. In the case of the "destroyers for bases" deal, the trade did of course help equip England with a sufficient naval force for escorting convoys across the Atlantic with their cargo of U.S. war supplies under the Cash and Carry Act. Meanwhile, it threw the Americans' net even wider, giving them control over new territories, above all in ocean zones until then beyond the horizons of U.S. strategy.

Thus, with the idea of Great Britain as a "forward base" for the United States, a threshold had been crossed, and the multiplication of U.S. bases followed, not only in the United Kingdom itself ("launch pad" for the invasion of continental Europe), but also throughout the British Empire. Once the United States moved into the war, this process accelerated, and the number of bases rose steadily, with the occupation of more and more territories previously belonging to nations crushed by Germany (including Belgium, Holland, and France) and even the territories of neutral countries, as one by one they came to be regarded as falling within the radius of U.S. "interests," which became so extended that potentially those interests stretched across the whole world.[14]

Coming Closer: Conflict or Cooperation

Many notes and writings of the time betrayed the first signs of an emerging sense of global strategy,[15] but the embryos of the new concept were most explicit and organically laid out in the papers of the CFR. Besides Memorandum P-B19, discussed above, Memorandum A-B51 of the Security and Armaments Group, April 16, 1942 (also written by Major Eliot) provided key insights on this development. In a single page,[16] the document presented the array of possible options on the "future of American bases and relative installations on foreign soil" and even suggested a further extension of the number of installations to cover all continents, hypothesizing the possible permanence after the war of U.S. bases in former enemy territory, as well as in allied and liberated countries.[17]

The bases were a focal point of the discussions on the foundation of a corps for "international policing" by forces from all three of the Great Powers (United States, Soviet Union, and Great Britain); the corps was envisaged as the armed force of the United Nations Organization, which was in its nascent phase.[18] The inherent political and conceptual ambivalence of establishing these bases caused some misinterpretations and diverging opinions on the matter even within the administration. The debate between departments and agencies on "security" and "location" was vociferous. The basic issue was political rather than military. Given that the British Empire continued to hold its dominion over a quarter of the world, the bases were just one of the many problems in Anglo-American power relations. Some members of the State Department favored decolonization and independence for British territories (or at least some of them), but the General Board of the Navy, the Joint Chiefs of Staff, and the Strategic Survey Committee all felt it was imperative to keep the British Empire alive in its entirety.[19]

As numerous scholars have pointed out, the working philosophy behind many of the U.S. government's decisions in those years was greatly molded by Anglo-American relations as the two countries moved toward permanent interaction and by the solutions found to the problems that arose from this political and diplomatic framework. One might even state that the forms U.S. "globalism" took during the war were largely dictated by this "special relationship" between Washington and London. The problem of how to divide the spoils between the United States and Great Britain (and eventually with the Soviet Union) was a far more complex issue than the fate of the German Reich and Japanese empire, which was already potentially in the hands of the Americans (who, after Pearl Harbor, never had any serious doubts as to the outcome of the war). But even during the two-year period 1940–1941, the Americans were prompted to impose their own rules on the British and block any ambitions the latter might have had.

W. R. Louis, who studied this covert wrangling very closely, recalled a comment by a high-level British official that epitomized the awkwardness between the two nations: In the face of what he considered a mania on the part of Cordell Hull and Sumner Welles for free trade and the Open Door Policy, the British secretary of state for India and Burma, L. S. Amery (who was also a well-known statesman of the Conservative Right), exclaimed that he far preferred "Hitler's New Order to Cordell Hull's Free Trade system."[20] Reading through Keynes's papers and the copious records and memoirs of the British diplomats (Winston Churchill's included), one can see that ever since their first debt to the Americans because of Lend-Lease, the British realized that Washington was gradually forcing their hand and imposing formulas and briefs whose content was humiliating.[21] The network of bases, providing a fundamental structure of U.S. political strategy, and the international emphasis on trusteeship[22] as a legal structure, replacing the traditional internal norms of colonial dependence (almost as an antidote to British imperialism), were clear indicators of the anti-British streak in U.S. foreign policy.

The CFR documents examined the friction and divergences between Washington and London, and analogies to the kind of historical discord between pairs of naval powers operating in tandem were noted. Because both governments upheld similar philosophies of international relations, the documents concluded that the convergence of the two countries' strategic interests and economic conflicts could hardly keep them antagonistic for long. Open conflict would thus be avoided. Unlike the confrontation between "navalism" and "continentalism" in the "whale versus bear" metaphor of the cold war between the United States and the Soviet Union,[23] there was no contention of opposing international or political vocations between the two English-speaking countries. Nor did the documents predict the development of the conflict situation that had pitted certain pairs of maritime powers (Holland and England, England and France) against each other in a mortal struggle or, more recently, had characterized the U.S.-Japanese conflict, insofar as there was no strategic complementarity in those cases.[24] Nonetheless, U.S. relations with Great Britain were objectively divergent and seemed to be on a potential collision course.

The United States tended to capitalize on this friction to expand its area of intervention toward nations and territories under London's influence and control. Meanwhile, the British government was rapidly reducing its own capabilities of command and control, especially over the more distant and turbulent areas of the empire.[25] Britain was sorely in need of U.S. money and could no longer sustain the burden of the empire.[26] The steady eclipse of London's authority, even where British troops were stationed and the Union Jack was still officially flying, was creating a power vacuum that slowly allowed for U.S. penetration, though this was sometimes solicited for contingent reasons and then made permanent by necessity.[27] But all the while, the historical, institutional, ethnic, and cultural affinities between the two powers prevented them from misinterpreting each other, and there was never any threat of outright conflict, as would arise between nations with less-reciprocal flows of communications.[28]

It is therefore comprehensible that since the fight to the death is interrupted only when two adversaries cease to fight and start talking (i.e., begin negotiating),[29] the United States and Great Britain had found a common language capable of defusing and circumscribing their differences. They created institutional structures and codes of behavior valid for both parties, with the express aim of establishing the rules of the game, an essential requirement for the two founding states of the new system.

The "universal" international order (the United Nations and its specialized agencies), although it arose out of the Anglo-American alliance, was bound to sanction U.S. supremacy unambiguously—a supremacy made necessary by the vacuum left by Germany and Japan. Such an order presumed for Washington an apparently neutral authority, so as to avoid the pitfalls (ideological and otherwise) of the Versailles legacy. However, the scheme was also aimed at protecting Britain from weakening to the point of collapse. Owing to this set of new structures and rules— the fruit of long negotiations, particularly between the Americans and the British (Placentia Bay, Dumbarton Oaks, Bretton Woods, and San Francisco)—the British felt sure the rate of geopolitical and economic decline would level out after the war was over.[30]

However, as pointed out by W. R. Louis, "the wartime archives have amply revealed that the historical feeling of antagonism between Great Britain and the United States continued to exist, in parallel with the spirit of cooperation generated in the course of the war."[31] Furthermore, it is certain that in some circles of the U.S. administration, the hostility and diffidence toward Great Britain were even stronger than the ideological distrust of the Soviet Union—a feeling even President Roosevelt seemed to share.[32]

The effects of this mixture of conflict and cooperation on economic matters are well described in the lengthy account of a discussion that took place within the Economic and Financial Group on July 19, 1941. The text considered all the existing "areas of conflict" one by one: "Joint development of backward areas; disposition of surpluses; raw material export controls; competitive trade; tariff problems; international investment (direct and indirect, governmental and private); capital movements; shipping; air routes; the British balance of payments and freer trade; and the status of equipment shipped under the lend-lease program."[33]

The list of controversial topics shows that the Anglo-American divergences entailed virtually all sectors of the economy. But the impression is one of a tolerable and superficial kind of conflict spread out fairly evenly through a broad range of themes, with few real peaks. It is almost as if the Americans saw these ill-feelings and potential controversies as the inevitable product of two specific factors: (1) the resumption of inter-Atlantic trade and financial relations, which had been virtually interrupted during the 1930s, and (2) the signing of the Lend-Lease agreement in March 1941. It was evident that the new system of economic interaction needed time to settle. However, it was an indispensable tool for Britain's survival, even as it indicated that country's dependence on Washington.

The Economic and Financial Group's texts vividly convey the emergence of this completely new political bond between the two shores of the Atlantic, a tie that was to gradually take on the form of "asymmetrical interdependence."[34] But not everyone was aware of the unusual configuration of the bond. One of the more lucid members of the EF Group commented on the long list of conflicts with the British: "Americans do not seem to be aware of the humiliation the British feel at simply being told 'we will take care of your needs' and having no definite understanding of how they are going to be enabled to meet their commitments."[35]

The critical awareness of certain more attentive observers to the historical change taking place is representative of a special American "perception" of British sensitivity, often missing from much of Washington's treatment of other European and Asian countries. This spirit of understanding explains why the dwindling of British power, which in 1944 was fairly obvious to everyone, did not occasion open disputes with the United States. This "special relationship" between the United States and Great Britain, which had originated in the nineteenth century,[36] took on the appearance of a painless dynastic succession of commitments and roles from one generation to another.

Anglo-American relations were viewed by both the administration and the "internationalist" pressure groups as an inseparable combination of economic needs and political opportunities. This perception was embodied in the notion of "total defense," i.e., the need to defend oneself to the limits of one's own ability.[37] The theme is dealt with most explicitly in a document drafted in August 1940 by Mordecai Ezekiel, then economic adviser to Roosevelt's secretary of agriculture, Henry Wallace. In his document, Ezekiel (a leading figure, who played a major role during the New Deal years) developed a concept that had already been sketched out in broad terms by the president himself less than a month before. On the premise that despite the increase of four million new jobs since February 1940, in July there were still nine million unemployed, Ezekiel maintained that "England is our present front line of defense."

The Political Group of the CFR had expressed similar views in some of their memoranda. In itself, it was not such an original statement, considering that by June 10, 1940, some had observed that the frontier of U.S. national interest "is now on the Somme."[38] This time, however, the argument was more elaborate, stating that "it is far cheaper and more effective to help England fight over there, than to fight alone over here." But to help Great Britain defend itself, it was vital to initiate "a carefully coordinated program of total defense." That implied mobilizing "the maximum industrial and military power of which we are capable . . . and the rapid utilization of every available person to that end. . . . A program of total defense need not reduce the standard of living of our people. On the contrary, if we employ effectively our idle men and resources, we can make ourselves impregnable from attack, and at the same time establish higher living standards."[39]

Though its tone was somewhat unusual, this document was significant because it was written in the wake of a great many discussions between "a number of political and governmental leaders," as stated in the accompanying letter sent to the Department of State. It recorded the type of debate going on in the "liberal" circles of the administration at this very early stage in the long-term analysis of the future aims of U.S. foreign policy. Ezekiel's text also reflected the ideas of the dwindling ranks of New Dealers still active within the administration and was the product of a group of intellectuals and functionaries that did not agree, culturally or stylistically, with the majority of CFR members, who represented the more moderate wing of the internationalist elites.

But Ezekiel's document and others like it revealed the different political weight of the ideas developed by the CFR, compared with those that emerged from the lively intellectual debate on foreign-policy issues in those years. The fact that Ezekiel's text anticipated (even more so than the CFR memoranda) a theme such as the "war economy" for a "total war" (of which the concept of "total defense" was simply the mirror image) was indicative, not of greater political clout, but of the opposite. Basically the document was one of rupture rather than of persuasion.[40]

This was not so of the CFR documents. They nearly always showed some correlation between the frame, or context, a carefully gauged mixture of different factors (political climate, maturity of the administration and the public), and innovation, i.e., the ability to develop new arguments from official draft schemes, from words or phrases in papers and speeches of government figures, without breaking (at least apparently) the current political rationale.[41] This correspondence of form was absent from Ezekiel's document (his idea of "total defense" must have come like a thunderbolt for the State Department in August 1940, when even Roosevelt and Hull were still assessing whether and how they might coexist with German Europe); however, the form and contents of the CFR texts demonstrated just how closely they tied in with the language of the executive branch.

When the notion of "total defense" finally began to filter through the administration, it was dressed up as part of an expansionist political economy based on the stimulation of the domestic demand through public spending. It therefore avoided appearing as a global project of foreign and military policy aimed at a general mobilization of the country's resources against the Germans. In fact, at the same time as the president, with this motivation in mind, was asking Congress (on July 10, 1940) for more money for defense (which was only formally referred to as "total"), the State Department had begun to formulate ideas and scenarios for "peaceful coexistence" with Germany, probably drawing on CFR memoranda.[42]

The Transformations of U.S. Neutrality

The ensuing clash between two ways of life and schools of thought within the administration relative to the problems of peace and war was largely due to reciprocal ignorance of the other's culture. On one side stood the New Deal lobby—intellectuals, consultants, and functionaries lured into the administration by Roosevelt and by his "brain trust."[43] On the other side were the Cordell Hull–style "free traders" and the members of a group bearing the ironic name of the Pretty Good Club, taken from the title Martin Weil affixed to his book on the founders of the U.S. diplomatic service in the interwar years. Apparently the president was fully aware of this divergence between the State Department and the White House and shortly after Pearl Harbor wryly commented that "his State Department was neutral in this war, and hoped it would remain so in future."[44]

The split within the administration was not a question of opposition between isolationists and internationalists, a battle that was fought in the arena of public opinion and in official politics, but a clash between different kinds of internationalists, who for many reasons had varying pictures of the U.S. role in international relations.[45] The most important operation that the CFR helped initiate was the settlement of dissension in the internationalist camp. Within this design emerged the first sparks of "bipartisanship" in U.S. foreign policy, a joint party stance that took hold during the war and lasted at least until 1968.[46] Because of the more mature perception of the need to unite the forces of the country's elites during the war, and especially in view of the coming world responsibilities, the language and themes of the CFR had to be more tempered than those of other circles at the time—they had to avoid bias, to appear more credible. Nonetheless, despite their appearance, semantically they were clearly "war arguments" and thus "persuasive strategies" to convince both Democrats and Republicans and sideline only the more rigid among the traditional isolationists and pro-German neutralists.

The internationalist establishment was a step ahead of the administration in developing its awareness of the role that the United States would have to play on a global scale,[47] and the successive stages of its progress can be tracked in the output of the CFR. In the first phase, the internationalists already displayed a deeply innovative concept of international relations and began to develop their first long-term projects for the postwar world. In the second phase (which continued to the end of 1940), there was great uncertainty as to the outcome of the war in Europe, and hence of the ways to address the emerging international situation—namely, whether to accept coexistence with Germanic Europe or reject and therefore fight it.[48] In the third phase, Anglo-American relations intensified as the U.S. commitment in the Atlantic increased; meanwhile relations in the Pacific with the Japanese were worsening. The situation provided the context for the conceptual groundwork for the new international order with which the United States would have to contend.

The German invasion of the Soviet Union accelerated this process, shifting the conflict's center of gravity toward the eastern edge of Europe and upsetting the erstwhile European balance of power. The Allies' view of the hostilities, which had so far been entirely "western," with offshoots in North Africa and the Balkans, was necessarily modified, becoming more "eastern."[49] As we shall see, the United States felt that the Soviet Union's entry into war inevitably entailed U.S. intervention, and it was considered necessary at this juncture to devise some "war aims" to begin constructing a political and ideological armor for future U.S. action.[50]

The first step was to tidy up the country's friendships and alliances, which were gradually expanding as the United States became a political and strategic sanctuary for larger and larger areas of the world (starting with Latin America). Meanwhile Washington was increasingly obliged to support Canada, the only American state actually at war,[51] and found itself forced to develop an alternative to the outdated official stance of "neutrality," while at the same time imposing a conceptual framework solid enough to justify the gradual mobilization of resources and eventual U.S. entry into war.[52]

The problem was not an easy one, as the political and strategic equation had to juggle a set of variables of uneven importance, size, and order. The somewhat recalcitrant U.S. public accepted the idea of the United States as the "arsenal of democracy," as long as the country was not directly involved in the war itself. But it was also necessary to define just what the United States intended by participation in the war, in terms of both propaganda and national interest. Drawing up a package of propaganda goals was complicated. Roosevelt's foreign policy, unlike that of the Axis powers, had always flaunted neutrality and pacifism, which were held to be central to the official government philosophy.

For the government to make an about-face turn and mobilize men and resources—even with becoming the "arsenal of democracy" as the goal—was a delicate operation that could be actuated only through a sophisticated scheme of persuasion.[53]

It was less difficult, however, to put together a set of war aims that fit within the flexible concept of national interest. The schemes of analysis used had already enjoyed considerable success in the United States during the fifty years prior to World War II, particularly in the expansionist doctrines of U.S. foreign policy since the Civil War, in the notes on the Open Door Policy, in the Dollar Diplomacy philosophy of Presidents William Howard Taft, Calvin Coolidge, and Herbert Hoover, and in Cordell Hull's free-trade doctrine. In all these cases, U.S. national interests had been made credible by presenting the United States as the world's number-one generator and sustainer of democracy and liberty.[54]

Hence it was not hard to blend propaganda—which was essentially based on the crusade for a free world—with the national interests linked to the expansion of international markets and control of international resources. The keystone of this equation was a set of concepts, such as growth (i.e., economic and social prosperity), a rise in living standards, and collective security (a guaranteed magnet for consensus)—principles that were reinforced at the end of the war and the years that followed through copious assistance and aid programs, culminating in the Marshall Plan.

Discussions of War Aims and the Role of the CFR

The nation's war aims (which some insisted on calling "peace aims") were part of the cultural baggage of the internationalists and got their first airing during the third phase of U.S. neutrality,[55] which coincided roughly with the twelve months of 1941. Here again the CFR took up a pioneering position. In June 1941 it set up a special group (the European Nations [EN] Group) with the explicit task of identifying the main objectives for which each European nation was actually fighting. It would appear that Memoranda E-B32 and E-B36, drawn up by the Economic and Financial Group in the first half of 1941, were probably the first papers drafted in the United States on the issue of war aims and were seen as such by the State Department.[56]

Ever since the outbreak of hostilities there had been much debate, especially in Europe, over war aims. Some governments (especially the British government) had been bitterly criticized in the press and political circles for omitting to make official declarations of the country's war aims, as belligerent and neutral nations alike had done during World War I. In answer to those who criticized him for not defining the war aims of the British government, on March 27, 1941, Winston Churchill told the Central Committee of the Conservative party, "everyone knows what we are fighting about, but if you try to set forth in a catalogue what will be the exact settlement of affairs in a period which is unforeseeable, you will find that the moment you leave the area of pious platitude you will descend into the arena of heated controversy."[57]

Roosevelt demonstrated basic agreement with this evasive interpretation, though in some of his speeches in the early months of 1941 he seemed to be on the point of giving more detailed indications of the future "peace settlement."[58] In the CFR documents, the debate on war aims, unhampered by prejudices and political restrictions, became something more than a vague declaration of intentions such as those served up by the administration.[59] In the spring of 1941, the problem was given due attention by the U.S. government, as it began to test out various schemes for the reconstruction of the world order. Even the first principles outlined by Cordell Hull were complex and innovative compared with the traditional, inflexible, and blinkered free-trade outlook he had always vociferously supported.

On May 18, 1941, he had stated that "international agreements regulating the supply of commodities must be so handled as to protect fully the interests of the consuming countries and their people" and that "the institution and arrangement of international finance must be so set that they lend aid to the essential enterprises and the continuous development of all countries, and permit the payment through process of trade with the welfare of all countries."[60] The more traditional concepts were enhanced with new ideas that swiftly took hold and were, as Harley Notter admitted, the fruit of the work of a small staff of high caliber researchers and officials who had individually reflected on the long-term aspects of the current events.[61]

In various quarters, it was clear that something had to be developed to replace the old Eurocentric balance-of-power system, which had so miserably failed twice in twenty-five years, in 1914 and 1939. Moreover, there was widespread sense of the need for a more effective framework of international economic relations than the one in force since 1929, which had both contributed to and resulted from the collapse of the political system. There were, however, vague hints at the need for future institutions, bodies, and structures and at the construction of new rules, decision-making procedures, and norms; nothing more concrete emerged in the way of political proposals.

Very few staff members worked in the various departments and agencies on postwar planning or on designing possible frameworks for the future world order. If there had not been an outside body acting as an ongoing workshop, the ideas of the policymakers might have been even more general and uncertain than they were at the time.[62] In the State Department there were, in fact, no more than six officials in all, including Leo Pasvolsky (director of the division over the period February– December 1941), who were assigned to the Division of Special Research, under the guidance of Deputy Secretary of State Sumner Welles, to study postwar planning. In the other government departments and agencies, planning in 1941 was even more irregular, often improvised at the whim of the officials, with no system; an even smaller number of officials or researchers were working full- or part-time. It is not hard to imagine that the memoranda of the WPS study groups influenced the formation of ideas (and even decisions) of the administration on these matters. If during this period the CFR was alone in producing specific documents on this vast range of issues and in drawing up for each issue memoranda and discussion digests, often rewritten numerous times, then we can assume that the material the administration began to put together, at first hesitatingly and then with increased self-assurance, was mostly derived from the CFR papers.

In a systematic comparison of the WPS output on postwar planning and the State Department documents of the same period on the same subject, their similarities are self-evident. Very often the themes and arguments in State Department documents follow along the lines of CFR memoranda drawn up beforehand. Obviously, in the latter the general principles followed were those indicated by the government, but there was plenty of room left for devising new scenarios and structures. Cordell Hull himself considered a "broad program of world economic reconstruction," which did not have the characteristics that made U.S. aid to Europe ineffective after World War I.[63] However, he would not have been able to go beyond that vague idea had it not been for the detailed papers drawn up by federal or private study groups on postwar planning.

Historians are not unanimous on this point. Some scholars of the intellectual background of World War II and the origin of the postwar order, like Robert Divine, Ruth Russell, Mark L. Chadwin, Gabriel Kolko, Ernest R. May and John K. Galbraith, Walter Isaacson, Evan Thomas, and Richard M. Ketchum, attributed the gradual formation of these concepts and ideas to a broader range of cultural influences and input.[64]

Without a doubt, the multitude of councils, clubs, and foundations of internationalist stamp played a significant role in swaying public opinion, usually through the media and a host of public initiatives. But the ad hoc documents worked out secretly along the lines of those same internationalist ideas, documents compatible with the language of the administration and sent directly by their authors to the White House and the State Department, must surely have had an incisive influence (albeit discreetly achieved) on the action of statesmen and government members. Unlike the pressure of public opinion on the government, in the case of the CFR the communication was interactive, with feedback on both sides. To give an example, if the EF Group turned out a memorandum like E-B32, summarizing original, innovative solutions and political formulas (such as the idea of "restrictions on sovereignty" in order to achieve a more closely integrated international economic order), it is unlikely that the discussion deriving from it was generated solely within the CFR or was its exclusive reserve.

This two-way relationship was demonstrated by a series of documents attesting to the frequent correspondence between CFR members, WPS Group members, and prominent figures in the administration. One particularly interesting example is a letter written by Hamilton Fish Armstrong (director of *Foreign Affairs*, the quarterly journal of the CFR) to Leo Pasvolsky on July 14, 1941, in which Fish informed the director of the Division of Special Research of the constitution of a new study group (the EN Group), whose job was to gather and compile the various aspirations of all the countries of the Europe, so as to have a solid basis on which to "adjust" U.S. policy. Armstrong informed Pasvolsky that the EN Group was already operational and attached its first memorandum (on "Polish War Aims"), informing him moreover that Armstrong had personally supplied Sumner Welles (Pasvolsky's immediate superior as deputy secretary of state) with a copy that Saturday, reminding him also that Welles himself had "expressed the opinion that the new series of memoranda would be most useful to the Department."[65]

Another letter of the same period, in the same tone, provided confirmation of the keen interest of the CFR regarding the special relations between the British and U.S. governments. The author, Francis P. Miller, administrative secretary of the CFR, explicitly stated to Leo Pasvolsky (on September 20, 1941): "We have reached a stage in the work of the Political Group on a program of joint action between the American and British Governments where it is essential for us to know more than we do about what is going on. We need a list of points at which joint action is taking place now, with a brief description in each case of procedures employed."[66] The letter was quite blunt in its request for information, which must have been quite restricted. At the same time, the tone of the missive seems to confirm the fact that between the CFR and the State Department there existed a long-standing communication system and even the awareness (at least on Miller's part) that it was indeed the CFR that was "doing a favor" for the State Department and not the other way round.

It seems logical therefore that the CFR often acted upon the request, albeit informal, of the State Department, orienting its research along the basic guidelines laid down by the administration, studying issues and analyzing questions suggested by politicians and officials, rather than acting autonomously on its own initiatives. In some ways, given the lack of appropriate personnel or expertise in the official bodies, the CFR was virtually "contracted" to do the background work for the State Department, often anticipating the government's need for long-range analyses. After the war, when the Policy Planning Office was set up, this arrangement became permanent.[67] Thus the outstanding contribution of the CFR was to translate the general ideas of the establishment into an almost "technical" language, at a time in history when the establishment was about to take on new and much wider functions.

Although the study groups' work was prompted from above, their output in turn provided vital feedback and material for debate and the persuasion of the politicians themselves. Anticipating the policy reviews of the postwar decades, the CFR acted as a scout in the as-yet-uncharted territory of future U.S. foreign policy, without risking the pitfalls of utopianism.[68] As a rule, the study groups did not stray far from the limits imposed on them from above and hence maintained constant links with the government. Communications were guaranteed by the network of relations (including personal and informal) linking CFR members with the Roosevelt administration.[69]

This closeness to the government can be found throughout the WPS material drafted in relation to immediate issues (like the question of Greenland) and more complex questions, such as the future of Germany. The WPS groups had begun working on future U.S. foreign policy in autumn 1939, long before the departmental and interdepartmental committees were set up (between 1940 and 1941). They were also ahead of numerous private and nonofficial research centers, which generally began operating from 1942 on.

The formulation of the nation's war aims in the second half of 1941 is a good illustration of the constant exchange of ideas between the CFR and the State Department. The complex set of questions arising from the need to define Anglo-American relations was gradually transformed into a broader discussion on overall war aims. This transposition of issues germinated through internal discussions within each study group and the special intergroup meetings. Their material, coupled with that of the State Department, provided the groundwork for the summit between Roosevelt and Winston Churchill at Placentia Bay in August 1941.[70]

It is clearly not possible to gauge how much WPS material actually found its way into the dossiers Roosevelt took with him to Placentia Bay or its influence on the agenda of the bilateral meetings with the British prime minister. Churchill claimed to have sketched out the preliminary draft of the "Joint Declaration" himself, a declaration that was subsequently called the "Atlantic Charter."[71] It is certain, however, that the working agenda of the two statesmen paralleled in method and topics the debates that had taken place, including those in the CFR in the weeks prior to the summit. There were two items on the agenda: the current issues directly affecting the Anglo-American alliance and the long-term issues revolving around the theme of establishing a more cohesive "statute" for relations between the two countries, and in particular the "settlement" of the war in political and institutional terms. This latter part of the discussion, which became the Atlantic Charter, ran parallel to various discussions that had taken place in the meetings of the Political Group, the Economic and Financial Group, and the Territorial Group of the WPS.

The Anglo-Saxon Foundations of
the Atlantic System

U.S. relations with Britain and U.S. war aims were really two different facets of the same issue. This is an essential point for understanding World War II, because that issue was the load-bearing and generative "framework" of the postwar international system.

Even before war events caused the Anglo-American coalition (which was both anti-German and anti-Japanese) to include the Soviet Union, China, and then France and other minor countries, the kernel of the Grand Alliance, and therefore the conceptual core of the postwar world order, had already largely been decided. No variation or later ideas added to the initial scheme by the advent of new allies and adversaries affected the original concept of the postwar world sketched out at Placentia Bay by the two Atlantic statesmen.[72] Neither the events of war nor the internal diplomacy of the Grand Alliance would alter this basic scheme (at least until Yalta and Potsdam). Not even relations with the Soviet Union, which were largely structured on the architecture of the relationship between the United States and Great Britain, caused any substantial alteration to this model. The Anglo-American conference at Malta preceded the Anglo-Soviet-American conference at Yalta, just as the consultations between the British and Americans had always preceded openings to other Allies (as at Cairo and Teheran).

Many more conferences were held between the British and Americans than there were meetings of the three and four powers. The Anglo-American summits aimed to maintain an umbilical link between the two powers, to prevent the development of conflicts that could waylay their common program.[73] The special nature of the bond, which wavered between interdependence and integration, consisted largely in the multifaceted communication flows between the two governments and their respective elites.

The constant exchange of messages as well as the affinities between the communication codes they used (because they shared a common language, cultural references, some democratic values, Protestantism) enabled both parties continually to adjust their perceptions of each other's intentions and thus avoid the accumulation of differences of opinion and interests on general political matters, such as the question of Western leadership, or on specific issues. Clearly, this system was bound to become unbalanced over time, provoking marked asymmetries and the growing dependence of one side upon the other.[74] During the summer of 1941, U.S. "war aims" and the U.S.-British partnership[75] were compatible in action and in the memoranda and discussion digests of the different study groups.[76]

On June 4, 1941, the Political Group put out a memorandum[77] that analyzed the three alternative courses of action that the U.S. government could follow in its relations with the British, assuming that (1) sooner or later the United States would find it necessary to become a "military" participant in the war and that (2) the U.S. government would therefore be forced to consider the problem of its "political" relations with the governments of the British Commonwealth, not only for the duration of the war but probably for the long term as well. This went beyond the subject matter of Memorandum P-B18, of May 2, 1941, which proposed the more limited objective of developing above all "joint administrative arrangements for aid to Britain in such a way as to facilitate American-British cooperation after the war."[78] The proposal devised by the Political Group consisted of a set of political guidelines showing far more commitment to the partnership, in the awareness that in one way or another the United States had to conduct the war in league with Great Britain.

Furthermore, the issue is not merely a technical one, i.e., confined to the level, quantity, and type of bond to establish with London. Behind the institutional formulas and hypotheses, in fact, there was a decidedly innovative orientation at work regarding U.S. commitments compared with the tradition of "nonentangling alliances." This tradition wielded such psychological power that, during World War I, it forced President Wilson to participate in the war and in the peace negotiations of 1919 in the odd role of head of state of an Associated Power rather than of a full member of the Quadruple Alliance. However, the authors of the document made no attempt to conceal their internationalist bias, showing an unequivocal preference for a defensive alliance, as opposed to an association or a permanent political association, the first being the choice they considered more mature and practicable.

The debate over the level of institutionalization of Anglo-American relations was grafted onto an earlier conceptual and political debate that had witnessed some interesting developments in Europe during the interwar period. A variety of federalist utopias had emerged over the years, from the Koudenhove-Kalergi formula in the 1920s to the Anglo-French Political Union in 1940. Even in the United States, back in the 1930s and again at the beginning of the war, the "federalist" theme (more Atlantic than European) had had some backers, though it was interpreted in the Hamiltonian form dictated by the constitutional history of the American Revolution.[79] But on a political level, a permanent bond of this kind was utterly unthinkable in a country so averse to "entangling" itself institutionally with the outside world or even to entertaining formal alliances in peacetime.[80]

In any case, although an Associated Power status, like the one set up in 1917–1918, was the easiest to realize (as it could be deliberated by the president himself through a simple executive order without involving Congress), it entailed certain operative drawbacks since it would prevent any postwar extension of "the fruits of wartime collaboration." Such was the verdict of Memorandum P-B20: "If special care were not taken in handling popular psychology, the American government might find it difficult to guide its wartime partnership with the British along such channels as to be able to 'sell' to the American people a program of sustained American-British collaboration on the task of postwar reconstruction, let alone for the establishment of a new international order under American-British auspices."[81] There was some hesitation and perplexity also over the third option, involving a long-term American-British partnership. The memorandum pointed out the risks that could arise from establishing a "permanent political tie-up" with the United Kingdom.

By scaling down the enthusiasm shown in the more emphatically pro-British currents of public opinion and the press during those months, the Political Group's document attempted to outline the limits to the possible "partnership," defining it as an association with limited liabilities, with the scope of coordinating the two governments only in some specific functional spheres. The partnership basically entailed deploying both air forces and navies in mutual assistance in the "international policing" of certain areas of the globe. Further action included the development of policies of cooperation on trade issues, such as raw materials, shipping, civil aviation, currency systems, and investment policy, as well as broad-based cooperation on health programs, food, immigration, and the development of underdeveloped areas.[82]

This list of potential issues was soon to find a practical application during the ensuing negotiations with Great Britain (and the Allies). The list also served later as a model for the institutional foundations of the United Nations and other international postwar organizations,[83] even though, of course, it specified that "the establishment of a common citizenship would probably be out of the question."[84]

The preferred option could therefore only be for an "American-British Defensive Alliance." The question had been much debated since February by the Political Group and others. Major Eliot stated that "the trusteeship of civilization is now largely in our hands. As the first naval power of the world, the United States would inevitably become the senior partner in any projected Anglo-American association. Control of the sea would ensure an adequate flow of raw materials."[85]

The concepts, though ostensibly of an "imperial" character, were in some cases rather traditional, especially in the idiom adopted. Using the three groupings suggested by David Calleo regarding the mixed American feelings toward Europe during the war, i.e., "Europeanists," "Geopolitical Atlanticists," and "Rump Hullians,"[86] without doubt, many CFR members (especially those in the Political and Territorial groups) were among the Geopolitical Atlanticists. Others, however, were more or less Rump Hullians, whereas only those in the Economic and Financial Group had a strong Europeanist inclination.

The rationale for this differentiation in analytical method was fairly clear. It was a period of change for all concerned, and many of those concerned harbored an inextricable mixture of old and new ideas. In this document, Eliot stressed the geopolitical nature of the control of the sea-lanes rather conventionally, although realizing full well that, sea routes aside, the United States was assuming an ever-greater role in international relations and "would emerge from the struggle with an overwhelmingly superior industrial productivity."

It was this superior productivity, rather than the explosion of industry instigated by the war effort, that would have kept the United States ahead of both winning and losing countries after the war, including the United Kingdom.[87] For this reason, Memorandum P-B20 urged "a more formal and less restrictive type of wartime partnership, comparable in substance to the Anglo-French military alliance of 1939–40."[88] This formula would give the Americans a dual escape route. Such a bond would work perfectly if things proceeded well and Great Britain managed to keep the Germans at bay. On the other hand, it would allow the United States to recoup its autonomy should the British buckle under the onslaught, as had happened with the Anglo-French alliance in June 1940. In that case, Washington could simply slide out of its commitment without a troubled conscience, putting the entire Atlantic Ocean between itself and Europe, instead of just the English Channel: a broad and complex psychological and political Dunkerque.

As for the procedure to adopt, the defensive alliance "might take the form of a treaty, preferably a brief, simply phrased document, or of a joint resolution."[89] Basically, the final objective of Placentia Bay in August 1941 had already been amply outlined in Memorandum P-B20, in which it was stated that "the nature of this type of partnership might put us in a relatively stronger diplomatic position to influence the peace settlement along American lines. In proportion as the war dragged out, the United States would increasingly become the 'senior partner' in the alliance."[90]

This idea of "seniority rule," of great importance in U.S. congressional committee rules, translated to mean "primacy" in a bilateral international alliance with the former mother country, was clearly something quite new in U.S. history.[91] Until the end of World War I, the power of the United States (which intervened late in the conflict) had been considered a decisive factor, but always a surrogate for its European counterpart— the Americans contributed that extra quota of might necessary to tip the scales but not to win the war by itself. Hence, Washington's previous voluntary abstention from intervening in European political affairs seemed even to the more enlightened Europeans (and to the British above all) as the absence of one of the necessary props in the European order, though certainly not the loss of the keystone of the balance of power, as provisionally restored after the war's end at Versailles in 1919.[92]

The U.S.-British alliance of August 1941 deeply altered this organic network centered on Europe. American "seniority" was no longer simply an external buttress to the European system caught in a moment of crisis, but the cornerstone of a new global structure of international relations centered on the Atlantic and the common Anglo-Saxon heritage. However, U.S. "primacy"[93] was not simply a geopolitical or strategic matter. The concept had had its first airing in terms of economic policy and institutional methodology in Memorandum E-B36, dated June 22, 1941, presented by the EF Group the day Germany attacked the Soviet Union. The memorandum was brief (five typewritten pages) but covered a great many new ideas, more than can be found in other documents of the same period produced by similar groups.

In its attempt to sketch out the basic guidelines for dealing with the problem "of the economic organization of the postwar world desired by the United States," i.e., to define one of the country's chief war aims, the document adopted a functional-dynamic "presystemic" approach, instead of the customary "structural" approach describing the system of negotiation or institutions to be set up. After clarifying the concept of war aims, the memorandum separated out the functions that the war aims could perform, according to whether they were to be used as propaganda or as tools for defining the national interests. Having decided against the propaganda function, the memorandum identified the following as being of U.S. national interest in economic matters: (1) "the full use of the world's economic resources: implying full employment and a reduction in business-cycle fluctuation"; and (2) "the most efficient use of world resources: implying an interchange of goods."[94]

Thus far there is nothing particularly new, except for the coupling of the concept of "full employment" of resources and manpower and the reduction of business-cycle fluctuations with the concept of using resources more efficiently (i.e., the international division of labor according to specialization criteria and to comparative costs). This combined two different lines of economic philosophy (Keynesian and neoclassical) whose theoretical and practical "coexistence" had never been hypothesized, let alone tested.[95]

But the real innovation of the memorandum was its method of analysis. Unlike many other members of the East Coast Establishment, who were anxious to establish U.S. primacy in traditional geopolitical terms, the EF Group emphasized the fact that the economic war aims "do not require that the United States should have a special privileged position in the world." Presaging the concept of worldwide interdependence, it added "that the long-run interests of the United States are identical with those of all other countries: that is, securing the fullest possible development of the world's economy."[96] According to this thesis, the real "national interests" of the United States lay in the construction of a world economy and in overcoming the trade and economic barriers among different regional areas.[97]

Large sectors of the business community saw two sides to the problem of the postwar order: On the one hand, it was vital to avoid a crisis after demobilization; on the other, crisis could be avoided only if the world markets opened themselves to U.S. goods, and if the demand for investment and consumer goods throughout the world was great enough to absorb the gargantuan output capacity of the U.S. economy. However, the gradual opening of economic frontiers and the creation of a climate of free-trade universalism could hardly come about by using old shibboleths but would have to follow principles like those in J. Hay's Open Door notes or those of agricultural free traderism, championed by Cordell Hull and the southern senators. "It is more important," the memorandum stated, "to emphasize the profitable interchange of goods than conditions of free trade."

Judging by their advanced understanding of the matter, the authors of the memorandum may well have read some of the eminent sociologists and social scientists of the day, such as Max Weber and Talcott Parsons, whose work presaged a full-fledged revolution in American thinking in the postwar years.[98] One also senses a certain new experimental and empirical awareness, consonant with the restructuring of large corporations and business management that began after the Crash of 1929 and the Great Depression of the 1930s.[99]

The documentation of the State Department and of the Federal Economic Administration, set up ad hoc to oversee mobilization, plus the memoranda of the CFR, seem to confirm the belief of Alfred Chandler, Jr., that "the mobilization of the war economy brought corporation managers to Washington to carry out one of the most complex pieces of economic planning in history."[100] The form itself of the institutions, the organization of public spending, and the government legislative process were all deeply transformed by the way big business was working.

This managerial conversion of Washington's bureaucracy did not stem from the officials working within the administration but from the leaders of industrial, banking, and service industries, who were put at the government's disposal as consultants and advisers during the war.[101] These people operated from within government agencies and the administration, passing straight over the heads of the officials, fleshing out the ranks, bringing in entirely new experiences, and often even outnumbering the somewhat meager prewar staff of the shoestring federal bureaucracy, to which the New Deal policy had brought few new administrative workers.

In the arena of international politics and postwar strategy, the innovative procedures borrowed from the "managerial revolution" under way catalyzed new institutional inventions and architectures that reflected the legacy of the great legal experience of the Wall Street law firms. With their decades of training in formulating legal procedures and commercial and financial rules, and continually adapting them to the changing environment of manufacturing and service industries, the East Coast lawyers were garnering a growing "market share" in politics.[102]

Even the government's philosophy was affected, at least in part, by this professional and intellectual environment, a change that was amply reflected in Memorandum E-B36, which exposed the debate between the two leading schools of economic theory—one Keynesian–New Dealist, the other neoclassical-monetarist. However, the clash of these two doctrines was diluted in Memorandum E-B36, as the two cochairmen, Hansen and Viner, attempted a conceptual compromise: "It will be necessary to concentrate on the positive role governments can play in increasing the production and interchange of goods, and avoidance of the restrictive role they have played in the past."[103] The delicate balance introduced by this pragmatic outlook was to lend greater flexibility to U.S. postwar policy-making in matters of mixed economies and the political coalitions representing them: "Sometimes the state can function best by supervising private enterprises, sometimes by direct intervention in economic processes. The economy of the postwar world will clearly be a 'mixed economy' rather than one which approximates either pure socialism or complete laissez faire capitalism."[104]

In their sweeping new economic and political design, the authors of Memorandum E-B36 felt that it was of paramount importance to clear the ground first of any traditionalist residues and asserted that a "reversion to the economy of 1939, 1925, of 1913 will not solve the world's problems." Gone was the nostalgia for the good old days of the balance-of-power system. The depression and the scattered conflicts leading to World War II between 1931 (Manchuria) and 1939 (Czechoslovakia and Albania) had made it plain to the ruling class in the countries of the West that there was no room for any regression to the past.

It is hardly surprising therefore to find affinities between the theories of British economist Lord Keynes and those of the EF Group,[105] but with the difference that while the Americans of the EF Group favored a return to free trade, the British economists preferred the idea of a "clearing union" between the United States and Great Britain. Had the choice been made for the latter (as Keynes dearly hoped), the "Americanization" of world economy would have taken a very different course.[106]

The bare bones of the war aims presented in Memorandum E-B36 cover issues already much debated in the United States and Great Britain in both the normal press and in the specialized publications. Some of these topics (and their solutions) had already been thrashed out during preparatory discussions on the Lend-Lease Act. Some had cropped up in discussions leading to the Atlantic Charter. And some acquired greater definition and depth in the coming years, both before and during the debate at Bretton Woods (on monetary policy) and Dumbarton Oaks (on institutions), prior to the founding of the United Nations and the other specialized agencies.

Points 4, 5, 7, and 8 of the Atlantic Charter (whose first draft, according to Churchill, was "flour from the English sack") showed affinities with the concepts and style of Points 1 to 5 of Memorandum E-B36. This parallel is evident, although the Atlantic Charter, a document whose contents were in part improvised and therefore general, consisted of "container ideas" rather than binding provisions. It was, in substance, only a legal "framework," as the norms had yet to be defined, according to criteria that had, however, already been developed.[107]

Through long and drawn-out negotiations, punctuated by spates of tension and conflict, and after some significant revisions, the gaps in the Atlantic Charter were gradually filled in. What did not change was the idea of an Atlantic System led by an Anglo-American partnership (with U.S. primacy, however), around which the rest of the world would gather, according to the unwritten laws of economic interdependence and national or collective security.

8

The Expansion of
the Western Hemisphere

Economic Interdependence

Although initially the economically interdependent Grand Area was conceived as a counterweight to the growing integrated commercial and economic area of German-dominated continental Europe, it was soon seen as a viable alternative of economic interdependence in its own right. It was not until after the war that the supposedly cohesive Germanic area was revealed to be insubstantial. Little success had actually been achieved in integrating and streamlining the economic systems of the controlled European states to the needs of the "central" German economy. Nor did the situation improve after 1942 under Albert Speer's regime of "domination/dependence," which proved to be inefficient and badly organized by nature.[1]

And yet, in the spring of 1940 the seeming perfection of the German war machine led some observers to believe that the same sleek efficiency demonstrated in the blitzkrieg could be readily applied by the Reich to the economies of its allied nations or occupied territories. The very concept of a Grand Area expressed the West's acknowledged technical and organizational inferiority compared with the apparent physical and political compactness of the German economic and financial system. The geographical distances between the different regions of the Grand Area and the limited effectiveness of clearing agreements further emphasized the absence of commercial areas (or blocs) with a unified tariff system. The differences between the procedures adopted within the British Empire and those existing in Latin America hampered the functioning of the Grand Area. In addition, there were the extra transport costs when cargoes were diverted from normal peacetime transit routes.

Perhaps for these reasons, the scheme for the Grand Area now appears more significant for its futuristic ideas than for its workability at the time. Its philosophy then went far beyond the need to counterbalance a Germanized *Neue Europäische Ordnung* (New European Order). The idea of setting up an interdependent network of commercial, financial, and (in the long run) industrial ties, with the purpose of readjusting the existing relations in the intercontinental division of labor, had been gradually forming in the minds of many economists, including the members of the Economic and Financial Group. The project began to assume the implications of a complex full-fledged scenario rather than a short-term political solution. In fact, since the mid-1930s such a possibility had been a favorite topic in New York business circles. Articles, essays, pamphlets, and books appeared, including those of Allen W. Dulles and Hamilton Fish Armstrong in 1935 and 1939 and a volume by James T. Shotwell, published in 1940.[2]

Of course, the scheme for a trade bloc was still only a rough sketch, but it was destined to have some application in the postwar world if the method of establishing "interdependent" economic ties among nations was politically accepted by all those involved. To work, the Grand Area presupposed that each country, including the United States, update its economic relations with others, and hence there would have to be a complete reworking of the essentially banking-oriented approach of U.S. dealing with the outside world—a practice that had proved ruinous in the clumsy handling of the war debts the Allied countries had run up during World War I.[3] The strictly financial nature of U.S. transactions and the rigid accountancy that had always accompanied them had often compromised the resounding political successes of the Dollar Diplomacy (especially between 1920 and 1933) achieved by the private bankers, who had handled the country's foreign economic policy on behalf of the administration, especially with respect to dealings with Europe.[4]

The debate on the Grand Area radically altered this attitude. The bipartisanship that characterized the CFR from its inception, symbolized by the cochairmanship of Viner and Hansen, allowed all manner of projects and scenarios to germinate. Doctrines and practical experience of many kinds were laid out for comparison: from those based on strictly free-trade and financial criteria, which were profoundly internationalist, to those that were semiprotectionist and in the New Dealer tradition, which could have provided a practical operational framework directly suited to the needs of the wartime and postwar planning.

An example of the program's flexibility was Hansen's idea of building a North American highway system from north to south, from Canada through Mexico, and financed collectively by the United States and its allies. There was also a far-fetched idea of a great railway going east to west across China, Indochina, and India. These highly utopian schemes greatly contrasted with the more down-to-earth proposals for trade policy geared to economic interdependence between countries and regions, without any loss of sovereignty or freedom of action.

During this period, there were various options as to the reorganization of world economy. But the Establishment (and the CFR's Economic and Financial Group) tended to waver between the schemes of integration and those of interdependence. In conceptual terms, the dilemma was utterly new. However, it is harder to establish whether in these documents the conceptual outline of interdependence, in terms of permanent mutual, if asymmetric, dependence, was formulated; this concept would affect not only the balance of payments but also the internal dynamics of the domestic productive system of all the actors.

The Inter-American Model

The New Dealer doctrine, which involved a transposition of domestic economic policy methods to the field of economic relations with Latin America (essentially through the creation of international, regional, or sectorial public agencies), had been rejected on various occasions by opposition factions within the administration, and in particular by the more ardent free traders, who imposed a much more traditional line, even on the president.[5] However, despite the old-fashioned character of the free traders' views, during World War II those special ties between the United States and Latin America were enhanced with a set of new functions that rapidly reached out beyond the conventional geographical boundaries of a diplomatic relationship that had endured for at least a century.

Diplomatic records covering those years tracked the metamorphosis of the basic structures of that relationship. On the one hand, they revealed the theoretical character of the debate on the general perspectives of U.S. foreign economic policy, and on the other, they highlighted the updating of the means of influence employed by Washington on Latin American countries during the first phase of U.S. neutrality. U.S. relations with Latin America symbolized the working correlation between the political use of economic supremacy and the dynamics of strategic influence.

Washington's method of dealing with the subcontinent from the mid-1930s to the early 1940s represented the first systematic use of U.S. political influence and economic superiority to secure relations that were not merely bilateral, but that reinforced collective (or multilateral) ties among the countries of the American continent, under the aegis of the United States. Washington made a concerted effort to transform the network of its existing relations (in economic and commercial terms) with this specific region into something more complex, to create a political-institutional framework (with conference schedules and a permanent secretariat) capable of mobilizing resources and ensuring the strategic security of the whole continent.

The scheme of inter-American relations, at least since the 1936 Buenos Aires conference, which established a better understanding between the United States and the Latin American countries, had tended to change radically as the crisis in East Asia and Europe escalated. A new model of political behavior was gradually being pieced together, a kind of prototype for the "special relationship" of a mixed economic and political nature that the United States later established with the various parts of the world once it had joined the war, and that became a standard feature in the chessboard of regional alliances and ties with individual allied countries.[6]

The task of coordinating the international behavior of the republics in the Western Hemisphere became a key political issue for Washington once the war broke out in Europe and the pattern of international relations was fundamentally altered. Meanwhile, the specter of German (and to some extent also Italian) influence on some of the South American countries (such as Argentina, Brazil, and Uruguay) threatened to become a concrete reality.[7]

At an Inter-American Conference in Panama (September 23–October 3, 1939), the United States had decided to set up an Inter-American Financial and Advisory Committee, whose very title stressed a traditional style of intervention based on financial (and not political) aid to Latin American countries. But the key word was "advisory," which suggested a more modern idea of economic relations with friendly countries, in which technicians and experts were sent as "advisors," generally paid from federal funds. The shift in outlook was confirmed by the rapid transformation of the advisory committee into the Inter-American Development Commission, which drafted an early scheme for an Inter-American bank.

After the fall of France, it became immediately apparent that Pan-American relations could be furthered only through innovative intervention in both economic and political matters. The reason was that over half of Latin American exports was channeled toward Europe and only a third was absorbed by the U.S. market. Furthermore, this imbalance did not take into account that the principal exports from the Southern Cone of Latin America (Argentina, Uruguay, and Chile) were competing directly with U.S. produce in the same markets (notably cereals and meat).

Historian William Langer—an active CFR member in the Political and in the Peace Aims Group, who at the war's end wrote a monumental history of U.S. neutrality between 1937 and 1941—recalled that, as of

May 1940, the State Department, the Treasury, the Departments of Commerce and Agriculture, the Federal Loan Agency, and the Federal Reserve System were all busy looking into the question. He also observed that "outside the Government, numerous private organizations were pursuing researches and drafting suggestions."[8] "The president himself was snowed under by plans and proposals," added Langer, "until the confusion became so great as to threaten all systematic planning."[9] But although he passed over groups supporting the work of government departments, Langer referred to a document of the Division of American Republics (of the State Department) dated June 10, 1940, reporting statistics and analytical material, much of which originated with the Council on Foreign Relations (Memorandum E-B12), plus a series of bibliographical references to authors who, except for one, were actively involved in the War and Peace Studies project (Alvin Hansen, Percy W. Bidwell, and Arthur R. Upgren).[10]

But the stance the government assumed under the incisive leadership of Adolf Berle—an assistant secretary of state and an early New Dealer—was quite different. Following a scheme Berle himself devised,[11] the official line was based on principles that were strikingly innovative for their time. The following excerpts testify to the boldness of his design: "The obvious answer to this [the German trade menace] is an immediate agreement between the twenty-one Republics that commercial negotiations shall be carried on not by individual countries, but by all of them en bloc." For the first time, here was an official mention of a full-fledged "multilateralization" of inter-American trade. This was openly confirmed further on in the document, when it is suggested that the Inter-American Economic Committee take up a proposal for a joint agreement on any trade arrangements with Germany, Italy, or Russia—or, possibly, with any countries outside the Western Hemisphere. But this was not enough. And it is here that the scheme encountered its greatest hurdles: "I suggest that, immediately, plans are drawn up by which the necessary amounts of money are made available for the time being to purchase certain amounts of exports from countries which live on such exports, these commodities to be pooled and stored, and handled much as we handle our own surplus commodities."[12] The idea in question was the "cartel scheme" borrowed from the New Deal national farm surplus programs set out in the Agricultural Adjustment Act (AAA) and first implemented in 1933.[13]

The Berle project displayed a certain integrationist view of the various national economic systems, which went far beyond a simple scheme for a custom union, like the old trade bloc of the Hull era. In its definitive form, the cartel envisaged "the establishment of an Inter-American Trading Corporation, with strong central direction, with an organization appropriate for achieving the desired objectives, and with control equitably distributed among the participating countries. It should be contemplated that the Corporation should from the outset operate as an effective agency for joint marketing of the important export staples of all the American Republics."[14]

There were contrasting reactions to this scheme, both in the United States and among the Latin American countries. Criticisms hinged on two basic points: U.S. financial circles feared that the cost of the operation would be exorbitant (there was talk of several billion dollars for 1940 alone), whereas the agricultural lobby was worried that American money might be used to buy goods that directly competed with U.S. agricultural products.

But the chief objections came from the more conservative sectors in the United States and from the governments of many Latin American countries. The former were against extending the perimeter of the AAA's operations and system of farm management to the entire hemisphere, as such a move would have endorsed certain types of state intervention the conservatives had been campaigning against for years. Meanwhile, the Latin American critics viewed the scheme as an updated version of "Yankee imperialism," which, in the first place, "entailed the loss of economic independence of the American Republics."[15]

It may be that the plan appeared a little too revolutionary in its premises and too onerous a commitment on a financial level. However, it was a taste of the future and tied in well with the "One World" myth touted by the Republicans.[16] For example, reflections may be discerned in the various means the United States employed both during and after the war to absorb surplus farm produce in various countries around the globe, and in Washington's direct contribution to efforts to limit the sale of certain food products during periods of crisis. The rules of the European Economic Community farm policy for market intervention are very similar to those originally suggested by Berle.

Such an innovative document was bound to raise some hackles within the administration, including those of the secretary of state, who had championed a program for bilateral clearing agreements based on lists of items and compensatory devices to reduce currency exchange to a minimum. Therefore this pioneering integrationist project was abandoned despite the enthusiastic support it had received from the president. The Pan-American cartel, whose very title betrayed the protectionist sympathies of its New Deal author Berle, failed before it ever got off the ground, but many of its insights on the advantages of monopoly were taken up later and served as a framework for the plans drafted in ensuing years by the administration[17] and private organizations like the CFR.[18]

One plan in particular, similar and almost contemporary to Berle's, was drawn up by an advisory group, the Coordinator of Inter-American Affairs (CIAA), under the direction of the youthful Nelson A. Rockefeller. The plan was sent to Secretary of Commerce Harry Hopkins and to Sumner Welles and the Division of American Republics, on June 10, 1940.[19] Alongside emergency measures and proposals to set up a pool for handling agricultural surplus (and mining surpluses, as Rockefeller wisely added), the scheme envisaged a broader program for U.S. international economic policy in Latin American countries "in the frame of hemisphere economic cooperation and dependence."[20]

This juxtaposition of the terms "cooperation" and "dependence" hinted at the historical origins and conceptual framework of "interdependence," a notion that has had such a far-reaching influence on U.S. policy since the war. However, it was not a question of integrating the economies as in the theory of European integration. The latter was developed after the war with the somewhat remote idea of the political and institutional unification of the countries involved in the program, as a kind of prelude to the voluntary renunciation of national sovereignty, complemented by the institution of common federalist supranational organs. Instead, in Rockefeller's scheme, the purpose was to establish a "reciprocal dependence" on a formal and normative contract basis rather than a structural basis (given the disproportionate disparities among the countries of the hemisphere), which would allow the hegemonic leader to retain full legal independence and complete freedom of choice, leaving it to the objective asymmetry of interdependent relations to determine the rules of the game.

The memorandum, signed by Rockefeller on June 14, 1940 ("Hemisphere Economic Policy"), was a kind of embryonic summary of a future long-term operational program. It also provided suggestions on the kind of approach that could be applied to various sectors of future U.S. international economic policy.

The catalogue of possible issues is long and complex. Initiatives include: (1) the reduction and/or elimination of customs tariffs and other nontariff barriers to trade, accompanied by compensation for U.S. agricultural and industrial interests affected by these policies; (2) the definition of guidelines for investment policies of (private or governmental) in Latin America toward developing and exploiting local resources of raw materials; (3) the financing of the conspicuous public debts of the Latin American republics; (4) the expansion of government services; (5) the coordination of U.S. administrative agencies operating in the area; and (6) the encouragement of cultural, scientific, and educational relations.[21] The cultural programs aimed at Latin America were also prototypes of programs for dissemination of information and propaganda that were exported worldwide after the war through agencies like the United States Information Service (USIS).

The CIAA program was an important example of the innovative activities of groups in the East Coast Establishment in formal support of the politics of the State Department—basically over the heads of the bureaucracy. CIAA initiatives stimulated the ideas of an administration that was both conservative and on the whole ill equipped to deal with the global role that the United States was actually assuming.

In this sense, together with the texts and proposals of the CIAA and other organizations, the CFR documents[22] were the source of future U.S. foreign and international economic policy. The strategic positions outlined in these writings provided the rudimentary guidelines and impulse that caused the pure free-trader line and the Keynesian integral New Dealer line to be scuttled, paving the way for the "neoclassical synthesis." The groundwork covered in these texts furthered the identification and definition of the basic form of interdependence, the theoretical pillar of postwar U.S. foreign policy.

The Monroe Doctrine and the Problem of Security

The Western Hemisphere, however, was more than a laboratory for experimenting with new forms of international political economy that would enhance the U.S. role in the world. During the years of U.S. neutrality, the hemisphere, which was a sort of "rural periphery" to the U.S. "core," also became the experimental terrain of a singular "geographic" (and only later "geopolitical") revision, a conceptual reorganization, in which the second conceptual pillar of U.S. foreign policy, national security, was to be strengthened.[23]

It is only by reviewing the "special" attitude of the United States toward the Western Hemisphere that it is possible to show that the concept and context of U.S. national security had been steadily expanding. A full understanding of the historical and cultural origins of this formula would require a general survey of the behavior, rules of conduct, and decision-making procedures that the U.S. administration used vis-à-vis the Western Hemisphere, starting with the Monroe Doctrine.[24]

In its broadest sense, the concept of security had in fact been present since Monroe's presidential address of December 2, 1823. Commenting on the text of the speech, Dexter Perkins[25] observed that Monroe's words "unequivocally formulated the theory of the separation of the New World from the Old." This schism was not simply geographical or political. It involved a marked divergence between U.S. and European perceptions of international politics, a divergence that would grow as time went on. Much of the lack of comprehension, or the "misperceptions," that characterized relations between Allied and Associated Powers at the Paris Peace Conference, and in particular between President Woodrow Wilson and his European colleagues, probably stemmed from different interpretations of the same concepts and formulas.

According to Perkins,[26] Monroe "built American policy on the right to self-defense—that is, on a right that has always been fundamental to international law." But the concept of "self-defense" is open to radically differing interpretations. Even Perkins, who was writing during the years of U.S. neutrality (his book was published in 1941), noted that "the decision of Adams, the Secretary of State, who had in turn made his own interpretation of the Monroe Doctrine, instructing U.S. Ambassador Rush, who was leaving for his London office, is cause for much reflection. Could it perhaps justify today's isolationists or those who suggest a policy of cooperation with England? All those supporting the two divergent opinions naturally try to invoke the work of the men of 1823 for their own side."[27] The concept of "self-defense" can mean various things, not only with respect to its legitimacy or to the gravity of the acts provoking such reactions. It can above all be used to define the legitimate interests and subjective rights the actors intend to defend and the forms these can assume.

In the light of this, the interpreters of the Monroe Doctrine adopted self-defense as a cardinal point of U.S. foreign policy—regarding not only Latin America but also the rest of the world—and managed to link it to "national interest" and "security," themselves equally blurred concepts. The product of this merger was the more complex notion of "national security" in force today.

U.S. historians, especially those of the revisionist school, have tended to interpret the rise of the United States from colony to empire[28] as an unbroken process of expansion, which they consider intrinsic to the program of independence of the American republic and to the political culture of the Thirteen Colonies. According to this view, expressed by Magdoff, Williams, L. Gardner, LaFeber, Van Alstyne, and others in a compelling debate developed in the 1950s and 1960s, the movement toward empire status seemed to be caused by the linear expansion of American influence, an expansion that began with the demise of the myth of the frontier and with the surplus of capital in an economic system that had become the most powerful in the world by the close of the nineteenth century.

It was no coincidence that in his 1959 essay on U.S. foreign policy,[29] Williams opened with the Spanish-American War of 1898 and the successive fate of Cuba to describe the forms and objectives of U.S. imperialism, exploring the idea that "imperialist" culture is rooted in strictly economic needs, endorsed ideologically by the drive to export democratic and anticolonial "idealism." However, this interpretation of the facts is unconvincing.

The history of concepts such as national interest and national security reveals an American view of the world that is substantially different from that of the Europeans. The very term "security" implies a defensive rather than an offensive approach to foreign relations. In the United States this attitude in fact dates back long before Monroe spoke out against U.S. involvement in territorial disputes among European powers.

A certain wariness toward Europe can be noticed in Williams's text, driven perhaps by the proud but parochial sense of difference the Americans felt in regard to Europeans—a difference that was accentuated by the great distance and communication difficulties, as well as by the enduring U.S. isolationist ideology, which harked back to George Washington's "Farewell Address." This would suggest that U.S. expansionism was a kind of by-product of the country's being drawn into the tide of world history and justified simply through questions of self-defense— the defense of "national interests" and "national security."

This process was clearly not linear, nor was it even consciously active as such. Instead it appears to be essentially action-reaction, a dialectical process with sudden periods of fervent activity punctuated by intervals of relative stasis. These fluctuations in the cycle were noticeable even after World War II, though the sheer lack of leeway in the bipolar system for more than four decades prevented Washington from the isolationist backpedaling it effected between the wars.[30]

Basically, U.S. expansionism was not merely determined by the "need" for new sources of profit and outlets for investment for domestic (and later multinational) capital. It was also dictated by strictly political and strategic motives, by restrictions inherent to the international system, and by the perception that U.S. security was under threat. Relations with the Western Hemisphere during the two-year period of neutrality demonstrated how this philosophy unfolded and offered detailed insights into the emerging globalist view of national security that, together with interdependence, would dominate U.S. foreign policy after 1945.

One of the more generally accepted accounts of the history of U.S. international relations described the expansion of the U.S. "frontier" from the end of the nineteenth century as a set of stages, marked first by U.S. intervention in Mexico, Central America, and the Caribbean (with Cuba), and then in the Pacific Ocean (Japan, the Philippines, and China). (U.S. relations with Canada are a separate story.) According to that accepted account, expansion toward Europe and Africa was a natural complement to processes already tried out in the Pacific and China, rather than a reworking of those traditionally used in relations with Latin America.

However, it is likely that the cultural model and political techniques behind U.S. decisions to intervene in Europe during World War II and after actually stemmed from the ongoing selection and perfection of formulas adopted specifically in the Western Hemisphere, rather than an updated version of methods used in the Pacific and East Asia, for which a substantially different scheme of action had been devised. The difference between the two philosophies was self-evident from the behavior of the U.S. government toward Asia on the one hand, and toward Europe on the other. The war in Indochina was perhaps the most blatant case of this divergence.[31]

On the other hand, ever since the nineteenth century, the special relationship between the United States and Latin America had reflected the basics of a regional system with its own rules, a system that was latently interdependent and of course "asymmetrical," founded on preserving the U.S. hegemony and on the desire of the Pan-American elites to ensure their own protection. It was, basically, a special type of "regional system" and as such could be copied after 1945 for U.S. relations with Western Europe.[32]

The American "Butterfly" and the Forms of Expansion

The key to understanding the transition from a restrictive and "defensive" interpretation of the concept of Western Hemisphere to an "expansive" and interventionist one lies in the events that span the months between the spring of 1940 and early 1941. The transformation of U.S. foreign policy from that of a country geographically peripheral vis-à-vis the core of the Eurocentric international power system—a nation with negligible military power and constitutionally bound from establishing "entangling alliances" in peacetime with other countries—to the global foreign policy of a superpower, can be compared to the metamorphosis of a larva into a butterfly, which finally rises and spreads its wings, just as the United States rose and spread its power over two-thirds of the globe. Therefore, the long period from the 1823 proclamation of the Monroe Doctrine to its gradual implementation in the course of the nineteenth century until the war with Spain (1898) could be described as the "larval" phase of U.S. foreign policy.

The twentieth century, which has on occasion been called the "American Century," saw the butterfly emerge. After the "body," i.e., the Western Hemisphere, matured, the first wing opened out over the Orient— the first phase of U.S. "imperialism," when Washington was able to control a fair portion of the Pacific Ocean and acquired a set of key naval bases (stretching from Hawaii to the Philippines to the Polynesian

Islands), consequently making its influence felt—first in Japan and then in China, from the mid-nineteenth century to World War I.[33]

With the advent of World War II, the other wing of the butterfly unfurled toward the Atlantic Ocean and out to the British Isles, then to the western coast of Africa, and finally over the European mainland. The dynamics of this were quite different from U.S. activity in the Pacific, the development of which was in many respects unprecedented (until the attack on Pearl Harbor). The transformation of the concept of Western Hemisphere into the "Atlantic System," however, followed a line of development largely borrowed from the earlier experience of relations between Washington and the Latin American capitals.

The Pan-American model was tentatively exported even before the defeat of France had triggered a rash of questions on the fate of European colonial territories in and around the American continent. In October 1937, for instance, Sumner Welles drew up a plan in preparation for the Brussels conference scheduled for the end of that year. In his plan, Welles urged the constitution of a "League of Neutral Countries" that would influence international relations (founded on an antiwar idealism), under the illusion that, after the resounding failure of the League of Nations, a new multilateral version of pre-1914 "good offices" diplomacy might still work.

Welles had hoped the document would be translated into a Charter of Principles to be applied to international relations between the Great Powers without jeopardizing the minor nations. Such a charter would list the scope and application of regulations on land and sea warfare, together with the rights and obligations of neutral parties, and guarantee the access of all countries to raw materials, even during times of international wars. The naïveté of the document—which was submitted to the European powers in the middle of the Spanish Civil War, a war whose internal and international developments openly rejected (and to some extent changed) the very character of war[34]—tended to obscure the innovative character of the method Washington was adopting, namely, to apply to their relations with Europe a principle of international behavior borrowed from U.S. policy toward the American continental region. Welles's document in fact explicitly stated that the proposal was intended as "the extension of the Pan-American doctrine of collective isolation from war pronounced at the Conference of Buenos Aires in 1936."[35]

In his 1981 book, C. A. MacDonald commented that the Welles plan, typical of U.S. "appeasement," was nevertheless based on a solid give-and-take logic. On the one hand, it hinted at U.S. willingness to revise the 1919 treaties, but on the other, it suggested the possibility of setting up an Open Door Policy in Europe, just when the United States was trying to prevent the institution of a "closed door" in the Far East.[36]

This position was still, however, basically part of a "defensive" strategy. The weak and abstract appeasement and pacifist proposals had little chance of succeeding in Europe, from which the United States had deliberately distanced itself in 1920, even more so in 1931. The bargaining models and techniques drawn from Rooseveltian diplomatic style (and sometimes even New Dealer style)—which had been in use since the Good Neighbor Policy was announced in FDR's first inauguration speech and defined in greater detail on Pan-American Day on April 12, 1933, when the president first depicted the Western Hemisphere as an interactive structure based on equality and cooperation[37]—were utterly unworkable outside the context of Latin America.

The lack of U.S. strategic (or economic) influence on prewar Europe thwarted U.S. proposals to "normalize" the international balance-of-power system in a phase in which irreconcilable national and ideological interests were hastening its demise. The American continental system managed to function as a semi-institutional structure, owing to the homogeneity of the Latin American regimes and to the undisputed hegemony of the United States over the entire area—and, above all, because there was no real military threat to the area's security net.[38]

To shrewder American thinkers, the structural impotence of the Welles plan was self-evident. Its abstract proposals of free trade, unaccompanied by any guarantee of collective security for the European system, made the plan little more than a verbal exercise. It appeared patently unworkable even to certain Latin American governments (Argentina and Uruguay in particular) that, in spite of their enduring dependence on the United States, had been pursuing relations (though not "special") for some time with the Axis powers. That development caused alarm in Washington and in the many nongovernmental institutions, such as the Council on Foreign Relations.[39] It was not until the blitzkrieg of May–June 1940, turning military hostilities into full-blown war, that the pattern of power relationships in the Atlantic Ocean and, consequently, in the Western Hemisphere started to be redrawn.

9

Defending the Continent

The Two Shores of the Atlantic

The outbreak of war in September 1939 not only drastically upset relations between Europe and the United States but also wrought a strategic change in the power hierarchy within the Western Hemisphere and other areas round the globe. Britain's entry into the war had almost eliminated Germany's chances of persuading the South American governments to support a pro-Nazi policy. With vigilant British squadrons patrolling Atlantic waters, German expansionist aspirations in Latin America were effectively thwarted, as demonstrated in December 1939 when the German warship *Graf Von Spee*, having been cornered by the Royal Navy, was sunk by orders of its own commander. Suddenly the U.S. public had to acknowledge the statement—first voiced by the internationalist lobby and then by Roosevelt himself—that the United Kingdom was indeed the "first line of defense" for the Western Hemisphere and hence for the United States itself.[1]

In Memorandum P-B19 (May 16, 1941) for instance, Great Britain was called an advance fortress in the emerging U.S. strategic defense system. Moreover, G. F. Eliot wrote that "if Britain falls, the United States would have to deal with German aggression of all sorts from bases no further advanced than Iceland, Bermuda and Sierra Leone; and perhaps from Newfoundland only in the North, or Trinidad in the South."[2]

This new integrated view of the Atlantic region in mid-1941 was quite clear in the minds of the more forward-looking groups. Yet barely a year before, few had contemplated it. Toward mid-1940, the emerging system, referred to in the memorandum as the "Atlantic System," with a tripod structure planted firmly in the continents of America, Africa, and Europe, was only a "navalist" concept and not yet perceived as a global scheme. Rather than the British Isles themselves as a kind of advance military stronghold, the main bastion was seen as the Royal Navy, whose task during the first phase of the conflict was to bolster

U.S. bargaining power vis-à-vis the Latin American countries, which were occasionally influenced by the political and military might of the Axis, as amply testified by the records of the Pan-American conferences, from Lima, to Panama, to Havana, to Rio de Janeiro in 1942.

But the Royal Navy had a further implicit politico-military function in U.S.–Latin American relations. In the face of the inadequacy of U.S. naval force (at least until 1943), the British fleet (patrolling alone or in conjunction with Latin American ships) enabled the Allies to keep a close watch on the entire Atlantic shoreline of the Western Hemisphere. Most of the U.S. fleet had in fact been stationed in Hawaii as a deterrent against Japanese expansionism in the Pacific. Consequently, the means at the disposal of the government on the Atlantic side were meager, to say the least. Before Congress went ahead with any mass naval rearmament scheme, it was therefore essential to establish (1) that the danger of invasion or systematic penetration of the Latin American subcontinent was not a fantasy; (2) that Great Britain was truly the front line of U.S. defense and as such needed all the help the United States could offer; and (3) that U.S. naval weaknesses in the Atlantic could gradually be redressed by a naval program geared to establishing a "two-ocean navy," something the United States had never before attempted.

The months from June to September 1940 were decisive. Between July 10, when the administration's "Total Defense" program was first put before Congress, and September 9, when the new defense bill went through, the government managed to obtain over $5 billion more than it had requested.[3] The bill for the constitution of the two-ocean navy presented on June 17, 1940, was approved in just over a month, and Congress authorized the construction (over a six-year period) of 1,325,000 tons of navy hardware. In addition, the manpower was upped to 1.2 million, and a further 18,000 aircraft were ordered.[4]

This sudden leap in arms expenditure, under the umbrella title of Industrial Mobilization Plan (IMP), clearly led to recruitment and training problems, together with complex industrial conversion programs, the institution of Selective Service (a partial conscription system), and the creation of the National Defense Research Committee (NDRC), which inaugurated direct collaboration between the scientific world and the war industry. Summer 1940 heralded the start of the "defense period" of U.S. neutrality, a phase of transition between the prewar "planning period" of 1930–1939—during which the conceptual lines of the IMP were drawn up, ready for streamlining the entire economy to the war effort—and the official "war phase" that opened with the bombing of Pearl Harbor.[5] The deep concern over the fall of France had certainly speeded the transition, and funds were suddenly available for a host of schemes formulated in step with the rapid succession of events. The rearmament program was of epic proportions, quite incomparable with the arms expenditure of the 1930s.

However, in spite of the leap in military outlay, the resulting army of little more than 1 million men (as confirmed during the debate in Congress prior to the approval of the new military bills[6]) was scarcely enough to defend the nation's frontiers—let alone protect the more exposed sections of the Western Hemisphere and the islands. The same shortcomings applied to the new two-ocean navy, whose planned implementation time was so long that intervention, let alone offensive action, was still unthinkable.

Not even the conspicuous increase in air power was a real sign of U.S. desire to push beyond the ocean. The bulk of the air force's stock were transport craft and reconnaissance planes. The production of strategic bombers had been very limited, just enough to meet the minimum defense requirements of the bases in the Pacific and the Philippines.

The very name of the Munitions Program (June 30, 1940) implied the limits and partial nature of its objectives. The main difference was that whereas in eighteen years from 1922 to 1940 the U.S. military budget had been no more than $6 billion, the new rearmament program alone topped that figure and, added to the $3 billion approved the previous month, pushed the War Department's total expenditure up to an unprecedented $9 billion. A further allocation of funds on July 18, 1940, guaranteed an impressive overall budget for the Total Defense effort, and yet it was still not enough to contemplate offensive measures, even in the Pacific, where the United States was effectively best organized and equipped. Moreover, until the middle of 1940, this surge in military outlay was not accompanied by a commensurate change of approach in strategic matters. Outside of special closed groups like the CFR, attitudes remained locked in a strictly continental vision of defense, consistent with the country's long-standing neutral tradition and laws, which had always considered any foray beyond the Western Hemisphere (including U.S. intervention in Europe in 1917–1918) as an excursion, a wholly provisional operation of an Expeditionary Corps.

But the fall of France and thus the destruction of the last vital props of the "intermediate system" in Europe did not influence only the willingness of the United States to rearm itself, albeit for purely defense purposes.[7] The collapse of the Eurocentric balance-of-power system raised the more urgent issue of the strategic reorganization of the geopolitical analyses of international relations. The crisis spurred warring and neutral nations alike to rethink their understanding of territorial priorities in the light of the emerging pattern of power in Europe, as they sized up the new alignments and adversaries and developed schemes for combating and neutralizing them.[8]

Strategic Defense in 1940

In view of all the changes, Washington adjusted its strategy to three main objectives: (1) the continental defense of the United States; (2) the joint defense of Canada; and (3) the Pan-American defense of the Western Hemisphere. These three objectives are worth looking at individually.

The first system, aimed at defending the "continent," was a straightforward scheme devised by the army and the army air force for defending U.S. national territory (including Hawaii, Alaska, Puerto Rico, and Panama). This was yet another version of the plan instituted by the National Defense Act of 1920 and its modified versions. A central feature of the legislation was the creation of the General Headquarters (GHQ) of the army (and its air force), which was programmed to function as General Command of the Field Forces in wartime. The GHQ was able to cover one or more separate theaters of war, with commanders in full power over all military activity within each theater.

This infrastructure was based on experience gained during World War I, when the United States found itself having to coordinate military operations in several continents at once. Such a setup facilitated the movement of troops and the conduct of operations over the main theaters, enabling a geographically unlimited expansion of U.S. war activity around the globe. As such, this continental defense scheme served as a model for U.S. military activity throughout the war.[9]

The second system, affecting "North America," i.e., a joint defense operation with Canada (at the time still a British dominion) was more political than strategic, as the linking of two defense systems against possible external threat raised diplomatic and legal snags because of the official neutral position of the United States—Canada had been at war with Germany since 1939. There was some contradiction with the Monroe Doctrine too, which, although allowing for the existence of colonies, endorsed their gradual "liberation."

The third system of defense focused on the Western Hemisphere as a whole. The U.S. decision explicitly to defend the entire hemisphere had great political import, taken just before the United States itself was plunged into war. There again, the turning point was the summer of 1940, when President Roosevelt applied a series of defensive measures for the hemisphere, giving a historical, albeit approximate, definition of its boundaries.[10]

The system of relations established between the United States and the rest of the American countries (especially during the two years of neutrality) clearly served as a working model for later postwar alignments with allied European countries. It also provided the basic structure for the strategic paradigm that, from 1947 to 1950, would lead to the U.S.

national security policy, the paradigm on which the United States modeled the management of its area of influence and even its relations with the Soviet Union.

Given the status of the U.S. armed forces in 1940, this new strategic pattern for the Western Hemisphere signaled a shift, if only in part, from traditional defense schemes. The country's defense was now divided into three "zones," the first being the North (Canada, plus access from the Atlantic and Pacific); the second included the Panama Canal and U.S. strategic outposts in Central and South America on both coasts— with a defense triangle formed by Alaska-Oahu-Panama on the west side and Panama–Puerto Rico–Virgin Islands on the east; the third zone was the Latin American subcontinent, below 10–15° south latitude.

The defense of the first two zones was guaranteed by the forces already available (depending mainly on the navy and the marines); the defense of the third zone was still under discussion. In this case too, discussions held in the military departments (and reflected in the minutes of the Security and Armaments Group's meetings) brought forth a spectrum of new ideas and concepts that were not put to practical use until later.

The "Americanization" of Canada

Regarding the defense of the first zone, even the public took it for granted that the Americans would play a major role, despite their ingrained aversion to foreign intervention. Despite Canada's being a British dominion (and officially at war with Germany), the linguistic and cultural affinities meant that it was considered to be an appendage to the United States. To some extent, owing to its status as a European semicolonial territory, Canada actually posed a possible threat to stability in the Western Hemisphere, since the defeat of Great Britain would have supplied the Germans with a legitimate point of access to the United States through internationally recognized "rights of succession" between states.

Whatever the reasons, even before the United States was drawn into the war, over two-thirds of the public was in favor of U.S. intervention in Canada's defense, should the Germans ever threaten to invade. A poll carried out by *Fortune* magazine in three different periods in 1940 amply illustrated this view. Those interviewed were asked which of three countries—Canada, Mexico, or Brazil—if invaded, the United States ought to defend with force (see Table 1).

But the "Americanization" of Canada was a relatively novel phenomenon. After World War I, Canada strengthened its ties with Great Britain and had been openly critical of U.S. isolationism, especially when the

TABLE 1   Percentage of U.S. Public Favoring U.S. Troop Deployment in Three Western Hemisphere Countries

	January 1939	January 1940	August 1940
Canada	73.1	74.2	87.0
Mexico	43.0	54.4	76.5
Brazil	27.0	36.8	54.2

Source: Wilfred Hardy Callcott, *The Western Hemisphere* (Austin: University of Texas Press, 1968), p. 384.

Americans refused to join the League of Nations. Nevertheless, in 1938, although certain British observers had begun to take Canada's irreversible assimilation into the sphere of U.S. influence for granted, there were still a great many issues over which the two countries disagreed.[11] However, Canada needed guarantees on its arms supply, and the United States needed guarantees of defense for its northern frontier and the control of coastal approaches to the dominion.

The deliberations resulted in a treaty, with the institution of a very anomalous body, the Joint Board of Defense, between a neutral country and a country at war that was also a member-state of the British Empire. Demonstrating a shift of emphasis from a soft "diplomacy" approach toward a harder line based on "security," the United States took the first steps in building the theoretical and methodological approach to international politics that, together with the concept of interdependence, would provide the two pillars of U.S. foreign policy in the postwar world.

The Declaration of Ogdensburg on August 18, 1940 (a formal treaty that was never signed), marked Canada's entry into the U.S. defense program for the Western Hemisphere. Although clearly dictated by events, the decision was a milestone, a striking break with tradition, if we consider that in 1914–1915 Canada had asked Japan (at the time allied with Great Britain) rather than the United States for protection of its western coastline.

Coupled with the treaty, the agreement for Britain to hand over to the United States military bases in Newfoundland, Bermuda, and the Caribbean in exchange for fifty outdated destroyers (the "four pipes") was crucial. The United States thus was able to expand the perimeter of its strategic interests permanently. On September 3, Roosevelt himself said emphatically, "This is the most important action in the reinforcement of our national defense that has been taken since the Louisiana Purchase."[12]

The issue was also dealt with in the CFR study groups, especially in the form of an exemplary case study for the hypothetical expansion of the perimeter of the Western Hemisphere beyond its natural borders, and hence the reworking of the principles of U.S. defense security.[13] The evolution of these concepts was therefore gradual, though fairly continuous. In fact, the CFR memoranda seized upon the analogies between Canada and Latin America, making a bolder logical link than that made by the officials of the State Department, whose line of approach continued doggedly to be bilateral relations and/or purely economic cooperation.

The Caribbean and the
Destroyers-for-Bases Agreement

The U.S. attitude to the second zone of its new strategic defense scheme took a different slant. In the spring of 1940, political concern for the central zone, which stretched from Mexico to the Guianas and Brazil, induced Washington to revise its criteria for security for the entire sector south of the United States itself.

The problem took a more concrete turn when, as German forces plowed through Denmark and Norway, and then France, Belgium, Holland, and Luxembourg in May–June 1940, the fate of the European colonial territories suddenly became a burning issue. At first the question was confined to purely political, ideological, and legal, rather than strategic, terms, given the acute U.S. sensitivity over the question of colonialism (a concern shared by other countries in Latin America). Washington in fact preferred to keep a low-profile approach to the entire issue, as the fate of the colonies of Nazi-occupied countries posed a problem that could have assumed immense proportions.

There were precedents, however. In 1916, when the United States was still uninvolved in World War I, Washington had pressured the Danish government to sell certain small Caribbean islands to the United States (the Virgin Islands, as they came to be called, with St. Thomas), a move that involved writing continental strategic and defense clauses into the treaty of sale. The formulas differed little from those used in 1940.

The issue had cropped up even earlier, at the time of Secretary of State W. H. Seward and the end of the American Civil War. Attempts to purchase or, failing this, to rent small island territories had also been made at the end of the century (1898), under the influence of A. T. Mahan during the Cleveland presidency. The United States was then at the peak of its "navalist" expansion and had defined the Caribbean as "the very domain of sea-power."[14] A further incident came in 1902, when a treaty of sale for $5 million (already signed) was turned down by the Danish parliament.[15] Finally, in 1916, and once again under pressure from the United States, Copenhagen resolved to sell off its residual splintered empire in Central America for $25 million. The purpose behind the operation was exclusively strategic, and the enormous cost of maintaining the islands (which were in utter economic and social decay) bore out the comment made by a famous author of the time, who said that the island of St. Thomas was the U.S. "Gibraltar."[16]

The complex negotiations over the Danish territories in the West Indies were symbolic of American desire to reinforce its defense of the continent, even through the purchase of foreign territories, which had been clear since the occupation of Puerto Rico in 1898. The method employed was peaceful and negotiated. It eventually led to further development of the U.S. strategic conception of the Western Hemisphere, but more important, it introduced a form of "modern" political action toward the whole chain of European colonies in the Atlantic, of which the island of St. Thomas was the first and weakest link.

However, neither the problem of the European colonies (and not only European) nor the need to build up a constellation of naval or air bases throughout all areas of access to the American continent (even between the wars) was a new issue; each had been tackled before on several occasions. Spurred on by the navy and other military interests, this expansionism had found some sympathetic ears among certain members of the civil administration, although during the New Deal years, most proposals had been shelved for political reasons. The rationale used for galvanizing the government's attention, and the sympathy of the public, had always centered on the vital importance of ensuring that this or that island or territory would not fall into non-American hands. Thus, from 1917 on, in addition to the isolated foreign territories dotted around the Atlantic, the military turned its sights on certain Pacific domains, such as the Galapagos Islands (property of Ecuador), the Cocos Islands (Costa Rica), and Easter Island, off the coast of Chile.[17]

No real action had been taken during the twenty years between the two world wars, but the seeds sown earlier soon germinated. In 1939, faced with a new demarche on the part of the navy, the president was highly cautious but suggested that the question be examined in the context of the new legal framework of Pan-American trusteeship, which he felt would provide a formula for the eventual acquisition of the territories in question.[18] And thus it happened that, in April 1940, when a proposal drawn along similar lines was advanced to the president through his wife, Eleanor, suggesting the occupation of British, French, and Dutch Guiana, with the purpose of cultivating tropical products in a "new American frontier," the president's answer was the same. With the backing of Sumner Welles, he again promoted the idea of "Pan-American trusteeship," a term that neatly joined the two highly workable concepts of "Pan-Americanism" (as a prototype of multilateral inter-dependence), and "trusteeship," as an effective substitute for the pre- and postwar colonial hierarchies established between 1915 and 1922 (including, among others, three types of mandates [A, B, and C] as well as dominions).[19]

For the time being, Roosevelt's "trusteeship" was essentially limited to the Western Hemisphere. It was not until later that the concept came to be applied to all colonial empires. Here it was still closely tied to the evolving concept of national security, which was gradually extending its scope in time with the increasing availability and improved technology of weaponry and with the growing crisis of the entire international system.

It was not, therefore, simply a formula conjured up to justify legally (and therefore camouflage) U.S. semicolonial ambitions, as many historians have claimed. It has been said that under the guise of this presumed "multilateral" Pan-Americanism, guaranteed by the fact that it represented a provisional and educative political regime for the subject nations, trusteeship was simply a means of achieving political control over foreign territories. But the theory is not very convincing.[20] The use of the term "trusteeship" was instead the starting point of a gradual process in which the United States identified its own security interests with the fate of the entire globe.

In the postwar world, this new awareness was to become a cardinal feature of U.S. foreign policy and was cogently manifested by the Truman Doctrine. The war, and the final victory in 1945, left the United States with a legacy of global responsibilities. It was the only world power to come out of the war stronger than when it had first entered, in utter contrast with the appalling decline of all the other nations involved. This state of affairs in a sense "obligated" Washington to revise radically the concept of national security and its sphere of action. The expansion that took place was nothing more than the systematic consequence of filling the power vacuums left behind by collapsing nations in Europe and in the Pacific.

The question arises, however, as to why such a transformation in the U.S. notion of security had not happened in the previous forty years, when the United States had already extended its influence to the east, obtaining the complete control of the Pacific Ocean and securing in East Asia what had all the appearance of a full-fledged colonial empire. What was the real motive behind the change in the philosophy of U.S. presence around the world? The initial phase of this new view, the series of acts and acquisitions that marked the shift, began in summer 1940 and lasted until the end of the following year.

TABLE 2   Naval Deployment, 1922, 1936, and 1941

	United States	Great Britain	Japan	France	Italy
A. Naval Deployment Allowed by the Treaty of Washington in 1922 (in thousands of tonnes)					
Battleships	526	559	301	221	182
Aircraft carriers	13	88	15	25	0
Cruisers	183	393	142	142	85
Torpedo boat destroyers	363	245	65	36	33
Submarines	49	76	24	31	18
Total	1,134	1,361	547	455	318
B. Naval Deployment (excluding obsolete ships) upon the Expiry of the Limitation Treaties, in 1936 (in thousands of tonnes)					
Battleships	464	475	312	186	87
Aircraft carriers	81	115	68	22	0
Cruisers	249	359	242	147	172
Torpedo boat destroyers	216	191	96	115	97
Submarines	68	52	66	78	55
Total	1,078	1,192	784	548	411
C. Naval Deployment (excluding obsolete ships) in 1941 (in thousands of tonnes)					
Battleships	534	443	357	177	164
Aircraft carriers	135	161	178	22	0
Cruisers	329	471	299	150	119
Torpedo boat destroyers	237	268	154	114	101
Submarines	117	55	107	61	84
Total	1,352	1,398	1,095	524	468

Source: Samuel Eliot Morison, *History of United States Naval Operations in World War II* (Boston: Little, Brown, 1947), vol. 1, p. lxi.

At a first guess, it was a move to block the threat arising from France's fall and the possible defeat of Britain. War events had seriously impaired the security of the Western Hemisphere and the Atlantic Ocean, a vital bulwark of U.S. security. Comparisons of the five major naval powers, as established at the 1922 Washington Conference (and confirmed at other meetings) had recorded an increasingly powerful Japanese fleet and a growth (albeit limited) of French and Italian naval hardware, whereas no increase at all was registered for the British Navy and only a small rise in the U.S. capacity (see Table 2).

As things stood, the Atlantic was the most exposed front because the bulk of U.S. warships had been stationed in Hawaii. When war broke out in Europe, the Atlantic Squadron was a negligible force composed of four old battleships (the *New York,* the *Texas,* the *Arkansas,* and the

Wyoming), a division of heavy cruisers (the *San Francisco*, the *Tuscaloosa*, the *Quincy*, and the *Vincennes*), a squadron of destroyers, and the carriers *Ranger* and *Wasp* (still under construction). In all, the fleet was completely inadequate for the expanse of water it had to cover.

Nonetheless, there was a general feeling during those months that the Atlantic coast was not so much protected by this motley assortment of U.S. war vessels as it was by the Royal Navy. The situation was further aggravated by fears, whether imaginary or real, of possible pro-Nazi coups in certain Latin American states, and people even suggested the somewhat imaginative possibility of a German invasion of the Latin American subcontinent.

The press meanwhile stressed the danger of European possessions passing into enemy hands. U.S. government concern about the loyalty of the governor of Martinique to the Vichy government was symptomatic of this climate of uncertainty, together with the question of the Caribbean islands of Curaçao and Aruba and of Suriname.[21] Endless calculations were made to show that the German, Italian, and French fleets together represented a grave threat to the Atlantic convoy routes. Such a situation would become desperate if the Royal Navy were to fall into German hands.The most important official strategic document of this period, "The Basis for Immediate Decisions Concerning National Defense," dated June 27, 1940, was emphatic about the U.S. Army's inability to undertake military action south of Venezuela—at least not before December.[22]

Opinion polls (*Fortune*, *Life*, and Gallup) confirmed that the public indeed feared a German attack on the Western Hemisphere. According to *Fortune* magazine (June 1, 1940), 78 percent of those interviewed were convinced that Germany would attempt to occupy some territory or other in the hemisphere, directly, using their own troops. According to *Life* magazine of July 29, 75 percent of those interviewed wanted the United States to use arms against any invasion of Mexico or Central America, the country's traditional backyard; and 69 percent (an exceptionally high figure for the time) favored direct intervention in South America too. The Gallup survey recorded 67 percent affirmative replies to the question whether it was appropriate to employ the army and navy in Latin America, if the threat of German invasion arose.[23]

The chances of Germany's actually attacking while the Royal Navy remained strong and continued to patrol Atlantic waters actively in addition to the U.S. Navy's Atlantic Squadron were, according to the specialists, practically zero. Writing in 1947, in his semiofficial history of the U.S. Navy, Adm. Samuel Eliot Morison stated, "Thus, in September 1939, there was even less hope than in 1914 of the German Navy's winning command of even the narrow seas."

Indeed, despite the ostentatious German shipbuilding program drawn up by Adm. Kurt Fricke on mandate from the High Adm. Erich Raeder in those very months,[24] the German fleet in operation at the time was not only inadequate for gaining control of the Atlantic but also would have been hard put to keep the English Channel clear for more than twenty-four hours. For the German Navy to achieve its overall objectives, it would have needed a further 60–80 warships, 15–20 aircraft carriers, 100 cruisers, and 150 submarines, with the backing of a privateering fleet of 115 cruisers, 250 destroyers, and 1,200 support ships. Aware that such a building program was sheer fantasy, Fricke proposed a scaled-down version of his program for the first phase of rearmament (to last fifteen years), during which the country would build 25 battleships, 8 aircraft carriers, 400 submarines for the home fleet, and 65 cruisers, 150 destroyers, and 500 support vessels for the privateering fleet.[25]

But even this reduced program was swept aside by the need to meet demands for the "Battle of the Atlantic" (supply and transport ships), which started in autumn 1939. Alfred von Tirpitz's hopes (later shared by Hitler and Raeder) for a traditional fleet based on battleships was soon dashed as all raw materials and technical and financial resources were plowed into the construction of submarines (which rose from 4 to 20–25 units per month). Approval was given for the production of 300 vessels ranging from 500 to 750 tons for surprise tactics in and around the internal and coastal waters, to be completed in 1942, with an increase to 900 units for 1943. This program was also left incomplete, and even if it had succeeded, it would not have been sufficient.

Leaving aside reasons of propaganda, there must have been other reasons why the political elites decided to stoke the national psychosis about a possible German invasion. Defense and security in the Western Hemisphere were insufficient reasons to explain why President Roosevelt and his administration had gradually begun to expand U.S. presence through the Atlantic, both eastward and southward.

The collapse in the summer of 1940 of the "intermediate system" had provoked a new situation that contrasted considerably with the setup since Versailles. The equation of forces operating on the continent (France and Great Britain against Germany and Italy, plus the smaller "revisionist" states and member-states of the "Petite Entente" divided equally among the larger nations) was being supplanted by a new system centered on Berlin. Although this Germanic continental "pole" exerted considerable power on land, its naval strength was not at all comparable. This led to a vacuum of power in the Atlantic, in contrast to the surplus of power on the continent.

The vacuum in the Atlantic was certainly not going to be filled by Germany, for the reasons outlined above. But neither was Great Britain equipped to cover all the gaps left by the disappearance of the French fleet (and by the defeated Belgian, Norwegian, and Dutch fleets). The real problem then was the lack of sufficient guarantees for the Western Hemisphere, irrespective of the risk of a German invasion.

In other times, this lack would have prompted the United States simply to reduce its area of security for the Western Hemisphere. But in 1940 the advances in naval technology, the increased deployment of airborne forces, and the growing deployment of aircraft carriers meant that Washington could not afford to ignore the possibility, however remote, that the latent power vacuum in the Atlantic could gradually turn into a real threat to the continent. Faced with this development of sea power in the Atlantic, policymakers had a valid reason to change their traditionally defensive line. The area of defense crept almost imperceptibly in the direction of Europe, passing from a purely defensive stance to a defense-offense philosophy.

The problem of introducing a greater military presence was quickly translated into the crucial question of air and naval bases, as we have seen. First the United States had to face the question of its bases in the central zone of the Western Hemisphere. These bases had always been the mainstay of the entire continental defense system, both to provide intercontinental communication and to be a shield for the "soft underbelly" of the United States. Although they remained important for the forward protection of the Panama Canal, the islands of the Pacific, Atlantic, and Caribbean suddenly acquired further strategic significance. The perimeter of control and security steadily expanded, or became denser with the installation of more bases, as two new factors were added to the geopolitical changes and latent power vacuum: (1) the spreading of new technology, weaponry, and war machinery for sea and air forces, with ever-increasing fire power and penetration capability; and (2) the dwindling political and military presence of defeated European powers (France, Holland) or those in the throes of a strategic crisis (such as Great Britain).

At this point, the U.S. "discovery" of the crucial strategic importance of Martinique (belonging to France), which provided the only major port between Trinidad and Puerto Rico,[26] seemed to be prompted by fears that the vacuum left in the Caribbean by the fall of France might be filled by others (the British, perhaps, or some South American country). Washington also hoped that the Vichy government in France, being unrecognized, could be supplanted by the United States itself. There was a widespread feeling of insecurity, even among the public, and a growing conviction that the United States could remedy its problems by acquiring new naval and air bases. To some extent, that conviction was merely the consequence of the debate (initiated in the 1920s and

1930s and inflamed by the campaign in Ethiopia and then the war in Spain) over the possibility of integrating the new strategic theory of air power with the more traditional theory of sea power, combining the two in a single formula: "sea-air power."

On June 5, 1940, the *New York Herald Tribune*, under the hail of bad news from France, explicitly suggested that the joint resolution debated in Congress two days earlier, stating that "the United States would not recognize the transfer, nor would accept peaceably any attempt to transfer any geographical region of this Hemisphere from one non-American power to another non-American power," should have been extended to include areas outside the Western Hemisphere. It listed some of those territories—Iceland, the Azores, Cape Verde, the Canary Islands, and even the westernmost tip of Africa, with Dakar.[27] Congress instead approved only the original draft of the joint resolution.[28] However, the idea grew that the complete chain of islands and territories in mid-Atlantic from coast to coast, even outside the Western Hemisphere, should be kept in check. The U.S. deal with the British for control of their bases in the Caribbean and Newfoundland in exchange for fifty old torpedo-boat destroyers was a consequence of this line of thought.

The operation was twofold: (1) strategic consolidation of the U.S. position within the Western Hemisphere for a long-lasting period (ninety-nine years); (2) political as well as military backing for the United Kingdom, to prime the nation for the consequences that acts such as leasing the bases (clearly hostile toward the Axis) would sooner or later invite. The extended term established in the rental of these bases, and the fact that the United States was taking them over from a still strong and active power, belied the explanation given to the public—that the operations were "urgent" and "temporary."

The Southern Cone

U.S. concern about the security of the Western Hemisphere was particularly grave regarding the south. The archives of the State Department (and in greater detail in the papers of the Joint Chiefs of Staff) showed that the military considered the Nazi threat in South America to be one of the most immediate perils to the nation. The Liaison Committee of the Joint Chiefs of Staff, which held approximately 100 meetings over the period 1939–1940, assigned top priority to questions concerning Latin America in all but six meetings.[29] Although further research showed that there were no such plans for invading Latin America, there was some talk in German circles in South America of a "Patagonian Anschluss" and a "German Antarctica."[30]

The debate on the geopolitical and strategic importance of the third zone of the hemisphere was initiated by Clarence Streit and continued by Nicholas J. Spykman, who thought up the idea of a South American buffer zone, in which the hemisphere was to be defended through the control of northern Brazil.[31] On an operational level, the Inter-American Defense Board was set up in April 1938 to coordinate the various military aspects of such a problem.

In spite of the limited ability of U.S. military power to use force to defend this third region, the general attitude in the U.S. was to defend the entire American continent against any direct outside threat.[32] Six weeks after the 1938 Munich agreement, President Roosevelt himself had declared that "the United States must be prepared to resist attack on the Western Hemisphere from the North Pole to the South Pole, including all of North America and South America."[33]

Spykman's studies into the possibility of defending the Western Hemisphere were widely known by 1940, though his book *America's Strategy in World Politics* was not published until 1942. Spykman's views, together with those of Isaiah Bowman (chairman of the Territorial Group), were undoubtedly decisive in the official definition of the actual boundaries of the Western Hemisphere, boundaries that had never really been clearly defined before, especially as regards the northeastern frontiers of the continent.

The Influence of Geopolitics

The basic conceptual tools fueling this new expanded vision of the Western Hemisphere were new theories (and countertheories) that had germinated from the ongoing debate between the "continental" and the "navalist" schools of geopolitical thinking (Mackinder, Mahan, Haushofer, and others). Another major influence in revising the defense doctrine for the Western Hemisphere was the evolution of military technology and particularly the rash of new theories on "air power" drawn from the book by the Italian General Giulio Douhet, whose ideas were taken up by Colonel Mitchell and his student, Major Alexander De Seversky.[34]

In the course of a bitter interwar debate between the progressive vanguard that championed air power, and the conservative lobby of the army and navy,[35] new ideas and strategies emerged for air and sea warfare regarding the Western Hemisphere. The debate also provided essential material for the growing doctrine of an autonomous air force, which after World War II led to the foundation of the United States Air Force (USAF)—an independent body within the framework of the new Department of Defense—and the unification of the three services.[36]

The fabled successes of air power also prompted the United States and its aeronautics industry to adopt strategic bombing (which was already official doctrine in Britain) as the key strategy of modern warfare.[37] Once its importance was recognized, medium and heavy bomber aircraft (B-17, B-24, B-29, and so on) were designed and built. Their range and autonomy offered a powerful reservoir of strike power over the entire globe—a force that would be used during and after the war in the changing perspective of bipolarity, a legacy of the atomic bomb, the new "absolute weapon."[38]

In the meantime, war developments and the realization of the limited range of action of the navy's battleships compared with the power of the aircraft and their carriers, gradually caused strategists to defect from the traditional Anglo-Saxon theories of sea power in favor of the complex strategy of "air-naval warfare" and the use of floating and fixed bases. In 1942 De Seversky had observed that "since the beginning of the war, British and American shipyards have been jammed with warships disabled by aerial bombing. With battleships like the *Prince of Wales*, the *Repulse* and the *Arizona* on the floor of the Pacific, that old argument is ended once and for all."[39]

The growing importance of aviation led to a noticeable change in U.S. perception of the physical dimensions of the Western Hemisphere and of the priorities among its various regions. In 1941, Hans W. Weigert, geographer and faithful pupil of the geopolitician Mackinder, wrote a brief but highly cogent description of the change that new technology and military doctrines had engendered in strategic thinking and especially in U.S. geopolitics. Weigert's article was published first in *Harpers* magazine and then in 1942 in *Foreign Affairs:*

> Our strategy is not beginning to comprehend a vital lesson which will be considered elementary tomorrow, the North Pole is, in the age of air power, close to the pivot of world strategy, whether one looks at it from Washington, Tokyo, or Berchtesgaden. Such a geographical view, based on an azimuthal projection, inevitably makes Eurasia and North America an almost continuous continental landmass, the landmass of future world domination. Flanked by the United States (Alaska), Canada and Russia, which rule the Arctic Sea, this immense continent holds the inner lines and bends the Axis Powers to the outer crescent.[40]

This view of the globe is almost prophetic. Weigert undoubtedly had a "northcentric" perspective of the Eurasian landmass. His vision went far beyond that of Mackinder and later of Haushofer, which placed the English and American "islands" at the outer rim. The new perspective signified a revolution in the very concept of landmass, which privileged the industrial North (United States, United Kingdom, Soviet Union, and Japan) at the expense of the central and southern band (Germany, Italy, the Mediterranean, and the colonized lands). This futuristic and para-doxically "modern" vision of postwar relations between the "strong" countries and their "poor" counterparts presaged the accentuated North-South polarity of the contemporary world. The new "horizontal" division of the world contrasted with the concept of the "vertical" isolation of the American Western Hemisphere, consisting of former colonies and external to the center of world politics, i.e., Europe. This azimuthal projection centered on the North Pole upset the established Mercator projection of world geography, altering the notions of centrality and periphery according to geopolitical parameters of far-reaching potential.

Weigert's words opened a window on the pattern of power in the postwar world. Bipolarity in fact is a traditional way of interpreting world order. The vertical view of distances and political compartments is still a residue from the past. A good example is the division of the world between Spain and Portugal, made by the pope at the beginning of the sixteenth century. That division, along the meridian axes, reflected the east-west trend of geographical discoveries. There is relatively little change in climate and customs along the same horizontal band of the globe. But moving vertically from continent to continent involves marked changes in climate and culture. This diversity of living conditions, climate, and socioeconomic indicators is what determines both affinities and differences. The "northernness" of the West, and the potential "southernness" of the East, is a very recent discovery. It reveals the influence and cultural effects of the new polar routes, the new international communication network that had been growing hand in hand with the development of aeronautics in the 1930s,[41] which enabled Weigert (whose book included pieces that had previously appeared in the CFR's *Foreign Affairs*) and others like him to bend the central idea of Mackinder's geopolitical theory on landmasses and the "island of the world" to American ends.[42]

In the British interpretation of geopolitics, and likewise in that of General Haushofer's "magical" *Geopolitik*, the "landmass of future world domination" pivoted on Russia and Europe, thus Germany (hence Hitler's *Drang nach Osten*). Weigert saw things differently. He applied his research to the altered needs of U.S. strategy and security, shifting the pivot to include North America in the landmass. With Weigert's azimuthal pro-jections, the American continent (and particularly North America) became a natural extension of the Eurasian landmass centered on the North Pole.

Weigert coupled this political use of geography with special cartog-raphy, with reference to the 1942 article "Maps" in *Life* and to the set of maps drawn up by R. E. Harrison and published in *Fortune* in 1941.[43] In this new vision of global geography, the Western Hemisphere was no longer seen as the isolated and peripheral new continent (i.e., rimland versus heartland) or as external (i.e., the outer crescent) to the old Asiatic center of gravity of the world. Europe (or at least the northern half of it) was finally pushed out to the periphery, and it was possible to assert with geographical objectivity: (1) that Central and South America were situated in a peripheral zone by definition; and (2) that, together with a section of the British Empire (Canada) and the Soviet Union, the United States was destined to dominate the world, endorsing the Grand Alliance in force at the time of publication of his book.

In an attempt to expose the errors of Haushofer's geopolitics, Weigert stressed the general's failure to grasp the real situation of the Western Hemisphere, since he had erroneously focused his analysis of the American continent exclusively on the Pacific. The Germans had in fact devoted many geopolitical studies to the American continent, but always from an "oriental" standpoint, emphasizing Chile's role in South America (with its small but highly outspoken German population) and California's in the United States, which they judged to be heavily influenced by immigration from Japan.

As did other geopoliticians of the era, Weigert was critical of not only Haushofer for these macroscopic errors. Weigert had numerous targets and accused even Spykman of cultural subordination, together with other American authors who had exercised considerable influence in forging U.S. strategic thinking during and after the war. His targets included James Burnham (author of *The Managerial Revolution*) and George T. Renner (for his article in *Collier's* magazine entitled "Maps for a New World"). Weigert's contention was that each of them had identified completely with the principles of Realpolitik and power politics that they had officially condemned in the German analyses. Owing to this oversight, they could hardly share the future vision of Roosevelt's "Four Freedoms."[44] To some extent, Weigert reinstated the methodological framework of traditional geopolitics, adapting it to a new vision of world politics and future U.S. foreign policy, purging it of the more blatant colonialist and/or imperialist components and of the formulas typical of the pre-1914 "gunboat diplomacy," which had influenced the work of Haushofer and certain American geopoliticians between the wars.

Considerable coverage has been given here to the work of Weigert because it added an innovative dimension to the debate on U.S. foreign policy and strategy in this particular phase of rapid transformation. In fact, many authors reflected a general ambivalence in these matters, which were not the reserve of a closed number of academic geopoliticians but a question that united the political and social elites in common research. In this melting pot of ideas, a mixed recipe of realism and idealism, of the American Creed and the U.S. global role, gradually came into being as new forms of political behavior were sought, for which traditional geopolitical concepts seemed inadequate, though they could not be completely overlooked.[45]

The new philosophies were varied: "federalism" in Streit, "air power" in De Seversky, "neonavalism" in the thinking of Adm. Harold R. Stark and even more so in that of Adm. Ernest J. King, "universalist institutionalism" in Shotwell, economic and commercial, as well as productive, "interdependence" in the pioneering work completed by Francis P. Miller and his wife, Helen Hill, in 1930 on the Atlantic Community, "common war" and "military aid" (lend-lease) to Great Britain in the political behavior of Roosevelt and General Marshall. All these facets of the crystal being formed would finally culminate in the two pillars of U.S. foreign policy, "interdependence" and "national security."[46]

The dual image of the United States in 1940, at once isolationist and interventionist, was also reflected within the military establishment, just as it had been in the politico-cultural elites and the public. Those army officials who shared the opinions of the America First Committee continued to be influential. They held that "true patriotism enjoined strict adherence to Washington's admonition to stay clear of foreign quarrels."[47] This sector of the armed forces had the firm conviction that a well-prepared nation "could successfully resist any outside power or combination of powers."[48]

However, there was a growing group among the military (which included Chief of Staff Gen. George C. Marshall) who were ready to step in and help Great Britain in its battle for survival, "but only on the firm understanding that American viewpoints would be considered first. The Joint Army-Navy planners spoke for this element when they issued instructions to American representatives engaged in conversations with the British." This prudent statement was pronounced in the summer of 1941 during the Atlantic conference in Placentia Bay, when a sense of the imminence of U.S. involvement was widespread.[49]

The reluctance of the armed forces to open the U.S. arsenal to the British, in the fear of compromising security and interests, can also be noticed in the attitude of the Security and Armaments Group of the CFR in its first two years of activity. The group's feelings were in stark contrast to the general farsightedness of the politicians, especially to the "internationalists" of the Century Group and the more famous Committee to Defend America by Aiding the Allies. In his endorsement of the "Summons to Speak Out," Francis P. Miller, for instance, also a highly active member of the Century Group, had openly petitioned for war against Germany as early as June 10, 1940, when the Italians joined the fray.[50]

As with many other of the old internationalist guard, Miller's views were representative of the militant U.S. internationalism of the period. Convinced of the need to establish a permanent bridge between the United States and the other industrialized countries, Miller had spoken of "Americanizing" Europe right from the start, calling for an economic, social, and political union between the United States and the European continent. Of particular interest were the ideas expressed on July 12, 1940, in the "Tentative Draft" Miller prepared for the meeting of the twelve "centurions," the leading members of the New York Century Club. In the draft he remarked: "The Latin American countries do not practice our way of life. There is no basis—political, cultural, economic, geographic or strategic, for close alliance between the countries of South America and the United States. . . . The English-speaking people on the other hand, do practice our way of life."[51] This was tantamount to an outright denial of the traditional close ties among the American republics, a critical notion for the idea of the Western Hemisphere and the ideological bedrock for the Monroe Doctrine. It was an equally outspoken acknowledgment of the umbilical cord tying the United States to Europe.

For the time being, given the political atmosphere, Miller spoke only in terms of "English-speaking people" in his address to the centurions. It would have been too problematic, during the war, to speak of Europe as a whole. Ten years earlier, however, in *The Giant of the Western World*, Miller and Hill had not hesitated in referring to the northern Atlantic as a whole, including Europe in its entirety (a point Streit was also to make eight years later): "The very fact of the existence of the United States renders obsolete the European balance of power and the sufficiency of the present European nation-states as an economic unit."[52] And then: "The United States is the strongest single power in the world today. While we hold ourselves aloof from European affairs politically, we are, at the same time, developing and exploiting foreign markets and establishing a stranglehold on the European economic situation, thus creating for ourselves a responsibility that cannot be ignored."[53]

But Miller and Hill did not stop there. In 1930 they had openly attacked U.S. foreign policy, its technical structures, and the diplomatic staff for not being equipped to deal with the new situation: "One of the scandals of our national life has been the failure of successive administrations to build up a State Department, capable of constructing the new type of foreign policy which is needed, and to invest the Department with the authority and dignity necessary to commend its activities to the country."[54] In a harsh indictment of the evils of the

State Department,[55] Miller and Hill pointed out that the Republican diplomacy of the 1920s had run its term, and that the management of the Department of Commerce under Herbert Hoover, before he was elected president in 1928, had all but eliminated the State Department. The idea that began to grow in the minds of these pioneers of the new internationalist foreign policy between the economic crises was (1) to bring the United States closer to the other developed countries, a closeness that alone would guarantee a bigger and more sophisticated market for the future; (2) to update the conceptual and political tools of U.S. activity vis-à-vis the outside world, by pinpointing specific themes and regions of interest in which to concentrate efforts; and (3) to reshuffle the entire body of professional and appointed staff in the State Department and hence overhaul the machinery that defined the handling of the country's international affairs.

The list ignored a matter of fundamental importance, namely, the country's strategic security. Hence it overlooked the question of the means and doctrines necessary for effecting the conversion of U.S. foreign policy. But this was 1930, and despite the crisis under way, the state of the world was far less pressing than it would be ten years later.

Nonetheless, these premises for intervention in Europe—lasting premises founded on precise conceptual and political assumptions—provided a potential strategic program that would eventually lead to the radical reworking of the entire political and military setup of the United States. The decision to turn the sights from the underdeveloped countries to the industrial ones in itself meant creating a defensive-offensive structure. That structure would make possible the formation of suitable "Expeditionary Corps" to send out to distant lands to dissuade (or combat) industrially advanced nations with modern war equipment.

The few existing battalions of U.S. Marines in the Antilles and a group of cavalry squadrons in Mexico would no longer be sufficient to resolve problem situations.[56] The U.S. defense system in Asia, Hawaii, the Philippines, and China in 1940 was utterly outnumbered by the swelling Japanese force. The rapid fall of all the U.S. bases in the Far East between the attack on Pearl Harbor (December 7, 1941) and the Battle of Midway (May 1942) was conclusive proof of the shortcomings of the U.S. war machine in the face of modern war requirements. U.S. involvement in Europe, although ostensibly to help Britain, inevitably entailed the definitive transformation of the U.S. military system, a transformation that would have taken place even had the country remained neutral. In 1940 the world was a ready seedbed for the new ideas and irrevocable demands engendered by the sudden implosion of the Eurocentric international system.

10

Greenland and Iceland

Military Plans

In 1940, four major geopolitical developments dominated traditional U.S. foreign policy. First, the strategic structure of the three regions of the Western Hemisphere had to be redrawn with new and more suitable parameters and standards. At this juncture it was also imperative to establish a means of legal and political legitimation for the acquisition of new naval and air bases in the Caribbean and Central America, an area Spykman had dubbed "the American Mediterranean."[1]

Second, it was accepted as fact that the nation's security was inextricably entwined with the security and control of the Arctic sea-lanes, in accordance with the new doctrine of air power. Third, the internationalists were growing in number and political leverage. They were a mixed bag of individuals of diverse origins and political orientations who were increasingly convinced that the real geopolitical bedrock of U.S. national security lay in creating tighter bonds with the Northern Hemisphere and ensuring close inter-Atlantic relations. Fourth, there was an increasingly horizontal emphasis on the east-west axis (as opposed to north-south) and hence a shift of the center of the security system, and its underlying "philosophy," to the north and to the Atlantic. This shift was evident in the changing order of geopolitical priorities manifested in the formulas of Spykman, Weigert, and Streit, which found concrete expression in the revision of the war plans of the general staffs of both army and navy.[2]

Answers to the question that had troubled U.S. politicians and strategists for some time finally began to appear in 1940. The concept of the "security zone," which had remained unaltered since the times of Theodore Roosevelt, was finally being expanded. Whereas originally U.S. strategy had been limited to the North American area (including the Caribbean), which had been subsequently extended to become the "Western Hemisphere," at this time a decisively global accent was emerging as the security zone progressively spilled across the Atlantic in the direction of Europe.

As the range of strategic bombers continued to increase, so the area of the U.S. security system spread out in all directions, and particularly toward Europe. It is hardly surprising therefore that when the United States joined the war at the end of 1941, the immediate priority of Roosevelt and the armed forces[3] was to crush Nazi Germany, despite the Japanese attack on Pearl Harbor.

The shift from the Pacific to the Atlantic (and hence from Japan to Germany) resulted, however, from a doctrine that still did not venture outside the traditional "oceanic" defense outlook of the U.S. Navy, a philosophy that was successively translated to a general strategic level. Given that the United States possessed a "one-ocean navy," if the country had to face an enemy on both oceans, it made sense to tackle the stronger of the two adversaries first. The approach was reminiscent of the "orange" and "red" strategies that the United States had planned against Japan and Great Britain respectively, prior to World War I. When Germany ("black") supplanted Great Britain ("red") as the primary foe, the relative weakness of the former's navy in no way altered the decision to award absolute priority to the Atlantic. This timeworn theory remained a staple in the war plans that the Joint Army-Navy Board had been studying since 1939. The board had detailed all the possible alternative scenarios on the assumption that there would be a U.S.-British alliance (with or without France's participation) against Germany and Italy or against the tripartite enemy in both oceans.

The different "colors" (red, blue, and orange) were shuffled in various combinations to form a total of five Rainbow Plans, covering all possible outcomes. The first was geared to "preventing the violation of the Monroe Doctrine, and protecting the United States, its possessions and its trade." The second aimed to "realize Plan no. 1, and give backing to the authority of democratic powers in the Pacific zone." The third was to "insure control over the Western Pacific." The fourth was aimed at "reinforcing the defense of the Hemisphere by sending U.S. task forces to South America and the Eastern Atlantic where this is deemed necessary." The fifth plan was geared to "achieving the aims of Plan nos. 1 and 4, and to providing troops for Africa or Europe in order to obtain the final defeat of Germany, Italy, or both."[4] This last plan presupposed cooperation with Great Britain and France.

The Rainbow Plans, many of which were scuttled before the details were worked out (the second and third plans never got beyond the preliminary draft stage), contained themes and strategies that had emerged in the course of the widespread debate on foreign policy throughout the country. The fifth plan, which shortly before the attack on Pearl

Harbor became the basic plan for U.S. entry into war, was a highly ambitious program that presupposed the globalization of U.S. intervention in the war.

General Strong, who had participated in drafting the original plan, was also an influential member of the Security and Armaments Group of the Council on Foreign Relations. But the revamped strategy only came into its own, operationally speaking, after the fall of France. It was first formalized in the June 22, 1940, memo,[5] which General Marshall and Admiral Stark presented jointly to President Roosevelt. The document contained both philosophies of the U.S. military establishment, which was ready to adopt an expansionist approach to the Western Hemisphere, including the occupation of English, French, Dutch, and Danish islands in the Atlantic and Pacific. There was, however, considerable reluctance to boost the export of arms to Great Britain—essential for London to survive, but which, Marshall and Stark argued, would drain the reserves of the U.S. armed forces.

A boost to the defense budget was sufficient to quell the vacillations and uncertainties in military circles. But the mood had spread to the public, and in order to make this new and somewhat conflicting strategy between security and expansion more palatable (and to keep it in tune with the public's eternal self-deception on foreign-policy issues[6]), the political elites had to become familiar with this type of reasoning and the various points of view had to be harmonized before the message was transmitted to its hesitant target.

On a strictly military level, the internal struggle between the "neo-navalism" of the U.S. Navy and the U.S. Air Force's obsession with "air power" was mitigated by a substantial investment in the carrier fleet and naval aviation. However, on a geopolitical and strategic level (i.e., on the relationships between war and politics), the unrest was less easy to allay, and there were hints of an imminent U-turn in traditional thinking.

The final orientation of U.S. military decisions during and after the war was therefore the product of a complex interaction of ideas, facts, person-alities, and one-time events. But most of all it was the result of internal discussions within the various command centers of the political system and the academic, professional, and press circles, which pragmatically settled each controversial situation as it arose, carefully defining the theoretical and critical concepts, or tools, that would serve in the future.

Precedents

One of the major issues in which the work of the CFR study groups influenced the decisions of the administration—and perhaps those of the president himself—was the inclusion of Greenland and Iceland in the Western Hemisphere's zone of defense. In this particular case, the WPS documents of the first two years showed a marked difference from the output of other centers and study groups and demonstrated the council's ability to influence the decision-making processes of the federal administration and the course of its policy planning. The issue of the inclusion of the Caribbean and the two Atlantic islands (Greenland and Iceland) virtually coincided with the German invasion of Denmark in April 1940 and with the crushing defeat of France in June. But the two areas posed separate problems. Whereas the Caribbean was quite clearly well within the Western Hemisphere, geographers were divided on the exact positioning of Greenland but agreed that Iceland was outside the hemisphere.

In any case, the first official diplomatic documents on the Greenland issue—which betrayed a keen interest on the part of both the administration and the State Department in Arctic and sub-Arctic zones and their importance to the war in Europe—were all subsequent to the German conquest of Denmark and Norway, unlike the memoranda of the Council on Foreign Relations, which were written earlier. Further indication of this interest can be inferred from the paperwork on the territorial status of the Antarctic and surrounding areas.[7] In his letter of August 1, 1940, to President Roosevelt, commenting on the valuable services of Rear Adm. Richard E. Byrd (who was also a world-renowned explorer of the polar regions) as commanding officer of the United States Antarctic Service, Secretary of State Hull noted:

[Byrd has] two bases in the Antarctic regions, and active scientific and economic investigations at each base are either now being carried out or will be initiated as soon as weather conditions permit. The establishment of these bases, together with the noteworthy flights made by Admiral Byrd early this year, which resulted in the discovery of a great extent of hitherto unknown stretches of the Antarctic coast, goes far toward strengthening any territorial claims which the United States may desire to make in the American segment of the Antarctic Continent. In this connection it should be observed that West Base is situated in an area which has been claimed by New Zealand, although American activities have been extensive in that general region, and the East Base is in an area claimed by Great Britain. The United States has never recognized either British or New Zealand sovereignty in the Antarctic areas claimed by those Governments.[8]

As the letter explicitly stated, the Antarctic was not part of the official definition of the Western Hemisphere and was considered as a separate continent. However, for some time the United States had been contending with other powers for portions of the region.[9]

Apart from Roosevelt's "declaration" of April 14[10] deploring the Reich's latest enterprise (the invasion of Norway on April 9 and the invasion of Denmark on April 6), the first State Department document to discuss seriously the subject of the Arctic landmasses—and Greenland in particular—was dated April 24. And even then, the issue was discussed in terms of the legality of installing a provisional U.S. Consulate on the island. The Office of the Legal Adviser of the State Department[11] maintained that it was advisable to defer such action, although formal procedures had begun August 17–22, 1929—long before war broke out in Europe. Showing some political boldness, the Division of European Affairs suggested that, in absence of a rightful Danish government, the United States address its request to set up a consulate to the "de facto authority in Greenland, which is now vested jointly in the Resident Commission for the Provinces of North Greenland and South Greenland."[12] By adopting this stance, Washington was patently refusing to recognize German possession of Denmark and likewise disregarding the substitute Danish government authorized by Berlin. Furthermore, this interpretation implied an informal removal of Greenland from Danish sovereignty, albeit provisional and due to force of circumstance.

The message of assent from the Danish administration in Washington four days later, made without consulting Copenhagen, with direct reference to the two governors of North and South Greenland[13] (doubtlessly in agreement with the State Department), showed that Washington was bent on considering the island an appendage that was no longer attached to occupied Denmark and hence qualifying for a different administration—for legal as well as strictly geopolitical reasons. Apart from this reference, the issue was summarily ignored in official archives. Notter himself[14] failed to give it any real attention until May–June of the following year.

Greenland had cropped up in earlier debates, however, albeit somewhat fleetingly, in the context of a list of European-owned territories and possessions to be watched regarding possible transfers of sovereignty following events in Europe. The theoretical terrain was therefore already staked out and even received the endorsement of the isolationists, whose stubborn defense of the Western Hemisphere obviously made them more sensitive to European interference in U.S. affairs and more anxious than their internationalist counterparts to rid themselves of the surviving residue of the old colonies.[15]

The Two Memoranda

Until March 1940, however, things had never proceeded beyond this point. And so it is somewhat surprising to find two memoranda (T-B3 and T-B4) of the Territorial Group (among the first in chronological order of the WPS papers, dated March 27, 1940, and April 8, 1940, respectively) entirely devoted to a careful preview of the problems these two undefended but crucially strategic islands represented.

The title of each followed the same formula: "The Strategic Importance of Greenland" and "The Strategic Importance of Iceland." The dates attributed to the two documents, immediately prior to the occupation of Denmark and Norway (the Greenland text coming a mere fifteen days before the sudden and unforeseen invasion of Denmark), do not correspond directly to the period the material was actually put together but to the meeting of the Territorial Group in which the texts were discussed and approved. Normally, the author of a document (in this case Philip E. Mosely) submitted the text some time earlier to members of the group, who were allowed time to read it through and make notes (March 7 for T-B3 and April 1 for T-B4).

We can reasonably assume therefore that the topic had been discussed with Mosely some time earlier (probably in February), when no one imagined that in the space of a few weeks the Germans would storm Norway and Denmark, making the entire issue urgent. This timing made the texts almost prophetic in their concern with problems and possible outcomes of the incipient war. But they also confirm the speed with which the concept of "security" was developing within certain specialized Establishment circles and with security, the evolving conceptualization of the Western Hemisphere's geographical delimitation, and a growing U.S. military presence in territories that had previously been considered, a priori, outside the area of U.S. national interests.[16]

In the SA Group's digest (Memorandum A-A10, dated April 18, 1941, a full year later) of discussions on the possibility of establishing military bases in Ireland, and on the question of escorting convoys across the Atlantic, Adm. Harold Pratt proffered a definition of the perimeter of the Western Hemisphere: Its easternmost border began at longitude 30° west, "officially" enclosing most of Greenland, whereas Iceland (as well as Ireland) was cut out completely. However, that new perimeter was soon made redundant by the White House—on April 10, 1941, President Roosevelt spoke privately to a group of key individuals and cabinet secretaries (Stimson, Frank Knox, Hopkins, and others), declaring that U.S. ships would patrol the Atlantic from longitude 25° west, thereby extending the Western Hemisphere's range even further.[17] Although the president made no public announcement, he had taken a significant step toward anchoring the final arches of that strategic "bridge" across the Atlantic linking the United States definitively with Europe. The day before this secret discussion, Roosevelt stated officially to the nation's press that "the United States Government had signed an executive agreement with the Danish minister in exile, placing Greenland under the protection of the United States and authorizing the construction of American air and naval bases there";[18] he made no mention of the strategic position the island had in the definition of the Western Hemisphere.

But such a political outcome was the result of a long policy-making process that had begun the previous year. Memorandum T-B3 (the first to deal with the argument) had in fact tried to link the fate of Greenland with certain historical "precedents," in the hope of alleviating qualms over the issue. This is confirmed by the fact that the author adopted a juridical tone, which evoked a more traditional U.S. prewar legalist diplomacy.

The first part of the text was devoted to the political line adopted by Washington in the accord with Copenhagen during World War I, stressing the fact that the United States had formally renounced all claims to Greenland with the declaration of August 4, 1916, regarding the purchase of the Danish West Indies (the Virgin Islands). It must be said that even then Washington had expressed reservations over the agreement, noting that the U.S. explorers Robert E. Peary and Elisha Kane had first reached areas to which, theoretically, the United States could have claimed some rights, along similar lines to what was happening to the Antarctic. That area was being divided according to the individual spheres of influence of the various powers. On this particular score, the memorandum quoted a passage from the 1916 declaration signed by Secretary of State Robert Lansing, pointing out that in 1905 Senator Henry Cabot Lodge had urged President Theodore Roosevelt to pursue the acquisition of the territories.

Mosely also hinted at the potential U.S. interest in securing influence over the island. The chief issue was fishing rights. The Danish government had instituted a state monopoly on the western coastal waters, awarding exclusive rights to national fishermen to trawl the waters.[19] During the 1920s and 1930s, the dispute over fishing rights was further exacerbated by the fact that for some time it had been envisaged that Greenland would be an obligatory stopover for flights between Europe and the United States. Such was the conviction of Greenland's importance in aviation that between 1932 and 1938 the U.S. airline Pan American Airways had an agreement with the Danish government for long-term permission to carry out flight tests in the area and to complete in-depth meteorological studies on the subcontinent.

In 1933, Col. Charles Lindbergh, the first person to fly nonstop across the Atlantic (financed by Pan American Airways), had completed a long flight across Greenland with his wife to assess the viability of commercial air routes. Lindbergh was doubtful, owing to the summer fogs and intense winter, and Greenland was subsequently discarded as a port of call for civil aviation. However, the reconnaissance flight undertaken by the Lindberghs had far-reaching political repercussions as well. The couple flew thousands of miles around the Atlantic between July 9 and December 19, 1933, a sequel to a similar expedition they had made in China and Japan in 1931. It is interesting to note this flight around the Atlantic in search of civil air bases gave rise to a new sort of "Atlanticism," although the strategic importance of the Pacific was beyond all doubt.[20] The Lindberghs took off from Flushing Bay in Newfoundland, flew up to Canada, Greenland, and Iceland, over the British Isles and Scandinavia, then made stopovers in the Soviet Union, the Netherlands, France, and Portugal, going as far south as the Azores, the Spanish Sahara, Cape Verde, then across to Natal in Brazil, Port of Spain (Trinidad), Puerto Rico, the Dominican Republic, and finally back to Miami and up the East Coast. The Lindberghs' flight path and choice of landings largely anticipated the ensuing debate on the defense of the Western Hemisphere, a debate that was soon to become a central issue in political and military spheres.

Another outstanding flight around the Western Hemisphere, this time more traditional in scope, had been completed some years earlier, in October 1929, by Junius B. Wood. In a mere sixty-seven hours Wood covered a distance of over 8,000 miles.[21] The flight was carried out as a propaganda gimmick to promote the airmail service but tied in well with the general intensification of communications throughout the Western Hemisphere during the four years of the Hoover administration, when Stimson (secretary of war 1940–1945) had been head of the State Department.

No longer the focus of fishing objectives, or considered suitable terrain for civil air bases, Greenland suddenly became the object of purely strategic and military interests. It was only in this light that Greenland's importance was given due consideration in 1940, as evidenced by Mosely's memorandum for the CFR. Using very precise terms, the document asserted that if Germany were to occupy Denmark, then Greenland could logically pass into German sovereignty by treaty. In that case, if Germany used the island as a base for its own aviation, Canada would be immediately vulnerable and with it the security of the entire American continent would be at risk.

The question assumed a dual importance. On the one hand, it was an eminently strategic issue that demanded a military solution. On the other, it provided a concrete case for international law based on the political application of the Monroe Doctrine. At the heart of the debate was Secretary of State Lansing's interpretation of the Monroe Doctrine spelled out in 1917 in a letter to President Woodrow Wilson: "The

Monroe Doctrine, settled national policy of the United States, would have caused this country to look with disfavor upon the transfer of sovereignty of the Danish West Indies to any other European nation."[22]

Ever since Wilson, it had been understood that the existing colonial territories in the Western Hemisphere definitely could not pass from one European power to another; it had also been stipulated that should a colonial power wish to negotiate, the United States would examine the possibility of "purchasing" territories sub judice. This policy was sanctioned even by the most determined and conservative isolationists. Acquisition has been a constant feature of U.S. diplomacy (and, less so, leasing), dating back to the days of the Louisiana Purchase of 1803. Once again, in March 1940, there were some individuals, such as the rather vaguely defined "leaders of American aviation" (as Mosely called them in Memorandum T-B3) who "express privately the view that, if Greenland could be secured for a moderate price, it would be desirable to purchase it in order to eliminate the military nuisance-value which it possesses as a potential menace to the security of the North American mainland and of North American commerce."

There was, however, a more immediate issue of a political and legal nature that the Territorial Group hoped to solve: "If Germany should win the current war and thus destroy British control over the North Atlantic could the United States contest the right of Denmark to transfer to German sovereignty or to joint German-Danish sovereignty the possession of Greenland?"[23] The Territorial Group's reply was unhesitatingly affirmative. In its summary of the possible international reaction to such a purchase, Memorandum T-B3 unswervingly upheld that such a move would have been favorably received by both Great Britain and Canada. Nor would it have caused misgivings among the Latin American states, although any signs of returning to the policy of territorial purchase south of the United States (in the Caribbean or South America, for instance) would have been met with immediate hostility.

But the development of this new "security" rationale was not going to halt at the borders of Greenland. The strategic importance of Atlantic control—justified in terms of the ever-growing range of the new aircraft, the necessity for safeguarding civil aviation routes, as well as the need for a framework of control and reconnaissance for maritime communication networks—inevitably led to the inclusion of Iceland among the nation's security strong points. One by one, new territories were added to the security network. And the inherent instability of the relationship between security and expansion made a balanced handling of developments practically impossible.

A full year ahead of Roosevelt and the War Department's decisions to include Iceland in the U.S. strategic system, Memorandum T-B3 pronounced: "Acquisition of Greenland as a defensive air-outpost would make the status of Iceland exceedingly important in terms of strategy, since the nuisance-value of Iceland is far greater than that of Greenland, while Iceland itself hardly falls within the geographical sphere within which the Monroe Doctrine is presumed to apply."[24] This is an important point, as it explicitly contested the most durable myth of U.S. foreign policy, namely, the limits to intervention under a "defensive" reading of the Monroe Doctrine. At the same time, the statement stressed the strategic interests represented by Iceland, as always, in terms of "national security."

The debate in the Territorial Group on this particular issue was so animated that it justified a second session. Faced with the utter novelty of the subject matter, the group proposed to do more research and draw up two more memoranda for the following sitting, expressly devoted to (1) U.S. policy on the transfer of "American" territories from one European sovereignty to another; and (2) the analysis of the political status of Iceland and its strategic significance for U.S. security.[25]

Discussion of the Events

During the period between the drafting and the discussion of the document on Greenland (T-B3) and the one on Iceland (T-B4), Germany won another astonishing victory, occupying Denmark in three days and then swarming into Norway. The fate of the two Arctic islands was abruptly catapulted into the foreground.

The sudden invasion of Denmark caught the Territorial Group members off their guard. Both they and the other CFR study groups had had a quite different sequence of events in mind. The memorandum on Iceland, which had been conceptually formulated ahead of events, was imbued with a "hypothetical philosophy" rather than true policy analysis. As such, it was substantially "prewar" in tone, even though it anticipated a view and a logic that would be adopted later on. For this reason, it was not entirely dissimilar to the paper on Greenland—in its layout (particularly in its division into legal, trade, and strategic issues) and in its working proposals, which were bound to be generic and summary.

On a conceptual level, however, the outline of the scheme to intervene in Iceland (despite its being far outside the perimeter of the Western Hemisphere, at longitude 30° west) was traced out for the very first time in this somewhat visionary document. As with Greenland, Washington's interest in Iceland depended neither on trade nor aviation. Indeed, most of Iceland's trade was with Europe and not the United States.[26] Had Washington so wanted, it could have redirected Iceland's overseas trade channels fairly easily by absorbing the island's sole export products, fish and bauxite. It would have been a purely political exercise, however, which would certainly have upset the U.S. fishing lobby. As for Iceland's contribution to civil aviation, as with Greenland, despite Lindbergh's flights and the funds spent by Pan American Airways, the island was discarded as a stopover for transatlantic flight routes in favor of the two existing paths, through Newfoundland and Ireland in the north, and Bermuda and the Azores in the south.

The only thing left was the island's possible strategic contribution. This image of a "bridge" across the Atlantic, largely used to convince the public (as well as the officials and policymakers in the administration) that intervention in Iceland was justified, became centered on the question of the security of the Western Hemisphere. "A strong air power in control of Iceland could control or destroy both air and sea traffic over the Great Circle Route. Its military nuisance-value with respect to North Atlantic shipping and flying could hardly be overestimated. While Iceland has few facilities adapted to large naval vessels, it offers usable facilities for hydro-planes throughout the year, and can develop facilities for land planes when those are required."[27] The sheer novelty of the hypothesis warranted considerable prudence in the proposals. It was noted that "although Iceland is sometimes described as an 'American Republic'[28] its connections with the American Hemisphere and, for instance, to extend to it the application of the Monroe Doctrine, would be to disregard the entire history of Iceland."

Any suggestion of intervention in Iceland at this stage seemed premature, to say the least. At the time, the war in Europe was still a "phony war," and the public was predominantly neutral. This hesitancy on the part of public opinion tended to curb the WPS groups' enthusiasm about the emerging concepts. In late June 1940, only 14 percent of the nation was willing to attack Germany. A look at the religious affiliation of the respondents to the various polls carried out reveals even more striking differences. Undoubtedly influenced by their ethnic origins (Italian and Irish), the nation's Catholics were the least in favor of entering the war. At the height of the Battle of Britain, after the "destroyers for bases" deal had been signed, 53 percent of the Catholics polled still felt it was more important "to try to keep out of the war ourselves" than it was "to help England win, even at the the risk of getting into the war"; whereas only 42 percent of the Protestant respondents, 32 percent of the Jews, and 45 percent of no religious affiliation were of the same opinion.[29]

Even the military exponents, being fully aware of the country's unpreparedness for war, were careful not to dream up extravagant schemes outside their own sphere of influence, so as not to court disaster.[30] The most they were prepared to advance was that "the United

States interest would then be, at bottom, to prevent any aggressive European power from exploiting Iceland as an air and sea base." Just how was not explained. It was thought that Canada might accept Iceland as a "political partner, perhaps as a Dominion, with the approval and support of the United States."[31] Though eccentric, the idea certainly showed imagination. If Iceland were made a dominion of Canada (in the same way that Canada was a dominion of the British Empire), with the added protection and safeguarding of the United States, Iceland would be under Canadian sovereignty (in the same way that the Ottoman Empire had ruled over dependent Egyptian territory, at least until 1882). An alternative idea was to set up a kind of "coprotectorate" of sorts, in league with Canada, over Iceland—legally detached from the third party, Denmark, whose sovereignty was suspended owing to the German occupation.

But little time was devoted to these specific juridical and formal problems during the discussions that followed the presentation of the memorandum. In the main, members' contributions avoided weighing down the text with formal and legal definitions and concentrated on the political reasoning and ways of mediating and persuading domestic opinion. The final draft was approved by the Council on Foreign Relations and subsequently submitted to the State Department.

However, the digest (T-A3) of discussions on Memorandum T-B3, which took place on April 18, 1940, in the Territorial Group, was filled with uncertainty and added new doubts of its own. Isaiah Bowman, for instance, avowed openly that "this was not a matter of geography, but of political interest; Iceland was far nearer to Great Britain than to Canada."[32] The renowned geographer also raised similar questions regarding Memorandum T-B3's proposed solutions for Greenland. What he most feared was that if the United States asserted its claims to the island, Argentina would make identical claims on the Falkland Islands and other British possessions in the Antarctic region. Furthermore, he felt that if the United States was not more consistent in sustaining its continental interests, by occupying the Dutch island of Curaçao, off Venezuela, the Japanese could move in as far as Batavia (Jakarta). In conclusion, Bowman asserted that since Iceland was completely outside the hemisphere's perimeter, it could at best be neutralized and/or demilitarized, but not occupied.

This cautious legalistic approach, which was fueled by fears of possible violations of international law over the geographical division of national territories, was hotly contested by certain members of the Territorial Group and by John C. Cooper in particular. Cooper, a civil aviation expert, took up Mosely's line that Iceland could turn out to be a much greater threat to the hemisphere's security than Greenland and argued that certainly the fate of the latter, and probably that of the former as well, was primarily a U.S. issue and only secondarily a Canadian problem. William L. Westermann, a professor of diplomatic history, struck a similar chord, claiming he was certain he could find ample support for the U.S. occupation of Greenland in international law through a procedure of analogy.

The discussion, which had first centered on the fate of the Arctic islands, then expanded to broader issues. In particular, a debate was begun over the conceptual and political foundations of U.S. policy during the war. Decisions had to be made as to how to meet new diplomatic demands arising from the war, and the fate of the Arctic islands was a case in point. New norms and procedures had to be established and developed without delay. A fundamental contradiction also came to light in the substantial "ideological" and cultural gap between European international law and American international law, which for over a century had been based on the Monroe Doctrine.

The problem was understanding whether the United States should apply the Monroe Doctrine in all cases that involved the Western Hemisphere, regardless of European international law, or whether it should act according to recognized international law within the hemisphere, insisting that others also respect the same statutes regarding areas outside the hemisphere. There was no easy answer. The case had shown that U.S. foreign policy could not continue with this double standard, applying "European" law to cases that involved non-American regions, while calling on a strictly "continental" (or even "national") principle such as the Monroe Doctrine for "American" issues.

The problem had arisen before 1940, however. There had been heated debate at the turn of the century, with the Open Door Policy, when the United States had irritated many European governments over the division of China into zones of influence by applying an unbending logic that was both abstract and opaque. Compared with the European approach, on many occasions Washington's philosophy toward the outside world seemed arrogant. The most striking episode of incompatibility occurred at Versailles in 1919, when the gap turned into open attrition, producing an unbalanced and incoherent international system based on a mixture of philosophies.

After two decades of semi-isolation (with the exception of Stimson's doctrine of 1932, dealing with U.S. interests in the Far East), in 1940 the unresolved problem of incompatibility between the U.S. and European approaches came to a head.[33] The dilemma really stemmed from the Monroe Doctrine. Originally devised as a tool of defense, the doctrine was pointedly anti-European. It rejected the rationale and authority of the existing Concert of Europe, at least with regard to territories within the arc of United States influence, above all, within the Western Hemisphere. The inherent contrast of Washington's approach grew as the country's international role grew, reaching a peak in 1940.

On this occasion, the editor in chief of *Foreign Affairs*, Hamilton Fish Armstrong, reminded the Territorial Group that "the United States would not base a policy on an illegal basis."[34] The problem was gauging what was legal and what was not: the "spirit of the law," as suggested by the logic of the Monroe Doctrine in its "extensive" sense, or an interpretation derived from traditional international legal statutes, which safeguarded rights to national sovereignty and laid down the principles of succession between states in dependent properties.

Bowman had no doubts at all and defended the imposition of the Monroe Doctrine for issues involving the Western Hemisphere but accepted the norms of international law for cases that involved other areas of the globe. He did, however, candidly admit that this attitude could give rise to a double standard in U.S. foreign policy with other states. To settle the argument, Armstrong explained that he saw no point in "abandoning the standpoint of American legal interests when the United States realistic interest coincided with legal principles." The problem was how to act in the opposite case—especially in international controversies over "border areas" (conceptual or geographical) between the Western Hemisphere and the rest of the world.

As the European system began to come asunder, a process hastened by the collapse of France, the more lucid internationalists were forced to lay the foundations for a new international "order," realistically based on the military outcome of the war itself. Consequently, the guiding criteria for the emerging globalist philosophy of the United States had to be U.S. "interests," as we have seen from War and Peace Studies records of the Political and the Economic and Financial groups' work regarding the Grand Area. However, the legitimacy of the Grand Area had to be sought in (and, where possible, interwoven with) internationally sanctioned legal principles. Such an endeavor was difficult but still feasible, given the new order established by the Nazis in Europe, thus paving the way for a wholesale revision of the foundations of the international system. On the basis of these ideas (which in no way contradicted the parallel work being done by the Security and Armaments Group on the question of the Arctic islands[35]), new arguments were formulated and gradually filtered up to Cordell Hull and the president through the channels linking the Council on Foreign Relations with the State Department and the White House.[36]

The arguments of the Territorial Group were confirmed en bloc and even bolstered by the SA Group. Gen. Frank R. McCoy had frequently stressed the idea that the greatest danger to the United States came from the north rather than from the south, and that the entire set of problems to be dealt with involved first defining relations with Canada—a country under partial control of a warring European nation, situated in a continent that had made neutrality one of its sacred principles.[37] Declaring his conviction that the German occupation of Greenland and Iceland was a real possibility, McCoy stated that Newfoundland and (according to reports from Hugh R. Wilson, U.S. ambassador in Germany until 1939) the two nearby French islands, St. Pierre and Miquelon, were under threat.

Although the attitude of the Security and Armaments Group was somewhat staid and less imaginative than that of the Territorial Group, it must be said that the concepts and basic principles of both groups regarding the defense of the Western Hemisphere—which provided the main fulcrum of U.S. strategy in this period—were by and large the same. The difference, if any, lay in the SA Group's realizing the lack of military readiness and in its respecting formally the strictly "continental" character of the military's defense planning, which made military within the SA Group and the SA Group as a whole proceed with greater caution and less ambition than its civilian counterparts. However, following the traditional U.S. strategic priorities, rather than adopting an "extensive" interpretation of the Western Hemisphere, the officials of the Security and Armaments Group tried to envisage any future intervention in the Arctic islands in strictly continental terms, accurately retracing the intermediate stages of rearmament and clearing the field of residual trouble spots—such as strategic relations with Canada, which implied a variety of different ways of deploying troops and hardware—before tackling new themes such as the organization of task forces, however small, to be sent outside the perimeter of the Western Hemisphere.[38]

Washington's Influence

In any event, these texts, and particularly Memorandum T-B3, seem to have had considerable weight in steering the State Department and even Congress onto the right path.[39] The first official documents to raise the issue were (1) a pro memoria from Harley Notter to Sumner Welles dated April 9, 1940, entirely devoted to the political question of the applicability of the Monroe Doctrine to the Danish possessions in the Western Hemisphere; and (2) another pro memoria for Cordell Hull, prepared by Green Hackworth, the State Department legal consultant, on April 12, 1940, on the same subject.[40]

Also on April 12, Cordell Hull had an interview with the British ambassador in Washington during which Hull confirmed that "there is the express application of the Monroe Doctrine by this country regarding Greenland; and that there appeared to be no serious question about Greenland forming a general part of this hemisphere as contra-distinguished from the European side of the Atlantic."[41] It is difficult to ascertain whether the two War and Peace Studies memoranda were studied by the administration before the two official pro memoria were drafted, or whether it was the State Department actions that prompted the Council on Foreign Relations to embark on a deeper study of the matter.

In this respect, Notter's memorandum of April 9 is the one that most interests us here, as Hackworth's examined the issue exclusively in terms of international law. However, on closer examination, not even Notter's supported the first hypothesis,[42] for two reasons—first, it was dated April 9 (Hackworth's was dated April 12), whereas T-B3 was dated March 27 and T-B4, April 8. Second, one gets the impression that Notter skirted the issue of the fate of the Danish territories, dealing lightly with the problem of including Greenland (and Iceland) in the Western Hemisphere—a problem that was to keep the federal administration busy for a good two years. It almost seems as if Notter was writing after the German invasion of Denmark, and even after Roosevelt's decision to expand the interpretation of the Monroe Doctrine and extend the Western Hemisphere's perimeter of security and deterrence.

Cordell Hull was recorded to have told the British ambassador that Greenland was part of the Western Hemisphere. But in saying this, he was merely respecting a traditional stand, referring to the verbal note from Washington to London on June 5, 1920, which stated that "this Government was not disposed to recognize the existence in a third Government of a right to acquire the territory of Greenland, should the Danish Government desire to dispose of it, and that this Government reserved for future consideration the position which it might take in such an eventuality."[43]

Basically, it was a question of principle, rather than a real intention of expanding the U.S. strategic front toward the eastern Atlantic. But Notter boldly quoted an official from the State Department in a message to Welles on April 9, saying: "This single element of uncertainty which is believed to exist is whether the United States would desire to define the [Monroe] Doctrine as blanketing into its protection the entire area in the Atlantic which geographers include within the western hemisphere. That is a matter essentially of policy, of whether this Government desires to do so."[44] Unless he was expressing a personal view or deliberately trying to influence members of the administration on an issue that was to generate a great deal of discussion (and on which Roosevelt himself would speak, with the utmost circumspection, in the press conference of April 18, 1940, when he announced that most Americans saw Greenland as falling "within the Monroe Doctrine"[45]), we can assume that the text in question was written after the period in which the first tentative approaches were made, though not long after.

In the context of the Pan-American declaration on Panama in 1939, Greenland was referred to as part of the Western Hemisphere, but that is insufficient proof of the hypothesis of active protection on the part of the United States, as Notter implied. In fact, the decision to occupy certain areas of Greenland was not taken until a year later, with the agreement signed by the plenipotentiary minister for the Danish government, Henrik de Kauffmann, in Washington on April 9, 1941, despite requests on the part of the islanders for U.S. military presence on May 3, 1940. Actually, that agreement coincided with (1) the initiation of a program based on the Lend-Lease Act that took the form of vast convoys of merchant ships navigating offshore; (2) the decision taken in Berlin on April 25, 1941, to extend the German war zone out across the Atlantic to include Iceland's waters and the east coast of Greenland; and (3) the careful surveillance by German aircraft of the territory for possible strategic sites for constructing air bases to use in their search for British supply convoys.[46]

In the spring and summer of 1940, though Greenland had been officially considered inside the Western Hemisphere, the Americans' main concern was not so much in establishing strategic control of the island themselves as in preventing others from doing so. However, the Germans were not the only ones with designs on Greenland. The British, and the Canadians in their stead, had also shown an interest. Canada's status as a dominion of a belligerent nation to some extent undermined the coherence of the neutrality of the American republics. The anomaly of the situation virtually justified the possible German occupation of Greenland.[47]

It was not until September 7, 1940, that the U.S. president spoke on the matter. He ordered the State Department to send a message to the British and Canadian governments (sent on September 23) specifying that "we consider Greenland as a part of the Western Hemisphere, and therefore that we could not acquiesce in any operations which constituted a permanent occupation or change in the status of the territory."[48]

As for Iceland, the entire question was more complex and was handled with greater caution: U.S. claims were less tenable, and there was also less chance of a German attack there since the British had already occupied strategic points across the island.[49] When the general consul of Iceland in New York became concerned that the war between Britain and Germany would reach his country, he approached the State Department, asking whether the United States might wish to extend the

Monroe Doctrine to cover Iceland, to give the island special economic status. The U.S. authorities did not act on the suggestion, saying that in geographical terms the perimeter of the Monroe Doctrine had never been officially defined and that the matter needed further discussion. In practice, Washington's reply was a rebuttal.[50]

This official attitude was respected to the letter, although even the Germans at the time would have preferred that Iceland fall within the protection area of the Western Hemisphere rather than become an outpost for the British forces. When the British did in fact land in Iceland (May 10, 1941), the German press (including the *Deutsche Allgemeine Zeitung*) voiced the Reichsminister's position in commenting that Iceland, being far closer to Greenland than to Scotland, belonged in the Western Hemisphere, placing it squarely within the influence of the Monroe Doctrine.[51]

This lengthy series of exchanges, texts, and arguments on the fate of the islands would seem to disprove the theory that the State Department's project for integrating the islands within the U.S. security network predated the papers of the study groups of the Council on Foreign Relations, despite the implications of Notter's notes of April 9. Notter's somewhat assertive tone really only echoed earlier official positions regarding Greenland's inclusion in the Western Hemisphere. Otherwise, it would seem to show unusual levity on the part of the author with regard to issues that provoked extreme caution in the administration, issues that touched vital nerve points of the entire U.S. foreign policy, particularly the country's neutrality.

11

The War and Peace Studies and the Concept of National Security

National Interest and National Security

The analyses of the process by which Greenland and Iceland came to be included in the Western Hemisphere, and of the origins of the basic concept that defines the latter, allow us to draw some preliminary provisional conclusions. The decision to intervene in the two Arctic islands marked the first tentative foray of the internationalist circles in U.S. foreign policy outside the traditional perimeter of the American continent. This provided a test case for domestic public opinion that was in fact of much greater importance than the strategic significance of the islands themselves.[1]

The memoranda of the Council on Foreign Relations, both T-B3 and T-B4 and their respective discussion digests, stressed the political nature of the Greenland question (and subsequently that of Iceland), rather than the technical implications of the commercial and aviation requirements and opportunities, or even the more specifically strategic and military aspects. This represents a qualitative leap in the logic and policy of the concept of national security, to be adjusted according to the requirements of the ongoing war and also to the size of the country and its unexpressed power.

It had become necessary to define the conceptual and territorial boundaries of the U.S. foreign projection and security interests, and hence the active policies, for the United States to adopt in the name of national interest, in its new technical and specialized formula, that of national security. The process by which the formula of national security was distinguished from the broader concept of national interest was gradual and complex. The formula was first defined in rather generic terms in 1943, when Walter Lippmann asserted, "A nation has security when it does not have to sacrifice its legitimate interests to avoid war, and is able, if challenged, to maintain them by war."[2] But this definition reflected a deeper and more articulated understanding, based essentially on ideas developed between the mid-1930s and the U.S. entry into the war in 1941.

A retrospective study of the foreign policy of the major powers in the 1930s convinced the planners that the war could have been avoided if the British and French had not opted for a line of "appeasement" with Hitler at the Munich meeting, and if the United States had not adopted such an intransigent isolationist and neutral stance. This conviction led to a more incisive definition of national interest, which became a kind of litmus test for U.S. foreign policy. It seemed obvious that the category of "national interest" should assume a more objective political dimension tailored to the situation, a reality that each state had to acknowledge in order to identify appropriate policies for it to pursue.

It then followed that the national interest might be more effectively protected if incorporated within the security question, which was the tactic adopted during and immediately after the war.[3] In 1962, for example, Arnold Wolfers linked the two formulas to form the hybrid concept of "national security interest."[4] Although the idea was not accepted, it ably expressed the affinities among national identity, foreign policy, and strategic policy.

Coming from different environments, the members of the various study groups of the Council on Foreign Relations brought a wide range of experience and expertise to their work—but also a mixed bag of mental attitudes, cultural prejudices, and preconceived ideas. These men were the pioneers of U.S. globalism, but only insofar as they were part of an intellectually and politically homogeneous group. As individuals, however, they were largely unprepared to be the continental "parents" of a "globalist" generation. At times, faced with the utter novelty of the situation unfolding in the United States, and because of the way these people's "internationalist" outlook had taken form, it was often the least professionally prepared for the task—the nonspecialists—and the least familiar with the internal rules of the various "sectors" who intuitively came up with new hypotheses and original solutions to the prevailing issues.

This should hardly come as a surprise. The restrictions imposed by the norms and codes of conduct handed down from an uncertain past, which Lippmann unhesitatingly labeled "The Bankruptcy of American Foreign Relations (1898–1941),"[5] were a great hindrance even to the more talented experts in their attempts to conquer uncharted areas in their own fields. Consider, for example, the limited imagination of the military figures in the Security and Armaments Group with regard to strategic questions or the weak formulations of the State Department career diplomats in postwar foreign-policy planning.

The flexibility of the collective effort of the WPS groups enabled nonspecialists to enter into the highly complex analytical fields in which imagination had the winning edge over routine. It was therefore the task of these "intruders" to shake things up. They borrowed a method from the academic world, in-depth analysis by study groups, that became a widely used device for analysis during the war, and above all they generated a set of working groups in direct contact with the operational "nerves of government,"[6] composed of both scholars and people of action. As the new concept of national security was gradually formulated, this approach turned out to be particularly suitable, especially in the first two phases of U.S. neutrality (until the end of 1940).

However, the Economic and Financial Group of the CFR had a solid tradition of the study and development of the concept of interdependence. Group members could also draw on their experience with internationalism, dating from the Wilsonian era of the previous decade. In contrast, their expertise on matters of national security was much more narrow and uncertain.[7]

As mentioned above, not even the Security and Armaments Group, which was assigned the task of developing formal proposals and analyses in this area, was particularly imaginative with regard to the security issue. Instead, it tended to be distracted by partial or minor issues or dealt with general problems, but from a very traditional perspective (especially in 1940). This is obvious in the SA Group's memoranda, which were little more than summaries of the prewar debate on disarmament and arms control and which, given the war under way in Europe in 1940, seemed rather dated. Memorandum A-B2, of May 1, 1940, for instance, was a "Survey of Significant Disarmament Proposals Prior to the World War" (i.e., World War I); Memorandum A-B5, of June 1, focused on "The Problem of Control and Supervision of Arms Limitation Agreements 1919–1934"; and Memorandum A-B6, of June 28, retraced the same ground ("Areas of Agreement in the Preparatory Disarmament Commission and the General Disarmament Conference") in reaction to the hypothesis (which was a dismal failure) of a conference to be held at the end of the war.

The first SA Group text that showed any political and imaginative commitment, without backsliding into the hazy area of neutrality and disarmament policy (a leftover from U.S. officials' experience in the international arena from 1919 on), was a memorandum on "Western Hemisphere Security" dated November 25, 1940. Though somewhat later than the other groups, the SA Group finally addressed the crucial theme of continental security and promoted rearmament.

This lag was probably due to a number of factors. Some Security and Armaments Group members were in fact professional soldiers, nearly all generals in the army or admirals in the navy. They were therefore all older men, and mostly in the reserves, such as Maj. Gen. Frank R. McCoy, Adm. William F. Pratt, Adm. William H. Standley, and Maj. Gen. George W. Strong. Although each one of these figures later had a major role during the war,[8] in 1940 they were not very innovative in their reading of the geopolitical and strategic potential of the war raging in Europe. The iron rules on neutrality made the security issue the most sensitive in terms of "political dangerousness" vis-à-vis the public, which was generally unreceptive to foreign-policy issues and largely pacifist, if not isolationist.[9]

Although the Security and Armaments Group contained certain distinguished figures, many of whom were later to play leading political or administrative roles both during and after the war (such as the Dulles brothers), or who were outstanding scholars and strategy analysts (Edward M. Earle, Harold Sprout, George Fielding Eliot, and Hanson Baldwin), the group's contribution was rarely comparable to that of the Economic and Financial Group or the Territorial Group. Moreover, the SA Group was less influential than the Political Group—especially during preparations for the Dumbarton Oaks and Bretton Woods conferences.[10]

Internationalists and Territorialists

To many of the leading internationalists, geopolitics and the emphasis on territorial issues seemed a holdover from the ancien regime rather than a basis for future international relations, given the acutely "ideological" character of the war under way between the three essential concepts of the world (fascist, communist, and liberal democratic). Furthermore, the chief cause of the conflict lay in the arbitrary and violent changes of sovereignty in contested territories. Finally, ever since the turn of the century and particularly during the Wilson era, an internationalist conscience had been gradually forming in the United States. The new internationalist philosophy was decidedly opposed to the European "patrimonialist" tradition of territorial transfer, which ignored the spirit of self-determination so frequently evoked by Wilson at the Paris Peace Conference and which prospered in the "spirit" of Geneva and in the League of Nations, despite the disappointments suffered in the twenty years between the wars. In the 1940s these sentiments were still strong. The friction between the United States and Great Britain over the fate of the colonies of the European powers, including the British Empire itself,[11] was ample testimony of this.

Thus, the constitution of a Territorial Group within the War and Peace Studies project seemed to hark back to a concept of the world that had flourished during the heyday of the pre-1914 balance of power.

However, as the Territorial Group evolved, and with it the material it tended to address, the more traditional aspects of geopolitics were displaced in favor of a "realist" philosophy of international relations, as discussed by E. H. Carr in a volume that soon became the "gospel" of the U.S. internationalist lobby, together with the works of Lippmann, Morgenthau, and Wolfers.[12] The new "territorialism" embodied a latent neoexpansionist and strategic tendency that stemmed from the objectivity of the role the United States was assuming in relation to the power vacuum that war and peace had created.

One more piece of the complex jigsaw of the ideals and cultural components of U.S. internationalism fell into place. But this new territorialism differed greatly from the turn-of-the-century imperialism forwarded by Presidents Grover Cleveland, William McKinley, and Theodore Roosevelt. The expansion of U.S. power (after the defeat of the major European powers and Japan) took place in an entirely different environment. Rather than a process of leverage between spheres controlled by the Great Powers, it was a natural dissemination of U.S. power over territories affected by a power vacuum, a void no other nation (at the time, not even the Soviet Union) was in a position to fill.[13]

The new territorialist philosophy did not spurn Wilsonian idealistic legalism or universalism (and indeed the United Nations was created amid a cloud of globalist and universalist rhetoric). Instead it was injected with a new pragmatism and realism, which subsequently found an outlet in Franklin D. Roosevelt and the internationalist elites both within and outside government spheres.

Not surprisingly, some of the more active members of the Territorial Group (but also Sprout, Earle, and Baldwin in the Security and Armaments Group) were later considered the "founders" of three interactive political science disciplines, which in the postwar United States engendered a new sector of social sciences, namely, "international political economy," "international relations," and "national security studies."[14] The new disciplines were distinctly American in character and derived from the application of a business management approach[15] that mixed political and strategic theory, political economy and accounting, geopolitics and operational research, systems and armament engineering, and simulation theories. It was a fusion of distinct kinds of knowledge, already deeply rooted and internalized in the collective U.S. culture, methodically reworked during the 1930s with the influx of European intellectual émigrés.[16]

The theory of national security became a specific "science" of the bipolar international order that emerged at the close of the war.[17] Eminently American, national security has also become the theory of the Western political subsystem operating within the bipolar international environment necessarily centered on the United States. Given that this theory was the main architecture on which the modern international system was grounded, it is likely that the ideas developed by the Territorial Group, fueled by the constant commitment of its more active members (Bowman, Mosely, Cooper, Hopper, Lattimore, and especially Armstrong) during the two years of U.S. neutrality, contributed in no small measure to molding the conceptual environment in which the postwar formula of national security came into being.[18] This model could have become (as to some extent it did) the determining premise for a globalist "theory of America," founded on a provisional system of world security determined by the outcome of the war—a system that could have drawn on U.S. experience of "overseas government" conducted in Europe and Japan during and after the war.[19] Hence the model could have become the permanent structure of international relations.

Of the Security and Armaments Group members, perhaps only Major Eliot, a distinguished American of Australian origin (who was also a member of the Political Group), had enough imagination to envisage some of those possible worlds. Many other important contributors in the Political Group were from the same cultural background as Eliot and showed an innovative mind and even a willingness to experiment. Besides Armstrong, Mosely, and Lattimore (who was also in the Territorial Group), other key figures included F. P. Miller, Shotwell, J. F. Dulles, and Altschul. These outstanding thinkers and leading exponents of the Eastern Establishment provided the real "brain trust" of the communications network headed by the War and Peace Studies.[20]

This constellation of proponents commuted between the business community and the administration, "inoculating" both with the ideology of U.S. internationalism. Their activity was more far-reaching, yet less visible, than the work of the Committee to Defend America by Aiding the Allies, set up by William Allen White and continued by Clark Eichelberg.[21]

These ingredients blended different ideological and cultural outlooks— from one of economic interdependence to one of expansive nationalism founded on a special way of handling "security." The formula was taking shape.[22]

The Era of "Magic Formulas"

The first authentically revolutionary formula the WPS groups provided was to turn U.S. economic and financial supremacy into permanent political, territorial, and strategic advantage. They meant to globalize political tactics, which had so far been experimented with exclusively on home soil. Not even in the days of Theodore Roosevelt or Woodrow

Wilson had such a momentous leap in horizons been made, even though Europe in those days already considered the United States as the world's breadbasket and "arsenal of democracy."[23] The United States was beginning to awaken to an idea of a world in its own image, just as it was itself changing its image and role.

Walter Lippmann, whose two slim volumes written during the war provided an uncluttered and cogent view of U.S. foreign policy, ably interpreted the transformed intellectual climate when he claimed that "the vulnerable part of the Western Hemisphere is the Atlantic which, compared with the enormous distances of the Pacific, is a small mass of water."[24] Thus, "it was necessary for us to have control over the Atlantic to reach our Ally, Great Britain."[25] He saw the possibility of establishing "an international order only through collective agreement between fifty or more separate nations," implicitly discarding the viability of the universalist idea of Wilson and the League of Nations, and of the United Nations, in favor of garnering the nations in regional groups with a coordinated program of alliances, a premise that underpinned the concept of the Atlantic Community.

This regional view of the international system, which Lippmann shared with the internationalists within the CFR, was really a formal and diplomatic cover for a globalist theory, based on the fact that at the time, the Atlantic Community, with its colonial territories scattered throughout the globe, signaled that it would install a system of global control. At bottom, Lippmann was not just saying, "Western Europe and the two Americas constitute an indivisible strategic system of security and defense." He explicitly stated: "The Atlantic Community stretches far beyond the Pacific. The reason for this, is that the power and authority of this community of States lies in both oceans, and their prevailing form of civilization, which reaches as far as Australia and New Zealand, stems primarily from the Atlantic region itself."[26]

Rather than to gain economic advantages alone from this war—as promised by Dollar Diplomacy, and before that by Hay's Open Door Policy notes and the imperialism of Cleveland and his successors—the idea behind the national security formula, i.e., the security of the "Atlantic system" and hence of the globe as a whole, was to obtain a more far-reaching political goal that combined idealism, universalism, an economic empire, democratic influence, and strategic power and that was founded on an American model of world management. The gap that had grown between the two currents of U.S. internationalism between 1898 and the end of the 1930s (with Wilsonian idealism on the one side and J. P. Morgan's and Thomas Lamont's finance-oriented free-trade approach on the other) had led both approaches up a blind alley and hence to failure first in 1920 and then in 1929. That gap was finally being closed.

The new internationalist formula was the product of the insights provided by the more open internationalist groups of the Eastern Establishment during the twenty years between the two world wars. In 1940, this formula was ready to bear fruit in political and strategic terms. The political leverage secured by the superiority of the U.S. productive capacity, its trained work force, and its wealth of management experience and know-how became the vital framework of this new philosophy.

According to many scholars, historians, and economists of the revisionist school (political scientists included),[27] the East Coast internationalists (with Sumner Welles acting as a kind of "lord protector")[28] were motivated by reasons of strictly domestic importance, i.e., the need to bolster a stagnating economy, to galvanize investment, and to boost employment. They also hoped to keep the country free of crippling depressions like the one of 1929–1932 and to develop investment and control in foreign economies through the "multinationalization" and diffusion of the U.S. production model.

The evidence overwhelmingly suggests, however, that what guided the CFR members in their work (and that of the more aware officials in the State Department and other federal departments and agencies involved in postwar foreign-policy planning) was principally the need to avoid the pitfalls of the interwar era regarding "collective security," miscalculations that had marred interwar diplomacy. Only secondarily were they motivated to check the threat of a postwar economic crash that would upset the balance of payments and the monetary exchange system, dragging employment and profits down with it.

The conditions that made it possible to bypass both threats safely were then partly external to the U.S. domestic political system. In fact, if a homogeneous area under German control in Europe had not come about and, as a counterweight, the building up of a system of national security and economic interdependence as a weapon for fighting the coming war, it would have been far more difficult to induce the U.S. public and government to accept the idea of U.S. permanence in Europe.

Among the many scenarios drawn up in the United States during the war, there was not one international political system that resembled the bipolarity that actually emerged after the war. The issues were essentially debated among (1) those who hoped to reinstate the traditional balance of power and extend it to extra-European countries (i.e., the United States and the Soviet Union); (2) those who hoped for a "universal" system, though something better than the hapless League of Nations; and (3) those who, like Walter Lippmann and others (including President Roosevelt), imagined the world as a kind of mobile checkerboard balanced between universalism and realism, whose mechanisms would have become permanent through the continuation of the Anti-Fascist Alliance after the war's end, tempered by a system of regional zones of influence. In this system, the United States, with its enormous economic and military prowess, would necessarily have played the role of referee.[29]

No one had foreseen the bipolarization of power and the competitive logic (typical of a two-player game) that materialized in the second half of the 1940s.[30] Therefore, what guarantees were there at the time that the same ghosts and problems would not reappear as they had after World War I and at the end of the 1930s? Who could have prevented the dominance of idealist philosophy in the drafting of the Charter of the United Nations (a philosophy that was rife among those involved in this work) or the hardening of the "financial aid" line comparable to that which had brought Herbert Hoover to the foreground at the end of World War I? Had postwar aid for reconstruction not been accompanied by the security issue of Soviet competition for the occupied areas, the funds might simply have taken the form of untrammeled grants with few political ramifications for the European governments.[31]

The overly simplistic revisionist accounts of the cold war historians (Fleming, Kolko, Williams, and others)[32] suggested that if the Soviet Union had not existed it would have had to be invented in order to prevent the United States from retreating a second time from Europe. But the Soviet Union did exist and rushed to fill the void left behind by the Nazi defeat in Europe. The bipolar system came into being almost as if by chance, at least in Europe, as a result of the collision of the two globalist doctrines facing each other over the River Elbe in the spring of 1945. The circumstances precipitated the system that was crystallizing around two antagonistic and unfulfilled war aims—the liberal-democratic doctrine of the United States, a form of "supernationalism" applicable to all, and of Soviet communism, a supranational model with internationalist leanings.

And what would have been the eastern frontier of the U.S. security area—perceived by this time as a national and vital area of influence— if there had been no threat of German continental hegemony in Europe (or the equally daunting prospect of a Greater East Asia Co-Prosperity Sphere, under Japanese rule)?[33] And what would have happened without the sudden and dramatic power vacuum provoked by the fall of the Third Reich, which brought the Allies and the Soviet Union to a face-to-face confrontation—not so much over territorial claims as over the type of international order to be established?

The resulting polarization of the two positions was also catalyzed by the collapse of the "intermediate system," an event for which the United States had been preparing itself ahead of the other Great Powers, including the Soviet Union, at least since 1940. It was certainly a gradual process, virtually imperceptible even to those piloting it (as in the case of the members of the study groups of the Council on Foreign Relations and the diplomats and advisers such as Leo Pasvolsky and Harley Notter), and engendered by the critical destabilization provoked by the German successes on the western front in 1940—with repercussions that not only affected Europe but also challenged the legal and political legitimacy of the European colonial empires and their traditional areas of influence. Thus, the United States systematically took over the role of each European power and Japan, stepping in first to combat and then to aid these ailing nations, depending on the case, but always with an eye to securing greater power.

The progressive expansion of the Western Hemisphere went hand in hand with this process. It was a kind of "potential" power, and almost despite itself, for the United States, it became actual power.[34] Likewise, ever since the beginning of the century, navalism (itself a careful balance of potential and actual power) had prompted the idea of taking the mantle from Great Britain, which was utterly drained. Once France was overrun by the Nazis, Britain was under even greater threat. Navalism had also promoted the idea of the progressive acquisition of bases for patrolling an ever-increasing number of shipping routes and stretches of water. It did so first as a means of enforcing the laws of neutrality and free navigation and later to exercise fundamental strategic control.[35]

The CFR study groups put each of these options to the test, mixing different ingredients, making the impossible possible, suggesting options and scenarios, clearing the field of the remaining obsolete ideologies and cultural backwardness. Their basic contribution—of which the destiny of the two Arctic islands is a minor example—seems to have been one of piloting an elite that was still divided over domestic issues and competing interests toward a large-scale project of structural conversion of U.S. foreign policy. That policy, because of the particular combination of political and historical circumstances, became a tool for reworking the very structure of the international political system from the foundations up.

12

Conclusion:
The Pearl and the Oyster

The sudden attack on Pearl Harbor on December 7, 1941, ushered in an entirely new phase in U.S. planning for the postwar period. War became the determinant factor of politics; all theories on the future depended entirely on military developments. Victory became an absolute priority, to which all other considerations were subordinated. But the intense reflection and development of ideas of the previous months were by no means wasted. On the contrary, they became the very conceptual groundwork for the alliance policy.

"The week after the attack on Pearl Harbor, our government put forward a proposal that incorporated the preceding initiatives in favor of uniting [our] ideas and actions with the Allies, which was put into the Declaration of the United Nations. . . . The Declaration, hastily drafted by the State Department and the White House, and negotiated with the Allies, bore the date January 1, 1942." It was signed by twenty-five countries, which accepted in full the contents of the Atlantic Charter, signed the previous August by Franklin D. Roosevelt and Winston Churchill.[1] Hence the scheme for reorganizing the postwar international system entered a political phase, posited for the first time in multilateral terms and establishing a framework for permanent consultation and the strategic planning of the coming world order, which three years later would lead to the San Francisco charter and the United Nations.[2]

The means to achieve globalism and its goals had largely already been traced out by the small circle of pioneers in the Council on Foreign Relations. Now that trajectory was about to be systematically explored by the federal administration and by a plethora of other public and private organizations, which in 1942 set about examining every possible aspect of the problem.

All minds were focused on the postwar world. But in the light of the topics analyzed and proposals developed, the three years leading to

1945 were perhaps less stimulating than the previous two. The definition of the form that the new world order could (or should) assume was in fact far simpler than the earlier analyses developed in relative freedom by the pioneering thinkers operating within the CFR study groups in New York. Although the subject was treated in far greater detail, the range of options under study became smaller and smaller. War developments also greatly influenced the course that the Grand Alliance, the U.S. government, and consequently the analysts of the State Department and other agencies had to follow. The advance of the Soviets toward the west, for instance, forced the planners to revise their schemes repeatedly, while the military and political weaknesses of the Chinese in the face of the war somewhat thwarted Roosevelt's hopes of a Washington-Peking axis against any future infiltration by other powers in the Pacific.[3] Meanwhile, the Western world was gradually shifting its focus to the Atlantic, because of that special alliance between the United States and Great Britain, but the sharing of power between the two partners was as yet unclear.

In spite of the patriotic fervor and intense planning catalyzed by the country's entry into war (multiplying the centers for creating and developing initiatives), the work of the WPS groups continued—in fact, links between the CFR and the administration grew even more complex. Many members of the study groups began to commute between New York and Washington as acting members of the Advisory Committee on Post-War Foreign Policy, set up by the State Department.[4]

Planning activity in Washington followed basically the lines previously established by the CFR in New York, readjusted pragmatically to the changing needs of politics and the war. In general terms, one might say that from these studies and projects, a "model" emerged, albeit an informal one, of foreign-policy behavior. Notwithstanding the disappointments of the postwar era and the birth of the bipolar system (which at the time no one could have predicted), this model continues to provide the framework for U.S. activity in the world.

The case study on the War and Peace Studies project has also shown that the proposals contained in the CFR memoranda found a conceptual confirmation in the "mirror" theories of growth and power, which have formed a permanent base for U.S. global policies in the twentieth century. On the one hand, the CFR proposals reflected the idea-criterion of growth and hence interdependence, echoing the logic of U.S. domestic economic history since the mid-1800s. This trajectory continued into the Open Door Policy, thence to advocacy of free trade, to the New Deal and the different forms of relief, aid, loans, and sanctions, through the European Recovery Administration, the Organization for Economic Cooperation and Development (OECD), the International Monetary Fund, and the World Bank.[5]

The CFR proposals also amply reflected the idea-criterion of power, and hence national security (a cross between national interest and collective security[6]), which drew on the principle of law and order according to the rules of the U.S. political system. The principle of national security grew and spread outward, extending the area of application of the Monroe Doctrine from the Western Hemisphere toward the east, first to Greenland and Iceland, then to the Atlantic System, and finally to the foundation of a "Euro-American" security system based on the formula of "extended deterrence" heralded by NATO.[7]

During the more than fifty years since the outbreak of World War II, U.S. international "globalism" has continued to oscillate between the two integrated philosophies of interdependence and national security, as the political and operative incarnations of the notions of growth and power. But even on a purely theoretical level, the duality of U.S. foreign policy, first established in the 1940s, was prolific. Many American scholars (from Hans Morgenthau to Richard N. Cooper, Joseph Nye, Kenneth Waltz, and others) have constructed models for interpreting the international system, basing them at times on the first and at others on the second of the two theoretical pillars, interdependence or national security. But the overall debate on the theory of international relations, as interpreted by U.S. scholars, has always unfolded within the conceptual sphere of these two principles, growth/interdependence and power/national security.[8]

In a 1986 study, Richard Rosecrance attempted to determine the extent of this oscillation between growth and power. He criticized any form of single-cause explicative theory for the dynamics of international relations, whether it be from the realist school, or based on "hegemonic stability," on international "regimes," on a Marxist-Leninist analysis, or on imperialism.[9] Rosecrance concluded that only a dualistic theory is able to explain the entire range of international behavior.[10]

Rosecrance's hypothesis stemmed from the assumption that the comparison between the cost-benefit ratio of trading (i.e., from growth and interdependence in a broad sense) and the cost-benefit ratio of war is a highly influential factor in nations' choices in terms of reciprocal emphases.[11] This interpretation highlighted an essential aspect of the trade-off between the concepts of interdependence and national security, namely, their permanent reciprocal interaction. Rosecrance also stressed the nation-state as the basic decision-making unit of the international political system[12] and discarded the optimistic view of those who consider that the era of national actors is definitively over because they are about to be replaced by a universal or even merely regional modern power order.[13]

Like nearly all those who have studied the subject, Rosecrance tended to overlook the fact that the U.S. political culture underpinning the rationale of these two concepts also implicitly influenced their operational logic and method of action, making them markedly different from each other. In actual fact, they have two different histories, as the case study of the Council on Foreign Relations demonstrates. To assume that the two concepts are perfectly interchangeable is to underestimate their different historical and structural evolution. The emphasis on one or the other of the two fundamental principles is a cyclical trend that can be detected in the political guidelines of every U.S. administration since 1945. Some of these administrations tended to stress the security issue (Eisenhower, Nixon, and Reagan), others were more focused on interdependence (Kennedy, Carter), and still others wavered between the two principles (such as Truman, Johnson, and Bush), though without ever choosing to follow both simultaneously. The only authors who attempted to construct a model based on the alternation and integration of the two principles—albeit in different forms and languages—were Robert Keohane and Joseph Nye, who tried to keep the conceptual distinction between power and interdependence.[14]

Nevertheless, historical dynamics have developed these concepts and given them more definition, illustrating their limits. The association of the theory of interdependence with the U.S. economic system has, for example, multiplied the effects of trade liberalization, monetary stability, and the control of raw material prices, through the aggressive exportation of these concepts to all corners of the world after the war. As a result of this relentless campaigning, concepts such as economic nationalism, protectionism, and the neomercantilist conceptualizations of economic and trade policy became by definition negative symbols. Terms such as "autarchy" and "trade barriers" became synonymous with political and cultural backwardness. The growth of the multinational company has undoubtedly galvanized U.S. productivity, efficiency, and technology. But it has also catalyzed the competition of its leading partners in Europe and Japan, which in turn helped spread the gospel of interdependence.

The relative decline of the U.S. economy since 1945 despite the country's continued technological supremacy has also proved that interdependence was not altogether geared to serving the interests of a hegemonic or imperial power; it also stimulated the economic capacity of the more advantaged regional areas, bringing them into direct competition with the United States itself. The decline has shown that the hegemony of a bloc leader within its own subsystem is not simply a constraint to sovereignty or to the economic independence of the allied (or client) countries, but an incentive to stability and a guarantee of correct international relations.[15] Likewise, with national security, the evolution of the U.S. role proceeded in step with the dynamics of security on global level. U.S. security has gradually become the security of the entire world or at least of that part of the world that has been incorporated into its subsystem within a rapidly changing bipolar environment.

The first decisive leap forward came shortly after the war, when the disbanding of the Grand Alliance forced the Allies to find their own national or regional role, this time not necessarily within a coalition. The special relationship linking the United States with Great Britain soon showed just how precarious the equality of roles and responsibilities actually was. London was no longer able to govern its traditional area of influence, nor could it fill the vacuum left behind by Germany and Japan, not in the Balkans, the eastern Mediterranean, the Middle East, or in East Asia, or indeed in India.

From 1945 to 1947, the United States therefore took over the role of Great Britain everywhere—in Iran, Turkey, and Greece—a function that was a by-product, so to speak, of the role the United States had performed during the war, and this obliged Washington to define the perimeter of its action and policies. It was during the period between 1945 and 1950 that the debate on the U.S. global role really began, and with the debate the first institutions were set up to develop the national security bodies that continue to define U.S. security to this day.[16]

The legacy of concepts to draw on was by no means abundant. The relatively scant experience of the United States in handling international relations in distant lands led to improvisation, which was not always successful. Often, unused schemes drafted during the war were dusted off and reexamined, including the memoranda of the study groups of the Council on Foreign Relations.

The final fruit of this dramatic self-questioning was a mature doctrine of security and national interest, a doctrine that still determines the strategic hierarchy of the various regions and the forms of deterrence and defense models to be adopted.[17] National security became a means of measuring the existence not only of the United States itself but also of the entire bipolar international system, which, because of its inherent belligerent nature,[18] had to be kept under constant observation; the "regime" of nuclear deterrence had to be adjusted to the dynamics of the superpowers' technology, doctrine, and interests.

The two conceptual pillars also symbolize the way in which the U.S. domestic political philosophy (with interdependence as a mix of market rules and political checks and balances, and national security as an adjustment of the concept of law and order) was shifted out to an external political culture, i.e., translated to specific forms of foreign policy. The CFR texts exposed the links between the facts and the theories behind them, explaining (at least in part) the factors that determined the international bipolar system.

The sudden collapse of the "intermediate system" in the summer of 1940, a system that had so ineptly guided the world through the twenty years between the wars, triggered new theories on security that evolved as the dynamics of the war and postwar developments gradually increased the field of application. The security of the Western Hemisphere expanded to cover the collective security of the Allies, then of the United Nations, and then became the postwar security of Western Europe, of the Far East, of the many other decolonized zones, and of the sea-lanes. At the same time, a new meaning of power began to take shape—it came to be conceived as an extension of national security. For a global superpower, this was the equivalent of control over the entire subsystem of its bloc.

The risk and fears of another recession, the need to boost the war effort, and the need to keep both Europe and East Asia within the U.S. political and social sphere of influence resulted in a new theory of interdependence between nations, based on economic, monetary, and financial interaction. Hence the World Bank, the International Monetary Fund, the GATT (which replaced the International Trade Organization), and finally the Marshall Plan for European recovery. And so the concept of interdependence matured and effectively became the rationale of economic relations in the Atlantic-American subsystem.

The drive to curb Nazi hegemony in continental Europe required an implicit acceptance of prewar geopolitical theories of the kind advocated by Mackinder, Spykman, and Mahan, carefully combined with the rising doctrine of air power (developed by Douhet, Mitchell, and De Seversky). These would in turn serve as the basis to the later doctrines on nuclear power and deterrence.[19]

The outcome of the war and the relative failure of the scheme for a utopian, "universal" government based on international law gave impetus to the theory and practice of bipolarity, a system based on a trade-off between the U.S. policy of containment and Soviet expansionism.[20] The innate war-proneness of the "dual" international system, including the distortion caused by the presence of nuclear weapons, quickly became clear. Hence the capital importance of new strategic theories on the conduct of world affairs, which often forced adjustments in politics and even in the economy. The major change was of course the use of nuclear deterrence as a principal means of managing international politics, in peacetime as well as in moments of crisis.[21] As such, the new doctrine contrasted vividly with the traditional interaction of force and diplomacy.[22]

Paradoxically, nuclear deterrence engendered a peaceful regime within a belligerent system.[23] The oscillating pattern of conflicts and crises that had characterized the pre–atomic age[24] was supplanted by a strange stalemate that was neither peace nor war, a limbo of waiting and fear, a means of maintaining the nuclear "truce."[25] The new international political system that emerged lay utterly outside the functional schemes of world organization envisaged by the CFR study groups, whose whole working praxis was based on the idea of restoring sanity to a world gone mad. As such, they upheld that the international order should be guaranteed by a system of mutually agreed-upon interactive rules and procedures, a system founded on the reciprocal guarantee of collective security and on Ricardo's theory of comparative costs and benefits between specialized and complementary economic systems—an approach based on optimism and realism.

The partial failure of the built-in automatic or semiautomatic mechanisms of the system of collective security, and those of the economic and monetary machinery developed at Bretton Woods, in no way affected the Americans' long-standing notion of foreign policy. They thus tried to salvage its central concepts by adapting them to reality through the use of the privileged means that their role as a hegemonic power put at their disposal.

As the bipolar system established itself, the United States transformed the original concept of security into a paradigm of a two-player game, as in a duel. The concept of national security for the United States had by nature become somewhat different from that of its Allies. On the one hand, U.S. national security concentrates on the security of the minor actors under its protection, defining this security in terms of the safeguarding of their primary national interests. And yet on the other, the basic perimeter of U.S. national security is essentially established by an interactive relationship with the other bloc leader (the Soviet Union).

Hence the inherent ambivalence of a concept of security that stemmed from the combination of three contrasting factors: (1) the domestic concept of security culled straight from the tradition of U.S. politics; (2) the country's position as bloc leader ensuring the security of the Allies; and (3) the agile shifts of emphasis in the country's interplay with its main antagonist to ensure a reasonable level of reciprocal nuclear deterrence. Almost the same may be said of the automatic mechanisms of economic interdependence, which tends to buckle whenever political decisions on domestic economy are made that block the regular trade flow or when such decisions (as in 1917) overturn the monetary system.

Perhaps it was all a narcissistic illusion, one that time has pared down to size, forcing U.S. policy to come to terms with the political cultures of the rest of the world. One outcome has been the ambivalence of the U.S. relationship with the world, which seemed to justify the views of the third and fourth generation internationalists and those of the neoisolationists of the 1980s.

The metaphor of the pearl and the oyster captures that sense of duality, the mixture of "diffidence and ambition" toward the outside world that has characterized U.S. policy since World War II. Fully aware of its status as the richest nation on earth, a glistening pearl tightly set in its hard shell, the United States has often had the impression that that shell might suddenly slam shut and transform what was a protective cradle into a suffocating prison. The United States has yet to find a solution to this enduring dilemma.

Notes

Introduction

1. This apt definition comes from Mayer (1981), p. 1.

2. Cf. especially Chapter 12 of J. G. Miller (1978) on "The Supranational System," pp. 903–1024.

3. See Petitot (1977), pp. 894–954 and relevant bibliography on the structure and theory of "a-centric" organizations. This term, also found in Rosenstiehl (1979) in reference to the concept of "labyrinth," has been adopted here because it seems useful in the theoretical analysis of the international system. The use of the concept of "a networked, a-centric society," as Rosenstiehl defined it (p. 29), as with Petitot's "myopic automaton," is helpful in tracking the "diffusion of power" and the decay of the bipolar system.

4. Cf. J. G. Miller (1978). See especially "processes of matter-energy interaction" at work in the structure of the subsystems belonging to the "supranational" system (pp. 910 and 999).

5. A great many studies have been made into the notion of "misperception," combining psychological analyses with internationalistic research. See Jervis (1976) in particular and the work of Janis and Mann (1977), as well as Lebow (1981).

6. In the vast literature on war written in more recent times, works focusing on international "crises" or "near wars" have outnumbered others. These studies have occasionally produced interesting new approaches helpful to both analysts and politicians. Among the many thought-provoking works, see Snyder and Diesing (1977).

7. The "efficiency" of the international system can be measured by its ability to stabilize the ratio between conflict and cooperation and to handle the communication flows among the different actors, in each of the various regional areas. On this meshing of "conflict" and "cooperation," see Keohane (1984), who tackled the issue in terms of international political economy; see also Krasner (1982), which outlines the state of the art in organization morphology regarding the contemporary international structures.

8. For insights into the behavior of the United States in Latin America, see the chapter on events in the Dominican Republic from 1961 to 1966, written by Jerome N. Slater, in Blechman and Kaplan (1978).

9. For an overview of historical studies in Italian on the cold war, see the volume edited by Agarossi (1984). One of the most compelling accounts of World War II is by Terkel (1984). Forty years after the war, the author assembled a series of interviews with ex-combatants, with a few touches of latter-day radical

ideology; the volume testifies as to how deep the cultural heritage of the Americans still is regarding that war.

10. The concept of the "diffusion of power" is explained in more depth in Santoro (1981).

11. Besides Bobbio's well-known work (1979), see also Bonanate (1976b) and in particular his theory of the "source-war." "The inevitability of war," wrote Bonanate, "soured people's attitude toward international relations, believing their nature to lead to anarchy. But the same reasoning can lead in the opposite direction, namely, that war's task is to instill order, not anarchy, as at the end of each war it is necessary to reestablish the rules of the game or the structure of the international system that derives from the outcome of the conflict."

12. For a perspective on the various theories on international systems, see Rosenau's anthology (1969), which, though in need of revision, is still one of the most complete guides. For a more up-to-date overview of the different schools of thought on the subject, see the many texts listed in the Bibliography herein.

Chapter 1

1. George Liska's four-volume work (1977, 1978, 1980, 1982) provides an imposing and highly comprehensive summary of the elusive question of international balance and crowns a lifetime's research. In the first two volumes, which are also the most compelling, Liska compares the United States and the empires of Rome and Great Britain to pinpoint the constants inherent to the "forms" and "phases" that the international system has gone through to the present day. For a summary, see vol. 1, chap. 12 (pp. 203–217), on the "Conceptual Environment of American Foreign Policy."

2. Cf. Bobbio (1979) and Bonanate (1976b).

3. According to Robert A. Dahl, "polyarchy" signifies that the first and crucial variables to which political scientists should turn their attention are the social and not the constitutional variables; see Dahl (1950: 83). In other words, the polyarchies can be understood as relatively (though not completely) democratized regimes (Dahl 1971, 1973: 32). This formula has been adopted here regarding the international system, as the status of many national and minor actors, set in a more or less rigid checkerboard of alliance or dependence with the major powers and/or superpowers, induces behavior that is comparable to that of internal "polyarchic" regimes in Dahl's sense.

4. The concept of isolationism stems from a political and cultural debate that continued throughout the twenty-year interwar period. See the series of essays on the phenomenon of isolationism by Cole (1953, 1957, 1962, 1974, 1983). See also the two recent volumes by Dallek (1979, 1983) on Roosevelt's foreign policy, Adler (1957), a classic on U.S. isolationism between the wars, and Adler and Paterson (1970) and Tucker (1973). For more detailed information on relations between America and the world, see Gallup (1972), especially vol. 1, which summarizes the polls made between 1935 and 1948. Finally, see Doenecke (1972) for a bibliography on the issue.

5. Cf. in Holsti and Rosenau (1984) the birth and death of consensus in U.S. foreign policy between 1941 and 1968.

6. Cf. Hofstadter (1963, 1964), A. K. Weinberg (1935), Nouailhat (1980), Merk (1963), Williams (1980), Bairati (1976), Magdoff (1969), and LaFeber (1963). See also notes on method supplied in E. May's article (1983).

7. Sources included the classical works of Deutsch (1963), Aron (1962), Waltz (1979), and Jensen (1982).

8. Among others, see Knox (1980, 1982), Hildebrand (1979), and Hillgruber (1965a, 1965b).

9. See also, however, J. E. Miller (1984: 746ff.); Link (1957); and Maier (1981: 327–352).

10. Cf. Yergin (1977), Dallek (1979), Russell (1958a), and Divine (1967).

11. Cf. Notter (1949) for a synthesis of the activities of U.S. postwar foreign-policy planning from the start of the war; see also the memoranda drafted by the Council on Foreign Relations for 1942 and 1943.

12. Cf. Gaddis (1982: 3–24), for a conceptually systematic summary of this particular topic.

13. There are a number of views on this subject. Elsewhere, I have argued that the U.S. economic and productive model, which had been developing steadily until the 1929 crisis, needed a more open political and institutional framework for it to be effectively exported around the globe. It was therefore vital to establish a postwar international order that could lay open European and Asian markets to the penetration of the "culture" of mass production and consumption, which had previously found no foothold even in the more advanced countries of Western Europe. For a more in-depth analysis, see Santoro (1980).

14. Even among the papers of Harley Notter and Leo Pasvolsky (in USDD, RG-59, National Archives, Washington, D.C.), the number of postwar policy planning documents on strategic and military issues is relatively few. The same goes for the bulk of the documents of agencies working on the future order, whether governmental, academic, or private. For relative data see below. The limits to the military approach to U.S. analysis of international policy during 1940–1941 is borne out by the role of intelligence regarding Germany and Japan: See Kahn (1980: 39–41); F. Pratt (1939); and Puleston (1941); as well as Wohlstetter's classic study (1962) on Pearl Harbor.

15. For concepts related to "war systems" see Santoro (1984b). For an analysis of U.S. postwar strategic planning carried out during the war see Sherry (1977).

16. Cf. M. A. Kaplan (1957) and Liska (1977).

17. The reference is to Notter (1949) and the memoirs of the various leading figures, including Hull (1948), Sherwood (1948), and Truman (1955, 1956).

18. Cf. Jensen (1982: 231ff.) and Rosecrance (1963).

19. Cf. Notter (1949). See also Gaddis (1982).

20. In researching the material for this book, I interviewed a number of key surviving figures from the period under study. Among the more important interviews are those with J. K. Galbraith (October 1979) and with certain leading members of the CFR, such as W. Diebold (interviewed on several occasions between 1977 and 1985); important (albeit controversial) figures from the State

Department, such as Alger Hiss (October 1979); and scholars who were highly active during the war such as W. T. Fox (May 1980). Although the responses were quite varied, a basic outline of an implicit project to which all the above contributed began to emerge.

21. For a reconstruction of this, see Gaddis (1978 and 1982) and the chapter entitled "Franklin D. Roosevelt's Plans for a Postwar System of Security" in Craig and George (1983: 101ff.).

22. Cf. George (1979: 43–68).

23. For a striking comparison, see Lippmann (1943, 1944) and D. S. Blum (1984), whose fresh biography on Lippmann is second only to that of Steel (1980). The similarity and in some cases outright transposition of phrases or political formulas may be found in the records of the New York–based Council on Foreign Relations, and in certain diplomatic papers (see USDD, RG-59, "Notter File" and "Pasvolsky File," National Archives, Washington, D.C.).

24. See the literature on U.S. postwar foreign policy. Of particular interest are C. S. Campbell (1976), J. F. Campbell (1971), and Jensen (1982), the two volumes by S. Hoffmann (1968, 1978), Allison and Szanton (1976), and Bloomfield (1984: 23–39).

25. It is worth mentioning an anthology of documents (with a foreword by Michael Ledeen and Herbert Romerstein) prepared for the State Department and the Department of Defense regarding the U.S. invasion of Granada. The volume, entitled *Overview and Selection* (September 1984, Washington, D.C.: USGPO) tends to demonstrate the correctness of Washington's action and the faults of the local government. But it is interesting to note that U.S. intervention is justified on the basis of the assumption that it is the necessary consequence of the unrightful expansion of the "Soviet Empire" in Central America, a zone that traditionally belonged within the "American Empire."

26. Cf. Karnow (1983), Gelb and Betts (1979), and Holsti and Rosenau (1984).

27. Cf. Agarossi (1984) and bibliography herein.

28. Cf. Gaddis (1978, 1982).

29. In fact, the period specific to war has for some time been considered an extension of the prewar, or an anticipation of the postwar, period. Historiographical research on World War II was no exception. See, for instance, the debate on the "origins" of the war, in Robertson (1971), or the later works by Schlesinger (1967, 1979). The same can be said for the origins of World War I as discussed by Koch (1972).

30. For an account of the role played by the press and mass media during 1940–1941, see Steele (1984) and bibliography herein; see also B. C. Cohen (1963, 1979).

31. An important account of the theoretical basis of U.S. foreign policy is given in the series of studies and edited volumes by Rosenau (1961, 1967a, 1967b, 1980).

32. Cf. DePorte (1979: 115–141); Parrini (1969); Feis (1961); and F. L. Paxton (1948).

33. Texts on the subject include Yergin (1977), Clemens (1970), Sherwin (1973b), and D. F. Fleming (1969).

34. Which I shall not be dealing with here; please refer to the "revisionist" and "postrevisionist" literature on the origins of the "American Empire" by Williams (1952, 1969, 1972c, 1980), Kolko (1969), E. N. Peterson (1978), LaFeber (1963), and Van Alstyne (1944, 1952, 1965, 1970).

35. Cf. E. May (1973 and especially 1961).

36. Cf. Allison (1971) and his three models for analyzing foreign policy; see also Halperin (1974) and his "bureaucratic" model; or Waltz (1979) and his "systemic" theory; the "six models" of M. Kaplan (1957); and Deutsch (1963) and his cybernetic theory of international decision making. See also Jensen's categories (1982); Rosenau's schemes (1980); and Brecher's (1979) and Panebianco's (1977) models.

37. See writings on U.S. neutrality by Langer and Gleason (1952, 1953), Dulles and Armstrong (1935, 1939), and Beard (1940).

38. Besides Blechman and S. S. Kaplan (1978), who give a breakdown of postwar intervention, see Karnow (1983) and especially Gelb and Betts (1979); all these show the constant contradiction present in U.S. foreign policy owing to the frustration arising between the desire to intervene and the duty to intervene.

39. Cf. work edited by Krasner (1982) for an anatomy of the various "regime-archetypes"; see also P. Kennedy (1987).

40. Krasner (1982: 185).

41. Liska (1977: 32).

42. Rosenstiehl (1978).

43. Cf. Easton (1953, 1971).

44. Liska (1978: 31). This study differs greatly from those of the revisionist school of Williams, Kolko, LaFeber, and Magdoff; see also P. Kennedy (1987).

45. See Rosenstiehl's double labyrinth theory (1978: 14, fig. 9), for an effective description of the way the bipolar system works.

46. Besides the pioneering work of Carr (1939, 1946; 1978), for more on this theoretical point, see Deutsch's classic study (1953) on "nationalism" and the equally significant work of Liska (1962) on the alliances; see also the more recent volume by Gilpin (1981) on the transformations of the international system.

47. The above-mentioned study by Merk (1963) and the classic by A. K. Weinberg (1935) illustrate well the chain of ideas that led to the theory of the Manifest Destiny of the United States in the world. See also the literature on national interests, including Rosenau (1968) and Neuchterlein (1973), and the latter's conceptual separation of national, public, strategic, and private interests (pp. 6ff.).

48. A great deal has been written on this in both the U.S. and Europe. Refer to Ellwood (1982) for a definition of the concept of "growth," and to Spykman (1942, 1944) for more on the concept of "power."

49. For a breakdown of studies, see Rosenau (1980). See also Feis (1960, 1965, 1966); Gaddis (1972, 1978, 1982); Yergin (1977).

50. The reference here is to Santoro (1980) and the theory of the U.S. economic "model" exported to Europe after the war. See especially pp. 76–78 and accompanying bibliography.

51. Cf. Karp (1979), E. May (1961), Aquarone (1973), and Testi (1984).

52. Cf. Karp (1979: 13).

53. Cf. Blechman and S. S. Kaplan (1978).

54. See Ellwood's volume (1977a) for the Allied Military Government stationed in Italy from 1943 to 1947 and the work edited by Krippendorff (1981) on U.S. involvement in the reconstruction of Italy and West Germany from 1943 to 1949. See also Balfour and Mair (1956).

55. Cf. memoirs of Ortona (1984) and Louis (1978) on the origins of the notion of trusteeship in Roosevelt's politics.

56. Cf. Connery (1951), Stettinius (1944), D. M. Nelson (1946), and Boutwell (1941).

57. Refer to the analysis of Hopkins and Wallerstein (1982) on the "World System" for a more complete examination of relative theories and working methods.

58. Ibid., pp. 83 and 91.

59. Raymond Aron (1962) had sensed this cultural continuity, though his classification of international systems includes variances and factors of change that on the whole tend to negate it. Other authors have been more cautious in maintaining that the "continuity" of international systems is acquired by definition. For this view, see Liska (1962, 1977, 1978, 1980, 1982), Morgenthau (1948), and Deutsch (1968, 1978).

60. Cf. Carr (1939, 1946) and Aron (1962) and the theoreticians of the "realist" school, headed by Morgenthau (1948), Wolfers (1962), Niebuhr (1952), Kennan (1951), Strausz-Hupé (1942, 1972; 1945).

61. An in-depth study of specialist international language was made during a seminar at the Faculty of Letters and Philosophy of Bologna University in the academic year 1980–1981. The analysis of texts was based on a series of documents produced in the United Nations during the 11th Special Session devoted to global North-South negotiations, held in August-September 1980. The research was directed by Umberto Eco and myself.

62. The term "newspeak" is borrowed from George Orwell's 1984.

63. Numerous studies have been made on the expression "interdependence," particularly in economic terms. See R. N. Cooper's fundamental work (1968), Keohane and Nye (1977), and indirectly also Machlup's discussion of "integration" (1977). For a full bibliography on "interdependence" see Santoro (1984a: 126–132).

64. Cf. J. M. Blum (1976b: 6). See also Terkel (1971, 1984), Perrett (1973), and Polenberg (1968, 1972).

65. For a nearly exhaustive overview of the complexities of U.S. international relations in the first half of the 1940s, see Kennan's renowned work (1951) on U.S. diplomacy from 1900 to 1950. Ambassador Kennan, the founder of the doctrine of containment, interpreted the past in such a way as to allow a coherent interpretation of the future postwar world on an ideological and even conceptual level. For a reasoned selection of U.S. political documents from 1945–1950, see Etzold and Gaddis (1978). Another attempt at such an analysis much later than Kennan's, taking a highly different approach, is the work by Gamson and

Modigliani (1971), who attempted to test a series of theories of the cold war, and hence U.S. behavior, studying them in terms of "action-reaction" with the Soviet Union. This system of decoding the various theories, integrated with the use of events data, only directly reveals the two fundamental concepts of interdependence and national security.

66. For more on the "unification" of the various military departments completed in 1950, see Caraley (1966), who focuses on the internal conflicts (between the U.S. Navy and the War Department), the episodes of bargaining at the executive level, and the influence of the legislature and nongovernmental actors on the decisions made. The limits and history of the unification generated many problems affecting national security in the years that followed. See also Rearden's work (1984) on the creation of the Office of the Secretary of Defense, 1947–1950.

67. See the famous work by Paul Hoffmann (1951) describing how the Americans intended to "win the peace"; see also Gimbel (1976) on the origins of the Marshall Plan.

68. Cf. Offner (1969), MacDonald (1981), F. Kaplan (1983), and L. Freedman (1981).

69. For a study into the concepts and etymology of national security, national interest, international integration, international relations, international politics, and international organization, see separate entries in the *International Encyclopedia of the Social Sciences* (New York: Free Press, 1968).

70. For a list of the main official documents on postwar planning see Notter (1949), especially the list of documents on pp. vi-ix.

71. There are various publications covering the activities of the Council on Foreign Relations. See the work by Schulzinger (1984), a historian more interested in the formation of ideas and groups than in the decisions themselves, who first delved into the question in an earlier work (Schulzinger 1975) devoted to the mental processes of U.S. diplomats from 1908 to 1931. For a less mature, "revisionist" study into the same field, see Shoup and Minter (1977).

Chapter 2

1. Cf. Duroselle (1953, 1957, 1978) for a chronology of events; see also Carr (1939, 1946), and M. Kaplan (1957), for a description of the essential rules of the balance of power. An in-depth critique of the theories underlying the balance is found in Bonanate (1976b) and (1979).

2. The expression "intermediate system" refers ostensibly to the twenty years between the two world wars, which some, including Mayer (1981), have defined as an "armistice" within the "Thirty Years War of the general crisis of the 1900s," which ran from 1914 to 1945.

3. Cf. Duroselle (1960) and Feis (1950a, 1965; 1950b). See also bargaining procedures for the treaties of Washington of 1921 and 1922, in the volumes of Foreign Relations of the United States (FRUS) for the same years published by the USGPO, Washington.

4. See M. Kaplan (1957: 23).

5. The "de-Europeanization" of the international system was a hidden, ongoing process. It only became noticeable after the economic depression of 1929–1932. On this question, see Ferrell (1957, 1970; 1985); Feis (1950a); L. Gardner (1964); and Nearing and Freeman (1925, 1966).

6. Cf. Keynes's prophetic work (1919, 1971) on the *Economic Consequences of Peace.*

7. In addition to authors mentioned in previous notes, for further reading on the period 1919–1939, see W. Newman (1968); cf. Gulick (1955, 1967: 3–89), and Liska (1977) for further reading on the balance of power.

8. For more on the crucial year 1940, cf. Gulick (1955, 1967), DePorte (1979), and Collier (1979).

9. Cf. C. A. MacDonald (1981); J. V. Compton (1967, 1972).

10. The list that follows is simply a taxonomic extrapolation of ideas and hypotheses drawn from various sources over time, including the press (dailies and periodicals) and archives.

11. Cf. Offner (1969), Langer and Gleason (1952, 1953).

12. Cf. F. C. Jones (1954) on Japan, also Lebra (1979), Herzog (1973), Morley (1980); on the Soviet Union and its geopolitics see Mastny (1979) and Maiskij (1968 It. ed.), Mackinder (1942), Spykman (1942, 1944), Miller and Hill (1930); on Germany, see Speier (1941), Staley (1937), Haushofer (1932, 1933–1941), Hildebrand (1969), M. Howard (1968).

13. Cf. Shirer (1969), Speer (1969), and Santoro (1984b).

14. Cf. Borg and Okamoto (1973) and Farago (1942).

15. Cf. Divine (1967); Russell (1958a). For bibliographical sources, see Divine (1967: 316ff.), as well as Feis (1966).

16. For a breakdown of the political and diplomatic aspects see the two volumes by Langer and Gleason (1952, 1953), which despite their age are still an indispensable source. See also Dallek (1979) and Tansill (1938, 1952), Beard (1946, 1948), and A. K. Weinberg (1940), which offer source reading immediately following events. For questions of customs and social history, see Perrett (1973) and J. M. Blum (1976b); for an account of public opinion polling, see Leigh (1976) and Gallup (1972).

17. For a study of the political process leading up to the Lend-Lease Act signed by Roosevelt on March 11, 1941, with H.R. 1776, see Dallek (1979: 258ff.). The most exhaustive text is still Kimball (1969).

18. See Part 1 of Kimball (1969), Nelson (1946), and Stettinius (1944). The book by Boutwell (1941), on the defense effort under way after the European crisis in 1940, was probably commissioned by the administration and was published before war broke out. It was nonetheless prowar propaganda.

19. Cf. Deane (1947) on aid to the Soviet Union; see also Boutwell (1941) on the drive toward "total defense." See also Feis (1966); Lash (1976: 346–370); and Erickson (1975, 1983). For a nonorthodox view see Tansill (1952) and Beard (1948), the last of the progressive isolationists.

20. Cf. F. D. Roosevelt in the book edited by Gantenbein (1975: 252ff., "Message December 8, 1941, to Congress").

21. Cf. again 1941 opinion polls in Levering (1976, 1978) and Gallup (1972) for the evolution of U.S. public opinion. On relations with Nazi Germany, see

Bailey and Ryan (1979), as well as Morison (1947) and Herwig (1976) for the operations at sea. See also Gatzke (1980: 126–153) and Offner (1975: 215–245 and the bibliographical section of the Appendix). See also Compton (1967: 85–105). For relations with Japan see Borg and Okamoto (1973), as well the various volumes by Iriye (1967, 1981 in particular), as well as Ienaga (1968, 1978), Feis (1950a), Prange (1981), and Wohlstetter (1962).

22. Cf. Adler (1957), Rieselbach (1966), and Cole (1953, 1957, 1962, 1974, 1983).

23. Cf. Liska (1978: 108ff.), as well as Merk (1963), Perkins (1941, 1955), and Williams (1969).

24. Cf. Wiltz (1968) for a (now out-of-date) summary of the major works on this issue, together with the bibliographies in Paterson (1979), Dallek (1979), and Cole (1983).

25. In the first instance, see Langer's volume (1947b), written under pressure from Cordell Hull, who was accused in many quarters of not having distanced himself sooner from Pétain and therefore for having hindered the French Resistance and the Free French in London. See also Lottman's biography of Pétain (1984), as well as some documents quoted in Gun (1979); for an overview of collaborationist France, see Paxton's well-known work (1972), Churchill's memoirs (1949), vol. 4, and the first volume of de Gaulle's memoirs (1954), entitled *L'appel*. There is some interesting coverage by DePorte (1968) on Gaullist foreign policy during the war, and also vol. 1 of the best critical biography of General de Gaulle by Lacouture (1984).

26. Cf. FRUS (1941, vol. 2), as well as Leahy (1950).

27. The same attitude prevailed again during the denazification process and the Fascist purges. Cf. Bower (1981) and Higham (1983).

28. Cf. Dallek (1979: 290–292); Burns (1970) and Lash (1976), among others.

29. Cf. Erickson's two volumes (1975, 1983) on the German-Soviet war, which is the most complete summary to date.

30. Cf. Craig and George (1983).

31. See Allison (1971) for the "three models" of behavior, especially the functional rules for "rational actors," pp. 10–38.

32. It is remarkable how most of the research into U.S. foreign policy of this period has focused on analyzing the "internal" causes of American behavior and has neglected to check on the influence of "external" factors and the international context. Even Dallek (1979), who has been referred to several times, as well as Roosevelt's biographers—Burns (1970), Divine (1969), Freidel (1973), Cole (1983), Schlesinger (1957–1965), and Kimball (1973)—and Vaudagna (1981a, 1981b) all tend to underestimate the international factors that influenced presidential action.

33. Cf. A.J.P. Taylor (1961) and, for the debate it provoked, Robertson (1971).

34. Cf. A.J.P. Taylor (1961) and Hauner (1978) for the first orientation, plus the classic work by Hugh Trevor-Roper (1960) for the second. See also Robertson (1963) for an analysis of Hitler's military plans between 1933 and 1939 and Rich (1973) for his plans during the war (pp. 121–252). The controversy surrounding Taylor's (1961) thesis is equal only to that provoked by the publication

of the first volume of F. Fischer's (1961) volume on German plans during WWI (see also 1969). For a thoroughgoing analysis of the interpretative debate on responsibility during World War I, and for an analysis of the positions of Zechlin, Ritter, Joll, Jensen, and Enstein, see also Koch (1972).

35. Trevor-Roper (1960: 121–133).

36. Rich, cited in Hildebrand (1979: 219), as well as Erdman (1976).

37. Hillgruber (1965a, 1965b: 197–222).

38. Cf. again the debate on F. Fischer's 1961 and 1969 theories.

39. Cit. in Hildebrand (1970, 1973 Eng. ed.: 97).

40. P. E. Schramm (1961–1965) cited in Hildebrand (1970, 1973: 109). See also chaps. 7 and 8, pp. 183–248, in Herzstein (1982), on the proposals for a "European Charter" and a continental "confederation"; Goebbels' diaries (1977, 1982); and Speer's memoirs (1969) and his last book (1981).

41. Cf. Ciano (1946, 1948, 1980).

42. The papers of the Ministry of Foreign Affairs and the General Staff between 1939 and 1943 offer a somewhat spare documentation, which I briefly consulted only to grasp the main trends. See in particular the papers of the "Ciano Cabinet" and those of the offices and services created ad hoc during the war (such as armistice and peace, Dalmatia, France, and Greece). See also the magazine edited by Giuseppe Bottai between 1939 and 1942, with the imposing title of *Geopolitica*. This magazine attempted to outline an Italian geopolitical line based on the German model. See, in the first issue, the inauguration letter written for the occasion by General Haushofer, editor in chief of the journal *Zeitschrift für Geopolitik*. See also De Felice (1981), Bottai (1982), and Knox (1982); and bibliographies in J. Petersen (1973a, 1973b) and Pieri and Rochat (1974).

43. See again the collection of essays edited by Borg and Okamoto (1973), especially the essay by Mitani Taichioro, pp. 575–594; also Morley (1980: 13–104). For documentation on the "Greater East Asia Co-Existence Sphere," later renamed the "Greater East Asia Co-Prosperity Sphere," see Lebra (1975: 31, 71, 154, and 164). An original interpretation of the Japanese aims during the war is provided by Iriye (1981: 96–148), which seeks to explain the conflict with the United States in terms of temporary "misperceptions" that, once clarified, led to the current close relationship between the two nations. A more critical examination of U.S. behavior in East Asia can be found in the work of British historian Thorne (1972, 1978) and in W. R. Louis (1978).

44. Cf. among others, Mastny (1979) and Erickson (1975, 1983), Clemens's classic 1970 study, Yergin (1977), Ulam (1968), Kuniholm (1980), and also the memoirs of the protagonists as well as U.S. diplomatic sources, FRUS (1945–1948). The relevant literature is vast and expresses many different views.

45. Cf. Hinsley et al. (1979, vol. 1, pp. 45–88), as well as Butler (1957: 247–265).

46. Cf. Lash (1976, especially chaps. 15 and 21, pp. 271ff. and 357ff.). For colonial issues, see also W. R. Louis (1978) and Churchill's memoirs (1949); compare Gibbs's volumes (1976a, 1976b), and the other volumes of the six-volume *History of the Second World War: Grand Strategy*, published as the official

history of the conflict, by Her Majesty's Stationery Office (HMSO) in London, especially vol. 2, by Butler (1957: 341–364 and 547–588).

47. Cf. the volumes of the major biography of Churchill edited by M. Gilbert (1983, 1986).

48. Cf. Coffman (1968); E. May (1959: 371–386); D. Kennedy (1980: 197); and Keegan (1976).

49. Cf. Liddell Hart (1970) and the evolution of the Italian "War Bulletins" during the war, which denounced the rapid degeneration of the "parallel war." Cf. Ministero della Difesa (1973).

50. Sundquist (1973, 1983) has best analyzed the process of dealignment and realignment within the U.S. political system (pp. 240–269 for the transformation effected by the New Deal). In this context, the two terms are used to mean the structural modifications in the international patterns of coalitions and/or alliances that the war provoked. See also Riker (1962).

51. See again Divine (1967) as well as Chadwin (1968), Cole (1983), and Geoffrey S. Smith (1973).

52. Cf. Coffman (1968), who used this widely publicized slogan as the title of his book.

53. Cf. the classic work by E. May (1959).

54. Letter from Woodrow Wilson to Cleveland D. Hodge, dated April 4, 1917, in Woodrow Wilson's Papers, Library of Congress, Washington D.C., cited in D. Kennedy (1980: 11).

55. On the concept and the history of the "war system," see Santoro (1982, 1984b, 1984c).

56. See also Schelling (1960).

57. Using this term, Brodie (1946) was the first to refer to the atomic bomb as a weapon that could revolutionize the way war was waged. See also L. Freedman (1981) for a history of the U.S. nuclear policy in the postwar period, and F. Kaplan (1983) for a description of the social and cultural background of the first generation of American strategy analysts in the postwar period.

58. C. S. Campbell (1976).

59. Hofstadter (1956), but also Testi (1984).

60. Karp (1979) called this shift "the despotism of professional politicians upon the free men," p. 311.

61. Rieselbach (1966), Cole (1983), Adler (1957), Fish (1919), D. Friedman (1968), Hoover (1939, 1958).

62. Chadwin (1968: 39, n. 17) recalled the text of one of these messages, specifically the one published on June 10, 1940, in twenty national dailies, including the *Washington Post* and the *New York Times*.

63. In addition to Kindleberger (1973) and Adler (1965), see also Terkel (1970), Allen (1931, 1959), and Ellis (1968). The last-named, which deals with Republican foreign policy between 1921 and 1933, includes an excellent bibliography of contemporary secondary sources. See also Soule (1947).

64. See Ellis (1968).

65. Howland (1928) and Lippmann (1932). See also Osgood (1953: 309), who quoted Curti (1936) and claimed that in 1926 there were no fewer than 1,200 organizations involved with international issues, as against 120 in 1914.

66. Ware (1934).
67. Ibid., pp. 223–306.
68. Cf. Miller and Hill (1930), Streit (1938), and also G. F. Eliot (1938), Dulles and Armstrong (1935, 1939), Gelber (1938, 1961), Hill and Agar (1940), Dennis (1936), and E. J. Young (1936).
69. See also Galloway (1942) as well as the International Student Service (1942).

Chapter 3

1. Cf. Santoro (1982); also R. Gardner (1956, 1969), Gimbel (1968, 1976), and Diebold (1952, 1959).
2. The idea of a world order in which the armies of the Great Powers policed the globe was expounded by Roosevelt at the Tripartite Conference in Teheran in December 1943. The special working party set up on this occasion took the name of the "Four Policemen Group," and it comprised, besides the United States, the Soviet Union, Great Britain, and China. See Feis (1966: 269–271).
3. Cf. Huntington (1981: 15ff.).
4. D. Rosenberg (1973: 143–195).
5. Huntington (1981: 15).
6. Ibid., 21.
7. For more on this point, see Crabb (1968: 79–81). The term "bipartisanship," with all its ambiguity, originated in the war years, stemming from the necessity to avoid using current terms like "unpartisan" or "nonpartisan" because of their negative implications. According to Crabb (1968), bipartisanship suggests the desirability of positive cooperation between the major political groups on necessary programs of global impact and the understanding that some consultation between the leaders of each party is undertaken before foreign-policy decisions are made (p. 80). See also relevant literature in Santoro (1984a); note also the wave of interest among U.S. elites for erstwhile bipartisanship in Holsti and Rosenau (1984) and the White Paper in the *Washington Quarterly* (1984) entitled "Forging Bipartisanship," with contributions by R. Reagan, Z. Brzezinski, H. Kissinger, J. R. Schlesinger, and D. P. Moynihan. See also Russett and Hanson (1975).
8. Striking examples of this "natural" assonance on Atlantic issues and the contrasting dissonance of U.S. relations with the Third World are contained in the volume by R. N. Cooper (1968), which discusses the problem in Atlantic terms; see also the article by R. N. Cooper (1977), which discusses how this affects developing countries. See also Santoro's bibliography (1982).
9. Cf. Mahan (1890, 1957; 1897, 1970: 107ff.), but also the essay by W. Neumann (1952) on F. D. Roosevelt, who was a "disciple" of Captain Mahan. Mahan had spoken of an Anglo-American union back in 1894 in an article in the *North American Review*, embarking on a debate that pivoted on three chief alternative formulas: (1) a federal state; (2) a naval alliance; and (3) a defensive alliance.
10. Cf. E. J. Young (1936) and his talk of "Robust Americanism" in 1936.

11. See Santoro (1980) for his theory of "transition phase"; see also Kindleberger (1973), L. Gardner (1964).

12. Cf. Machlup (1977) and Santoro (1984a: 67ff.).

13. Santoro (1984a: 71).

14. Ibid., p. 72.

15. Cf. Rappard (1930), R. Cooper (1968), Angell (1914b, 1952), and Muir (1933), who entitled his book *The Interdependent World and Its Problems*.

16. Cf. F. D. Roosevelt (1941–1950: 406). A historical-political analysis of FDR's speech is contained in Borg (1957: 405–433).

17. Cf. E. J. Young (1936) for a more contemporary "internationalist" interpretation of Roosevelt's politics.

18. The formative years of the United Nations and the role played by the men behind it have been carefully studied by Divine (1967) and Russell (1958b).

19. Besides R. Cooper (1977), see also Caporaso (1978a, 1978b) and Rosenau (1980).

20. Cf. Keohane and Nye (1977).

21. Cf. again E. J. Young (1936) and the work of A.D.H. Kaplan (1944), who examined the technical and economic aspects of "liquidating" the armaments industries and converting their output. The book was part of a series of studies promoted by the Committee for Economic Development, whose members included Paul Hoffmann and Thomas Lamont, among the leading figures of the U.S. financial world.

22. Besides E. J. Young (1936: 356), see also Maynes, Yankelovich, and Cohen (1976).

23. Cf. Beard (1934).

24. Cf. Neuchterlein (1973: 13).

25. Rosenau (1968).

26. Cf. Neuchterlein (1973: 6–29; 1979).

27. See the two volumes by Langer and Gleason (1952, 1953) for a detailed description of government dynamics; see also Dallek (1979), Cole (1983), and Chadwin (1968).

28. Cf. Liska (1977, 1978). In the 1978 book especially, Liska examined the various phases and forms of U.S. "imperial" expansion, starting with a study of the "international determining factors," then of "domestic" and "economic" factors, to which he correctly attributes secondary importance.

29. Cf. Berkowitz and Bock (1968).

30. Cf. Neuchterlein (1973), for a hierarchical classification of the different levels of "national interest" among "Survival Interests," "Major Interests," and "Peripheral Interests," pp. 10–24; note also how the vital interests were actually determined, pp. 30–56.

31. Cf. National Security Congress (1916: 407ff.).

32. Cf. National Security League (1917).

33. Cf. Cashman (1931). The *National Security Quarterly* was published in New York from 1927 to 1932.

34. Besides Caraley (1966), see also NSC text no. 68, April 14, 1950, entitled "United States Objectives and Programs for National Security," in Etzold and

Gaddis (1978: 385–442), which sanctions the unification of military departments and the future strategic approaches of the administration.

35. Cf. National Security League (1917).

36. Cf. E. J. Young (1936: 320–345).

37. Ibid., p. 371.

38. Cf. Lippmann (1943: 121).

39. See the distinction given in the summary by Dougherty and Pfaltzgraff (1971, 1981).

40. Cf. S. Hoffmann (1978: 32–76).

41. Cf. Etzold and Gaddis (1978: 1–23).

42. Cf. once again the 1976 and 1980 surveys carried out by Holsti and Rosenau (1984) on the "belief system" of the U.S. elites regarding the pattern of power relations in East Asia.

43. For an analytical interpretation of U.S. policy in Asia see Thompson, Stanley, and Perry (1981), whose appropriately titled book, *Sentimental Imperialists*, traced Washington's political trajectory also from the point of view of the history of ideas.

44. For further details on U.S.-British relations in this area see mainly Thorne (1978) and his article (1976) on the Indochina affair during World War II.

45. For U.S. policy in China, see Barnds (1977: 196ff.); Barnet (1977: 153ff.). See also Borg (1964) and Borg and Heinrichs (1980), plus Chern (1980), Schaller (1979), Davies (1972), and an account of General Stilwell in Tuchman (1970). The most important document on U.S. relations with China is the "China White Paper." See Department of State (1949).

46. Cf. Davies (1972); Thompson, Stanley, and Perry (1981: 217, 234); and Fairbank (1948, 1979), whose work has been for decades an American classic on information on China.

47. The publication that has met with most success (on a formal level also) is the book by Brzezinski and Huntington (1964) on the "mirror-image" nature of the two superpowers. Much has been written in the United States on these aspects. See especially the collection of essays edited by Nye (1984).

48. Cf. Groh (1961), Ulam (1968, 1971), and Uldricks (1980). Fairbank's (1948, 1979) volume on China complements the work of Hough and Fainsod (1953, 1979) on the Soviet Union. Whole generations of U.S. students were brought up on these two fundamental texts. See the well-known work of Brzezinski (1960) and Brzezinski and Huntington (1964).

49. The reference here is to Etzold and Gaddis (1978).

50. On containment, Gaddis (1982) is the best overview. See also Kennan (1967), and Donovan (1977), who studied the first three years of Truman's presidency; see also the two-volume biography of Eisenhower by Ambrose (1982, 1984).

51. See especially the bibliography on national security in Larson (1973) and the one in Russett and Stepan (1973: 196–371), with over 2,500 titles.

52. Those who have written on the "narcissistic" image of U.S. culture and foreign policy include Merk (1963), Perkins (1941), Kohn (1957), Hofstadter (1963, 1964), and Huntington (1981); in particular, see Lasch (1979).

Chapter 4

1. Here I will be concentrating mainly, though not exclusively, on the gradual formation of a trans-Atlantic system of interaction. This system arose out of necessity and matured during and after the war into a permanent functional structure. I will attempt to show the historical origins, even in the terminology (see the pioneering work of Miller and Hill [1930]), of this interactive Atlantic System, which was based on an enduring political model that presumed: (1) the existence of an international bipolar system; (2) the dominant role of the United States within the Atlantic System; (3) the strategic and economic influence of the United States on the entire Western subsystem (extended deterrence, dollar standard, etc.).

2. For further reading on the asymmetry of international relations, see the bibliography in Santoro (1981) and (1982).

3. The inherent pragmatism of U.S. foreign policy during World War II is clarified in Dallek (1979, 1983), who supplied a detailed chronology of Roosevelt's policies (especially in the 1979 volume) as an expression of the domestic political system and its forms of mediation.

4. See Santoro (1980) for a breakdown of themes and projects that the economic expansion of the 1920s and the New Deal aimed to address by developing ideas that influenced the country's foreign economic policy at the start of the 1940s. See also the classic pre- and postrevisionist studies of the postwar period, including L. Gardner (1964), Hawley (1966, 1974), and Maier (1975).

5. The expression "internationalism" here is intended to mean the ideas, groups, and men who had clearly expressed and supported an outward stance on the part of the U.S. government (at least after 1931, when Japan occupied Manchuria, and more vociferously in 1935 when Italy occupied Ethiopia); the "internationalists" condemned right-wing dictatorships in Europe and Japanese militarism in East Asia, and advocated U.S. participation in the great international debate. The strength and role of these internationalist groups have been studied by Chadwin (1968), Divine (1967), G. S. Smith (1973), among others. It is nonetheless interesting to note that even during the long phase of U.S. isolationism, internationalist activity was intense.

6. Controversy over the "globality" of U.S. foreign policy is certainly not a product of the war but dates back to the 1890s; see LaFeber (1963), Aquarone (1973), Duroselle (1960), and E. May (1961). The strong emergence of U.S. globalism began during World War I but suffered a sharp reversal in 1920, at least in terms of the political and diplomatic activity of the federal administration. But there is something decidedly different about the domestic debate over the role the United States began to play at the end of the 1930s and early 1940s, in connection with the outbreak of war in Europe.

7. The decision to set up the study groups and organize the work in the form of a specific broad-based project (lasting from September 1939 to the end of 1945) was taken on September 1, 1939, during a meeting of the Council on Foreign Relations. Hamilton Fish Armstrong (director of the institute's magazine,

Foreign Affairs) and Isaiah Bowman (president of Johns Hopkins University) both participated in the meeting. The War and Peace Studies Project (WPS) was quickly defined. Twelve days later, Armstrong and Walter Mallory (another eminent leader of the CFR) went to Washington to announce their intentions to the State Department and certain members of the administration, offering to supply the various departments with the results of their work. On December 8 of that year, another meeting was held at the home of the assistant secretary of state, George S. Messersmith, to establish on what basis the WPS might collaborate with the State Department. We can therefore assume that until the Division of Special Research run by Leo Pasvolsky and Harley Notter within the State Department was set up (February 1941), the administration regularly consulted with the CFR for analytical forecasting and policy planning, as this was the only trusted organization of high-level experts operating systematically in the field. For sources, see the volume published in 1946 by the CFR describing the activities of the WPS Project: CFR (1946) and Notter (1949). Additional information came from William Diebold, who was the research secretary of the CFR study groups at the time. The division directly reflected the structure of the main WPS Groups. It was divided into four sections, on economic, political, territorial, and security issues. In 1942, contacts between the State Department, the other federal agencies, and the CFR members became even more intense. Furthermore, other members of the CFR and WPS worked in special divisions and had a leading role in the evolution of later policy decisions. These include Percy W. Bidwell and the economist Jacob Viner (both in the Economic and Financial Group), who were summoned to Washington to work on European regional issues; many others operated in specific areas, such as the OSS, in the Treasury Department. The long list of federal agencies with which CFR members were in constant contact includes the Board of Governors of the Federal Reserve, the Department of Civil Aviation, the Economic Defense Board, the Board for Economic Stability, the Federal Loan Administration, the Joint Chiefs of Staff, the Joint Economic Committee of U.S.A. and Canada, the National Power Policy Committee, the Office of Production Management, the Office of Strategic Services, the Office of War Information, and the War Production Board. The WPS groups produced a series of memoranda grouped under five categories: (1) current situation; (2) possible developments of the situation; (3) studies on the background of general and/or noncurrent problems; (4) policy papers, i.e., recommendations and proposals to the various government departments; (5) documents outlining general principles useful in the formulation of future government policy approaches. During the six years of activity, the WPS turned out a total of 682 memoranda: 172 were produced by the SA Group, 161 by the EF Group, 148 by the P Group, 128 by the T Group, 65 by the PA Group, and 8 by the Steering Committee. A total of 362 meetings were held among the groups, as follows: 51 by the SA Group, 64 by the EF Group, 52 by the P Group, 48 by the T Group, 34 by the PA Group, 10 by the Steering Committee, 2 plenary sessions and 4 intergroup meetings, as well as 96 staff meetings.

8. For more on the role played by Inquiry members, see Levin (1968: 60, 69, 82, 203). The three elements of U.S. internationalism between the wars were

(1) universalist-idealist (of Wilsonian origin); (2) economicist-monetary, or dollar diplomacy; (3) geopolitical-strategic.

9. I have collected the biographies of all WPS members, including the less prominent ones. For reasons of space these are omitted. However, the standing and level of specialization in international affairs of each one is considerable.

10. Many members who left the WPS groups entered straight into service in the administration itself to work on the war effort.

11. Cf. Notter (1949: 19). Notter's book is the most authoritative résumé of postwar foreign-policy preparation in the United States. For a detailed analysis of State Department papers on postwar planning see the Record Group 59 (RG-59), "Notter File" and "Pasvolsky File" (National Archives, Washington, D.C.). The idea of the postwar planning committees came about for various reasons, both internal (in the struggle against isolationism) and external to the country. In 1939, it was commonly assumed that the war in Europe ("phony" in 1939, the "blitz" in 1940) could not last long. This meant that the the United States had to prepare itself to deal with the resulting configuration. The first systematic studies of the State Department were on raw materials and were very similar in content and layout to the WPS work, especially that of the EF Group. On February 3, 1941, the State Department's Division of Special Research was charged with "the analysis and appraisal of developments and conditions arising out of present day disturbed international relations and requiring special study as an aid to the formulation of foreign policy" (Notter 1949: 41). The division's staff was nevertheless very small, consisting in all of eight people, including economists, diplomatic functionaries, political scientists, a young research assistant, and a typist. It was not until Pearl Harbor and the end of the year that the State Department decided to inaugurate a proper planning operation, creating the Advisory Committee on Post-War Foreign Policy, set up by Cordell Hull in December 1941. The proposed committee would include Hull himself, and Under Secretary of State Sumner Welles, Norman H. Davis (president of the CFR and the American Red Cross), Hamilton Fish Armstrong, Adolf A. Berle, Jr. (assistant secretary of state), Isaiah Bowman, Benjamin V. Cohen, Herbert Feis, Green H. Hackworth, Harry C. Hawkins (three State Department functionaries), Anne O'Jare McCormick (from the *New York Times*), and Leo Pasvolsky. This list, which was submitted to Roosevelt, was slashed to six members (Bowman, Armstrong, and McCormick, plus Taylor, Davis, and Shotwell). Thus the CFR participation on the committee became 50 percent.

12. For more on the concept of perceptions and misperceptions in international relations, see Jervis's classic volume (1976). My analyses of the perceptions of members of the CFR Study Groups are based on interviews with and letters of those members who were still alive while I was doing the research for this book, in particular, interviews with William Diebold.

13. Cf. A. C. Coolidge (1908, 1971), Miller and Hill (1930), Streit (1938).

14. Apart from the internationalists' fantasies à la Miller, there were a few fundamental politico-strategic concepts on which U.S. security had rested for decades. The Atlantic role of the United States was deeply rooted in the country's subconscious, and even more so in military and naval spheres ever since the

British fleet had been interposed between Europe and the United States. To some extent, there was a kind of negative sense of the Atlantic, which had to mutate into a positive one because the "intermediate" system was disintegrating. Washington's concern that first the French fleet, then the British, would fall into German hands is a cogent indication of U.S. Atlanticism during and after World War II.

15. Here I have accepted M. A. Kaplan's interpretation (1957) of international system models. See especially his analysis of the balance of power and its essential rules. With the fall of France in 1940, the balance collapsed, as there were no longer five essential actors to sustain it.

16. For an analysis of Nazi attitudes to the reorganization of postwar Europe, see Herzstein (1982, especially pts. 1 and 3). On Nazi war aims, inasmuch as they foreshadowed the envisaged postwar order, see Chapters 2 and 7 of this book.

17. Cf. Divine (1967), Kolko (1968), Dallek (1979, 1983), Chadwin (1968).

18. An example is Roosevelt's official position on Greenland in spring 1940, as will be shown later.

19. Consensus diplomacy has been analyzed in depth by S. Hoffmann (1978). It is sometimes also referred to as "bipartisan policy." See also Santoro (1984a) on this point. The final disintegration of U.S. bipartisanship over foreign policy came with the Indochina war. In the 1980s there have been attempts at patching up the consensus. See contribution by specialists in the ad hoc paper produced by the *Washington Quarterly* (1984).

20. On the links between government and the academic world, see F. Kaplan's fine work (1983), which analyzes the formation of the groups that created the U.S. doctrine of nuclear strategy from 1945 through the 1960s. See also Isaacson and Thomas (1986). Some of the academics, including Bernard Brodie and William T.R. Fox, were members of the Institute of International Studies of Yale University, which began to produce papers on postwar planning in 1942 (p. 19ff.). In his interview with me, Fox stressed the important contribution made by these intellectuals in the formation of U.S. global policy (interview conducted on October 29, 1979).

21. By "new internationalism" I mean the new mixture of various tendencies that had arisen in the field of U.S. foreign policy, whether idealistic (Wilsonian), economy-based (dollar diplomacy), or geopolitical-imperial.

22. Cf. R. Gardner (1956, 1969).

23. Cf. Russell (1958b), E. May (1959, 1968).

24. Cf. L. Gardner (1964) and Aldcroft (1977) on the state of the international economy in the 1920s.

25. Cf. Kindleberger (1973) on U.S.-European relations in the 1930s.

26. Cf. Santoro (1980) on the exportation of the U.S. economic model to Europe in the 1920s.

27. The idea that globalist foreign policy was used deliberately to Americanize the European production model is hard to prove. Nonetheless, the process of Americanization, which began during World War I (though only in certain productive and social areas), became universal after the war and is still going on. However, this is a different topic and needs investigating elsewhere.

28. Cf. Weil (1978) and Schulzinger (1975).

29. Cf. Kennan (1951), Hans Morgenthau (1948), Wolfers (1962), Lippmann (1943), Strausz-Hupé (1945), Niebuhr (1947, 1953).

30. For a lengthier discussion, see Vaudagna (1981b) and Santoro (1984a: 15–66).

31. It is certainly odd that one of the more "qualified" WPS groups should have two chairmen whose ideas were so irreconcilable (at least at the academic level). But apart from the differences between their two schools of thought, the joint presence of Hansen and Viner amply covered the requirements of all aspects of international economic policy (in which Viner was expert) and the problems of reconstruction and planning of the domestic economic systems (of which Hansen had extensive knowledge and experience).

32. For more in this topic, see Chapter 8, on the extension of the Western Hemisphere.

33. Cf. the series of volumes covering Versailles in FRUS (1919) for a reading of the official U.S. position.

34. I gleaned the information about the orientation of the T Group from various written and oral sources, in particular, my interviews with William Diebold.

35. Memoranda: E-B10, "The Postwar Trade Role of the United States" (April 15, 1940); E-B11, "International Influences on Imports of the United States" (April 15, 1940); E-B12, "A Pan American Trade Bloc" (May 27, 1940); E-B13, "The Balance of Payments Position of the United States" (June 3, 1940); and E-B14, "Economic Aspects of United States Interests in the War and the Peace" (June 7, 1940).

36. Memoranda: E-B56 "American Interests in the Economic Unification of Europe with Respect to Trade Barriers" (September 14, 1942); E-B61, "The Anachronism of Lend-Lease" (December 15, 1942); and E-B67, "Business Requirements with Respect to Postwar Foreign Trade in Relation to Proposed International Organizations" (April 1, 1944).

37. On the two tendencies of Roosevelt's foreign policy, see Yergin (1977) and Cole (1983); for the background to the Truman administration, refer to Gaddis (1972, 1974) and in particular his book on the strategy of containment, Gaddis (1982).

38. The title of Memorandum T-B55 of October 26, 1942, was "Russia and an East European Federation"; see also the memoranda on Greenland and Iceland of spring 1940, discussed in Chapter 10.

39. Not even Dallek (1979), who closely analyzed all aspects of Roosevelt's foreign policy from the point of view of the internal bargaining between the executive and the legislative branches, has delved into this corner and reconstructed the conceptual trajectory of those involved.

40. For a highly detailed account of the Allied debate over the fate of occupied countries, refer to Ellwood (1977). The first list of permanent bases to be kept ready (even after the war) is in Memorandum A-B80 of February 12, 1943, entitled "Strategic Bases for the United Nations." After the war, the network of bases served as a preliminary skeleton of future U.S. bases throughout the world.

41. Cf. Memoranda A10 (later EN-A10) of December 15, 1941, "Italian Peace Aims," and P-C3 of February 11, 1941, "Germany's War Aims." Though Memorandum P-C3 is not the work of the PA Group, it belongs to a special category of the P Group's output, as Germany was not in fact among the European countries included in the Peace Aims series. The pattern of the first part is the same in both documents, however, as they were not developed by the CFR members alone but included the contribution of a foreign reporter. The two memoranda in question are emblematic of the same type of analysis and of certain interpretative limitations.

42. For a detailed examination, see the PA Group memoranda drafted between June 2, 1941 (A1) and May 14, 1942 (EN-A16). During these twelve months, the group analyzed the peace aims of the following countries: Poland, Czechoslovakia, Norway, Austria, Yugoslavia, Romania, Hungary, the Baltic countries, Italy, France, Greece, Denmark, and Belgium.

43. For more on the parallels between U.S. policy toward Latin America and U.S. policy toward Europe during and after the war, see Chapter 8, on the growth of the Western Hemisphere, and relevant bibliographical material.

44. Memorandum E-A17 of September 1, 1942, "Digest of Preliminary Views Regarding the Peace Aims of European Nations" (a revision of Memorandum A9 of December 15, 1941), which summarizes a year of the PA Group's meetings and categorizes the topics discussed under major headings: (1) Political and territorial international collaboration: It was necessary to understand the attitudes of the various foreign rapporteurs on the role of the United States and Great Britain and the prospects of building an international organization of universal application (the United Nations); (2) Regional agreements: The various opinions on the solutions for particularly disturbed areas and zones were sought; in the case of the Balkans in particular, the opinions of the rapporteurs differed greatly; (3) Attitudes toward belligerent countries or potential belligerents: A compendium of the thorny questions of postwar order with the defeated countries and the problems of transition from war to peace was collected; (4) Reestablishment of the sovereignty of European nations: This subject was only apparently free of contradictions (i.e., "the sovereignty of all occupied countries will be restored"). As it turned out, the issues created a tangled mesh, which, in some cases, not even forceful decisions managed to unravel; (5) Foreigners' opinions on the hypothesis of future international economic cooperation: Given the complete imbalance of effective power, opinion was basically unanimous.

45. Cf. Memoranda: P-C3 of February 11, 1941, "Germany's War Aims," and EN-A10 of December 15, 1941, "Italian Peace Aims." The question of war aims is dealt with in more detail in the first few chapters of this book. Here I should just point out that the East Coast establishment and the more aware public (nonisolationist) had understood the German war aims, even before the United States entered the war.

46. Cf. two volumes issued later, in early 1942, which typify the kind of political and propagandistic framework that was imposed on the public at the war's start. The first was an anthology of texts culled from German journalism of the period, edited by Ladislas Farago (1942), with the collaboration of a

group of intellectuals and experts of various origin, including George Fielding Eliot (Major Eliot of the SA Group of the WPS), Robert Strausz-Hupé, Kimball Young, and even the Brechtian composer Kurt Weill. The second was a volume written by Derwent Whittlesey (1942), which illustrated the Nazi strategy for world conquest, based on the continuity between Hitler's objectives and those of the Kaiser before him.

47. Cf. the famous work by Hughes (1975) on the immigration of European intellectuals to the United States and their role in the analysis of contemporary society from 1930 to 1965.

48. See the books of Fraenkel (1941, 1974) and F. Neumann (1942) on Nazi totalitarianism. Neumann's work came out during the war, but the intellectual climate it reflected could already be detected in some sections of Memorandum P-C3.

49. Cf. Migone (1980), Prothro (1954), and E. W. Bennet (1962), and many other works on U.S. economic diplomacy between the wars.

50. For an in-depth and controversial analysis of the forms taken by the politico-economic-institutional system in Europe during the 1920s, see Maier (1975).

51. Cf. Memorandum P-C3, p. 2, no. 8.

Chapter 5

1. The implicit corollary to this second structural innovation was the fact that the double line of defense of the United States—which was based on (1) keeping a foothold in France and thereby securing a potential bridgehead for the American Expeditionary force and (2) the protection of the United States in the Atlantic Ocean by the British Royal Navy—had been considerably reduced, and even the screen provided by the British Merchant Marine was now under threat by the events of the war.

2. There is no lack of literature available on the German "new order" in Europe. Particularly notable works are Milward (1977) on the economies of the major powers involved in World War II, the fruit of research undertaken by this distinguished academic since the mid-1960s. See also Freymond (1974) on the economic reorganization of German Europe in the first years of the occupation (1940–1942). On the main points of Hitler's strategy from 1940 to 1941, see Hillgruber (1965a, 1982; 1965b, 1977), Rich (1973), and Hildebrand (1970).

3. For the early years of the German economy see Eichholz (1969, vol. 1). A good outline of *Grossraumwirtschaft* is provided in Daitz (1938). The conceptual link between the German economic area and plans for European unification under national socialism is examined by Herzstein (1982), who looked specifically at the issue of the different interpretations given by the leading Nazi figures, such as Rosenberg, Himmler, Goebbels, and Von Ribbentrop, to the concept of the "new order" in Europe.

4. A general synopsis of the evolution of the decision-making processes, political bargaining with Congress, as well as increasing support for the economic mobilization of the country in view of the imminent war is to be found in

Dallek (1979). See chaps. 9, 10, and 11 in particular. Another interesting source is D. M. Nelson (1946). Nelson, as chairman of the War Production Board, was one of those responsible for the rearmament and for the mobilization that took place between 1940 and 1944. For a detailed analysis of the economic mobilization of the army and the navy, see R. E. Smith (1959); see also R. H. Connery's (1951) volume in the same series. The official version of the history of aid given to the allies and to Great Britain in the first instance is found in Stettinius (1944). In this book, which was written while the war was under way, Under Secretary of State Stettinius (the future secretary of state), who had handled the Lend-Lease Act between the U.S. and Great Britain in 1941, gave a highly propagandistic, but detailed, account of the act and the way it operated during the war. See W. F. Kimball (1969) on the same subject. Historical perspective did not prevent the author from sometimes framing his interpretations according to the canons of the revisionist school.

5. Despite the difficult times, the future order of the world was high on the British agenda also. On reforms in the international economy (trade, tariffs, and monetary policy), for example, see vol. 25 of the *Collected Writings of John Maynard Keynes* (Keynes 1980a), especially the first chapter, which includes all the documentation relating to "The Origins of the 'Clearing Union,'" pp. 1–144.

6. Cf. Schacht (1966) and Fest (1973).

7. Cf. Milward (1965).

8. Cf. Speer (1969).

9. See Part 3 in the volume by Gibbs (1976) in the series *History of the Second World War* (that volume gives the official British publication on the politics of rearmament), on the increased momentum in British rearmament after Munich. See also Butler (1957), in the same series, which looks at British armaments expansion and the control machinery necessary for their development in the period from September 1939 to June 1941.

10. Cf. Calvocoressi and Wint (1972).

11. Cf. Speer (1969: 312).

12. Cf. Milward (1965: 58).

13. Cf. Kindleberger (1973: 211ff.) and Kindleberger (1978: 114–122).

14. Cf. Keynes (1980a: 1–5).

15. Memo E-B12 of May 27, 1940 ("A Pan-American Trade Bloc") looked at the various possible options for increasing commercial and economic interdependence with Latin America, using the Germanic Europe idea as the yardstick for comparison. Memo E-B12 was followed (July 15 and 26, 1940) by two analytical supplements, which quantified the different possibilities in statistical terms. See Supplement 1, "A Study of Bloc Combinations Varying According to Importance of Economic and Defense Problems," and Supplement 2, "Position of the Western Hemisphere as a Supplier of European Imports of Specified Commodities."

16. The discussion digests of the EF Group meetings are particularly illuminating on the different positions taken by the members. These are archived in sequence according to the date, with the letters E-A.

17. As we shall see, Memorandum P-B13 contained the P Group's examination of proposals put forward by the EF Group in E-B19 ("Needs of Future United States Foreign Policy").

18. Facts would shatter this illusion. On the less than brilliant performance of the German economic sphere, see Milward (1965; 1977: 153–168) and Michel (1968, vol. 1, pp. 181–200). For the French situation in occupied Europe, see Sauvy (1978); for the Soviet Union, see Erickson's two volumes (1975, 1983).

19. See in particular C. Higham (1983) on the economic and financial relations with Germany of some of the managerial and administrative elite, including during the war.

20. Cf. Russell (1958a, 1958b) and Yergin (1977, passim).

21. A number of other historians who examined U.S.-Japanese relations during the years before Pearl Harbor also shared this opinion. See Herzog (1973) on the role of the U.S. Navy in closing the "Open Door" toward the Pacific, or Iriye (1981), who contradicted other traditional historical interpretations, suggesting that U.S.-Japan positions were not irreconcilable either before or during the conflict.

22. See again Santoro (1980), which discussed the fact that structural reasons, dictated by the quality of production and consumer patterns within the United States, made it impossible for the U.S. economic model to be exported to Europe at the war's end.

23. Cf. Memoranda P-B5 and P-B7, dated May 17, 1940, and September 12, 1940, respectively, entitled "American Attitudes Toward the War and the Peace," and "Survey of American Attitudes Toward the War and Its Relation to the United States."

24. Cf. Memo E-B10 of April 15, 1940, entitled "The Post-War Trade Role of the United States."

25. This was a set of six memoranda approved by the EF Group between March 1 and April 15, 1940, each focused on a specific issue. Memorandum E-B4 dealt with "Trade Dislocation and Economic Effects"; E-B5 talked about "Price Fixing by Belligerents"; E-B6, "Exchange Control: Structure and Mechanism"; E-B7, "Wartime Exchange Control"; E-B8, "Rationing"; and finally, E-B9 drew the first conclusions on "The Impact of War: Summary and Interpretation."

26. Cf. Notter (1949: 23).

27. Ibid., p. 24.

28. Cf. Notter (1949: 30) and S.J. Resolution no. 271, H.J. Resolution no. 556, 76th Congress, 3rd Session. The resolutions were not in fact harmonized until April 10, 1941. See Public Law 32, 55 Stat. 33.

29. Cf. T-B3 of March 17, 1940, and T-B4 of April 1, 1940. For a detailed analysis of these texts, see Chapters 10, 11, and 12.

30. On that occasion, President Roosevelt said, "We of this hemisphere have no need to seek a new International order; we have already found it." See F. D. Roosevelt (1941–1950, vol. 9, pp. 161–162), also cited in Langer and Gleason (1952, vol. 1, p. 435, n. 74). On this point see Chapter 8.

31. The first Political Group memoranda, which went over the issues already discussed by the Economic and Financial Group, confirmed this implicit "hi-

erarchy" in the influence of the various study groups. See especially P-B2 of July 11, 1940, "American and British Press Opinion of an Earlier Attempt (1931) to Set Up an Economic Bloc in Europe"; P-B8 of October 5, 1940, "An Examination of Western Hemisphere Affinities"; and P-B13, a more complex document discussed in greater detail later in this chapter.

32. See also Memoranda T-B3, T-B4, and T-B5 (April 18, 1940), "Treaty Basis of United States Rights with Respect to Mandates Territories."

33. Cf. E-B12 of May 27, 1940, "A Pan-American Trade Bloc," and especially its two supplements, "A Study of Bloc Combinations Varying According to Importance of Economic and Defense Problems" (July 15, 1940) and "Position of the Western Hemisphere as a Supplier of European Imports of Specified Commodities" (July 26, 1940).

34. Memo T-B11 of May 28, 1940.

35. Ibid., p. 3.

36. Memo P-B8 (Final) of October 5, 1940.

37. Ibid., pp. 4–5.

38. This series of memos starts with E-B16, dated June 20, 1940, and ends with E-B36 of June 22, 1941.

39. E-B16.

40. For this definition, see also memo P-B19 of May 16, 1941, which was explicitly entitled, "The Island of Great Britain as a Factor in the Strategy of American Defense."

41. Cf. Gallup (1972, vol. 1); Levering (1978: 65–91); Leigh (1976: 172), for a list of sources.

42. Despite the efforts of the "White Committees" and the Committee to Defend America by Aiding the Allies (see Chadwin [1968]), public opinion was firmly opposed to a U.S. entry into the war. For an in-depth analysis of the more systematic findings, see again Gallup (1972: 226–231) and Cantril and Strunk (1951) on the methods and results of the surveys carried out during the Roosevelt era as reported by one of the president's closest aides in the field of information.

43. Cf. Gallup (1972: 224, 252, 276, and 282). When at the end of April 1941, Gallup asked whether the United States would go to war, 13 percent of the respondents said, "We are already at war!"

44. The long preparatory phase of the Atlantic Charter and the Lend-Lease Act of March 1941, which preceded the Placentia Bay meeting in August, was minutely described in Russell (1958b) and in Kimball (1969).

45. For a detailed analysis of the "Allied Military Governments," and those referring to Italy in particular, see Ellwood (1977: 47).

46. Cf. E-B16, p. 7.

47. Ibid., p. 21.

48. The reduction in the number of essential actors, which was a foregone conclusion in this new version of the international system, increased the complexity of the inner workings of bipolarity, whose range of interactions could have escalated inordinately in relation to the increase in differentiation levels. Schelling (1960, 1966) and Waltz (1964, 1979) recognized that a bipolar system could

lead to the creation of a communications system that combined cooperation and conflict. This idea was extensively developed in the postwar decades, especially by researchers into interdependence.

49. The peripheral position attributed to the Soviet Union and Japan in relation to the international system based on "Western" power groups (including Germany) was not just due to the different cultural orientation of the U.S. establishment of the time; it also reflected the marginal involvement of these two countries in international economics from the beginning of the 1940s on. See Langer and Gleason (1952, vol. 1) and Tansill (1952: 616–645); see also the essays collected by Borg and Okamoto (1973) and Morley (1980).

50. The possibility of a Russo-German conflict was mentioned in memo T-B21 of October 28, 1940, "Significance for American Policy of Soviet Technique of Expansion." Another interesting memorandum, T-B22, of December 9, 1940, "Alternatives of American Policy Toward Russia," offered a summary of the discussions of the T Group of the CFR on U.S. foreign-policy options toward East Asia. The document effectively put forward two options, that the U.S. could either make the Soviet Union the departure point for the start of negotiations with China and Japan, or make China the departure point for negotiations with the Soviet Union (pp. 4–5).

51. American distrust of any kind of institutional link with other countries is well known. For an analysis of the ways this idea developed, particularly of the concepts that led to the analytical category of "interdependence," see Santoro (1982), Machlup (1977) and Cooper (1968).

52. Cf. Streit (1938).

53. Cf. E-B16, p. 9.

54. On the question of "imperial preferences" and the covert competition between the United States and Great Britain for markets, see W. R. Louis (1978) and Thorne (1978), especially in regard to Anglo-American interaction in the Far East during the war years.

55. In 1940, this figure had dropped to 8,200,000 as a result of the preliminary mobilization of resources and the effect of substituting imported goods (especially from Germany and the commonwealth countries) for domestic products. This was still 14.6 percent of the overall work force, however, and accounted for 21.3 percent of workers in the industrial and services sectors. See the Department of Commerce (1976, vol. 1, pp. 126–127, tables D, 1–10).

56. Cf. Memo E-B16, p. 10.

57. In June 1940, when Wallace was still secretary of agriculture, the idea of an economic and commercial union within the Western Hemisphere had been opposed by the farmers' interest groups, which feared dumping of surpluses by Latin American farmers. One of the more interesting proposals was put forward by Wallace's assistant Milo Perkins who, in the course of a meeting at the White House with Hull, Morgenthau, Harry Hopkins, and the president himself, suggested a scheme for centralized control over purchasing and sales for agricultural products throughout North and South America, which would have a special payments system. See documents on American Foreign Relations (1940, vol. 2, p. 163), cited also in Langer and Gleason (1952, vol. 1, p. 634, n. 68).

58. Cf. Memoranda E-B10 to E-B15.

59. This approach is, in some ways, a remarkable conceptual leap compared to the way documents were usually produced by the State Department. See the first internal documents of the Interdepartmental Group and especially the two reports, dated June 15 and July 2, 1940, relating to the proposals for the Economic Plan for the Western Hemisphere, also in Notter (1949: 32–33).

60. Cf. Memorandum E-B16, p. 19.

61. The memoranda analyzing the different possible scenarios are E-B17 of June 28, 1940, "The Resources of Germany and the United States. A Comparison Between a German-dominated Europe Including the Mediterranean Basin and the United States Including the Western Hemisphere: Minerals"; E-B18 of August 1, 1940, "The Future Position of Germany and the United States in World Trade: Introduction," with its three supplements, "Foreign Trade Needs of a German-dominated Europe," of September 6; "A Western Hemisphere–Pacific Area Economic Bloc," dated August 15; "Foreign Trade Position of Europe in Crude Materials and Foodstuffs," of October 30; and especially E-B19, of September 16, 1940, "The War and United States Foreign Policy: Needs of Future United States Foreign Policy," of October 9, 1940, with its supplement ("A Comparison of the Trade Position of German-dominated Europe and a Western Hemisphere–British Empire–Far East Trade Bloc," of September 16, 1940). The series of memoranda from E-B21 to E-B27 largely covered the same subjects, examining the areas and subareas individually on a more detailed basis.

62. Scenarios on coexistence with a Nazi economy were being weighed in official quarters as well, however. See Notter (1949: 28ff.).

63. The concept of "power" as "currency" in international politics was developed by Deutsch (1968, 1978). The process of "exchange" of politics is Talcott Parsons's idea.

64. Cf. Bailey and Ryan (1979, passim).

65. See first Beard's outstanding volume (1934) and then Beard (1948), which was highly critical of Roosevelt's attitude, leading the way for many revisionist reappraisals of the period. For a more recent interpretation that differed from both the usual orthodox and the revisionist lines, see Iriye (1981). Borg and Okamoto's collection of essays (1973), which took a close look at the approach to war both on the Japanese and the U.S. sides from 1931 to 1941, offered some interesting insights. Prange's major work (1981) confirmed mainstream viewpoints.

66. Cf. Memorandum P-B15 of December 18, 1940, "How Is Japan Likely to React to Economic Sanctions by the United States?" See especially the differences of opinion between the clearly pro-Chinese majority and the cautiously pro-Japanese minority, which favored moderation in initiatives or in reprisals against Tokyo. The predominance of the pro-Chinese faction was a foregone conclusion given the influence of the China Lobby and Roosevelt's overt sympathy for the Kuomintang party. See Koen (1974) on the importance of the China Lobby in U.S. politics.

67. For an examination of the complex international political situation in East Asia in the crucial period 1931–1933, see Thorne (1972).

68. Cf. Williams (1959) and E. May (1961).

69. The WPS groups were also closely involved with this issue, especially the Territorial Group. See again Memoranda T-B21 and T-B22.

70. All those interviewed, including the members of the WPS, have confirmed this observation on the prevailing mood at the time.

71. Cf. bibliography in Santoro (1980) and Rostow (1978).

72. Cf. Petzina (1968) on the politics of the autarchy in the Third Reich and in Germanic Europe; see also Pentzlin (1980) on Schacht's overseas trade policies.

73. Cf. Kolko (1968), Kolko and Kolko (1972), Louis (1978).

74. Cf. Thorne (1978) and R. Gardner (1956, 1969).

75. Cf. Notter (1949: 35).

76. Memorandum E-B19 is so important that I feel it relevant to quote a sizable extract: "Certain striking changes in the direction and nature of the national interests of the United States have taken place since the turn of the century and, more particularly, since the end of the World War in 1918. The resulting situation has not been adequately appraised in the determination of the present nature of our national interests. For example, even today the effects of greater urbanization and the occupational changes in the United States are not always realized. Most of the problems of agriculture of the last two decades are commonly attributed to the great stimulus and resulting expansion it derived from the last wartime period. Yet had there been no war, agriculture probably would have been depressed, relative to other lines. This follows from the fact that a combination of two factors—increased urbanization and enlarged standard of life—have adversely affected the relative position of our own agriculture. This can be illustrated by the situation in the two important products of wheat and pork. In the case of wheat, the per capita consumption has declined by about one-third since the 1890s. This decline is largely the result of increased urbanization because the dietary need of the urbanized population for bread is very substantially less than the need of a more rural population following agricultural and outdoor pursuits. The same situation exists in the case of hog-farming reflected by the great decrease of production of the lard-sized hog. Here again (especially in the obvious case of salt pork) per capita consumption has substantially declined as is also the case for all the other meats. Not only does increased urbanization profoundly affect the relative position of agriculture but increased productivity or enlarged income has the same effect. With higher income there is an introduction of variety into diet. This variety is secured largely through the use of semi-tropical and tropical fruits and foodstuffs—different and new products—rather than through an increased consumption of products of our own agriculture. It must be pointed out, however, that the problems of agriculture were relieved by the transference of labor from the farm to the factory, but this again only emphasizes the non-agricultural nature of such prosperity as we enjoyed in the 1920s.

"At the time that these changes have taken place, certain other changes have tended relatively to improve the position of the non-agricultural industries. Had it not been for the last wartime agricultural expansion, these changes would have gone far to ease the shock of readjustment by agriculture. The changes include the tremendous advance in our mechanized and mass-production industries, particularly the increased production of machinery of all kinds. This machinery was markedly stimulated in the years from 1914 to 1918. The pressing needs of our own war effort in 1917–18 served also to provide the necessary environment for a subsequent rapid growth of mechanical industries. Is this a growth that can attract surplus labor away from agriculture? A counterpart in agriculture has been its mechanization and the resulting economy of labor and land (i.e., the substitution of oil for oats as a source of power).

"As a result of these changes, the international or rather, the foreign trade interests, of the United States have undergone marked "directional" and "qualitative" changes.

"In the period prior to the last war, and more certainly prior to the turn of the century, the United States' foreign interests were focused almost wholly upon Europe. Export production for sale to Europe was then far more heavily agricultural. Finance and investment were conducted almost wholly with Europe and our debtor position was then represented by obligations owing to Europe. Enlarged productivity at home, represented largely by mechanical goods (or at least products of mass production), brought increased income that in turn resulted in a rapid increase of food imports from tropical and semi-tropical areas. The development of machinery products for export also resulted in a dependence upon non-European markets, primarily in areas that were even more recently developed than our own. Furthermore, the development of these new industries created a huge demand for industrial raw materials—again largely from the non-European areas of the Western Hemisphere and Southeastern Asia. Production of them was greatly facilitated by the tremendous export of machinery and related products to these areas.

"All this is reflected in the striking changes in the commodities that are now most important in the export and import trade of the United States. In the first two decades of the present century, the leading exports almost uniformly were cotton, wheat and meat, in the order named. The great changes since then are reflected by the fact that in 1938 cotton was in fourth, wheat in eighth, and meat in fifteenth place. The leading exports now are machinery, petroleum, automobiles, iron and steel mill products, chemicals, and copper. In fact the only maintained agricultural export is tobacco and the only increased agricultural export is fruit and nuts. In the case of imports today, the leading commodities are coffee, sugar, rubber, and silk, none of which is imported from Europe. In the final quarter of the last century, coffee and sugar were important, but cotton manufactures and wool manufactures were almost equally so. These last two areas are products of European industry.

"In 1938, however, cotton manufactures ranked seventeenth in our imports and wool manufactures twenty-ninth. Were it not for the import importance of Europe to us we would have declined even more sharply.

"Since the first five years of the present century, the average amount of our exports to Asia and Oceania have increased fifteen times as fast as our exports to Europe; exports to the Western Hemisphere have increased ten times as fast. In the case of our imports, those from Asia and Oceania have increased eight times as fast as those from Europe and those from the Western Hemisphere have increased ten times as fast. These comparisons are striking evidence of the great advance in trade importance to us of the rest of the Western Hemisphere and of Asia, and of our diminishing dependence upon Europe. From the point of view of the Western Hemisphere as a whole, the competitive production of Australia and New Zealand accounts for some of our difficulties and for the difficulties of integration, economically, with those areas."

77. Cf. E-B19, p. 16.

78. Cf. Gimbel (1976).

79. See Milward (1977) on the economies of the principal belligerents between 1939 and 1945; see also the figures included in League of Nations (1943, 1945), which were the source of many of the statistics used in the memorandum.

80. Cf. Williams (1969) and the role that he attributed to the agricultural interests in the development of American imperialism.

81. Cf. E-B19, p. 9.

82. The way international economics had in fact developed during the 1930s had highlighted the geographical and customs-based collaboration among the various commercial areas, or trade blocs, even within the capitalist world. This state of affairs certainly would not have facilitated larger economic and commercial areas, as envisaged by the document. The absolute lack of international convertibility of the national currencies (with the exception of the pound sterling) meant that the monetary flows could not work to make transactions easier, much less automatic. Another kind of remedy had therefore to be sought. This external factor could only be a political solution, with possible military overtones. Cf. Kindleberger (1973) and (1978). See also Hansen's two books (1938, 1945) that trace the great economist's theoretical development in the interwar years. Hansen and Kindleberger (1942) perfectly encapsulated the spirit of the Economic and Financial Group of the CFR in the early war years.

83. Cf. E-B19, p. 9.

84. Ibid. See also Divine (1967) and Russell (1958b).

85. See Louis (1978), including bibliography.

86. According to ibid. and the most recent historians, the question of dismantling the colonial empires was the main factor underlying Anglo-American relations during the war. For the status of Italian colonies and their fate, plus literature from Italian sources, see Del Boca (1976–1984) and Ellwood (1977).

87. For a definition of the "rigid" and "flexible" bipolar system, see M. A. Kaplan (1957: 89ff.).

88. On the more general issue of Anglo-American relations, see Gelber (1961), who looked at the basis of the "special relationship" between the U.S. and Britain and highlighted the process of "succession" of the "primacy" during and after the war (pp. 35–50).

89. This is Memorandum P-B13, dated November 10, 1940, "The Political Feasibility of the Proposal Advanced in Memorandum E-B19: Needs of Future United States Foreign Policy."

90. The two currents of opinion that emerged in 1940 could not yet be called interdependence and national security, in the sense that we discussed them in the first chapters of this book.

91. Cf. P-B13, p. 2.

92. Cf. Spiro (1968); for Hitler's global ambitions, see Hillgruber (1965a, 1982), Hildebrand (1970), and especially Rich (1973: 91–104).

93. Again in P-B13 W. C. Langsam quoted Karl Haushofer's remarks of March 3, 1940, on the Germans' political interest in Russian territories and resources (p. 4, n. 4).

94. As stated in the early chapters of this book, power and growth, two key analytical categories of U.S. political tradition, were becoming more and more closely linked during and after the war, as the idea of the United Nations and the Marshall Plan took shape. On the other hand, the idea of linking the institutional and legislative order (power) with the economic and productive (growth) opened up the way for collective bargaining for economic agreements and led to the creation of the international economic organizations of the postwar years. See Russell (1958a, 1958b, 1968), Divine (1967), Diebold (1952, 1959), plus the later works, Keohane (1984), and Krasner (1982).

95. This concern was furthered heightened with the signing of the Tripartite Pact of September 22, 1940, between Germany, Italy, and Japan, as well as the Soviet-Japanese Nonaggression Treaty of April 13, 1941.

96. Frequently, the behavior of the other national actors is interpreted in terms of the links between doctrine and political action. A prime example is the debate among historians on the "origins" of both the world wars and the bitter controversy on the issue of responsibility for the two conflicts. See the works of Fritz Fischer, James Joll, Gerhard Ritter, et al. in Koch (1972); see also Joll (1983) on the causes of World War I; and A.J.P. Taylor, Hugh Trevor-Roper, C. Robert Cole, Akira Iriye, et al., in Robertson (1971) on the causes of World War II. The problems that can arise from equating ideological positions and political and diplomatic actions, which are serious in historical interpretation, become almost insurmountable when it comes to constructing models for planning the behavior of the actors, as occurs in the case of the "perceptions" system. Cf. Jervis (1976), Janis and Mann (1977); Snyder and Diesing (1977).

97. There is a great wealth of literature on this subject, but here we can restrict ourselves to mentioning Yergin (1977), who offered a good descriptive summary of the much troubled history of U.S. relations with (and perceptions of) the Soviet Union from the late 1930s to the early 1950s. See his bibliography for further details. See also Nye (1984).

98. According to WPS figures, the relative levels of self-sufficiency of the two areas and the degree to which they complemented each other were 75 percent for the German area and 83 percent for the Grand Area. See E-B19, p. 13; and P-B13, pp. 7–8.

99. Cf. bibliography in Santoro (1984b: 622–660) on bipolarity as a war system.

100. Cf. Carr (1939, 1946), Q. Wright (1942a), Wight (1946, 1978).

101. Cf. P-B13, pp. 5–6.

102. As such, bipolarity is basically a war system. See Bonanate and Santoro (1986).

103. Cf. M. A. Kaplan (1957), as well as essays by Richard N. Rosecrance, Kenneth N. Waltz, Karl W. Deutsch, and Oran B. Young in Rosenau (1969),

which presented a detailed overview of the principal theories on the international system proposed by the first and second generations of scholars in this field.

104. Cf. Santoro (1984a) for the development of the debate on the U.S.-Soviet strategic balance from 1975 to 1983.

105. Cf. P-B13, p. 8. On the difference between "preventive" and "preemptive" attacks, see Freedman (1981).

Chapter 6

1. The first phase of neutrality lasted from September 1939 to June 1940. A Gallup opinion poll carried out in June 1940 (see Leigh [1976] for results) revealed that 65 percent of those questioned were convinced that if the Nazis succeeded in crushing France and Great Britain, they would then turn on the United States. Furthermore, five out of eight respondents expected that sooner or later the United States would find itself drawn into the war. Despite this, only one in fourteen citizens was in favor of the United States declaring war on Germany first. Although there was widespread awareness of the existence of the threat to the national economy, the nature and gravity of the threat were still too vague (at least on a public level) for any broad consensus to form regarding the measures to be undertaken. For readings on the evolution of public attitudes toward the war in Europe, see Leigh (1976: especially 62ff.), Levering (1978), and Perrett (1973).

2. This expression is normally used in reference to the two political initiatives piloted by William Allen White, editor of the *Emporia Gazette* and an important member of the Republican party. The first was the "Committee for Peace through the Revision of Neutrality Laws" (created in October 1939 and dissolved after the approval of the "Cash and Carry Act"). More important, however, was the "Committee to Defend America by Aiding the Allies," which materialized at the height of the French crisis (May 1940) with the declared objective to "fill the radio and newspapers and the Congressional mail with the voice of prominent citizens urging America to become the nonbelligerent ally of France and England." See Langer and Gleason (1952: 487).

3. Leigh (1976: 63ff.).

4. The declaration, entitled "A Summons to Speak Out," was drafted by Whitney Shepardson, a member of both the WPS Steering Committee and the Political Group since December 1939. The text of the declaration is reproduced in Chadwin (1968: 279ff.).

5. For more on this argument see Stromberg in Williams (1972c).

6. Cited in FRUS (1940, vol. 1, pp. 243–246).

7. A good example is what happened during the ensuing days. Roosevelt's speech excited such a rash of hopes in London and Paris that the U.S. president was forced to add a series of follow-up "clarifications" to check the "storm of Anglo-French appeals for all-out help." These requests became more pressing the more precarious the Allied military situation became. The president had a hard job explaining to Neville Chamberlain and Paul Reynaud that "his statement

carried 'no implication of military commitments,' because only the Congress could do that." See Dallek (1979: 228ff.).

8. For a critical view of this "establishment," see L. Silk and M. Silk (1980) and Shoup and Minter (1977).

9. Issues of *Foreign Affairs* published from 1938 to 1947 and New York and Washington newspapers (*New York Times, New York Herald Tribune,* and *Washington Post*) during the same period revealed this dual working method, which was basic to the philosophy of the CFR. We should not forget the CFR's concerted publishing effort: No less important than the journal were publications such as the annual *Political Handbook of the World, The United States in World Affairs, Survey of American Foreign Relations,* and *Studies in American Foreign Relations.* In the course of this book, further indications of the methods of selection and use of the printed material adopted by the WPSS groups will be given. See especially the bibliography put together ad hoc for the Economic and Financial Group by William Diebold between 1941 and 1945, which is highly revealing of the selection criteria adopted.

10. The start of the debate on "economic areas of free trade" and their "integration" (or better, "interaction") dates back to the period 1933-1934, after the turning point in the relations between the United States and Latin America, represented by the Montevideo Conference and by Hull and Roosevelt's Good Neighbor Policy, inspired by the principles of noninterference and "nondiscriminatory commerce." As Hull himself recalled in his memoirs (Hull [1948]), the creation of a Pan-American system of commerce was intended as a model for extended application, in opposition to the protectionist system of "imperial preferences" sanctioned for the areas of sterling currency in the Ottawa Conference of 1932: "The principles we were laying down and the agreements we were reaching were not exclusive. We should be more than delighted to share them with the nations of the rest of the world." See Cordell Hull, quoted in Calleo and Rowland (1973: 53). See also Higham (1983), on the secret collaboration of certain U.S. banks and industrial companies with Nazi Germany in the course of the war.

11. Cf. Willkie (1943). A general reconstruction still needs to be done of the gradual process of adherence of the "liberals" and "modernizers" of both parties to the policies of the executive, a convergence that came about between 1939 and 1941. The process is evident (though by no means exhaustively) in the change in the political profile of many leading figures, especially William A. White (a convinced isolationist throughout the 1930s), Reinhold Niebuhr, and Walter Lippmann (see his own account in Lippmann [1943]; see also Steel [1980]). Other useful points are contained in Yergin (1977) and Hoffmann (1978).

12. Author's interview with William Diebold.

13. Cf. the breakdown of the discussion, in E-A11 of November 3, 1940, p. 4.

14. Ibid. Of particular interest is the emphasis on the political instability of relations between the two blocs as a restriction on any form of integration and/ or coexistence, which was understood simply as a by-product of trade agreements between the two areas. It should be pointed out that the P Group's objections

were more specifically addressed to the "Rump Hullians," followers of "Economic Utopianism," who fantasized "a world order in which an economic system was abstracted from, and substituted for, the normal play of power politics among nation-states." See Rowland (1976). This criticism may perhaps also be applied, in part, to the "technologists" of U.S.-Soviet détente in the 1970s.

15. This line of research was never abandoned. All the reports compiled by the EF Group, starting with Memorandum E-B1 of March 1, 1940, can be read on two levels. On the one hand, they provided political proposals to be discussed, and on the other, they deepened understanding in matters of economic and trade relations between different blocs, with an eye to future developments.

16. See Memorandum E-B34 (and supplement) of July 24, 1941; Memorandum E-B27 of February 10, 1941; and E-B31 of March 7, 1941; as well as the summaries of discussions on these topics in the study groups, collected in E-A15 (April 12), E-A16 (May 17), E-A17 (June 14), and T-A14 (June 17).

17. On the other hand, the problem of defining forms of agreement and collaboration between highly developed countries (particularly between Great Britain and the United States) against the adverse effects of the protectionist outlook, was on the British agenda. Even Lord Keynes, over 1940–1941, was critically revising his previous position of the 1930s and his adhesion to the ideal of "national self-sufficiency." See Harrod (1951: 568).

18. Cf. Memorandum T-A14, p. 6.

19. It is worth noting that between 1934 and 1945, the Roosevelt administration successfully concluded bilateral agreements, based on the Trade Act, with about twenty nations, roughly half of which were Latin American. See R. Gardner (1956), L. Gardner (1964), Calleo and Rowland (1973) and B. Wood (1961: 310ff.).

20. On the second debate, besides R. Gardner (1956), see also Kolko and Kolko (1972) and Divine (1967).

21. Author's interview with William Diebold and a personal letter from Upgren to Diebold.

22. Cf. Memorandum E-B34 (Suppl. 1), p. 4. The study Diebold referred to is quoted in Memorandum E-B19. He suggested employing a new method based on a study conducted by the Royal Institute of International Affairs (Chatham House), the British equivalent of the New York–based Council on Foreign Relations.

23. Cf. L. Gardner (1964), Kindleberger (1973), Leuchtenburg (1963), Schlesinger Jr. (1957–1965), Dallek (1979, 1983), and Cole (1983).

24. See Milward (1977), especially chap. 2.

25. "There is a solidarity and interdependence about the modern world both technically and morally, which makes impossible for any nation completely to isolate itself from economic and political upheaval in the rest of the world, especially when upheavals seem to be spreading and not declining" (Roosevelt [1937, in 1932–1945]).

26. As A. J. Schlesinger, Jr., recalled (1957–1965, vol. 1, pp. 179–260), the first New Deal presumed that "the age of economic expansion was over" and that "the economy of the future would be less concerned in increasing production than in the management of what already existed" (p. 182). See also Vaudagna

(1981a, 1981b) and Tugwell (1968). But the possibility of realizing effective internal planning postulated the "impermeability" of the national economy to fluctuations (especially monetary) of the international economy. As explained by Walter Lippmann in 1933, the American people "rejected free trade between nations because they want and hope to establish a more controlled economic society" (Schlesinger (1957–1965, vol. 1, p. 187). It is highly significant that both sectors—conservative and progressive—of the New Deal reflected this "nationalist" tendency: The only real exception to this tendency was Cordell Hull, who remained isolated for a long time. See Gourevitch (1984), T. Ferguson (1984), and Dallek (1983).

27. Memorandum E-B34, p. 2.

28. Cf. Chadwin (1968) and the Ezekiel Memorandum in USDD, RG-59, "Pasvolsky File," Box 32.

29. Reams have been written on this fundamental juncture of U.S.-British relations. Here I limit my references to Rowland (1976), Langer and Gleason (1952, 1953), Dallek (1979), and T. Wilson (1969). For an "inside" account of negotiations, the papers of Keynes, who was on the British delegation, are fundamental reading (cf. vols. 23 and 25 of the *Collected Writings of John Maynard Keynes* [Keynes 1979a, 1980a]).

30. Memorandum E-B34, p. 2.

31. Cf. Gaddis (1982) for the historical evolution of the concept of containment.

32. On this issue, see the concepts of "Alliance" in Liska (1962) and the concept of "threat" in contemporary strategic literature, including Freedman (1981), Schelling (1960), and G. H. Snyder (1984).

33. *Life*, February 17, 1942.

34. Ibid. and Memorandum E-B34, p. 3.

35. Memorandum E-B34, p. 2.

36. Cf. for instance Memorandum P-B19, of May 16, 1941.

37. Chadwin (1968: 279ff.). The names of the thirty signatories of the "Summons" are included there.

38. Memorandum E-B34, p. 5.

39. Author's interview with W. Diebold. See Memorandum P-B19, "The Island of Great Britain as a Factor in the Strategy of American Defense" (May 16, 1941), and Memorandum P-B20, "The Political Conditions of American-British Partnership" (June 4, 1941), as well as those of the T Group: T-B26, "The Soviet-Japanese Treaty of Neutrality April 13th, 1941, and World Revolution in the Far East" (April 19, 1941), and Memorandum T-B29, "The Chinese Communists, the Comintern, and the Russo-Japanese Neutrality Agreement" (May 6, 1941).

Chapter 7

1. Cf. essays by Kolko (1972), W. R. Louis (1978), Gaddis (1982), Paterson (1973), Gimbel (1968), R. Gardner (1958) and Milward (1977).

2. This notion also turns up in the digest of discussions that took place on July 19, 1941 (E-A18). Since early April, the Economic and Financial Group had

been studying the hazards and advantages of U.S. intervention in support of the British. See Memorandum E-A15 of April 12, 1941, and E-B32 of April 17, 1941. For a closer analysis of Anglo-American disagreement over the future of the colonies (which included not only the Japanese-owned islands but also European and British properties in the Far East), see W. R. Louis (1978, pt. 2, chaps. 6–12, pp. 121–211), and Thorne (1978).

3. Memorandum PB-19, p. 1. For more on this argument, see the report compiled by the Harboard Board in 1920 (a special U.S. Army commission of inquiry) on the characteristics of the "coming war," reproduced in Watson (1950: 64).

4. Ibid., p. 65.

5. Ibid.

6. Cf. Mahan's theory of naval power (1890, 1897) with Douhet (1921, 1955) and De Seversky (1942) on air power.

7. For a clearer understanding of the origins of the "bases theory," see key contributions by Herwig, Grenville, and Hoggie in P. Kennedy (1979); see also Herwig (1976), S. Morison (1963), Bailey and Ryan (1979). Aquarone (1973) looked into links between navy and commerce and the "mercantilist" nature of these particular geopolitical doctrines. Among the vast amount of biographical material on Admiral Mahan, I suggest Earle (1943, 1973), Mahan (1890, 1957), and Till (1982, 1984).

8. Cf. Blechman and Kaplan's (1978) in-depth study of the forms, incidences, and methods of U.S. Army and Navy intervention outside the national boundaries after 1945; in contrast, see S. S. Kaplan (1981) for an account of Soviet behavior in similar circumstances. See also articles by D. Baldwin (1979, 1980) on the functions of "power."

9. Once the United States entered the war, the problem became more and more pressing. WPS Memorandum A-B80 of February 12, 1943, listed the possible bases available to the United Nations after the war. List of bases suitable for international policing purposes: "I. North and South America (including Caribbean area): A. West Coast: Alaska-Aleutian Area: 1. Fairbanks, 2. Dutch Harbor, 3. Adak; Canada-USA Area: 1. Seattle, 2. San Diego; Central American Area: Panama; Latin American Area. 1. Seymour Island, 2. Salinas, Ecuador, 3. Lima, 4. Quintero, Chile, 5. Falkland Islands; B. East Coast: Latin American Area: 1. Montevideo, 2. Rio de Janeiro, 3. Natal, 4. Belem; Caribbean Area: 1. Trinidad, 2. Puerto Rico, 3. Miami, 4. Corpus Christi; Canada-USA Area: 1. Norfolk, 2. Long Island area, 3. Newfoundland; Atlantic Islands: 1. Bermuda, 2. Azores, 3. Reykjavik. II. Africa: A. West Coast: 1. Dakar, 2. Cape Town; B. East Coast: Diego Suarez; C. Mediterranean Coast: 1. Cairo–Alexander–Port Said area, 2. Bizerte. III. European Area: British Isles: 1.Portsmouth, 2. Foynes, 3. Prestwick, 4. Scapa Flow; Western Europe: 1. Brest area, 2. Rotterdam; Western Mediterranean Coastal Area: 1. Gibraltar-Ceuta area, 2. Sicily–Southern Italy–Malta area, 3. Toulon; Central European Area: 1. Warsaw, 2. Prague, 3. Belgrade, 4. Constanza; Eastern Mediterranean Area: 1. Athens, 2. Eskisehir; Scandinavian-Baltic Area: 1. Stavanger, 2. Troms or Narvik, 3. Trondheim, 4. Göteborg, 5. Riga; Soviet Union in Europe: 1. Murmansk, 2. Kiev, 3. Astrakhan, 4. Crimea. IV. Far East

and Pacific: Asiatic Russia: 1. Vladivostok, 2. Gulf of Anadyr area; Manchukuo and Korea: 1. Mukden (Shenyang), 2. Fusan, Korea; China: 1. Shanghai, 2. Hong Kong, 3. Tsingtao; Japan: Paramushiro; India and Burma: 1. Calcutta, 2. Rangoon, 3. Ceylon, 4. Karachi; Arabia and Persian Gulf: 1. Bandar Shah, 2. Basra, 3. Aden; Southeastern Asia: 1. Singapore, 2. Manila, 3. Koepang; Australia and New Zealand: 1. Perth, 2. Sydney, 3. Auckland; Pacific Area: 1. Fiji Islands, 2. Truk, 3. Guam, 4. Wake, 5. Midway, 6. Hawaii."

10. The WPS groups continued to debate the issue: See Memorandum A-B5 of April 15, 1942 ("The Future of the United States Bases and Facilities in Foreign Territories").

11. As early as April 1940 the U.S. fleet was stationed in Pearl Harbor to deter Japanese encroachment in Indochina and the British and Dutch colonies. Soon after, numerous B17 bombers were stationed in the Philippines as a deterrent, and in December the president declared an embargo on the exportation of "strategic" goods to Japan.

12. The whole question of incorporating the two northern islands into the Western Hemisphere will be discussed in detail later on. Here it is important to note how the "global" definition of the U.S. strategic area actually followed rather than anticipated the events. In other words, it was the result of the perception of strategic opportunities and needs, a self-generating process because the expansion of the perimeter, although solving old security problems, created new ones. See W. R. Louis (1978) and Landes (1969).

13. Baily and Ryan (1979).

14. An exemplary (and to some extent conclusive) study of this early phase of defining a "highly sophisticated global defense scheme" was made in the Joint Chiefs of Staff paper entitled "On U.S. Military Requirements for Air Bases, Facilities, and Operating Rights in Foreign Territories," commissioned by the president himself for use on future occasions. According to this study (reprinted in Louis [1978: 272]), "In the East, the defense line ran through points in Iceland, the Azores, Madeira, the West Coast of Africa, and Ascension Island. In the West, the outmost western defense line ran from Alaska through Attu, Para-mashiru, the Bonin Islands, the Philippines, New Britain, the Solomons, Suva, Samoa, Tahiti, Marquesas, Clipperton, and the Galapagos to the West Coast of South America. In the Atlantic Area, secondary locations would exist in Greenland, Labrador, Newfoundland, Bermuda, Trinidad, French Guiana, and Brazil. In the Pacific Area, bases would be required in the Gilbert Islands, Canton Islands, Christmas Islands, Ecuador or Peru, Guatemala and Mexico." Louis also noted that a system of linkage for these "border positions" was considered, by establishing a complex network of "internal bases."

15. Unpublished bibliography of secondary sources, compiled by W. Diebold between 1941 and 1944.

16. The likelihood of the CFR documents' actually being read by those in the administration (i.e., Cordell Hull, Sumner Welles, and the president), was inversely proportional to their length.

17. Memorandum A-B51, p. 1. Details on the text's author are in Chadwin (1968). One can get an idea of the various interpretations of the policy of U.S.

bases round the globe from the debate on the war and postwar years that created a rift between the revisionist and orthodox historians in the United States in the 1960s and 1970s.

18. See T. Wilson (1969), Kimball (1969), and Lippmann (1944).

19. Cf. W. R. Louis (1978: 6–7). The U.S. military feared that the weakening of the British presence in East Asia would seriously destabilize this area of vital importance to U.S. trade and security. Roosevelt's position was more complex. Especially after 1942 (the military crisis and the "white" colony policy, involving Canada, Australia, New Zealand, and South Africa), he was convinced that the only way to achieve enduring stability was to begin a process of "decolonization," controlled by a regional power with political weight, which would have to act together with the other powers of the future international system. This explains Roosevelt's gamble in China, something the British failed to appreciate, given the disarray of the Kuomintang.

20. Ibid., p. 24. Many historians have underscored the harshness of this clash. For more on the Far East, see Thorne (1978: 57–91).

21. Hull's intentions and those of the State Department to use Land-Lease as a political lever against the Ottawa system is on record. Cf. Kimball (1969), who noted two facts: First, he distinguished the State Department's attitude from that of Morgenthau and the Treasury, which was more sensitive to the British arguments. Second, he was reluctant to uphold the so-called revisionist viewpoints. In his opinion, "the State Department position was not consciously cynical, but rather was based on a fervent belief in the justness and efficacy of the American form of economic liberalism" (p. 48). See Thorne (1978). For more literature on this difficult relationship, see M. Gilbert (1983), Lash (1976), and Feis (1950b); see Ellwood (1977) on the Anglo-American relations in occupied Italy.

22. The trusteeships were intended as an extension of the mandate scheme Wilson had devised for settling the question of the colonies of the former German empire (presented at the Paris Conference). These territories would have been governed by the victorious powers under mandate under the supervision of the League of Nations. The trusteeships introduced two crucial changes to this system: (1) the term of trusteeship was limited and geared explicitly to fostering political and economic conditions that would allow independence for the territories in question; (2) the "universal" organization (i.e., the United Nations) would be given executive power of supervision (power to inspect, direct contact with population, et cetera). On this argument, see the two volumes by Russell (1958a) and (1968).

23. Historical examples of the awkward balance are very common: Anglo-Dutch relations and Anglo-Portuguese relations in the 1600s were an example of conflict between naval powers; relations between Sparta and Athens or between Rome and Carthage were even earlier examples.

24. For the structure behind the "bear-whale" and "whale-whale" models, see Liska (1977), Mackinder (1919, 1942), and Weigert (1942).

25. Note the serious political crises in the Asiatic colonies in 1942, especially the crisis in India, during which (with Japanese help) Subhas Chandra Bose managed to muster a force of roughly 10,000 men against the British troops.

26. See Churchill (1949), W. R. Louis (1978) and M. Gilbert (1983), on the ongoing debate between the Labor and Conservative parties, and within the latter as well, regarding the fate of the British Empire.

27. Even in 1940, the British were well aware of their inability to defend their empire and tried on many occasions to involve the United States (still neutral at the time) in the defense of Singapore, a major access point to Indochina and India, but at the same time symbolic of white domination in the area. When secret talks began in Washington (January 1941), the British delegation asked the United States to join them against the Germans but also to "underwrite the defense of Singapore" by sending four heavy cruisers, an ancient carrier, a squadron of airplanes, and some submarines. See Matloff and Snell (1953, 1959: 34–38). The Americans rejected the request. See Thorne (1978), Gaddis (1972), Kolko (1968), and McNeill (1953).

28. The complex issue of "political communication" has been handled from various standpoints. See Deutsch (1963) on how it was structured, Jervis (1976) on reception and perception, and Schelling (1960) on the management and unilateral manipulation of the various forms of political communication.

29. Glucksmann (1967, 1969 Italian ed., p. 65).

30. This did not occur. After the war Britain was even more debilitated than it had been in 1940. See the classic study by Reitzel (1948) on the transfer of British power in the Mediterranean to the United States; see also Kuniholm's more recent volume (1980) on the same theme.

31. W. R. Louis (1978: 7).

32. Details of FDR's anti-British sentiments in 1941 are found in his brother's book (E. Roosevelt [1950]). Keynes also spoke of discussions with Americans he considered were "victims of current American mythology about British Imperialism." Many saw "Machiavellian projects" in every British proposal, bent on advancing "G.B. interests" and on making "rings around anyone who would oppose them." See Harrod (1951: 539).

33. Memorandum E-A18, p. 7.

34. On the concept of "asymmetrical interdependence," see Santoro (1984a).

35. Memorandum E-A18, p. 8.

36. Cf. C. S. Campbell (1976: 194 and 319); plus Thorne (1978) and Gelber (1961).

37. The term "total defense" was intended as a counterpoint to "total war" and was adopted by German writers in the 1920s and 1930s to denote the "nature" of twentieth-century war. For more on German strategic theory regarding the "war of the future" and on the links between Haushofer's ideas and those of Kjellén, see Speier (1943), Earle (1943), and Weigert (1942).

38. Cited in Chadwin (1968: 280). See L. Gardner (1964) on Ezekiel. Roosevelt made his Total Defense speech on July 11, 1940.

39. See the Ezekiel Memorandum in USDD, RG-59, "Pasvolsky File," Box 32, p. 2.

40. A text (or any "linguistic act" for that matter) is not solely or mainly the expression and communication of some precise subject matter. It can be used for effect, to modify situations, manipulating the beliefs and/or the

knowledge of the people involved in the interactive process. The ability of a text to produce the desired effect, i.e., its persuasiveness, also depends on a set of carefully chosen rhetorical strategies tailored to its audience, which is by no means an undifferentiated "public."

41. A brilliant example of persuasive argumentation was found in Memorandum A-B32 of April 17, 1941, "Economic War Aims: General Considerations."

42. Cf. Notter (1949: 32). See also FRUS (1940, vols. 1 and 2) and USDD, RG-59, "Notter File," Box 15.

43. Cf. Vaudagna (1981a, 1981b); Schulzinger (1975: 125–156).

44. Quoted in Weil (1978: 103). For more on the political and organizational aspects of the State Department in these years, see Hulen (1939).

45. Cole (1983: 6–7). According to Cole, the best definition of isolationism is in A. K. Weinberg (1940: 539–547). See also the volume by Cantril and Strunk (1951: 966–968), for a statistical breakdown of prewar isolationism.

46. See Crabb (1968).

47. But not Roosevelt, who on several occasions showed greater flexibility and foresight than many contemporary analysts.

48. Doubts on Britain's endurance were rife among the administration and diplomatic corps (see reports sent in 1940 to U.S. Ambassador Joseph Kennedy). Roosevelt eventually sent a personal delegation, led by Col. William Donovan (future director of the OSS), to assess British morale and readiness. See Beschloss (1980: 208–209). It was no coincidence that in this phase the question of relations with the Vichy government and Pétain was still open (see article by Langer [1947a]) and the biography of Marshal Pétain by Lottman (1984), plus Lacouture's (1984) biography of de Gaulle (vol. 1) and the memoirs of Leahy (1950); see also FRUS (1941, vol. 2, and 1959).

49. For the first time since 1919, the Anglo-Saxon powers were obliged to take a stand on the Soviet Union. Spurred by events rather than ideological motives, they set aside the anti-Russian feelings (at least in part) traditional in liberal Europe in the 1800s, feelings that were to spread to the other shore of the Atlantic the following century. See Groh (1961, 1980 Italian ed., "Introduction," pp. 3–11).

50. Actually, the CFR tackled the theme of war aims far more explicitly than the president or State Department ever did, or even the military departments (war and navy). However, the State Department was in fact talking of disarmament and economic welfare as a prime objective for the postwar period. Among the unexpressed aims were the strategic ambitions and political intentions of the United States, which had not been clearly traced out, even by the administration. See Notter (1949: 477) and USDD, RG-59, "Notter File," Boxes 1–10.

51. On August 18, 1940, Washington had set up a Joint Board of Defense with the Canadian government.

52. Discussions here will be limited to the formation of the conceptual guidelines behind Washington's actions, drawing largely on the State Department's theoretical planning work, rather than on diplomacy actually effected. Therefore I will not be tracing the history of allied relations as they matured into the Grand Alliance. This does not mean, however, that establishing some kind of

hierarchy among the Allies was not a focal issue affecting the dynamics of interaction of the various components of the U.S. war alliances. That was basically the first and most complex issue the Americans faced, as they were obliged to stress the unity of the "Allies," yet at the same time the special nature, thus the priority, of the relationship with Britain. Among the many studies into U.S. alliances, see Liska (1962) and Riker (1962), also Mastny (1979), Kolko (1968), Gelber (1961), W.R. Louis (1978), and Thorne (1978). For a more recent model, see G. H. Snyder (1984).

53. In fact, in this period FDR's attention was focused on propaganda. See documents reprinted in Perrett (1973: 173ff.); also Dallek (1979) and Cole (1983).

54. For a structural analysis of national interest see Neuchterlein (1973: 1–30). For more on national security, see Russett (1972), Larson (1973), and R. Higham (1975). For a chronology of democracy, see Williams (1980), L. Gardner (1964), Huntington (1981), among others.

55. See texts by Luce, Wallace, Willkie, and Lippmann collected in Polenberg (1968).

56. Memorandum E-B32, "Economic War Aims: General Considerations, the Position as of April 1, 1941," is dated April 17, 1941; E-B36, "Economic War Aims: Main Lines of Approach, Preliminary Statements," is dated June 22, 1941, the day the Germans launched their attack on the Soviet Union.

57. Quoted in Memorandum E-B32, p. 2. See also F. Fischer (1961, Italian ed., 1965) and P. Kennedy (1979) on war aims of World War I.

58. On March 7, 1940, FDR announced, "We cannot escape our collective responsibility for the kind of life that is going to emerge from the ordeal through which the world is passing today. We cannot be an island." And in his famous message to Congress on the "Four Liberties," on January 6, 1941, the president stressed the fourth, the freedom from need, which, in international terms, meant "an economic understanding which will secure to every nation a healthy peacetime life for its inhabitants" (quoted in E-B32, p. 8).

59. In two later statements, one on April 24 and the other on May 8, Hull announced that his department was working "on the task of creating ultimate conditions of peace with justice." See Notter (1949: 45).

60. Ibid., p. 46.

61. Ibid. Likewise, in a speech to the Chicago Foreign Policy Association on April 8, 1941, Vice President Henry Wallace forestalled contemporary statesmen in his explicit declaration of the general outline of a "lasting peace settlement," speaking on the need to construct an "international order" strong enough to block the rise of other aggressive powers.

62. Notter (1949: 45). See also p. 517 for a list of research staff between February 3, 1941, and January 14, 1944. The basic, if vague, hope was to set up a kind of international "regime." See Krasner (1982).

63. On aid to Europe during 1918 and 1919, see collection of essays edited by Lutz and Lutz (1983).

64. See Divine (1967), chaps. 1, 2, and 3; see also Adler (1957), Chadwin (1968), and Kolko and Kolko (1972). J. K. Galbraith's opinions were expressed during an interview with the author.

65. "Letter from Armstrong to Pasvolsky," USDD, RG-59, "Pasvolsky File," Box 1.

66. Letter from Miller to Pasvolsky, "Pasvolsky File," USDD, RG-59, Box 1. As early as 1930, Miller was among those in favor of a "North Atlantic Union." See Miller and Hill (1930).

67. The Policy Planning Office was set up in 1947, and George F. Kennan was appointed director. See Etzold and Gaddis (1978) and also Gaddis (1982).

68. See also FRUS (1940 and 1941), for an interesting comparison of the quality of these documents with those of the Council on Foreign Relations.

69. Until CFR members themselves entered the administration, as happened regularly after 1942.

70. I discussed the steady growth of U.S. "globalism" and U.S. global foreign policy in Chapter 1, which traces its development from early U.S. links with Britain to the definition of U.S. "war aims" and thence to the formation of the Grand Alliance and the definition of the aims for postwar order. In fact, U.S. globalism progressed in two geographical directions according to two quite different philosophies: the first being the special relations the United States had with the Western Hemisphere; the second, a specifically Anglo-Saxon direction, oriented on the Atlantic. Despite the structural parallels between the two subsystems, in some cases a "dual alliance" has sprung up in different regional areas, as in the case of the 1982 Falklands War.

71. Cf. Lash (1976: 391ff.).

72. Thus the "constitutive" effect of the system of Washington-London relations was only partially adjusted and the system was not scrapped, as happened in Central Eastern Europe, which was greatly affected by Soviet security needs and military events. See also Agarossi (1984), especially the introduction and essays by A. Schlesinger, Jr., E. R. May, and E. Mark.

73. As an indication of the weight of this "special relationship," note the voluminous exchange of messages, even within twenty-four hours, between Roosevelt and Churchill beginning in 1939. See Lash (1976), Feis (1966), Gilbert (1983), and the more recent three-volume publication of all the correspondence between the two statesmen, edited by Kimball (1984).

74. A clear indication of just how dangerous even a temporary division between the United States and Great Britain could prove to the "Western system" can be seen in the episode that determined the political fate of Poland after the war, along with that of other Eastern European countries. In Eastern Europe the British had a kind of historical "right of preemption" over the Americans. Churchill in fact felt himself authorized to deal directly with Stalin on the issue of defining respective zones of influence (at the Moscow summit in October 1944). According to both orthodox and postrevisionist accounts of the origins of the cold war (i.e., Clemens [1970], Feis [1966], Yergin [1977], and Gaddis [1982]), the lack of U.S.-British coordination prevented a more favorable arrangement for the West. The Moscow summit is held to have ratified, at least in part, the cardinal concepts of the policy of "zones of influence" (officially spurned by traditional U.S. policy) and helped to establish a precedent and an "affinity" of language and topics in the negotiations that Stalin was quick to

exploit. Furthermore, this episode supposedly aggravated friction between Washington and London, weakening their bargaining power against Stalin.

75. Cf. W. R. Louis (1978), Thorne (1978), Gilbert (1983).

76. Cf. especially the EF Group memoranda regarding the problem of relations with Great Britain: E-B38, August 29, 1941 ("England's Interests in Continental Europe and the Mediterranean Basin: Trade, Shipping, Investment"); E-B41, October 17, 1941 ("The Need for Elucidation of Point Four of the Atlantic Charter"); E-B42, October 20, 1941 ("Economic Aspects of Point Eight"); and E-B45, January 3, 1942 ("Tentative Draft of a Joint Economic Declaration by the Governments of the United States and United Kingdom"). P Group contributions included: P-B18, May 2, 1941 ("Note on a Program of Joint Action for the American and British Governments"); P-B20, June 4, 1941 ("The Political Conditions of American-British Cooperation"); and P-B32, December 3, 1941 ("A Comparative Analysis of the Wilsonian and Roosevelt-Churchill Peace Program"). The T Group memorandum on the subject is T-B41, November 17, 1941 ("Need for Immediate American-British Consideration of Postwar Issues"); and the Armaments Group memorandum was A-B33, December 4, 1941 ("The Atlantic and Postwar Security"). The CFR archives also yielded documents on the research and political forecasting of other U.S. organizations, such as the Institute of International Studies (at Yale), as well as foreign ones, for example, the British Royal Institute for International Affairs. It is worth noting that such reporting was kept up not only within the specific scope of the WPS but also by the CFR in general.

77. See also Memorandum P-B20.

78. Memorandum P-B18, p. 1.

79. As early as 1917 Henry Adams had envisaged an "Atlantic Community" based on Anglo-American partnership. The notion was really born around the turn of the century from the early reflection upon the United States as a true "power" (Mahan, Brooks Adams, and Turner). It really developed in the late 1930s, when the phase of U.S. insularity was coming to an end. See B. Adams (1900) and Turner (1893). See also the frequently cited volumes by Miller and Hill (1930) and by Streit (1938).

80. For an understanding of how these ideas were rooted in the American culture, see the works by Beard (1940) and Tansill (1952) and compare them with the works cited in the preceding note; see also Williams (1969).

81. Memorandum P-B20, p. 2. For a deeper analysis of the evolution of the concepts of "interdependence" and "integration" in U.S. politics, see Santoro (1984a), chap. 2.

82. In 1941, ex-president Hoover spoke of "food" as a potential weapon during and after the war. See L. Gardner (1964: 170).

83. For more on the United Nations, see R. Russell (1958) and R. Gardner (1956, 1979). See also Machlup (1977) for an account of a "world order" produced by the integration of the various economies into a supranational market economy. For the CFR, "universal" order and "Western" system were virtually synonymous. It was therefore not merely theoretical speculation, as the Wilsonian projects for a postwar order had been. It was more a question of constructing an

international postwar order in which the U.S. role was to be commensurate with its effective power and in which the worst risks of the previous system were to be avoided. See Calleo and Rowland (1973), DePorte (1979), and Carr (1939, 1946). The Western character of Europe and the world was in fact emphasized after 1919 by the political ostracizing of the Soviet republics in 1917 and the disintegration of the Ottoman and Hapsburg empires following the defeat of Germany and Austria in 1918. The German defeat had also pushed Europe even further West. Thus the pivot of the new order became the French-British axis. This westward drive continued between the wars. In 1940 Europe split in two. The eastern half pivoted on Berlin, and the epicenter of the western half shifted to the Atlantic, between London and Washington. This division of Europe, which became more accentuated after 1945, seemed to justify the semantic identity between "universal order" and "Western system," as clearly asserted in the CFR memoranda.

84. Memorandum P-B20, p. 4.

85. Memorandum P-A5, February 19, 1941, p. 2.

86. Calleo and Rowland (1973: 59ff., especially p. 63).

87. Cf. Milward (1977: 55–98).

88. Memorandum P-A5, p. 2.

89. The alliance between the United States and Great Britain was definitively ratified by a "Joint Declaration" on August 14, 1941, on the USS *Augusta*, a 10,000-ton U.S. naval cruiser, the last symbol of the Washington treaty on arms limitation of 1922. This text is a key document for tracing the political structures of World War II and for reconstructing the prominent moments of this "special" alliance; it was also the first formal act in U.S. history by which the United States accepted an "entanglement" in Europe in peacetime (albeit only for the duration of the "European war," as it was labeled). It is also significant that virtually the same formulas and definitions (especially that of "defensive alliance") cropped up in the debate over NATO between 1947 and 1949. For the latter, see Gimbel (1976) and Mee (1984).

90. Memorandum P-A5, p. 3.

91. For more on the details of seniority rule, see Toniatti (1983) and Franck and Weisband (1979).

92. For the cultural and political motives behind U.S. "abstention" from European affairs after World War I, see Duroselle (1960), Adler (1957), Cole (1983), Rieselbach (1966).

93. See S. Hoffmann (1968, 1978) on the concept of U.S. "primacy."

94. Memorandum E-B36, p. 1. See also Keynes (1980a), on the clearing union, and (1980b), in which the British economist openly criticizes Leo Pasvolsky.

95. A telling symptom of this state of affairs is Keynes's disappointment in the State Department economists' blind faith in nineteenth-century free-trade doctrines championed by Pasvolsky. To counter these "Rip van Winkles" of economy, as Keynes dubbed them, he cited a number of other economists who he felt were more aware of the practical and theoretical problems the previous twenty years of upheaval had caused to economic science. This list included the two EF Group presidents (Hansen and Viner), J. M. Clark, L. Currie, W.

Stewart, and M. Ezekiel. See Keynes's comment on Pasvolsky's memorandum "Possibilities of Conflict between British and American Official Views on Postwar Economic Policy" (December 1941), reproduced in Keynes (1979b: 239–242). See also British contributions to postwar planning in Keynes (1979b, 1980a, 1980b). See also Keynes (1980b: 239, and the list of American economists included).

96. Memorandum E-B36, p. 1, and Cooper (1968).

97. The need for globalizing the economy through the exportation of a model of production and consumption tested in the United States in the 1920s can be directly traced to the ideologies of the "idealist" school in the U.S. from Wilson to the Kennedy liberals and the dawn of multinational enterprises. In 1940–1945 this drive was embodied (see Polenberg [1968: 31ff.], the quote from *America Unlimited*, by Eric Johnston) in Roosevelt's universalist fantasies, in *One World*, by Wendell Willkie (1943), in the *American Century*, by Henry Luce (1941), and in *The Century of the Common Man*, by Henry Wallace (1942). It was no coincidence that FDR used these interdependence doctrines as a club against Stalin and Churchill's "regionalist" approaches (i.e., against the zones of influence).

98. For an account of the transformations in U.S. social sciences in the 1930s, especially through the influx of European social scientists (particularly of German origin), see Hughes (1975) and relevant bibliography. For an effective analysis of theory regarding relations between "state" and "market" within the political system, see the classic work of Lindblom (1977). Less has been written about the conceptual "transition" that took place in those years in the sphere of social science regarding the ability to abstract the "function" of economic interdependence (which allowed for structural or institutional difference between the various national and/or regional markets as long as they were "interfaced") from the traditional "structure" of "free trade" (i.e., an obligatory or almost normative form to be propagated in order to regulate economic activity in almost any part of the world market). The implicit dynamic of the function and the freedom from the traditional restrictions and conditions of free trade gave interdependence a creative slant and made it an unprecedentedly pragmatic proposition. In addition to the bibliography for the chapter on the origins of "interdependence" in Santoro (1984a, chap. 2), see Gilpin (1977), who delved into the links between interdependence and national security; see also the "world systems analysis" of Hopkins and Wallerstein (1982). In terms of intellectual history, the problem concerned the transfer of managerial know-how from the business context to that of public administration.

99. These were the years of the "managerial revolution," which prompted the new organizational and strategic structures typified by the modern "multiunit" company. One of the features of such companies is the differentiation and automation of the steps in production and particularly the integration of sectors (of the various units) in a single composite administration consisting of several levels (i.e., top, middle, and lower management). By means of this "vertical integration" (made possible through the development of ever more sophisticated "control instruments for supervision and monitoring") U.S. industry was able to obtain a "command/control" of both production and trade, after the crisis of the 1920s and 1930s demonstrated the obsolete nature of the existing

coordination mechanisms and of having separate production and/or distribution units. See Chandler (1962, 1977). Actually, as Chandler correctly pointed out, the idea that "the rise of big business has any relation to government and military expenditures (or for that matter to monetary and fiscal policies) has no historical substance." This clashes with the theories of many radical economists and sociologists (including Paul M. Sweeney and Seymour Melman, who thought that war expenditure acted as a kind of flywheel to the economy). But that does not mean that the effects of military outlay were negligible: "Only during and after the Second World War did the government become a major market for industrial goods." However, this claim, which is corroborated by the facts, helps confirm the assertion that with respect to the "multiunit revolution" in business structures and to the reasons behind it, the interaction between big business and government was simply an episode and was of limited importance.

100. Chandler (1977: 496).

101. For a "leftist" view on this idea, see Kaldor (1981).

102. See the memoirs and/or biographies of those involved in this operation. The autobiography of J. K. Galbraith (1981) is particularly relevant. Galbraith had a leading role in the handling of economic policy in wartime (price control). See also the chapter "Technology of Social Production" in Noble (1977: 257ff.) and Akin (1977: especially 149–170).

103. Memorandum E-B36, p. 2.

104. Ibid. The real originality behind these arguments was that while the Keynesian–New Dealist line had always been strictly national (or nationalist) and Hull's had been hostile toward direct state intervention in the economy, the "internationalist" line represented here embodied both schools of thought. The main consequence was the liberation from the residual American parochialism of the proposals and scope of the New Deal. For more on the conflict between the two positions in the Roosevelt administration, see Freidel (1973), Burns (1956), Schlesinger (1957–1965), Dallek (1979), Cole (1983), and Tugwell (1957, 1968).

105. See Keynes (1979a, 1979b).

106. On the origin and forms of the "clearing union" between 1940 and 1942 see Keynes (1980a: 1–144, especially p. 111, in which the first mention of the idea "Bancor" occurs). For further information there follows a list of U.S. "economic war aims" according to the EF Group before the Placentia Bay conference, and for comparison, the eight points of the Atlantic Charter.

107. Cf. Lash (1976) and T. Wilson (1969) for an in-depth analysis of the eight points of the Atlantic Charter.

Chapter 8

1. See the first-hand accounts of Schacht (1966) and Speer (1969) and the studies of Milward (1965, 1977).

2. Cf. Dulles and Armstrong (1935, 1939) and Shotwell (1944).

3. Besides Maier (1975), the chief texts on the argument are those of J. H. Wilson (1971, 1974). Further useful reading may be found in the studies of D.

Bishop (1965) and Migone (1980). See the "classic" revisionist text of L. Gardner (1964).

4. Besides those already cited, see also E. W. Bennet (1962) on American-German exchanges in 1931 regarding the Young Plan. See Machlup (1977) and Santoro (1982) on these two concepts.

5. For readings on the New Dealer line and the trade agreements and political measures it inspired, see Hawley (1966), Vaudagna (1981a), and Schlesinger (1957–1965).

6. See Liska (1962) on the theory of alliances.

7. Such as the attempted Fascist-style coup in Uruguay in 1938. See Connel-Smith (1966). See also Callcott (1968).

8. Langer and Gleason (1952: 630).

9. Ibid.

10. Ibid., n. 59. It is remarkable that the first document issued by the P Group on relations with Latin America (Memorandum P-B8) was dated as early as August 1940.

11. Ibid., n. 61, "Memorandum Berle to Welles," May 24, 1940; see also WPS Memorandum E-B12 of the same date.

12. Langer and Gleason (1952: 631).

13. Cf. Vaudagna (1981a: 34).

14. Langer and Gleason (1952: 633–634); the excerpt is taken from *History of the Office of the Coordinator of Inter-American Affairs* (Washington, D.C.: USGPO, 1947), Appendix.

15. Langer and Gleason (1952: 634).

16. The title of Willkie's book was *One World* (1943); Willkie ran for president on the Republican ticket, and his book became a political best-seller in its day.

17. Notter (1949: 133–146).

18. See EF Group memorandum on the problems of monopoly and cartels during these years and until the end of the war.

19. Cf. Langer and Gleason (1952: 632).

20. Cf. Memorandum C-B12 and supplements.

21. Cf. Ninkovitch (1981: 47–48), explaining how some of these initiatives were created as a countermeasure to the various cultural and propaganda activities of the Tripartite countries (Italy, Germany, and Japan) in Latin America. In 1941 these countries set up and financed an estimated 864 schools in the area, 670 of which were German, 134 Japanese, and 58 Italian. Fears of anti-American indoctrination prompted the United States to wage a more active education policy, and financial aid was given to the newly constituted CIAA, which issued grants to the American Council on Education to set up 200 American schools in South America.

22. See especially Memorandum E-B12, May 27, 1940, a comprehensive dossier of data and statistics on the question of a "Pan-American Trade Bloc."

23. For more on the concept of national security and its origins, see Berkowitz and Bock (1968).

24. For further reading, see essays by Perkins (1941), Van Alstyne (1965), Weigley (1973), Williams (1952, 1972a), and Jordan and Taylor (1981, 1984).

25. Perkins (1941: 31).
26. Ibid., 47.
27. Ibid., 49–50.
28. Williams (1972c).
29. Cf. Williams (1959), but also Magdoff (1969) and E. May (1959).
30. Cf. the studies of Tucker (1973) and Kennan (1951), together with the memoirs of Kennan (1967), who was constantly in the forefront of U.S. foreign policy after the war. For an analysis of the revival of isolationist leanings in the ongoing debate on strategic doctrine and U.S.-European relations, see Santoro (1984b); the later issues of *International Security* give a clear idea of the debate under way. For more on "national interests," see Neuchterlein (1973).
31. For more recent insights into the Vietnam experience, see Gelb and Betts (1979) and Karnow (1983).
32. Cf. Triska (1986). It may be stretching the idea, but a certain conceptual analogy can be seen in an "extensive" interpretation of the Monroe Doctrine. That is, it could be suggested that there is an affinity between this doctrine and the set of theories and interpretations inherent to the Atlantic Alliance, including the disputed doctrine of "extended deterrence." For a deeper examination see Freedman (1981).
33. Cf. Aquarone (1973), Karp (1979), and Westcott (1947: especially 237–292, "Geography and War Strategy" and "Sea Power, Lifelines and Bases," and 293–305, "A Navy Second Only to Britain").
34. See Santoro (1958). Examples of innovation are the complexities of civil war and international war, the new social figure of the volunteer, the issue of blockades and the submarine war.
35. See Welles Memorandum, October 6, 1937 (FRUS 1937, vol. 1, pp. 665–666), cited in Offner (1969: 191ff.); also C. A. MacDonald (1981: 39).
36. C. A. MacDonald (1981: 41).
37. Cf. Dallek (1979: 39).
38. The Chaco War of 1933 represented the most intense form of international conflict possible in that particular area.
39. For the administration's reaction, see Notter (1949). The debates within the various groups were recorded in the numerous texts written more or less at the same time: A-B7, "Western Hemisphere Security" (November 25, 1940); A-B9, "Joint Defense Commissions with Latin America" (October 9, 1940); A-B15, "Airfields Suitable for Military Uses in South America" (November 23, 1940); A-B8, "A United States Naval Base at Recife" (October 9, 1940); P-B8, "An Examination of Western Hemisphere Affinities" (October 5, 1940).

Chapter 9

1. See in USDD, RG-59, Pasvolsky's memorandum "Assistance to Latin American Countries" (October 6, 1939); this is the first example of explicitly anti-German intervention in Latin America. See Memoranda P-B19, "The Island of Great Britain as a Factor in the Strategy of American Defense" (May 16,

1941), and T-B12, "Bases of Possible American Participation in the War in Europe" (June 10, 1941). See also Bailey and Ryan (1979: 31ff.).

2. Memorandum P-B19, p. 4.

3. Cf. above all Langer and Gleason (1952: 548ff.). See also S. E. Morison (1947–1975), "The Neutrality Patrol of the Atlantic Squadron," in vol. 1. See Watson (1950: 168–171) and S. E. Morison (1963: 27ff.).

4. Cf. R. E. Smith (1959: 132, table 17).

5. Ibid., pp. 73ff., and p. 98, n. 1.

6. See Shepardson (1937–1941), chaps. 5, 7. It should be pointed out the Total Defense program was still part of the broader conceptual area of the Industrial Mobilization Plan and of the resulting logic of preparation for M-Day, namely the eventual day of mass mobilization, which originated at the start of the 1920s. See R. E. Smith (1959: 81ff., 132).

7. See note 6.

8. Cf. G. Snyder and P. Diesing (1977: 125, fig. 2-36), "U.S.-Japan 1940"; see also Langer and Gleason (1952: 702); Callcott (1968: 382ff.); Conn, Engelmann, and Fairchild (1964: 3, 16, 22).

9. For a broad analysis of and documentation on the U.S. continental defense system, see the official publication: Conn, Engelmann, and Fairchild (1964: especially 3–38 and map 3).

10. The Atlantic area included all territories of North and South America, Greenland, Bermuda, and the Falkland Islands (but neither Iceland nor the Azores), plus all islands east of longitude 180° and the Aleutian Islands in the Pacific area. Although the experience of World War I offered Washington some diplomatic precedents for intervention (owing to the cooperation established among the various states in the continent and with Canada), U.S. commitment in the Western Hemisphere and elsewhere was wholly original and theretofore untried. See Conn, Engelmann, and Fairchild (1964: 10 and 16).

11. Cf. Callcott (1968: 368). Disputes centered on air and postal routes between the continental United States and Alaska, on the Pacific Coast Highway, and on the course of the San Lorenzo River.

12. Cited in ibid., pp. 387–388.

13. Besides De Seversky and S. E. Morison, see also Memoranda A-B12, "Token Forces for the New United States Bases" (October 14, 1940), and T-B15, "Some Prospective Problems of U.S.-Canadian Relations" (July 18, 1940).

14. Mahan (1897, 1970: 99–100).

15. Cf. Tansill (1932).

16. Stoddard (1961: 292).

17. Cf. Conn, Engelmann, and Fairchild (1964: 304–305).

18. Memoranda: Welles to Roosevelt, March 14, 1939, and Roosevelt to Welles, March 25, 1939, both cited in Callcott (1968: 391). See also FRUS (1939, vol. 5, pp. 461ff.). See W. R. Louis (1978) for more on the political use of "trusteeship."

19. Louis Hart to Eleanor Roosevelt, April 20, 1940; Roosevelt to E. Roosevelt, May 4, 1940; Welles to E. Roosevelt, May 6, 1940; cited in Callcott (1968: 390–391, n. 98).

20. W. R. Louis (1978: 88, n. 1). See also Thorne (1978).

21. In February 1941 the command of the Atlantic Squadron was assumed by Admiral King. See T. B. Buell (1981), Watson (1950: 94–97). The Martinique episode and U.S. pressure on the French governor to accept a naval "observer" to monitor the French warships anchored there are also mentioned in Hull (1948, vol. 1, pp. 818ff.).

22. State Department, Diplomatic Documents, European War File, U.S. National Archives, Washington, D.C., also cited in Langer and Gleason (1952: 568 and 620).

23. See also *Fortune*, July 1, 1940, and *Life*, July 24, 1940; and the article by Cantril (1940) of the same period.

24. The set of war aims of the Kriegsmarine presented to the Foreign Ministry on July 27, 1940, reflected many earlier German aspirations from World War I and echoed a memorandum of Admiral Adolf von Trotha of 1917. See Herwig (1976: 207ff.).

25. Cf. Herwig (1976: 208).

26. Covered in detail in S. E. Morison (1947–1965, vol. 1, pp. 30–32).

27. Cf. Langer and Gleason (1952: 626–627).

28. The Congress approved the resolution after it received unanimous confirmation in the Senate and a vote of 408 to 8 in the House of Representatives.

29. Cf. E. R. May (1963, especially p. 759).

30. See essay by Conn and Fairchild (1960: 26–81); and Efron (1939).

31. Cf. Streit (1938), Spykman (1942: 411–460). The latter work presents an overview of Spykman's geopolitical thinking. See also Lieuwen (1960: 188–199).

32. While this kind of flirtation with Fascism and Nazism was not encouraged, it was not yet considered entirely unacceptable, as in the case of Argentina and Uruguay.

33. Cf. Conn and Fairchild (1960: 210); Langer and Gleason (1952: 615–617).

34. Cf. Douhet (1921, 1955) and De Seversky (1942). See Warner's essay in Earle (1943: 485–503), for an outline of the doctrine of air power.

35. Traces of this debate can be detected in De Seversky and even in the U.S. Navy Commodore Dudley Wright Knox's introduction to the first volume of *History of United States Naval Operations in World War II*, by S. E. Morison. See De Seversky (1942: 254–291) and Morison (1947–1965).

36. See study by Caraley (1966: especially 73–82) and also Yergin (1977: 193ff., "The Gospel of National Security").

37. Among others, see Terraine (1985: 251–300).

38. See Brodie (1946) on the concept of the "absolute weapon"; see also Freedman (1981).

39. De Seversky (1942: 51).

40. These and other writings are collected and cited in Weigert (1942), from which the citations were drawn (p. 195).

41. Accounts of the steady expansion of air communications can be found in A. M. Lindbergh, J. A. Macreddy, and J. B. Wood, all published in *National Geographic* between 1924 and 1934.

42. Cf. Mackinder (1919, 1942) for a collection of his geopolitical writings, including the important essay "The Geographical Pivot of History." For a more

recent Italian compendium of geopolitical theory see Portinaro (1982), Caligaris and Santoro (1986), and Ilari (1986).

43. Cf. *Life,* August 3, 1942; and *Fortune,* October 22, 1941. For a recent analysis of the importance of mapping in war, see article by Henrikson (1975).

44. Weigert (1942: 197–198 and 245–247). Similar ideas can be found in Strausz-Hupé (1945: vii) and in Gray (1977: 21).

45. It would be interesting here to try out the model developed by Huntington (1981: 61–79, and table 2, p. 64) of the values with which Washington handled that state of "cognitive dissonance" that marked the U.S. approach to the outside world in 1940. Huntington put forward a model based on four possible responses to the contradiction between "Ideals" and "Institutions" (the "I-v-I Gap"), a typical feature of 1980s or 1990s U.S. politics: Moralism and/or Hypocrisy (for those who felt intensely about their ideals), Cynicism and/or Complacency (for those who did not feel intensely about their ideals). See also in Bonanate and Santoro (1986, "Introduction").

46. Nearly all those mentioned detailed their analyses and political proposals in essay form. Besides the already cited De Seversky (1942), Miller and Hill (1930), Streit (1938) and Shotwell (1942), for more on the debate within the U.S. Navy, see T. Buell (1981). On Marshall, see Mosley (1982).

47. Pogue (1966, 1973, vol. 1, pp. 120ff.).

48. Ibid., p. 121.

49. Cited in ibid., pp. 121, 140ff. See also the papers of the chief of staff in USDD, RG-165.

50. As director of the CFR, in some respects Miller represented the "militant" wing of the internationalist cadre. As such, from the very outset he proved to be one of the more active members of the WPS, participating on the Steering Committee from December 10, 1940, through February 1942, and operating from within the Political Group from May 1940 to May 1943. For a brief biography of Miller, see Chadwin (1968: 45–46); see also eulogy given by William Diebold at the Century Club in New York on Miller's death.

51. Cf. Chadwin (1968: 44, n. 1; citation on p. 47).

52. Miller and Hill (1930: 3).

53. Ibid., inside cover.

54. Ibid., pp. 294–295.

55. This was in stark contrast to certain optimistic claims made concerning the State Department, claims that continued to be made at the start of World War II: see Hulen (1939) and M. Weil (1978: 75ff.). See Weil on pro-European diplomatic corps and the "Dunn Connection." See also Hoover (1951) and Ferrell (1957, 1970).

56. For a summary of the efforts to modernize and streamline the armed forces, which began at the end of the last century, see Abrahamson (1981); see especially chap. 9 on attempts and projects in the years following World War I, which were nearly always thwarted by the isolationist foreign policy and budget cuts.

Chapter 10

1. Langer and Gleason (1952: 708) called this operation "Hands across the sea." The marked interest in the Caribbean became a constant, even in the mass media and national press. Almost all the more widely circulated magazines carried articles and photographs of the area. Five out of the seven features in the September issue of the *National Geographic* were devoted to Central America—three articles on Mexico, one on the American Virgin Islands (Washington's latest purchase in the Western Hemisphere), and a full in-depth photographic report on the islands. Cf. *National Geographic* 78, no. 3; Langley (1983), and LaFeber (1963).

2. A map reproduced at the head of each chapter in Streit (1938) precisely demonstrated (perhaps unwittingly) the ensuing shift in the strategic epicenter of the United States. The map is based on an azimuthal projection over the North Pole and distinctly shows North America as part of the Eurasian landmass—and hence the emphasis on the north (as only the northern hemisphere is visible) and the Atlantic (as the Pacific is partly hidden).

3. Cf. Pogue (1966: 123ff.).

4. Detailed information can be found in Herwig (1976: 93–109) and in Watson (1950: 103–104).

5. "Basis for Immediate Decisions Concerning the National Defense," reproduced in Watson (1950: 110–113).

6. See the essay "Il governo della politica estera americana," in Santoro (1984a: 201–229).

7. See FRUS (1939, vol. 2, pp. 1ff.) and FRUS (1940, vol. 2, pp. 333–339), under the heading "Territorial Claims in the Antarctic Advanced by Certain Governments").

8. FRUS (1940, vol. 2, pp. 333–334).

9. This was not achieved until 1958, with the Antarctic Treaty, which is still in force.

10. FRUS (1940, vol. 1, pp. 157–158).

11. "Memorandum by Mr. Ralph W. S. Hill of the Office of the Legal Adviser," April 24, 1940; in FRUS (1940, vol. 2, pp. 333–334).

12. "Memorandum by Mr. Hugh Cummings, Jr., of the Division of European Affairs," April 24, 1940; in FRUS (1940, vol. 2, pp. 345–346).

13. "The Danish Minister Kauffmann to the Secretary of State," April 28, 1940; in FRUS (1940, vol. 2, pp. 347–348).

14. Cf. Notter (1949: 30).

15. Cf. Adler (1957: 250–290), Cole (1983), and Nouailhat (1980) on the isolationist view of U.S. foreign policy.

16. The lack of interest in Greenland in military circles during this period is evident in the negative response by the War Department to the Senate's request for an opinion in May 1939, during the discussions on the usefulness of purchasing Greenland for the strategic defense of the Western Hemisphere—"WPD's (War Department Division) findings at the time, supported by the

Navy's WPD, were that Greenland, mostly ice-capped and fogbound, has no natural facilities for operating either aviation or naval forces, and that strategic considerations offered no justification for [its] acquisition." Cf. Watson (1950: 485). The WPD made no further mention of the island until February 1941.

17. Cf. Divine (1965: 114–116) and a direct personal account in Stimson and Bundy (1948: 368).

18. Divine (1965: 115).

19. On the other hand, after its agreement with the United States, the Danish government won a favorable ruling at the International Court of Justice in the Hague on April 5, 1933, according Denmark full sovereignty of the island with all related rights. The ruling terminated a lengthy legal wrangle between Denmark and Norway that had begun in 1921 when Copenhagen extended its fishing monopoly to the east coast of the island—the act was much criticized by Oslo, which even sent in troops to occupy certain tracts of east coast land for a few years.

20. See maps on pp. 266–267, and the map of Greenland on p. 262 in A. M. Lindbergh (1934).

21. See route map in ibid., p. 267. The complete account of the flight is published in Wood (1930).

22. Lansing's letter is quoted on pp. 4–5 of the memorandum.

23. Ibid.

24. Memorandum T-B3, p. 5. Note the use of the expression "as a defensive air-outpost." For the time being, the question was seen in the light of the rising theory of air power, without sufficiently weighing the equally important naval implications of the island, despite the difficult meteorological and climatic conditions.

25. See Memorandum T-B5 (April 18, 1940), "Treaty Basis of United States Rights, with Respect to Mandated Territories"; Memorandum T-B7 (April 15, 1940), "The Interests of the United States and the Fate of Small Nation States in Europe"; and Memorandum T-B9 (May 20, 1940), "The Legal Situation of the Arctic."

26. See data in table 3 on p. 11 of Memorandum T-B4.

27. Ibid. Shortly after Denmark was occupied, British troops landed on the east coast of Iceland on May 10, 1940, as a means of controlling the Danish straits from the base at Seabol.

28. As Stefansson believed (1939a, 1939b).

29. These figures are taken from Hero (1973: 24). The rapport and influence between public opinion and the course of foreign policy is a topic that has been dealt with extensively by both journalists and scholars. Important contributions include the research of Levering (1978) and Leigh (1976), who concentrated specifically on the decade 1937–1947. The chief source of information on public attitudes and their evolution are the various opinion polls; for data on American opinion during the first half of 1940 see Gallup (1972, vol. 1, pp. 77, 84, 90, 131–132, 222–231, 252, 276, 282).

30. Cf. Watson (1950: 126–147).

31. Quote from Memorandum T-B3, p. 6.

32. Memorandum T-A3, p. 7. Many of Bowman's theories on territorial organization (Bowman [1947]) were formulated in the CFR, where he served as vice president for many years.

33. See Memorandum T-B18, "A Reappraisal of the Stimson Doctrine." In this memorandum the T Group carefully examined the principle sanctioned in 1932 by Secretary of State Stimson regarding the war in Manchuria, which stated that the United States would never recognize modifications to territories between states (China and Japan in this case) achieved through military conquest. The document asked whether the United States could adopt a dual political line, using the Stimson doctrine for the Western Hemisphere and a more flexible doctrine for the rest of the world, or whether it was more advisable to use a single standard for all situations. In an objective assessment of the pros and cons, the text suggested a more flexible case-by-case application for property transfers that continued to occur outside the Western Hemisphere but adhered to the above principle with respect to the American continent (pp. 3–4).

34. Memorandum T-A3, p. 9.

35. Cf. Memorandum A-A3, June 28, 1940.

36. During an interview with the author, William Diebold, commented that there had been rumors that when, on September 7, 1940, President Roosevelt made his pronouncement on the status of Greenland, that it was officially considered within the Western Hemisphere. See Langer and Gleason (1952: 686–687); he had Memorandum T-B3 on the reading stand in front of him.

37. For a commentary on U.S. relations with Britain and Canada, see Gelber (1961: 165–171) and W. R. Louis (1978: 102, 220–225).

38. Cf. Watson (1950: 110ff.).

39. For a comparison, see official documents in FRUS (1940, vol. 1, pp. 1, 333, 343, 352, 493, 675, 729).

40. See Langer and Gleason (1952: 430, n. 60).

41. FRUS (1940, vol. 1, pp. 352–353).

42. See Notter (1949: 30, 44). According to Notter, it was not until May 31 that the Subcommittee on Political Problems of the Advisory Committee on Problems of Foreign Relations (the first offspring of the State Department's postwar policy planning) actually began to consider the options regarding Germany's possible victory in Europe. In that session the subcommittee drafted the joint resolution of the president and the secretary of state on Greenland (but not Iceland, as Notter has pointed out), in which it was specified that the United States would refuse to recognize or passively accept "a transfer of territory in the Western Hemisphere . . . from one non-American country to another non-American country" (p. 30). The resolution was approved by the Senate on June 17 and by the House of Representatives the following day. The field into which Notter fit the argument was quite clearly more restricted than the one discussed by the CFR, more strictly "defensive" in tone than "offensive," and he therefore ruled out any military action except in the case of attempted German invasion of the island.

43. Telegram no. 590, June 5, 1920, 7 P.M., to the U.S. ambassador in Great Britain, published in FRUS (1922, vol. 2, p. 1).

44. Quoted in Langer and Gleason (1952: 430), which seems to imply Notter's memorandum came first. But Langer joined the Peace Aims Group only in June 1941 and therefore probably did not know of the memoranda in question.

45. See Bailey and Ryan (1979: 70) and F. D. Roosevelt (1932–1945, vol. 15, p. 280).

46. F. D. Roosevelt (1932–1945, vol. 15, p. 127); see also Ruge (1956: 64) and Morison (1947–1965, vol. 1, p. 58).

47. Cf. Langer and Gleason (1952: 430–435, and nn. 68, 69). For further reading on dealings with the British and Canadians between April and May 25, 1940, when the United States opened a consulate in Godthaap in Greenland, see also FRUS (1940, vol. 2, p. 343) and Hull (1948, vol. 1, p. 753).

48. Langer and Gleason (1952: 687, n. 36).

49. Be that as it may, in his article in *Foreign Affairs* of July 1940, Mosely himself foresaw the course of events and openly upheld that "Iceland's anomalous position shows that the concept of Western Hemisphere is at bottom a political concept, and that the privileges and duties connected with being a part of this Hemisphere cannot be defined by geography alone. For instance, the assumption that the United States could not conceivably allow any European state other than Denmark to possess Greenland needs to be weighed against the realization that Greenland could not be defended against a strong Power in control of Iceland." With this last comment, Mosely was hinting at the "domino theory." Cf. Mosely (1940: 746).

50. See FRUS (1940, vol. 2, pp. 675–684). Of special note is the "Memorandum of Conversation, by the Assistant Secretary of State (Berle)" dated July 12, 1940, which related the contents of an interview with the general consul of Iceland, Thor (ibid.: 681).

51. Cf. FRUS (1940, vol. 2, pp. 679–680).

Chapter 11

1. See map in Mosely (1940: 743), which clearly shows the string of submerged territories, islands, and subcontinents linking the American continent with Europe. The same azimuthal projection was used by Streit (1938). See also Bailey and Ryan (1979) for an analysis of the "naval" uses the two islands were put to by the U.S. Navy between 1940 and 1941.

2. Lippmann (1943: 5); see also Larson (1973), and Russett and Stepan (1973), especially the bibliography therein (Alcalà and Rosenberg [1973]: 193–371).

3. Cf. the studies on the birth of the so-called national security state: Yergin (1977) and Gaddis (1982). See also Bonanate and Santoro (1986).

4. Wolfers (1952), cited in Berkowitz and Bock (1968: 140). Cf. also Rosenau (1968: 34–40).

5. Cf. Lippmann (1943: 127ff.).

6. For a detailed case study on one of these centers, see J. N. Thomas (1974), which includes a sizable bibliography on the use of social sciences in political decision making and policy analysis.

7. It should be remembered that many members of the EF Group participated or had major roles in the Dollar Diplomacy of the 1920s and in later attempts at launching the New Deal model in the field of foreign policy. For key studies into economic diplomacy, see Ferrell (1957) and Aldcroft (1977); on New Deal diplomacy see L. Gardner (1964, 1984) and the early work of Nearing and Freeman (1925, 1966).

8. McCoy was later appointed president of a special investigation commission on the problem of foreign supplies; in May 1942 Strong became head of the Army Intelligence Department, G-2. Adm. Standley was transferred to Moscow to organize Allied convoys to the Soviet Union, and Adm. Pratt (chief of naval operations in the 1930s) became an adviser to Chester W. Nimitz, Ernest J. King, and Leahy.

9. The Gallup polls had revealed the U.S. public's low sensitivity to European affairs and to foreign politics in general. In the fifteen years between 1935 and 1950, the American Institute of Public Opinion carried out twenty polls on a sample of U.S. citizens, asking the same question each time: "What do you regard as the most important problem before the American people today?" The percentage of respondents who thought it was foreign affairs varied considerably over the years (see Almond [1961: 73]). The results follow: November 1935, 11%; December 1936, 26%; December 1937, 23%; January 1939, 14%; April 1939, 35%; December 1939, 47%; August 1940, 48%; November 1941, 81%; October 1945, 7%; February 1946, 23%; June 1946, 11%.

The answers would seem to indicate the marked dependence of interest in foreign affairs on dramatic and openly threatening events and the astonishing pressure of domestic and private affairs, even in periods of international crisis (p. 72). It should also be noted that the relative high percentage of respondents who thought that foreign affairs was the most pressing problem were still openly in favor of maintaining neutrality and in April and December 1940, in "keeping the country out of the war." This gradually began to change by the August 1940 poll, still only one percentage point up from preceding poll, although the August one was carried out in an intensely dramatic moment for the international system, after the fall of France and at the height of the Battle of Britain. Only 9% of those interviewed still felt that the main problem was a question of keeping the U.S. out of the war; 27% were concerned about national defense measures; 12% spoke of a "war problem" (p. 74). However, practically no one suggested that the United States enter the war alongside the Allies.

10. The P Group contributed hypotheses and solutions for postwar planning mainly in the second half of the war, during which (together with the EF Group) it assumed the leading role, especially regarding the preparatory discussion for postwar international order. The CFR study groups' contribution was recognized in R. B. Russell (1958b: 215ff., "Sources of Ideas on Post-War Organization"). In the first stages of the war, however, the P Group's work was somewhat limited. The only exceptions were the long and definitive debate with the EF Group on the proposed regional trade blocs and the question of coexistence with German-controlled Europe—as discussed in Chapters 5 and 6 of this book.

11. See W. R. Louis (1978).

12. Cf. Carr (1939, 1946), Lippmann (1943, 1944), H. J. Morgenthau (1948) and Wolfers (1952).

13. For an exhaustive examination of aspects of "imperial expansion," see Liska (1978); for more on the power vacuum in Europe in 1940, see pp. 108–157 of the same. See also Aquarone (1973), La Feber (1963), and E. May (1961, 1968).

14. Cf. Dougherty and Pfaltzgraff (1971, 1981) for an overview of the main "schools" (realist, idealist); see likewise Waltz (1979). See also the entry "International Relations" in Alger (1968: 61–69) and the anthology edited by Bonanate and Santoro (1986).

15. See especially R. E. Smith (1959: 48ff. and 73ff.) and Chandler (1977).

16. Cf. Noble (1977: 257ff., "Modern Management and the Expansion of Engineering," and 224ff., "The Industrial Process of Higher Education"). Noble looked closely into the birth of the early forms of interaction between industry and army in terms of human resources (during World War I, from the publication of the 1916 Defense Act), analyzing in detail the role of the War Department Committee on Education and Special Training (CEST), set up in February 1918 (pp. 214–225). The Defense Act actually authorized the constitution of an army education establishment along the lines laid down in the Morrill Act of 1861, which caused the number of engineering schools to leap from six to seventy. One of the first effects of the Defense Act was the creation of a Reserve Officers Training Corps (ROTC), which began at MIT in Cambridge, Massachusetts, in 1911 (pp. 225ff.). The specialization and training courses conducted by the CEST until 1919 and later continued by the ROTC (which in 1925 listed over 120,000 members) provided the handful of internationalist sympathizers both within and outside the armed forces great help in promoting the transition of the United States from being a continental power to that of global involvement.

17. See Bonanate (1976b) and Bobbio (1979) for a discussion on war not only as an "interval between two periods of peace" but also as a cusp in the relation of forces and power that lends structure (in historically different ways) to the system of international relations.

18. At the time, not everyone saw it this way. In an interview with me, Alger Hiss, who was a member of the U.S. delegation at Yalta, explained that except for President Roosevelt, the primary goal of the General Staff and of most of the politicians and diplomats present was to put an end to the war, without much concern for what came after (interview September 19, 1979).

19. These were the AMGs or Allied Military Governments. See David Ellwood's study on the American-British military occupation of Italy (Ellwood [1977]): His form of analysis could serve as a general model for interpreting Allied action regarding the future world order.

20. Cf. Deutsch (1963). Of particular interest is Deutsch's "cybernetic" interpretation of the growth of "intellectual power," in which he distinguished between the various levels of action. The first is labeled "manipulative reason" (*Verstand*), which involves the best deployment of available intellectual tools, the way a computer uses an existing program to solve a problem. Deutsch then examined the second level, commonly called "wisdom." This conceptual tool

does not solve problems directly but is used in deciding what problems are worth solving, what strategies and routines to develop, and what modifications to the program's structure are needed. The third level is "perceptive reason" (*Vernunft*), which the author used to denote the set of communications channels and existing memories that allow the reception of information from outside the system (from the "universe," through the process of "intelligence amplification," identified by W. Ross Ashby) and the capacity to combine the existing intellectual resources with "new" ones, with the purpose of increasing the system's performance on all three levels (see pp. xiv-xv). It would be interesting, though it strays somewhat from the scope of this work, to reconstruct a model based on Deutsch's three levels (*Verstand*, Wisdom, and *Vernunft*) to track the intellectual "growth" in U.S. foreign policy in the course of the war by examining the behavior of the major figures in the Council on Foreign Relations and the study groups of the WPS project. This approach could be used with the memoranda of 1940 and 1941 to determine whether they belong to the first, second, or third of Deutsch's levels.

21. For more on W. A. White, see the biography by Jerningan (1983) and White's own autobiography (1946). See also Chadwin (1968: 133–134) and G. Smith (1973: 164–165).

22. For the more distant political and cultural references, besides the numerous studies already mentioned, see W. Karp (1979), which examines the impact on the domestic political system of the two wars in which the United States was involved between 1898 and 1920, the Spanish-American War and World War I. The umbilical cord linking domestic affairs with foreign policy and the use of internationalist formulas and slogans for domestic political goals, as described in Karp, are more or less the same as the ones that would determine the overall configuration of the U.S. political system twenty years later (and perhaps even forty-five years later).

23. See Nelson (1946).

24. Lippmann (1944: 40ff.).

25. Ibid., p. 59.

26. Ibid., p. 60; see also Liska (1977, 1978).

27. A typical example is Shoup and Minter's book (1977).

28. See S. Welles (1944), with special reference to Chapters 3, 4, and 5. Compare also the interesting debate on the future world order and the United Nations in the making, led by Welles and Lippmann, which appeared in the August 21, 1944, issue of *Newsweek*; the debate focused on the question "How Can We Win the Peace?"

29. For more on Walter Lippmann and his concept of foreign policy, see R. Steel (1980: especially 379–418).

30. For an account of models for the international system, see the pioneering work of M. Kaplan (1957), which analyzed six possible types of system. The origins of the bipolar system are covered in Yergin (1977); see also the bibliography in DePorte (1979).

31. In addition to the fundamental essay by C. S. Maier (1975) on the interwar years, see Hoover (1951). This text carries some particularly revealing accounts

on the early days of "Belgian Relief" (pp. 152ff.), on U.S. Food Administration (pp. 240ff.), and finally on "The Relief and Reconstruction of Europe, 1918–1920" (pp. 282ff.).

32. D. F. Fleming (1969), Kolko (1969), Kolko and Kolko (1972), and Williams (1980).

33. There is a surplus of literature on the subject in the United States, and it is often not objective. Those listed here, both early and recent, represent some of the best historiographic representations of the argument, on both the American and the Japanese sides: Ienaga (1968); Iriye (1967, 1981); Borg and Okamoto (1973); Morley (1980); Prange (1981); Thompson, Stanley, and Perry (1981); Thorne (1978); Bergamini (1971); and Spector (1984). Also worth reading are two classic volumes, one by Beard (1948), the other by Tansill (1952). See also Ferretti's review (1982) of studies carried out by the Japanese.

34. On the distinction between potential and actual power, see the two articles by D. Baldwin (1979, 1980).

35. For a breakdown of naval strategy, see Till (1982, 1984: 19–74).

Chapter 12

1. Notter (1949: 61–62).

2. Russell (1958b); Divine (1967). See also the main memoranda of the CFR drafted by the EF Group and P Group on schemes for multilateral reorganization for the postwar era, which foreshadowed the actual political decision taken in 1945 by the government. Of special interest is the series of documents spawned by Memorandum E-B49, April 1, 1942 ("Postwar Economic Problems: International Relief, Labor Problems and Social Legislation, International Long-Term Investment"), and those that followed Memorandum P-B51, October 2, 1942 ("Alternative Bases for the Development of Postwar World Organization").

3. Cf. the note from the State Department, "What Do We Desire of China: Preliminary Considerations," dated December 1941 (signed SR:JM), reproduced in USDD, RG-59, State Department.

4. Notter (1949); also see the lists therein on pp. 69–78.

5. Refer to the bibliography on interdependence in Machlup (1977) and in Santoro (1982).

6. A deeper analysis of the concept of national interest and the relative hierarchies of U.S. regional priorities is found in Nuechterlein (1973, 1979). See also Hughes (1975: 25–48), who retraced the long history of internationalist sentiment in the United States, of which the Carnegie Foundation and the CFR were precursors in idealistic and normative terms, if not on a political-economic level.

7. Gaddis (1982).

8. Cf. H. J. Morgenthau (1948) and R. N. Cooper (1968); Keohane (1984).

9. Besides H. J. Morgenthau (1948) in particular, see the works of Lasswell and A. Kaplan (1950); M. Kaplan (1957), Liska (1962, 1977, 1978); Waltz (1979); Krasner (1982), Keohane (1984), and Axelrod (1984: 304–315).

10. Rosecrance (1986: 62).

11. Ibid.

12. Ibid.

13. For a classic definition of the essential characteristics and rules of this universal model, see M. Kaplan (1957).

14. Keohane and Nye (1977).

15. Keohane (1984); Gilpin (1981).

16. See the memoirs of Welles (1951); Truman (1955, 1956), and the volume by Rearden (1984) covering the formative years of the Office of the Secretary of Defense, from 1947 to 1950.

17. Freedman (1981); D. H..Rosenberg (1973); Kennan (1951, 1967); and Nuechterlein (1979); F. Kaplan (1983); Huntington (1959).

18. For more on the theory of the bipolar international system as a basic "war system," see Santoro (1984b) and Bonanate and Santoro's chapter, "The Bipolar System As a War System: The Logic of International Regimes," in Santoro (1988a).

19. Cf. Mackinder (1919, 1942); Spykman (1942, 1944); Mahan (1890); Douhet (1921); De Seversky (1942). See also the volume edited by Bonanate and Santoro (1986) for a list of the various levels and models of security.

20. The anthology of works edited by Etzold and Gaddis (1978) provides excellent source material; see also Gaddis (1982).

21. Snyder and Diesing (1977).

22. Craig and George (1983).

23. See the theory of the "Nuclear Deterrence Regime" by Bonanate and Santoro in Santoro (1988a: 9ff.).

24. For a review of the various theories in crisis management see the article by Gilbert and Lauren (1980) and O. R. Holsti's critique (1980) in the same issue of the *Journal of Conflict Resolution.*

25. For further analysis of this point, see Aron (1962) and Schelling (1960).

Bibliography

Aaron, Daniel (1983). "American Culture and the New Deal." Florence, June 4, 19 pp. (typescript).

Abosch, H. (1963). *The Menace of the Miracle: Germany from Hitler to Adenauer.* New York: Monthly Review Press.

Abrahamson, James L. (1981). *America Arms for a New Century: The Making of a Great Military Power.* New York: Free Press.

Acheson, Dean (1969). *Present at the Creation: My Years in the State Department.* New York: New York University Press.

Adams, Brooks (1900, 1947). *America's Economic Supremacy.* New York: Harper.

Adams, Henry H. (1977). *Harry Hopkins: A Biography.* New York: Putnam.

Adler, Selig (1957). *The Isolationist Impulse: Its Twentieth Century Reason.* New York: Abelard-Schuman.

——— (1965). *The Uncertain Giant, 1921–1941: American Foreign Policy Between the Wars.* New York: Collier.

Adler, Selig, and Paterson, Thomas G. (1970). "Red Fascism: The Merger of Nazi Germany and Soviet Russia in One American Image of Totalitarism, 1930–1950." *American Historical Review* 75, 1970, pp. 1046–1074.

Agarossi, Elena (1976). "Recenti orientamenti della storiografia americana sulle origini della guerra fredda: l'interpretazione revisionista," in *Italia e Stati Uniti durante l'amministrazione Truman.* Milan: Franco Angeli.

——— (1979). "Gli Stati Uniti e la divisione dell'Europa." *Storia Contemporanea* 10, no. 6, pp. 1157–1180.

———, ed. (1984). *Gli Stati Uniti e le origini della guerra fredda.* Bologna: Il Mulino.

Aigner, Dietrich (1978). "Hitler und die Weltherrschaft." In W. Michalka, ed. *Nationalsozialistische Aussenpolitik.* Darmstadt, pp. 44–69

Akin, William E. (1977). *Technocracy and the American Dream.* Berkeley: University of California Press.

Alcalà, Raoul H., and Rosenberg, Douglas H. (1973). "The New Politics of National Security: A Selected and Annotated Research Bibliography." In B. M. Russet and A. Stepan, eds. *Military Force and American Society.* New York: Harper & Row.

Aldcroft, Derek H. (1977). *From Versailles to Wall Street: The International Economy in the 1920s.* Berkeley: University of California Press.

Alexander, Charles C. (1969). *Nationalism in American Thought, 1930–1945.* Chicago: University of Chicago Press.

Alexander, John A. (1951). "The First World War in American Thought to 1929." American University (Ph.D. dissertation).

Alger, Chadwick F. (1968). "International Relations." In *International Encyclopedia of the Social Sciences,* vol. 8, pp. 60–68. New York: Free Press.

Allen, Frederick Lewis (1931, 1959). *Only Yesterday: An Informal History of the 1920s.* New York: Harper & Row.

Allison, Graham T. (1971). *The Essence of Decision.* Boston: Little, Brown.

Allison, Graham T., and Szanton, Peter (1976). *Remaking Foreign Policy: The Organizational Connection.* New York: Basic.

Almond, Gabriel A. (1961). *The American People and the Foreign Policy.* New York: Praeger.

Alsop, Joseph, and Kintner, Robert (1940). *American White Paper.* New York.

Ambrose, Stephen E. (1971). *Rise to Globalism: American Foreign Policy, 1934–1970.* Baltimore: Johns Hopkins University Press.

——— (1982, 1984). *Eisenhower.* Vol. 1, *The Soldier;* Vol. 2, *The President.* New York: Simon and Schuster.

American Economic Review (1940). (Special issue) "Economic Problems of War."

American National Committee on Intellectual Cooperation of the League of Nations (1934). *The Study of International Relations in the United States.* New York: Columbia University Press.

Americans United for World Organization (1944). *From the Garden of Eden to Dumbarton Oaks.* Stanford: Stanford University Press.

Angell, Norman (1914a). *The Great Illusion,* 4th ed. New York: Putnam's.

——— (1914b). *The Foundation of International Polity.* London: Heinemann.

——— (1952). "A Re-Interpretation of Empire." *United Empire* 43, no. 5.

Annals of the American Academy of Political and Social Science (1924). "American and the Post-War European Situation." No. 203.

Aquarone, Alberto (1973). *Le origini dell'imperialismo americano: Da McKinley a Taft (1897–1913).* Bologna: Il Mulino.

Arkes, Hadley (1973). *Bureaucracy, the Marshall Plan and the National Interest.* Princeton: Princeton University Press.

Armstrong, Hamilton Fish, ed. (1972). *Fifty Years of Foreign Affairs.* New York: Praeger.

Aron, Raymond (1962). *Paix et guerre entre les nations.* Paris: Calman-Lévy.

——— (1973). *République Impériale: Les Etats-Unis dans le monde, 1945–1972.* Paris: Calman-Lévy.

Artaud, Denise (1979). "La question des dettes interalliées et la reconstruction de l'Europe." *Revue historique* 30 (April-June), pp. 363–382.

——— (1980). "Protectionisme, libéralisation des changes et conquête des marchés extérieurs aux Etats-Unis, 1913–1934." *Relations Internationales* 31, no. 22.

Axelrod, Richard (1984). *The Evolution of Cooperation.* New York: Basic Books.

Bacchus, William I. (1974). *Foreign Policy and the Bureaucratic Process: The State Department's Country Director System.* Princeton: Princeton University Press.

Backer, J. H. (1978). *The Decision to Divide Germany: America's Foreign Policy in Transition.* Durham: Duke University Press.

Bailey, Thomas A. (1942). *The Policy of the United States Toward the Neutrals, 1917–1918.* Baltimore: Johns Hopkins University Press.

———— (1947). *Wilson and the Peace-Makers*. Vol. 1, *Woodrow Wilson and the Lost Peace;* Vol. 2, *Woodrow Wilson and Great Britain*. New York: Harper.

———— (1948). *The Man in the Street: The Impact of American Public Opinion on Foreign Policy*. New York.

———— (1961). "America's Emergence As a World Power: The Myth and the Verity." *Pacific Historical Review*, February.

———— (1977). *The Marshall Plan Summer: An Eyewitness Report in Europe in 1947*. Stanford: Hoover Institution Press.

Bailey, Thomas A., and Ryan, Paul B. (1979). *Hitler Versus Roosevelt: The Undeclared Naval War*. New York: Free Press.

Bairati, Pietro, ed. (1976). *I profeti dell'Impero americano*. Turin: Einaudi.

Baldwin, David A. (1979). "Power Analysis and World Politics: New Trends Versus Old Tendencies." *World Politics* 31, no. 2.

———— (1980). "Interdependence and Power: A Conceptual Analysis." *International Organization* 34, no. 4.

Baldwin, Hanson (1966). *Battles Lost and Won*. New York: Harper & Row.

Balfour, Michael (1979). *Propaganda in War, 1939–1945: Organizations, Policies and Publics in Britain and Germany*. Boston: Routledge and Kegan Paul.

———— (1982). "Personalities and Organisation in British Propaganda 1936–45." Bellagio Conference: April 5–9 (typescript).

Balfour, Michael, and Mair, John (1956). *Four-Power Control in Germany and Austria 1945–1946*. Royal Institute of International Affairs. London: Oxford University Press.

Bane, S. L., and Lutz, R. H., eds. (1943). *The Organization of American Relief in Europe, 1918–1919*. Stanford: Stanford University Press.

Bariè, Ottavio (1978a). *Gli Stati Uniti nel secolo XX. Tra leadership e guerra fredda*. Milan: Marzorati.

———— (1978b). *Gli Stati Uniti da colonia a superpotenza*. Milan: Mursia.

Barnds, William J., ed. (1977). *China and America: The Search for a New Relationship*. New York: New York University Press.

Barnes, Elmer Harry (1953). *Perpetual War for Perpetual Peace: A Critical Examination of the Foreign Policy of FDR and Its Aftermath*. Coldwell: University of Idaho Press.

Barnes, James T., and Barnes, Patience P. (1980). *Hitler's Mein Kampf in Britain and America: A Publishing History 1930–1939*. Cambridge: Cambridge University Press.

Barnet, Richard J. (1971). *Roots of War: The Men and the Institution Behind U.S. Foreign Policy*. Baltimore: Johns Hopkins University Press.

———— (1977). *The Giants: Russia and America*. New York: Simon and Schuster.

Barnhart, Michael A. (1980). "Japanese Intelligence Before World War Two: Best Case Analysis." Harvard University, 54 pp. (typescript).

Baruch, Bernard (1921). *American Industry in the War: A Report of the War Industries Board*. Washington: USGPO.

———— (1961). *The Public Years*. London: Macmillan.

Beale, Howard K. (1956). *Theodore Roosevelt and the Rise of America to World Power*. Baltimore: Johns Hopkins University Press.

Beard, Charles A. (1934). *The Idea of National Interest: Analytical Study in American Foreign Policy.* New York: Macmillan.

———— (1940). *A Foreign Policy for America.* New York.

———— (1946). *American Foreign Policy in the Making, 1932–1940.* New Haven: Yale University Press.

———— (1948). *President Roosevelt and the Coming of the War, 1941.* New Haven: Yale University Press.

Beaumont, Joan (1980). *Comrades in Arms: British Aid to Russia, 1941–1945.* London: Davis Poynter.

Bedarida, François, ed. (1979). *La Stratégie secrète de la drôle de guerre.* Paris: Fondation Nationale des Sciences Politiques.

Beitzell, Robert (1972). *The Uneasy Alliance: America, Britain and Russia, 1941–1943.* New York.

Bemis, Samuel Flagg, and Griffin, Grace Gardner, eds. (1935, 1963). *Guide to the Diplomatic History of the United States, 1775–1921.* Washington: USGPO, 1935; Gloucester: Peter Smith, 1963.

Bennet, Douglas J., Jr. (1978). "Congress in Foreign Policy: Who Needs It?" *Foreign Affairs* 57, no. 1.

Bennet, Edward M. (1979). *Recognition of Russia: An American Foreign Policy Dilemma.* Waltham.

Bennet, Edward W. (1962). *Germany and the Diplomacy of the Financial Crisis, 1931.* Cambridge: Harvard University Press.

Benoist-Mechin, Alain (1956). *Soixante jours qui ébranlèrent l'Occident: 10 Mai–10 Juillet 1940.* Paris: Laffont.

Benton, Wilbourn E., and Grimm, George, eds. (1955). *Nuremberg: German Views of the War Trials.* Dallas: Southern Methodist University Press.

Bergamini, David (1971). *Japan's Imperial Conspiracy.* New York: Morrow.

Berger, Jason (1979). "A New Deal for the World: Eleanor Roosevelt and American Foreign Policy, 1920–1962." City University of New York (Ph.D. dissertation).

Berkowitz, Morton, and Bock, P. G. (1968). "National Security." In *International Encyclopedia of the Social Sciences,* vol. 11. New York: Free Press.

Berle, B., and Jacobs, T., eds. (1973). *Navigating the Rapids: From the Papers of Adolf A. Berle.* New York.

Berman, Larry (1980). *The Office of Management and Budget, and the Presidency, 1921–1979.* Princeton: Princeton University Press.

Berman, Maureen R., and Johnson, Joseph E., eds. (1977). *Unofficial Diplomats.* New York: Columbia University Press.

Bernd, Martin (1981). "Amerikas Durchbruch zur politischen Weltmacht. Die Interventionistische Globalstrategie der Regierungs Roosevelt 1933–1941." *Militärgeschichtliche Mitteilungen,* no. 30, pp. 58–81.

Bernstein, B., and Matusow, A. J. (1969). *The Truman Administration: A Documentary History.* New York: Twentieth Century American.

Beschloss, Michael R. (1980). *Kennedy and Roosevelt: The Uneasy Alliance.* New York: Norton.

Bettelheim, Charles (1945, 1971). *L'economie allemande sous le nazisme.* Paris: François Maspero.

Betts, Richard K. (1982). *Surprise Attack*. Washington: Brookings.

Billington, Ray A. (1945). "The Origins of Midwestern Isolationism," *Political Science Quarterly* 9 (March), pp. 44–46.

Birnbaum, Karl E. (1958). *Peace Moves and U-Boot Warfare: A Study of Imperial Germany's Policy Toward the United States, April 18, 1916–January 9, 1917*. Stockholm: Almquist and Vicksell.

Bishop, Donald G. (1965). *The Roosevelt-Litvinov Agreements: The American View*. Syracuse: Syracuse University Press.

Bishop, John (1974). *FDR's Last Year, April 1944–April 1945*. New York: Morrow.

Blanchard, William M. (1978). *Aggression American Style*. Pacific Palisades: Goodyear Publishing.

Blechman, Barry M., and Kaplan, Stephen S. (1977). *The Use of the Armed Forces As a Political Instrument: Executive Summary*. Washington: Brookings.

——— (1978). *Force Without War: U.S. Armed Forces As a Political Instrument*. Washington: Brookings.

Bloomfield, Lincoln P. (1984). "What's Wrong with Transitions?" *Foreign Policy*, no. 55, Summer 1984, pp. 23–39.

Blum, John M. (1956). *Woodrow Wilson and the Politics of Morality*. Boston: Little, Brown.

——— (1965). *From the Morgenthau Diaries: The Years of Urgency, 1938–1941*. Boston: Little, Brown.

——— (1967). *From the Morgenthau Diaries: The Years of War, 1941–1945*. Boston: Little, Brown.

———, ed. (1973). *The Price of Vision: The Diary of Henry Wallace, 1942–1946*. Boston: Little, Brown.

——— (1976a). *Roosevelt and Morgenthau*. Boston: Little, Brown.

——— (1976b). *V. Was for Victory*. New York: Harcourt Brace Jovanovich.

Blum, Steven D. (1984). *Walter Lippmann: Cosmopolitanism in the Century of Total War*. Ithaca: Cornell University Press.

Bobbio, Norberto (1979). *Il problema della pace e le vie della guerra*. Bologna: Il Mulino.

Bohlen, Charles E. (1969). *The Transformation of American Foreign Policy*. New York: Norton.

Bohlen, Charles E., and Phelps, Robert M. (1973). *Witness to History, 1929–1969*. New York: Norton.

Bolt, Ernest C., Jr. (1977). *Ballots Before Bullets: The War Referendum Approach to Peace in 1914–1941*. Charlottesville: University Press of Virginia.

Bonacina, Giorgio (1975). *Comando bombardieri: Operazione Europa*. Milan: Longanesi.

Bonanate, Luigi (1973, 1979, 1983). *Introduzione all'analisi politica internazionale*. Turin: Giappichelli.

———, ed. (1976a). *Il sistema delle relazioni internazionali*. Turin: Einaudi.

——— (1976b). *Teoria politica e relazioni internazionali*. Milan: Ed. di Comunità.

——— (1979). "Sistema internazionale." In *Il Mondo Contemporaneo. Storia d'Europa*, vol. 7. Florence: Politica Internazionale, La Nuova Italia.

Bonanate, Luigi, and Santoro, Carlo M., eds. (1986). *Antologia di Relazioni Internazionali*. Bologna: Il Mulino.

Bonazzi, Tiziano, and Vaudagna, Maurizio, eds. (1986). *Ripensare Roosevelt*. Milan: Franco Angeli.

Boreisky, Michael (1975). "Trends in U.S. Technology: A Political Economist's View." *American Scientist* 63 (January-February), pp. 70–82.

Borg, Dorothy (1957). "Notes on Roosevelt's Quarantine Speech." *Political Science Quarterly* 72 (September), pp. 5–33.

——— (1964). *The United States and the Far Eastern Crisis of 1933–1938*. Cambridge: Harvard University Press.

Borg, Dorothy, and Heinrichs, Waldo, eds. (1980). *Uncertain Years: Chinese-American Relations, 1947–1950*. New York: Columbia University Press.

Borg, Dorothy, and Okamoto, S., eds. (1973). *Pearl Harbor As History: Japanese-American Relations, 1931–1941*. New York: Columbia University Press.

Borklung, C. W. (1966). *The Men of the Pentagon, from Forrestal to McNamara*. New York: Praeger (Italian ed.: *Gli uomini del Pentagono*. Milan: Il Borghese, 1969).

Borton, Hugh (1967). *American Presurrender Planning for Postwar Japan*. New York: Columbia University Press.

Bottai, Giuseppe (1982). *Diario, 1935–1944*. Milan: Rizzoli.

Boutwell, William Dow (1941). *America Prepares for Tomorrow: The Story of Our Total Defense Effort*. New York: Harper and Bros.

Bower, Tom (1981). *Blind Eye to Murder: Britain, America and the Purging of Nazi Germany*. London: Deutsch.

Bowman, Isaiah (1947). "The Strategy of Territorial Decisions." In *The Foreign Affairs Reader*. New York: Harper, pp. 428–449.

Boyle, J. M. (1972). *China and Japan at War, 1937–45*. Stanford: Stanford University Press.

Boyle, P. G. "The British Foreign Office View of U.S.-Soviet Relations, 1945–1946." *Diplomatic History*, Summer 1979.

Bradley, Omar N., and Blair, Clay (1983). *A General's Life: An Autobiography*. New York: Simon and Schuster.

Braisted, William R. (1971). *The United States Navy in the Pacific 1909–1922*. Austin: University of Texas Press.

Brandt, Peter (1976). *Antifaschismus und Arbeiterbewegung*. Hamburg: Christian.

Brebner, John Bartlett (1945). *The North Atlantic Triangle: The Interplay of Canada, The United States and Great Britain*. New Haven: Yale University Press.

Brecher, Michael (1979). "State Behavior in International Crises: A Model." *Journal of Conflict Resolution* 23, no. 3, pp. 446–480.

Briggs, Ellis (1968). *Anatomy of Diplomacy*. New York: McKay.

Brodie, Bernard (1946). *The Absolute Weapon*. New York: Harcourt, Brace.

——— (1959, 1965). *Strategy in the Missile Age*. Princeton: Princeton University Press.

Browder, Robert P. (1953). *The Origins of Soviet-American Diplomacy*. Princeton: Princeton University Press.

Brown, A. A., Jr. (1950). *The United States and the Restoration of World Trade*. Washington: Brookings.

Brown, Anthony Cave (1975). *Bodyguard of Lies*. New York: Harper Row (Italian ed.: *Cortina di bugie: Storia dei servizi segreti nella seconda guerra mondiale*. Milan: Mondadori, 1976).

———, ed. (1976). *The Secret War Reports of the OSS*. New York: Berkley.

———, ed. (1978). *Dropshot, The American Plan for WW3 Against Russia in 1957*. New York: Dial Press/James Wade.

Brown, Seymon (1968). *The Faces of Power: Constancy and Change in United States Foreign Policy from Truman to Johnson*. New York: Columbia University Press.

Brown, Stuart Jerry (1966). *The American Presidency: Leadership, Partisanship and Popularity*. New York: Macmillan.

Brzezinski, Zbigniew (1960). *The Soviet Bloc: Unity and Conflict*. Cambridge: Harvard University Press.

Brzezinski, Zbigniew, and Huntington, Samuel P. (1964, 1979). *Political Power: USA/USSR*. London: Penguin.

Buckingham, Peter Henry (1980). "Diplomatic and Economic Normalcy: America's Open Door Peace with the Former Central Powers 1921–1928." Washington State University (Ph.D. dissertation).

Buell, Raymond Leslie (1940). *Isolated America*. New York: Knopf.

Buell, Thomas B. (1981). *Master of Sea Power: A Biography of Fleet Admiral Ernest J. King*. Boston: Little, Brown.

Bulletin of the Commission to Study the Organization of Peace (1942). "Organization Working in the Field of Post-War Reconstruction." Vol. 2, no. 3-4 (March-April).

Bullit, Orwille H., ed. (1972). *For the President: Personal and Secret (Correspondence Between Franklin D. Roosevelt and William C. Bullit)*. Boston: Houghton Mifflin.

Bullit, William (1948). "How We Won the War and Lost the Peace." *Life*, August.

Bullock, Alan (1953, 1964). *Hitler, a Study in Tyranny*. New York: Harper (Italian ed.: *Hitler*. Milan: Mondadori, 1955, 1965).

Bundy, William P., ed. (1977). *Two Hundred Years of American Foreign Policy*. New York: New York University Press.

Burch, Philip H., Jr. (1980). *Elites in American History: From the New Deal to the Carter Administration*. New York: Holmes and Meier.

Bureau of the Budget, War Record Section (1946). *The United States at War: Development and Administration of the War Program by the Federal Government*. Washington: USGPO.

Burgwin, J. James (1977). *Fascist Revisionism: Mussolini Challenges the Great Powers in the Balkans and Danube, 1925–1933* (Italian ed.: *Il revisionismo fascista*. Milan: Feltrinelli, 1979).

Burns, James MacGregor (1956). *Roosevelt: The Lion and the Fox*. New York: Harcourt, Brace and World.

——— (1970). *Roosevelt: The Soldier of Freedom, 1940–1945*. (Italian ed.: *Roosevelt 1940–1945*. Milan: Dall'Oglio, 1972).

——— (1978). *Leadership*. New York: Harper & Row.

Butler, J.M.R. (1957). *History of the Second World War*. Vol. 2, *Grand Strategy, September 1939–June 1941*. London: HMSO.

Butow, Robert (1961). *Tojo and the Coming of the War.* Princeton: Princeton University Press.

Butz, Arthur R. (1980). "The International Holocaust Controversy." *Journal of Historical Review* 1, no. 1, pp. 5–22.

Byrnes, James Francis (1948). *Speaking Frankly.* London.

―――― (1958). *All in One Lifetime.* New York: Mayer.

Caligaris, Luigi, and Santoro, Carlo M. (1986). *Obiettivo Difesa.* Bologna: Il Mulino.

Callan, Charles (1932). *The Purchase of the Danish West Indies.* Baltimore: Johns Hopkins University Press.

Callcott, Wilfrid Hardy (1968). *The Western Hemisphere.* Austin: University of Texas Press.

Calleo, David P., and Rowland, Benjamin M. (1973). *America and the World Political Economy: Atlantic Dreams and National Realities.* Bloomington: Indiana University Press.

Calvocoressi, Peter, and Wint, Guy (1972). *Total War.* London: Allen.

Campbell, Charles S. (1976). *The Transformation of American Foreign Relations, 1865–1900.* New York: Harper & Row.

Campbell, John C. (1947). *The United States in World Affairs, 1945–1947.* New York: Harper.

Campbell, John Franklin (1971). *The Foreign Affairs Fudge Factory.* New York: Basic Books.

Campbell, T. M., and Herrig, G. C., eds. (1975). *The Diaries of Edward R. Stettinius, 1943–46.* New York.

Canizzo, Cynthia (1978). "Capability Distribution and Major-Power War Experience, 1816–1965." *Orbis* 21, no. 4, pp. 947–957.

Cantril, Hadley (1940). "America Faces the War." *Public Opinion Quarterly* 4, pp. 387–407.

Cantril, Hadley, and Strunk, Mildred (1951). *Public Opinion 1935–1946.* Princeton: Princeton University Press.

Caporaso, James A. (1978a). "Introduction: Dependence and Dependency in the Global System." *International Organization* 32, no. 1.

―――― (1978b). "Dependence, Dependency and Power in the Global System: A Structural and Behavioral Analysis." *International Organization* 32, no. 1.

Caraley, Demetrios (1966). *A Study of Conflict and the Policy Process.* New York: Columbia University Press.

Carell, Paul (1963, 1966). Vol. 1, *Barbarossa: Der Marsch nach Russland.* Frankfurt/M., Berlin: Ullstein, 1963 (Italian ed.: *Russia 1941–1945, Operazione Barbarossa.* Milan: Longanesi, 1972); Vol. 2, *Verbrannte Erde.* Frankfurt/M., Ullstein, 1966 (Italian ed.: *Terra bruciata.* Milan: Longanesi, 1972).

Carleton, G. (1967). *The Revolution in American Foreign Policy.* New York: Random House.

Carocci, Giampiero (1969). *La politica estera dell'Italia fascista, 1925–1928.* Bari: Laterza.

Carpinelli, Giovanni (1980). "Regime di Vichy." In *Il mondo contemporaneo. Storia d'Europa,* vol. 2. Florence: Politica Internazionale, La Nuova Italia.

Carr, Edward Hallet (1937). *Britain As a Mediterranean Power.* Nottingham: University College.

—— (1939, 1946, 1978). *The 20 Years' Crisis, 1919–1939: An Introduction to the Study of International Relations*. London: Macmillan.

Carrère D'Encausse, Hélène (1980). "L'Urss et le monde extérieur: Révolution et intérêt national, 1917–1941." *Relations Internationales*, no. 22, Summer 1980.

Carroll, Berenice (1968). *Design for Total War, Arms and Economics in the Third Reich*. The Hague.

Carroll, E. Malcolm (1938). *Germany and the Great Powers, 1866–1914: A Study in Public Opinion and Foreign Policy*. New York: Farrar, Strauss and Giroux.

Cashier, Philip Frederick (1980). "Natural Resource Management During the Second World War, 1939–1947." State University of New York (Ph.D. dissertation).

Cashman, Joseph T. (1931). *War of Defense Is Always Justifiable: An Argument for Preparedness*. New York: National Security League.

Caute, David (1978). *The Great Fear: The Anti-Comunist Purge Under Truman and Eisenhower*. London: Secker and Warlinry.

Caves, Richard (1964–1977). *American Industry*. Englewood Cliffs: Prentice-Hall.

—— (1980). "Industrial Organization Corporate Strategy and Structure." *Journal of Economic Literature* 18, no. 1. pp. 64–92.

CFR (Council on Foreign Relations) (1940 and thereafter). *The United States in World Affairs. 1940, 1941, . . .* New York: Harper.

—— (1946). *The War and Peace Studies of the Council on Foreign Relations (1939–1945)*. New York: CFR.

Chace, James, and Ravenal, Earl C., eds. (1976). *Atlantis Lost: US-European Relations after the Cold War*. New York: New York University Press.

Chadwin, Mark Lincoln (1968). *The Warhawks: American Internationalists Before Pearl Harbor*. New York: Norton.

Challenor, Richard D. (1973). *Admirals, Generals and American Foreign Policy, 1898–1914*. Princeton: Princeton University Press.

Chandler, Alfred, Jr. (1962). *Strategy and Structures*. Cambridge: MIT Press.

——, ed. (1970). *The Papers of D. W. Eisenhower: The War Years*. 5 vols. Baltimore: Johns Hopkins University Press.

—— (1977). *The Managerial Revolution in American Business, The Visible Hand*. Cambridge: Harvard University Press.

Chandler, Lester V., and Wallace, Donald H. (1951). *Economic Mobilizations and Stabilization*. New York.

Chern, Kenneth S. (1980). *Dilemma in China, America's Policy Debate, 1945*. Hamden: Archon Books.

Churchill, Winston S. (1949). "The Commonwealth Alone." London: Cassell.

—— (1950). *War Comes to America*. London: Cassell.

Ciano, Galeazzo (1946, 1948, 1980). *Diario, 1937–1943*. Milan: Rizzoli.

Civilian Production Agency (n.d.). "Industrial Mobilization in the Defense Period." National Archives, Washington.

Clark, John Maurice (1931). *The Cost of the World War to the American People*. New Haven: Yale University Press.

Clarkson, Grosvenor B. (1923). *Industrial America in the World War: The Strategy Behind the Line, 1917–1918*. Boston: Houghton Mifflin.

Clemens, Dyane (1970). *Yalta*. New York: Oxford University Press (Italian ed.: *Yalta*. Turin: Einaudi, 1975).

Cleveland, Harold van B. (1966). *The Atlantic Idea and Its European Rivals*. New York: McGraw-Hill.

CNSR (1979). "Français et Britanniques dans la Drôle de Guerre." Actes du Colloque franco-britannique de Décembre 1975. Paris: Centre Nationale de la Recherche Scientifique.

Coffman, Edward M. (1968). *The War to End All Wars: The American Military Experience in World War I*. New York: Oxford University Press.

Cohen, Bernard C. (1957). *The Political Process and Foreign Policy*. Princeton: Princeton University Press.

———— (1963). *The Press and Foreign Policy*. Princeton: Princeton University Press.

———— (1979). *The Influence of Non-Governmental Groups on Foreign Policy*. Boston: World Peace Foundation.

Cohen, Saul B. (1964). *Geography and Politics in a Divided World*. London: Methuen.

Cohen, Stephen D. (1977). *The Making of U.S. International Economic Policy*. New York: Praeger.

Cohen, Warren I. (1978). *The Chinese Connection: Roger S. Greene, Thomas W. Lamont, George E. Sokolski and American–East Asian Relations*. New York: Columbia University Press.

Cole, Wayne S. (1953). *America First: The Battle Against Intervention 1940–1941*. Madison: University of Wisconsin Press.

———— (1957). "American Entry into World War II: An Historiographical Appraisal." *Mississippi Valley Historical Review* 43 (March), pp. 595–617.

———— (1962). *Senator Gerald P. Nye and American Foreign Relations*. Minneapolis: University of Minnesota Press.

———— (1974). *Charles A. Lindbergh and the Battle Against Intervention, 1940–1941*. New York: Harcourt Brace Jovanovich.

———— (1983). *Roosevelt and the Isolationists, 1932–1945*. Lincoln: University of Nebraska Press.

Collier, Richard (1979). *1940: The Avalanche*. New York: Dial Press/James Wade.

———— (1981). *1941: Armageddon*. London: Penguin.

Compton, James V. (1967). *The Swastika and the Eagle: Hitler, the United States and the Origins of the Second World War*. London: Bodley Head.

————, ed. (1972). *America and the Origins of the Cold War*. Boston.

Conn, Stetson, Engelmann, Rose C., and Fairchild, Byron (1964). *United States in World War II: The Western Hemisphere, Guarding the United States and its Outpost*. Washington: USGPO.

Conn, Stetson, and Fairchild, Byron (1960). *United States Army in World War II: The Western Hemisphere, the Framework of Hemisphere Defense*. Washington: USGPO.

Connel-Smith, Gordon (1966). *The Inter-American System*. London: Oxford University Press.

Connery, Robert H. (1951). *The Navy and the Industrial Mobilization in World War II*. Princeton: Princeton University Press.

Coolidge, Archibald Cary (1908–1971). *The United States As a World Power.* New York: Macmillan.

Cooper, John Milton (1968). "The Vanity of Power: American Isolationism and the First World War, 1914–1917." Columbia University (Ph.D. dissertation).

Cooper, Richard N. (1968). *The Economics of Interdependence.* New York: McGraw-Hill.

——— (1977). "A New Economic Order for Mutual Gain." *Foreign Policy,* no. 26.

Corson, William R. (1977). *The Armies of Ignorance: The Rise of the American Intelligence Empire.* New York: Dial Press/James Wade.

Crabb, Cecil V., Jr. (1957). *Bipartisan Foreign Policy: Myth or Reality?* Evanston: Row-Peterson.

——— (1968). "Bipartisanship." In *International Encyclopedia of the Social Sciences,* vol. 2. New York: Free Press.

——— (1976). *Policy-Making and Critics: Conflicting Theories of American Foreign Policy.* New York: Praeger.

Craig, Gordon A., and George, Alexander L. (1983). *Force and Statecraft: Diplomatic Problems of Our Time.* New York: Oxford University Press.

Craig, Gordon A., and Gilbert, Felix, eds. (1953). *The Diplomats, 1919–1939.* Princeton: Princeton University Press.

Cruickshank, Charles (1979). *Deception in World War II.* Oxford: Oxford University Press.

Cuff, Robert D. (1949). "Bernard Baruch: Symbol and Myth in Industrial Mobilisation." *Business History Review,* no. 43.

Culberston, Ely (1943). *Total Peace. What Makes War and How to Organize Peace.* Garden City: Doubleday.

Current, Richard N. (1954). *Secretary Stimson: A Study in Statecraft.* New Brunswick.

Curry, Roy Watson (1957). *Woodrow Wilson and Far Eastern Policy, 1913–1921.* New York.

Curti, Merle (1936). *Peace or War.* New York.

Dahl, Robert A. (1950). *Congress and Foreign Policy.* New York: Harcourt, Brace.

——— (1971, 1973). *Polyarchy, Participation and Opposition.* New Haven: Yale University Press (Italian ed.: *Poliarchia.* Milan: Franco Angeli, 1981).

Daitz, W. (1938). *Der Weg zur Völkischen Wirtschaft und zur europäischen Grossraumwirtschaft.* Dresden: Meinhold.

Dallek, Robert (1971). "Franklin Roosevelt As World Leader." *American Historical Review* 76, no. 5.

——— (1979). *Franklin D. Roosevelt and American Foreign Policy: 1932–1945.* New York: Oxford University Press.

——— (1983). *The American Style of Foreign Policy.* New York: Knopf.

Daly Hayes, Margaret (1984). *Latin America and the U.S. National Interest.* Boulder: Westview.

Damiani, Claudia (1980). *Mussolini e gli Stati Uniti 1922–1935.* Bologna: Cappelli.

Dangerfield, George (1952). *The Era of Good Feeling.* New York: Harcourt, Brace (Italian ed.: *L'era dei buoni sentimenti. L'America di Monroe 1812–1819.* Turin: Einaudi, 1973).

Davenport, Russell W. (1945). "The Ordeal of Wendell Willkie." *Atlantic Monthly* 176, pp. 67–73.

Davies, John Paton, Jr. (1972). *Dragon by the Tail.* New York: Norton.

Davis, Forrest K., and Lindley, Ernest K. (1942). *How War Came: An American White Paper From the Fall of France to Pearl Harbor.* New York: Simon & Schuster.

Davis, Kenneth S. (1971). *FDR: The Reckoning of Destiny, 1882–1928, A History.* New York: Capricorn Books, Putnam.

Davis, Lynn Etheridge (1976). *The Cold War Begins, Soviet-American Conflicts in Eastern Europe.* Princeton: Princeton University Press.

Dawson, Raymond H. (1959). *The Decision to Aid Russia, 1941: Foreign Policy and Domestic Policies.* Chapel Hill: University of North Carolina Press.

Dean, Vera Micheles (1941). "Toward a New World Order." *Foreign Policy Reports,* May 15, 1941.

Deane, John R. (1947). *The Strange Alliance: The Story of Our Efforts at Wartime Cooperation with Russia.* New York: Viking.

De Conde, Alexander, ed. (1957). *Isolation and Security.* Durham: Duke University Press.

———— (1958). *Entangling Alliances: Politics and Diplomacy Under George Washington.* Durham: Duke University Press.

———— (1963, 1971, 1978). *A History of American Foreign Policy.* Vol. 2, *Global Power 1900 to Present.* New York: Scribner's.

————, ed. (1978). *Encyclopedia of American Foreign Policy: Studies of Principal Movements and Ideas.* 3 vols. New York: Scribner's.

De Felice, Renzo (1974). *Mussolini il Duce.* Vol. 1, *Gli Anni del consenso, 1929–1936.* Turin: Einaudi.

———— (1981). *Mussolini il Duce.* Vol. 2, *Lo Stato totalitario, 1936–1940.* Turin: Einaudi.

De Gaulle, Charles (1954, 1956, 1959). *Mémoires de guerre.* Vol. 1, *L'appel, 1940–1942;* Vol. 2, *L'Unité, 1942–1944;* Vol. 3, *Le Salut, 1944–1946.* Paris: Plon.

Deighton, Len (1979). *Blitzkrieg.* London: Jonathan Cape.

Delaisi, Francis (1925). *Political Myths and Economic Realizations.* London: Noel Douglas.

Del Boca, Angelo (1976–1984). *Gli Italiani in Africa Orientale.* 4 vols. Bari: Laterza.

Denison, Edward F. (1974). *Accounting for United States Economic Growth, 1929–1969.* Washington: Brookings.

Dennis, Lawrence (1936). *The Coming American Fascism.* New York: Harper & Bros.

DePorte, Anton W. (1968). *De Gaulle's Foreign Policy, 1944–1946.* Cambridge: Harvard University Press.

———— (1979). *Europe Between the Superpowers: The Enduring Balance.* New Haven: Yale University Press.

De Santis, Hugh (1979). *The Diplomacy of Silence: The American Foreign Service, The Soviet Union and the Cold War 1933–1947.* Chicago: University of Chicago Press.

De Santis, Vincent (1976). "Eisenhower Revisionism." *Review of Politics* 38, no. 2.

De Seversky, Alexander (1942). *Victory Through Air Power.* New York: Simon & Schuster.

Destler, I. M. (1972). *Presidents, Bureaucrats and Foreign Policy: The Politics of Organisational Reform.* Princeton: Princeton University Press.

Destler, I. M., Gelb, Leslie H., and Lake, Anthony (1984). *Our Own Worst Enemy: The Unmaking of American Foreign Policy.* New York: Simon & Schuster.

Deutsch, Karl W. (1953). *Nationalism and Social Communication.* Cambridge: MIT Press/Wiley.

———— (1957). *The Political Community and the North Atlantic Area.* Princeton: Princeton University Press.

———— (1963). *The Nerves of Government.* New York: Free Press (Italian ed.: *I Nervi del Potere.* Milan: Etas Kompass, 1972).

———— (1968, 1978). *The Analysis of International Relations.* Englewood Cliffs: Prentice-Hall (Italian ed.: *Le Relazioni Internazionali.* Bologna: Il Mulino, 1970).

Deutsche Institut für Wirtschaftsforschung (1954). *Die Deutsche Industrie im Kriege 1939–1945.* Berlin: Dunckes und Humbolt.

Dexter, Byron, ed. (1972). *The Foreign Affairs, 50-Years Bibliography, 1920–1970.* New York: CFR.

Diebold, William (1952). *The End of ITO.* Princeton: Princeton University Press.

———— (1959). *The Schuman Plan: A Study in Economic Cooperation 1950–1959.* New York: Praeger.

———— (1984). "Trade and Payments in Western Europe in Historical Perspective, A Personal View by an Interested Party." EUI Working Paper No. 85. European University, Florence.

Diggins, John Patrick (1981). "Power and Authority in American History: The Case of Charles A. Beard and His Critics." *American Historical Review* 86, no. 4, pp. 701–730.

Di Nolfo, Ennio, ed. (1976). *Italia e Stati Uniti durante l'Amministrazione Truman.* Milan: Franco Angeli.

Divine, Robert A. (1962). *The Illusion of Neutrality.* Chicago: University of Chicago Press.

———— (1965). *The Reluctant Belligerent: American Entry in World War II.* New York: Wiley.

———— (1967). *Second Chance: The Triumph of Internationalism in America During World II.* New York: Athaeneum.

———— (1969). *Roosevelt and World War II.* Baltimore: Johns Hopkins University Press.

———— (1974). *Foreign Policy and US Presidential Elections.* Vol. 1, *1940–1948;* Vol. 2, *1952–1960.* New York: New Viewpoints.

———— (1975). *Since 1945: Politics and Diplomacy in Recent American History.* New York: Wiley.

———— (1981). *Eisenhower and the Cold War.* Oxford: Oxford University Press.

Doenecke, Justus D. (1972). *The Literature of Isolationism: A Guide to Non-Interventionist Scholarship, 1930–1972.* Colorado Springs: Ralph Myles.

Donno, Antonio (1983). *Dal New Deal alla guerra fredda.* Florence: Sansoni.

Donovan, Robert J. (1977). *Conflict and Crisis: The Presidency of Harry Truman, 1945–48.* New York: Norton.

Dougherty, James E., and Pfaltzgraff, Robert L. (1971, 1981). *Contending Theories of International Relations.* New York: Harper & Row.

Douhet, Giulio (1921, 1955). *Il Comando dell'aria.* Rome: Rivista Aeronautica.

Drucker, Peter F. (1941). "The 1000-Year Plan." *Nation,* July 12.

Drummond, Donald F. (1955). *The Passing of American Neutrality, 1937–1941.* Ann Arbor: University of Michigan Press.

Dulles, Allen W., and Armstrong, Hamilton Fish (1935). *Can We Be Neutral?* New York: Harper & Sons.

_____ (1939). *Can America Stay Neutral?* New York: Harper & Sons.

Dulles, Foster R., and Ridiwger, G. (1955). "The Anti-Colonial Policies of Franklin D. Roosevelt." *Political Science Quarterly,* March 1955.

Duroselle, Jean-Baptiste (1953, 1957, 1978). *Histoire Diplomatique de 1919 nos jours.* Paris: Dalloz.

_____ (1960). *De Wilson à Roosevelt, la politique exterieure des Etas-Unis, 1913–1945.* Paris: Armand Colin.

_____ (1979). *La Decadence, 1932–1939.* Paris: Imprimerie Nationale.

_____ (1984). "Le Gouvernement de Vichy face à l'Italie." In J. B. Duroselle and E. Serra, eds. *Italia e Francia, 1939–45,* vol. 1, pp. 97–113. Milan: Franco Angeli.

Duso, Anna (1980). *Economia e istituzioni del New Deal.* Preface by M. D'Antonio. Bari: De Donato. Translation of *America's Recovery Program.* New York: Oxford University Press, 1934.

Dziuban, Stanley W. (1959). *Military Relations Between the United States and Canada, 1939–45.* Washington.

Earle, Edward Mead, ed. (1943, 1973). *Makers of Modern Strategy: Military Thought from Machiavelli to Hitler.* Princeton: Princeton University Press.

Easton, David (1953, 1971). *The Political System: An Inquiry into the State of Political Science.* New York: Alfred A. Knopf (Italian ed.: *Il sistema politico.* Milan: Comunità, 1973).

Eckes, Alfred E., Jr. (1973). "Open Door Expansionism Reconsidered: The World War II Experience." *Journal of American History* 59, no. 4.

_____ (1979). *The United States and the Global Struggole for Minerals.* Austin: University of Texas Press.

Efron, David (1939). "Latin America and the Fascist Holy Alliance." *Annals,* no. 204 (July), pp. 19–24.

Eichholz, D. (1969). *Geschicht der Deutschen Driegswirtschaft, 1939–1945,* vol. 1. Berlin: Akademie Verlag.

Eliot, George Fielding (1938). *The Ramparts We Watch.* New York.

Elliot, William Yandel, ed. (1952). *United States Foreign Policy: Its Organization and Centrals.* Report of a Study Group for the W. Wilson Foundations. New York: Columbia University Press.

Ellis, L. Ettran (1968). *Republican Foreign Policy, 1921–1933.* New Brunswick: Rutgers University Press.

Ellwood, David W. (1977). "Allied Occupation Policy in Italy, 1943–1947" (Ph.D. dissertation) (Italian ed.: *L'alleato nemico: La politica dell'occupazione anglo-americana in Italia, 1943–1947.* Milan: Feltrinelli).

——— (1982). "The Marshall Plan and the Process of Modernization in Italy." In *The Role of the U.S. in Postwar Reconstruction of Italy and West Germany, 1943–1949.* Berlin: Freie University.

Ellwood, David W., and Miller, James E., eds. (1975). *Introductory Guide to American Documentation of the European Resistance Movement in World War II,* vol. 1. Turin: University Institute of European Studies.

Emerson, William (1958). "Franklin D. Roosevelt As Commander in Chief in World War II." *Military Affairs,* Winter 1958–59.

Endicott, J. E., and Stafford, Ray W., Jr., eds. (1977). *American Defense Policy.* Baltimore: Johns Hopkins University Press.

Ennis, Harry F. (1980). *Peacetime Industrial Preparedness for Wartime Ammunition Production.* Washington: National Defense University.

Erdman, K. D. (1976). "Deutschland unter des Herrshaft des Nationalsozialisme und der zweite Weltkrieg." In *Die Zeit der Weltkriege,* vol. 4. Stuttgart.

Erickson, John (1961). *The Soviet High Command, A Military Political History, 1918–1941.* London: MacMillan (Italian ed.: *Storia dello Stato Maggiore Sovietico.* Milan: Feltrinelli, 1963).

——— (1975, 1983). *Stalin's War with Germany.* Vol. 1, *The Road to Stalingrad;* Vol. 2, *The Road to Berlin.* London: Weidenfeld & Nicolson.

Etheredge, Lloyd S. (1975). *A World of Men: The Private Sources of American Foreign Policy.* Cambridge: MIT Press.

——— (1978). "Personality Effects on American Foreign Policy, 1898–1968, A Test of Interpersonal Generalisation Theory." *American Political Science Review* 72, no. 2, pp. 434–451.

Etzold, Thomas H., and Gaddis, John Lewis, eds. (1978). *Containment: Documents on American Policy and Strategy, 1945–1950.* New York: Columbia University Press.

Evens Boe, Jonathan (1979). "American Business: The Response to the Soviet Union, 1933–1947." Stanford University (Ph.D. dissertation).

Fagen, Richard R. (1979). *Capitalism and the State in U.S.–Latin American Relations.* Stanford: Stanford University Press.

Fairbank, John King (1948, 1979). *The United States and China,* 4th ed. Cambridge, Mass.: Harvard University Press.

Farago, Ladislas, ed. (1942). *The Axis Grand Strategy.* New York: Farrar and Rinehart.

Fedyszin, Thomas R. (1978). "Liberal America and War Entry: A Study of the Propaganda Campaign Conduced Prior to the American Intervention in World War II." Johns Hopkins University (Ph.D. dissertation).

Fehrenbach, T. R. (1967). *FDR's Undeclared War, 1939–1941.* New York.

Feis, Herbert (1942). "Restoring Trade After the War." *Foreign Affairs* 20 (January), pp. 282–292.

——— (1950a, 1965). *The Diplomacy of the Dollar: First Era, 1919–1932.* Hamden: Archon.

——— (1950b). *The Road to Pearl Harbor: The Coming of the War Between the U.S. and Japan.* Princeton: Princeton University Press.

——— (1960). *Between War and Peace: The Postdam Conference.* Princeton: Princeton University Press.

_____ (1961). *The Atomic Bomb and the End of World War II*. Princeton: Princeton University Press.

_____ (1965). *Atomic Diplomacy: Hiroshima and Potsdam*. New York.

_____ (1966). *Churchill, Roosevelt, Stalin, The War They Waged and the Peace They Sought*. Princeton: Princeton University Press.

Fensterwald, Bernard, Jr. (1958). "The Anatomy of American Isolationism and Expansionism." *Journal of Conflict Resolution* 2 (June), pp. 111–139, and (December), pp. 280–309.

Ferguson, Eugene S. (1979). "The American-ness of American Technology." *Technology and Culture* 20, no. 1 (January).

Ferguson, Thomas (1984). "From Normalcy to New Deal, Industrial Structure, Party Competition and American Public Policy in the Great Depression." *International Organization* 38, no. 1, pp. 41–94.

Ferrell, Robert H. (1957, 1970). *American Diplomacy in the Great Depression: Hoover-Stimson Foreign Policy, 1929–1933*. New Haven: Yale University Press, 1957; New York: Norton, 1970.

_____ (1985). *Woodrow Wilson and World War I, 1917–1921*. New York: Harper & Row.

Ferretti, Valdo (1982). "Fra Inghilterra e Germania: un aspetto delle origini della seconda guerra mondiale secondo la recente storiografia giapponese." *Storia contemporanea* 13, no. 6.

_____ (1990). "La marina giapponese dal Patto Anti-komintern alla guerra contro gli Stati Uniti: un approfondimento documentario." *Storia contemporanea* 21, no. 3, pp. 439–462.

Fest, Joachim C. (1973). *Hitler. Eine Biographie*. Berlin (Italian ed.: *Hitler*. Milan: Rizzoli).

Fetter, Theodore Jonathan (1974). "Waging War Under the Separation of Powers: Executive-Congressional Relations During World War II." University of Wisconsin (Ph.D. dissertation).

Filene, Peter G. (1967). *Americans and the Soviet Experiment 1917–33*. Cambridge: Harvard University Press.

Finkelstein, Lawrence Stanley (1970). "Castles in Spain: United States Trusteeship Plan in World War II." Columbia University (Ph.D. dissertation).

Fischer, Fritz (1961). *Griff nach der Weltmach*. Düsseldorf: Droste Verlag (Italian ed.: *Assalto al potere mondiale. La Germania nella guerra 1914–1918*. Turin: Einaudi, 1965).

_____ (1965). *Weltmacht der Niedergang*. Frankfurt/M.: Europäische Verlag.

_____ (1969). *Krieg der Illusiones*. Düsseldorf: Droste Verlag.

Fischer, Louis (1972). *The Road to Yalta: Soviet Foreign Relations 1941–1950*. New York: Harper & Row.

Fish, C. R. (1919). *The Path of Empire*. New Haven: Yale University Press.

Fiske, John (1885). "Manifest Destiny." *Harper's New Monthly Magazine* 70.

Fleming, D. F. (1969). *The Origins and Legacies of World War I*. London: Allen and Unwin.

Fleming, Nicholas (1979). *August 1939: The Last Days of Peace*. London: Peter Davies.

Flood, Francis (1943). "Lend-Lease Is a Two-Way Benefit." *National Geographic* 83, no. 6, pp. 745–764.

Fox, Douglas M., ed. (1971). *The Politics of US Foreign Policy-Making.* Pacific Palisades: Goodyear Publishing.

Fox, Richard W. (1976). "Reinhold Niebuhr and the Emergence of the Liberal Realist Faith, 1930–1945." *Review of Politics* 38, no. 2.

Fraenkel, Ernst (1941, 1974). *Der Doppelstaat.* Frankfurt/M.: Europäische Verlag.

Franck, Thomas M., and Weisband, Edward (1979). *Foreign Policy by Congress.* New York: Oxford University Press.

Frankenstein, Robert (1980). "Intervention Etatique et réarmement en France, 1935–1939." *Revue Economique* 31, no. 4, pp. 743–781.

Freedman, Lawrence (1981). *The Evolution of Nuclear Strategy.* New York: St. Martin's Press.

Freidel, Frank (1952, 1954, 1956, 1973). *Franklin D. Roosevelt.* Vol. 1, *The Apprenticeship;* Vol. 2, *The Ordeal;* Vol. 3, *The Triumph;* Vol. 4, *The Launching of the New Deal.* Boston: Houghton Mifflin.

Freud, Sigmund, and Bullit, William C. (1967). *Thomas Woodrow Wilson: 28th President of the United States: A Psychological Study.* London: Weidenfeld & Nicolson.

Freymond, J. (1974). *Le IIIe Reich et la reorganisation Economique de l'Europe, 1940–1942: Origines et projets.* Geneva: Collection de Relations Internationales.

Frezza, Daria, ed. (1982). *F. D. Roosevelt: Il Presidente e l'opinione pubblica.* Siena: Università di Siena.

Friedlander, Saul (1963, 1967). *Prelude to Downfall: Hitler and the United States, 1939–1941.* New York: Knopf.

Friedman, Donald J. (1968). *The Road from Isolation: The Campaign of the American Committee for Non-Participation in Japanese Aggression, 1938–41.* New York: Knopf.

FRUS: See U.S. Department of State (various years). Foreign Relations of the United States (FRUS).

Frye, Alton (1967). *Nazi Germany and the American Hemisphere.* New Haven: Yale University Press.

Gaddis, John Lewis (1972). *The United States and the Origins of the Cold War, 1941–1947.* New York: Columbia University Press.

––––––– (1974). "Was the Truman Doctrine a Real Turning Point?" *Foreign Affairs* 52 (January), pp. 380–402.

––––––– (1978). *Russia, the Soviet Union and the United States: An Interpretative History.* New York: Wiley.

––––––– (1982). *Strategies of Containment: A Critical Appraisal of Postwar American National Security Policy.* New York: New York University Press.

Galbraith, John Kenneth (1981). *A Life in Our Times.* Boston: Houghton Mifflin.

Galloway, George B. (1942). *Post-War Planning in the United States.* New York: Twentieth Century Fund.

Gallup, George H., ed. (1972). *The Gallup Poll/Public Opinion, 1935–1971.* Vol. 1, *1935–48.* New York: Random House.

Gambino, Antonio (1972). *Le convergenze della seconda guerra mondiale.* Bologna: Il Mulino.

Gamson, William A., and Modigliani, André (1971). *Untangling the Cold War: A Strategy for Testing Rival Theories.* Boston: Little, Brown.

Gantenbein, James W., ed. (1975). *Documentary Background of World War II: 1931 to 1941.* New York: Farrar, Strauss and Giroux.

Gardner, Lloyd C. (1964). *Economic Aspects of New Deal Diplomacy.* Madison: University of Wisconsin Press.

—— (1970). *Architects of Illusion: Men and Ideas in American Foreign Policy, 1941–1949.* Chicago: Quadrangle Books.

—— (1976). *Imperial America: American Foreign Policy Since 1898.* New York: Harcourt Brace Jovanovich.

—— (1984). *A Covenant with Power: America and World Order from Wilson to Reagan.* New York: Oxford University Press.

Gardner, Richard N. (1956, 1969). *Sterling-Dollar Diplomacy: The Origins and Prospects of Our International Economic Order.* New York: Oxford University Press. 1956; New York: McGraw-Hill, 1969.

Garraty, J. A. (1953). *Henry Cabot Lodge: A Biography.* New York: Knopf.

Gattei, Giorgio (1976). "La Storiografia sulle origini della guerra fredda." *Studi Storici* 17, no. 4, pp. 185–210.

Gatzke, Hans W. (1980). *Germany and the United States.* Cambridge: Harvard University Press.

Gayda, Virginio (1943). *Gli Stati Uniti nella guerra mondiale.* Rome: Ed. Giornale d'Italia.

Geiger, T., and Van Cleveland, B. H. (1951). *Making Western Europe Defensible.* Washington: National Planning Association.

Gelb, Leslie, and Betts, Richard (1979). *The Irony of Vietnam: The System Worked.* Washington: Brookings.

Gelber, Lionel (1938). *The Rise of Anglo-American Friendship: A Study in World Politics 1898–1906.* London: Praeger.

—— (1961). *America in Britain's Place: The Leadership of the West and Anglo-American Unity.* New York: Praeger.

Gellman, Irwin F. (1980). *Good Neighbor Diplomacy: United States Policies in Latin America, 1933–1945.* Baltimore: Johns Hopkins University Press.

George, Alexander L. (1979). "Case Studies and Theory Development: The Method of Structured Forced Comparison." In P. G. Lauren, ed. *Diplomacy: New Approaches in History, Theory and Policy.* New York, pp. 43–68.

Gerber, Larry George (1979). "The Limits of Liberalism. A Study of the Conceptional and Ideological Development of Josephus Daniels, Henry Stimson, Bernard Baruch, Donald Richberg and Felix Frankfurter." University of California (Ph.D. dissertation).

Gibbs, N. H. (1976). *History of the Second World War. Grand Strategy.* Vol. 1, *Rearmament Policy.* London: HMSO.

Gideonse, Harry (1930). "Economic Foundations of Pan-Europeanism." *Annals,* no. 149 (May).

Giedion, Siegfrid (1946). *Modernization Takes Command.* New York: Oxford University Press.

Gilbert, Arthur N., and Lauren, Paul Gordon (1980). "Crisis Management: An Assessment and Critique." *Journal of Conflict Resolution* 24, no. 4, pp. 641–664.

Gilbert, Martin (1983, 1986). Vol. 1, *Finest Hour: Winston S. Churchill, 1939–1941*; Vol. 2, *Road to Victory*. London: Heinemann.

Gilpin, Robert (1975). *U.S. Power and the Multinational Corporation*. New York: Basic Books.

———— (1977). "Economic Interdependence and National Security in Historical Perspective." In K. Knorr and F. N. Trager, eds. *Economic Issues and National Security*. Lawrence: Regents Press of Kansas.

———— (1981). *War and Change in World Politics*. Cambridge: Cambridge University Press.

Gimbel, John (1968). *The American Occupation of Germany: Politics and the Military, 1945–1949*. Stanford: Stanford University Press.

———— (1976). *The Origins of the Marshall Plan*. Stanford: Stanford University Press.

Glucksmann, André (1967, 1969). *Le discours de la guerre*. Paris: Ed. de l'Herne (Italian ed.: *Il discorso della guerra*. Milan: Feltrinelli, 1969).

Goebbels, Joseph (1977). *Joseph Goebbels Tagebücher 1945: Die Letzen Aufzeichhungen*. Hamburg: Hoffman und Cape (British ed.: Hugh Trevor-Roper, ed. *The Goebbels Diaries*. London: Pan Books, 1978, 1979).

———— (1982). *The Goebbels Diaries, 1939–1941*. London: Hamish Hamilton.

Gooch, J. (1974). *The Plans of War: The General Staff and British Military Strategy, 1900–1916*. London.

Goodwyn, Lawrence (1978). *The Populist Movement: A Short History of the Agrarian Revolt in America*. New York: Oxford University Press.

Gordon, Colin, ed. (1978). *The Atlantic Alliance: A Bibliography*. London: Frances Pinter.

Gourevitch, Peter A. (1978). "The Second Image Reversed: the International Sources of Domestic Politics." *International Organization* 32, no. 4.

———— (1984). "Breaking with Orthodoxy: The Politics of Economic Policy Responses to the Depression of the 1930s." *International Organization* 39, no. 1, pp. 95–130.

Graebner, Norman A. (1956). *The New Isolationism: A Study in Politics and Foreign Policy Since 1959*. New York: Ronald Press.

————, ed. (1961). *An Uncertain Tradition: American Secretaries of State in the Twentieth Century*. New York: McGraw-Hill.

————, ed. (1964). *Ideas and Diplomacy: Readings in the Intellectual Tradition of American Foreign Policy*. New York: Oxford University Press.

———— (1969). "Cold War Origins and the Continuing Debate: A List of Recent Literature." *Journal of Conflict Resolution*, March.

Grafton, Samuel (1941). "A New Learned Society." *New Republic*, July 21.

Graham, Otis L., Jr. (1976). *Toward a Planned Society: From Roosevelt to Nixon*. New York: Oxford University Press.

Gray, Colin S. (1977). *The Geopolitics of the Nuclear Era*. New York: Crane, Russak.

———— (1982). *Strategic Studies, A Critical Assessment.* Westport: Greenwood Press.

Greenfield, Kent R. (1963). *American Strategy in World War II: A Reconsideration.* Baltimore: Johns Hopkins University Press.

———— (1969). *Command Decisions.* New York: USGPO.

Grenville, John A.S., and Young, George Berkeley (1966). *Politics, Strategy and American Diplomacy: Studies in Foreign Policy, 1873–1917.* New Haven: Yale University Press.

Grew, Joseph C. (1944). *Ten Years in Japan.* New York: Harper.

Griffith, Richard (1980). *Fellow Travellers of the Right: British Enthusiasm for Nazi Germany (1933–1939).* London: Constable.

Griffith, Robert (1975). "Truman and the. Historians: The Reconstruction of Postwar American History." *Wisconsin Magazine of History,* no. 59 (Autumn), pp. 20–25.

———— (1979). "Old Progressives and the Cold War." *Journal of American History* 66, no. 2, pp. 334–347.

Grigg, John (1980). *The Victory That Never Was.* London: Methuen.

Griswold, A. Whitney (1938). *The Far-Eastern Policy of the United States.* New York.

Groh, Dieter (1961). *Russland und das Selbstverständnis Europas.* Frankfurt: Luchterhand Verlag (Italian ed.: *La Russia e l'autocoscienza d'Europa.* Turin: Einaudi).

Gross, Gerbert (1942). *Amerikas Wirtschaft.* Berlin: Deutscher Verlag.

Grottle Strebel, Elizabeth (1981). "French Cinema, 1940–44, and Its Socio-Psychological Significance: A Preliminary Probe." *Historical Journal of Film, Radio and Television* 1, no. 1, pp. 34–45.

Gulick, Edward Vose (1955, 1967). *Europe's Classical Balance of Power: A Case History of the Theory and Practice of One of the Great Concepts of European Statecraft.* Ithaca: Cornell University Press.

Gun, Nerin E. (1979). *Pétain, Laval, De Gaulle.* Paris: Albin Michel.

Gunther, John (1950). *Roosevelt in Retrospect.* New York: Harper & Bros.

Haas, Michael (1974). *International Conflict.* Indianapolis: Bobbs-Merrill.

Hahan, Walter F., and Pfaltzgraff, Robert L., Jr., eds. (1979). *Atlantic Community in Crisis: A Redefinition of the Transatlantic Relationship.* New York: Pergamon Press.

Hailey, Lord (1944). *The Future of Colonial Peoples.* Princeton: Princeton University Press.

Halberstam, David (1979). *The Powers That Be.* New York: Knopf.

Hall, H. Ducan (1955). "North American Supply." In *History of the Second World War.* London: HMSO.

Halle, Louis J. (1959). *Dream and Reality: Aspects of American Foreign Policy.* New York: Harper & Row.

———— (1967). *The Cold War As History.* New York: Harper & Row.

Halperin, Morton H. (1974). *Bureaucratic Politics and Foreign Policy.* Washington: Brookings.

Hammond, Paul Y. (1961). *Organizing for Defense: The American Military Establishment in the Twentieth Century.* Princeton: Princeton University Press.

——— (1969). *The Cold War Years.* New York.

Hancock, W. K., and Gowing, M. M. (1949). *British War Economy.* London: HMSO.

Hansen, Alvin H. (1938). *Full Recovery or Stagnation.* New York: Norton.

——— (1945). *America's Role in the World Economy.* London: Allen and Unwin.

Hansen, Alvin H., and Kindleberger, Charles P. (1942). "The Economic Tasks of the Postwar World." *Foreign Affairs* 20, pp. 466–476.

Hardach, Gerd (1977). *The First World War: 1914–1918.* Berkeley: University of California Press.

Harriman, William Averell, and Abel, Elie (1975). *Special Envoy to Churchill and Stalin, 1941–1946.* New York: Random House.

Harris, S. E., ed. (1943). *Post-War Economic Problems.* New York: New York University Press.

Harrod, Roy (1951). *John Maynard Keynes.* London: MacMillan.

Hauner, Milan (1978). "Did Hitler Want World Domination?" *Journal of Contemporary History* 13, no. 1, pp. 15–32.

——— (1981). *India in Axis Strategy.* Stuttgart.

Haushofer, Karl (1932). *Welt-Geopolitik.* Berlin: Juncker und Dümpchaupt.

———, ed. (1933–1941). *Zeitschrift für Geopolitik.*

Hausrath, Alfred H. (1971). *Venture Simulation in War, Business and Politics.* New York: McGraw-Hill.

Hawley, Ellis W. (1966, 1974). *The New Deal and the Problem of Monopoly: A Study in Economic Ambivalence.* Princeton: Princeton University Press.

Haworth, Brian (1981). "The British Broadcasting Corporation, Nazi Germany and the Foreign Office, 1933–36." *Historical Journal of Film, Radio and Television* 1, no. 1, pp. 47–55.

Heindel, R. H. (1968). *The American Impact on Great Britain, 1898–1914.* New York: Octagon Books.

Heinrichs, Waldo H. (1966). *American Ambassador: Joseph C. Grew and the Development of the United States Diplomatic Tradition.* Boston.

Henrikson, Alan K. (1975). "The Map As an Idea: The Role of Cartographic Imagery During the Second World War." *American Cartographer*, no. 2, pp. 19–53.

Herken, Gregg (1981). *The Winning Weapon: The Atomic Bomb in the Cold War.* New York: Knopf.

Herman, John (1980). "Soviet Peace Effort on the Eve of World War Two: A Review of the Soviet Documents." *Journal of Contemporary History* 15, no. 3, pp. 577–602.

Hero, Alfred O., Jr., ed. (1973). *American Religious Groups View Foreign Policy: Trends in Rank-and-File Opinion, 1937–1969.* Durham: Duke University Press.

Herring, George C., Jr. (1969). *Lend-Lease to Russia and the American People.* New Haven. Yale University Press.

——— (1973). *Aid to Russia, 1941–1946: Strategy, Politics, the Origins of the Cold War.* New York.

Herwig, Holger H. (1976). *The Politics of Frustration: The United States in German Naval Planning 1889–1941.* Boston: Little, Brown.

Herzog, James H. (1973). *Closing the Open Door: American-Japanese Diplomatic Negotiations, 1936–1941.* Annapolis: Naval Institute Press.

Herzstein, Robert Edwin (1978). *The War That Hitler Won: The Most Infamous Propaganda Campaign in History.* New York: Doubleday.

———— (1982). *When Nazi Dreams Come True.* London: Abacus.

Hewes, James E. (1975). *From Root to McNamara: Army Organization and Administration, 1900–1963.* Washington: USGPO.

Higham, Charles (1983). *Trading with the Enemy: An Expose of the Nazi-American Money Plot, 1933–1949.* London: Robert Hale.

Higham, Robin, ed. (1975). *Guide to the Sources of United States Military Policy.* Hamden: Archon.

Hildebrand, Klaus (1969). *Vom Reich zum Weltreich: Hitler, Nsdap und koloniale Frage, 1919–1945.* Munich.

———— (1970). *Deutsche Aussenpolitik, 1933–1945.* (British Ed.: *The Foreign Policy of the Third Reich.* London: Batsford, 1973).

———— (1979). *Das dritte Reich.* Munich: Oldeburg Verlag (Italian ed.: *Il terzo reich.* Bari: Laterza, 1983).

Hill, Helen, and Agar, Herbert (1940). *Beyond German Victory.* New York.

Hillgruber, Andreas (1965a, 1982). *Hitlers Strategie, 1940–41.* Munich: Bernard und Graefe.

———— (1965b, 1977). "Der Faktor Amerika in Hitlers Strategie, 1939–1941." *Deutsche Grossmacht und Weltpolitik im 19 und 20 Jahrhundert.* Düsseldorf.

———— (1973). "La politica estera nazionalsocialista fra il 1933 e il 1941." In R. De Felice, ed. *L'Italia tra Tedeschi e Alleati.* Bologna: Il Mulino.

Hillman, H. C. (1954). "The Comparative Strengths of the Great Powers." In RIIA (Royal Institute for International Affairs). *The Economic Structure of Hitler's Power.* London: Oxford University Press.

Hilton, Stanley E. (1981). *Hitler's Secret War in South America 1939–45.* New York: Ballantine Books; Baton Rouge: Lousiana State University Press.

Hinsley, F. H., Thomas, E. E., Ransom, C.F.G., and Knight, R. C. (1979). *British Intelligence in the Second World War.* London: HMSO

Hirschman, Albert O. (1945). *National Power and the Structure of Foreign Trade.* Berkeley: University of California Press.

Hiss, Alger (1957). *In the Court of Public Opinion.* New York: Alfred A. Knopf.

Hoffmann, Paul (1951). *Peace Can Be Won* (Italian ed.: *Possiamo vincere la pace.* Milan: Mondadori).

Hoffmann, Peter (1969). *Wiederstand, Staatsstreich, Attentat.* Munich: Pier Verlag (U.S. ed.: *The History of the German Resistance, 1933–1945.* Cambridge: MIT Press, 1977).

Hoffmann, Stanley (1968). *Gulliver's Troubles, or the Setting of American Foreign Policy.* New York: McGraw-Hill.

———— (1978). *Primacy or World Order, American Foreign Policy Since the Cold War.* New York: McGraw-Hill.

Hofstadter, Richard A. (1956). *The Age of Reform: From Bryan to F. D. Roosevelt.* New York: Knopf (Italian ed.: *L'età delle riforme.* Bologna: Il Mulino, 1962).

———— (1963). *Anti-Intellectualism in American Life.* New York: Knopf (Italian ed.: *Società e Intellettuali in America.* Turin: Einaudi, 1968).

———— (1964). *The Paranoid Style in American Politics.* London: Jonathan Cape.

Hogan, Michael J. (1977). *Informal Entente: The Private Structure of Cooperation in Anglo-American Economic Diplomacy, 1918–1928.* Columbia: University of Missouri Press.

Hohlfeld, H. H. (1941). "Der Verrechnungskurs." *Der deutsche Volkswirt,* January 3, pp. 555–557.

Holborn, Louise, W., and Holborn, Hajo, eds. (1943–1948). *War and Peace Aims of the United Nations.* 2 vols. Boston.

Holsti, Ole R. (1980). "Historians, Social Scientists, and Crisis Management: An Alternative View." *Journal of Conflict Resolution* 24, no. 4, pp. 665–682.

Holsti, Ole R., and Rosenau, James N. (1984). *American Leadership in World Affairs.* London: Allen and Unwin.

Hooker, Harvison Nancy, ed. (1956). *The Moffat Papers: Selection from the Diplomatic Journals of Jay Pierrepoint Moffat.* Cambridge: Harvard University Press.

Hoover, Herbert C. (1939). *Shall We Send Our Youth to War?* New York.

———— (1951). *The Memoirs of Herbert Hoover: Years of Adventure 1874–1920.* New York: Macmillan.

———— (1958). *Ordeal of Woodrow Wilson.* New York.

Hopkins, Terence K., and Wallerstein, Immanuel (1982). *World-System Analysis.* Beverly Hills: Sage.

Horne, Alistair (1969). *How to Lose a Battle: France 1940.* (Italian ed.: *La campagna de Francia.* Milan: Mondadori, 1970).

Horowitz, David (1971). *The Free World Colossus: A Critique of American Foreign Policy in the Cold War.* New York: Hill & Wang.

Hough, James F., and Fainsod, Merle (1953, 1979). *How the Soviet Union Is Governed.* Cambridge: Harvard University Press.

Howard, Graeme K. (1940). *America and a New World Order.* New York.

Howard, Michael (1968). *The Mediterranean Strategy in the Second World War.* London: Weidenfeld & Nicolson.

———— (1970). *History of the Second World War.* Vol. 4, *Grand Strategy, August 1942–September 1943.* London: HMSO.

Howland, Charles P. (1928). *American Foreign Relations, 1928.* New Haven: Yale University Press.

Hoxie, R. Gordon (1977). *Command Decision and the Presidency: A Study in National Security Policy and Organization.* New York: Reader's Digest Press.

Hughes, H. Stuart (1975). *The Sea Change: The Migration of Social Thought, 1930–1965.* New York: Harper & Row (Italian ed.: *Da sponda a sponda, l'Emigrazione degli intellettuali europei e lo studio della società contemporanea, 1930–1965.* Bologna: Il Mulino, 1977).

Hulen, Bertram D. (1939). *Inside the Department of State.* New York: Wiley.

Hull, Cordell (1948). *The Memoirs of Cordell Hull.* 2 vols. New York: Macmillan.

Huntington, Samuel P. (1959). *The Soldier and the State.* Cambridge: Harvard University Press.

———— (1981). *The Promise of Disharmony.* Cambridge: Harvard University Press.

Ickes, Harold L. (1953, 1954). *The Secret Diary of Harold L. Ickes.* Vol. 1, *The First Thousand Days, 1933–1936;* Vol. 2, *The Inside Struggle, 1936–1939;* Vol. 3, *The Lowering Clouds, 1939–1941.* New York: Simon & Schuster.

Ienaga, Saburo (1968, 1978). *The Pacific War, 1931–1945: A Critical Perspective on Japan's Role in World War II.* New York: Pantheon Books.

Ilari, Virgilio (1986). "Politica e strategia globale." In C. Jean, ed. *Il Pensiero strategico.* Milan: Franco Angeli, pp. 21–64.

Institute of Pacific Relations (1945). *Security in the Pacific.* New York.

International Student Service (1942). "Post-War Planning. A Survey of Recent Organizational Activities."

Interrante, Joseph (1979). "You Can't Go to Town in a Bathtub: Automobile Movement and the Reorganization of Rural American Space, 1900–1930." *Radical History Review,* no. 1 (Fall), pp. 151–170.

Iriye, Akira (1967). *Across the Pacific: An Inner Story of American–East Asian Relations.* New York: Harcourt Brace Jovanovich.

―――― (1981). *Power and Culture, The Japanese-American War, 1941–1945.* Cambridge: Harvard University Press.

Irving, David (1955). *Hitler's War.* 2 vols. London: Macmillan.

―――― (1979). *The War Path, Hitler's Germany 1933–38.* New York: Viking.

Isaacson, Walter, and Thomas, Evan (1986). *The Wise Men.* New York: Simon and Schuster.

Jablon, Howard (1983). *Crossroads of Decisions: The State Department and Foreign Policy, 1933–1937.* Lexington: University Press of Kentucky.

Janeway, Eliot (1951). *The Struggle for Survival: A Chronicle of Economic Mobilization in World War II.* New Haven: Yale University Press.

Janis, Irving L., and Mann, Leon (1977). *Decision Making.* New York: Free Press.

Jensen, Lloyd (1982). *Explaining Foreign Policy.* Englewood Cliffs: Prentice-Hall.

Jerningan, Jay (1983). *William Allen White.* Boston: Twayne.

Jervis, Robert (1976). *Perception and Misperception in International Politics.* Princeton: Princeton University Press.

Johnson, Donald Bruce (1960). *The Republican Party and Wendell Willkie.* Urbana: University of Illinois Press.

Johnson, Walter, ed. (1952). *Turbulent Era, A Diplomatic Record of Forty Years, 1904–1945.* 2 vols. Boston.

Johnston, Eric (1942). *America Unlimited.* New York: Doubleday.

Joll, James (1983). *The Origins of the First World War.* London: Longman.

Jonas, Manfred (1966). *Isolationism in America, 1935–41.* Ithaca: Cornell University Press.

Jones, Byrd L. (1972). "The Role of Keynesians in Wartime Policy and Postwar Planning, 1940–1946." *American Economic Review* 62, no. 2, pp. 125–133.

Jones, F. C. (1954). *Japan's New Order in East Asia: Its Rise and Fall, 1937–1945.* London: Oxford University Press.

Jones, Robert Huhn (1969). *The Roads to Russia, United States Lend-Lease to the Soviet Union.* Norman: University of Oklahoma Press.

Jordan, Amos A., and Taylor, William J. (1981, 1984). *American National Security: Policy and Process.* Baltimore: Johns Hopkins University Press.

Kahan, Vilein (1976). "The Communist International, 1919–1943: The Personnel of Its Highest Bodies." *International Review of Social History* 21, pt. 2.

Kahn, David (1980). "Potential Enemies: The United States Views Germany and Japan in 1941." Paper for the Conference on Potential Enemies. July 11–13.

Kaiser, A.D.H. (1944). *The Liquidation of War Production.* New York: McGraw-Hill.

Kaiser, D. E. (1979). "Germany, Britain, France and the Arms Trade in South-Eastern Europe, 1935–1939." Magonza Conference: Sudosteuropa in Spannungsfeld der Grossmachte 1919–1939. December 6–8 (mimeograph).

——— (1980). *Economic Diplomacy and the Origins of the Second World War: Germany, Britain, France and Eastern Europe, 1930–1939.* Princeton: Princeton University Press.

Kaldor, Mary. (1981). *The Baroque Arsenal.* New York: Hill & Wang.

Kaplan, A.D.H. (1944). *The Liquidation of War Production.* New York: McGraw-Hill.

Kaplan, Fred (1983). *The Wizards of Armageddon.* New York: Simon & Schuster.

Kaplan, Morton A. (1957). *System and Process in International Politics.* New York: Wiley.

Kaplan, Stephen S. (1981). *Diplomacy of Power: Soviet Armed Forces As a Political Instrument.* Washington: Brookings.

Karnow, Stanley (1983). *Vietnam: A History.* New York: Viking.

Karp, Walter (1979). *The Politics of War: The Story of Two Wars Which Altered Forever the Political Life of the American Republic.* New York: Harper & Row.

Kasten Nelson, Anna (1985). "President Truman and the Evolution of the National Security Council." *Journal of American History* 72, no. 2, pp. 360–379.

Katzenstein, Peter J. (1975). "International Interdependence: Some Long-Term Trends and Recent Changes." *International Organization* 29, pp. 1021–1034.

Kaufman, Burton I. (1974). *Efficiency and Expansion: Foreign Trade Organization in the Wilson Administration, 1913–1921.* Westport: Greenwood Press.

Keegan, John (1976). *The Face of the Battle.* London: Jonathan Cape.

Keller, Suzanne (1968). "Elites." In *International Encyclopedia of the Social Sciences,* vol. 5. New York: Free Press.

Kenetz, Peter (1982). "Second World War Soviet Film Propaganda." Bellagio Conference, April 5–9 (paper, 26 pp.).

Kennan, George F. (1951). *American Diplomacy 1900–1950.* Chicago: University of Chicago Press.

——— (1967). *Memoirs, 1925–1950.* Boston: Little, Brown.

Kennedy, David M. (1980). *Over Here: The First World and American Society.* New York: Oxford University Press.

Kennedy, Paul M. (1976). *The Rise and Fall of British Naval Mastery.* London: Allen and Unwin.

———, ed. (1979). *The War Plans of the Great Powers, 1880–1914.* London: Allen and Unwin.

——— (1987). *The Rise and Fall of the Great Powers.* New York: Random House.

Kent, Alan E. (1956). "Portrait in Isolationism: The La Follettes and Foreign Policy." University of Wisconsin (Ph.D. dissertation).

Keohane, Robert O. (1984). *After Hegemony.* Princeton: Princeton University Press.

Keohane, Robert O., and Nye, Joseph S., Jr. (1977). *Power and Interdependence.* London: Pinter.

———, eds. (1970). *Transnational Relations and World Politics.* Cambridge: Harvard University Press.

Kester, Randall B. (1940). "The War Industry Board, 1917–1918: A Study in Industrial Mobilization." *American Political Science Review* 34.

Kevles, Daniel J. (1979). *The Physicists: The History of a Scientific Community in Modern America.* New York: Quadrangle Books.

Keynes, John Maynard (1919, 1971). *The Economic Consequences of the Peace.* London: Macmillan.

———— (1979a). *Activities 1940–1943: External War Finance.* Vol. 23. London: Macmillan.

———— (1979b). *Activities 1944–1946: The Transition to Peace.* Vol. 24. London: Macmillan.

———— (1980a). *Activities: 1940–1944, Shaping the Post-War World: The Clearing Union.* Vol. 25. London: Macmillan.

———— (1980b). *Activities 1941–1946, Shaping the Post-War World: Bretton Woods and Reparations.* Vol. 26. London: Macmillan.

Kimball, Warren F. (1969). *The Most Unsordid Act, Lend-Lease 1939–1941.* Baltimore: Johns Hopkins University Press.

————, ed. (1973). *Franklin D. Roosevelt and the World Crisis, 1937–1945.* Lexington: Heath.

———— (1974). "Churchill and Roosevelt: The Personal Equation." *Prologue,* Fall 1974.

———— (1976). *Swords or Ploughshares: The Morgenthau Plan for Defeated Nazi Germany, 1943–1946.* Philadelphia: Lippincott.

————, ed. (1984). *Churchill and Roosevelt: The Complete Correspondence.* 3 vols. Princeton: Princeton University Press.

Kincade, William, and Porto, Jeffrey D., eds. (1979). *Negotiating Security: An Arms Control Reader.* Washington: Carnegie Endowment for International Peace.

Kindleberger, Charles P. (1973). *The World in Depression, 1929–1939.* Berkeley: University of California Press.

———— (1978). *Manias, Panics and Crisis: A History of Financial Crisis.* London: Macmillan.

Kirk, Grayson (1947). *The Study of International Relations in American Colleges and Universities.* New York: Council on Foreign Relations.

Klein, B. H. (1959). *Germany's Economic Preparations for War.* Cambridge: Harvard University Press.

Knipping, Franz (1974). *Die Amerikanische Russland, Politik in der Zeit des Hitler-Stalin Pakts, 1939–1941.* Tübingen.

Knorr, Klaus, ed. (1976). *Historical Dimensions of National Security Problems.* Lawrence: University Press of Kansas.

Knox, MacGregor (1980). "Fascist Italy Assesses Its Enemies, 1935–1940." Oct., 28 pp. (typescript).

———— (1982). *Mussolini Unleashed, 1939–1941: Politics and Strategy in Fascist Italy's Last War.* Cambridge: Cambridge University Press.

Koch, H. W., ed. (1972). *The Origins of the First World War: Great Power Rivalry and German War Aims.* London: Macmillan.

Koen, R. Y. (1974). *The China Lobby in American Politics.* New York.

Kohn, Hans (1957). *American Nationalism: An Interpretative Essay.* New York.

Koistinen, Paul A.C. (1967). "The Industrial-Military Complex in Historical Perspective: World War I." *Business History Review* 41.

Kolko, Gabriel (1968). *The Politics of War: The World and United States Foreign Policy, 1943–1945*. New York: Random House.

———— (1969). *The Roots of American Foreign Policy: The Analysis of Power and Purpose*. Boston: Beacon Press.

Kolko, Gabriel, and Kolko, Joyce (1972). *The Limits of Power*. New York: Harper & Row.

Korb, Lawrence J. (1976). *The Joint Chiefs of Staff: The First Twenty-Five Years*. Bloomington: Indiana University Press.

Krasner, Stephen D. (1978). *Defending the National Interest: Raw Materials Investments and U.S. Foreign Policy*. Princeton: Princeton University Press.

————, ed. (1982). "International Regimes." *International Organization* 36, no. 2.

Krippendorff, Ekkehart, ed. (1981). *The Role of the United States in the Reconstruction of Italy and West Germany, 1943–1949*. Berlin: Freie Universität.

Kuniholm, Bruce Robellet (1980). *The Origins of the Cold War in the Near East: Great Powers Conflict and Diplomacy in Iran, Turkey and Greece*. Princeton: Princeton University Press.

Kuznets, Simon (1941). *National Income and Its Compositions, 1919–1938*. Princeton: Princeton University Press.

Lacouture, Jean (1984). *De Gaulle*. Vol. 1, *Le Rebelle*. Paris: Seuil.

LaFeber, Walter (1963). *The New Empire: An Interpretation of American Expansionism, 1860–1898*. Ithaca: Cornell University Press.

———— (1975). "Roosevelt, Churchill and Indochina, 1942–1945." *American Historical Review* 80.

———— (1983). *Inevitable Revolutions: The United States in Central America*. New York: Norton.

Landes, David S. (1969). *The Unbound Prometheus*. Cambridge: Cambridge University Press.

Langer, William L. (1947a). "Political Problems of a Coalitiion." *Foreign Affairs*, October, pp. 73–89.

———— (1947b). *Our Vichy Gamble*. New York: Knopf.

Langer, William L., and Gleason, S. Everett (1952). *The Challenge to Isolation, 1937–1940*, vol. 1. New York: Harper.

———— (1953). *The Undeclared War, 1940–1941*, vol. 2. New York: Harper.

Langley, Lester D. (1983). *The Banana Wars: An Inner Story of American Empire, 1900–1934*. Lexington: University Press of Kentucky.

Lapp, K. (1957). "Die Finanzierung der Weltkriege 1914–1918 und 1939–1945 in Deutschland: Ein Wirtschafts- und finanzpolitische Untersuchung." Nuremberg Universität (dissertation).

Laqueur, Walter, ed. (1976, 1979). *Fascism: A Reader's Guide, Analysis, Interpretations, Bibliography*. London: Wilword House.

Larson, Arthur D., ed. (1973). *National Security Affairs: A Guide to Information Sources*. Detroit: Gale.

Lary, Hal B. (1943). *The United States in the World Economy*. Washington: USGPO.

Lasch, Christopher (1968). "The Cold War: Revisited and Revisioned." *New York Times Magazine*, January 14, 1968.

———— (1979). *The Culture of Narcissism.* New York: Norton.

Lash, Joseph P. (1973). *Eleanor: The Years Alone.* New York: André Deutsche.

———— (1976). *Roosevelt and Churchill: The Partnership That Saved the West.* New York: Norton.

Laski, Harold J. (1940). *The American Presidency: An Interpretation.* New York: Harper & Bros.

Lasswell, Harold, and Kaplan, A. (1950). *Power.* New York: Free Press.

Latané, Holladay John (1918). *From Isolation to Leadership: A Review of American Foreign Policy.* Garden City: Doubleday.

Lattimore, Owen (1945). *Solution in Asia.* London.

League of Nations (1943, 1945). *The Transition from War to Peace Economy.* Report of the Delegation on Economic Depression, Part 1 (1943); Part 2 (1945). Geneva and Princeton: League of Nations.

League of Nations, Economic, Financial and Transport Department (1945). *Industrialization and Foreign Trade.* Princeton: League of Nations.

League of Nations, Economic Intelligence Service (1941). *Europe's Trade: A Study of the Trade of European Countries with Each Other and with the Rest of the World.* Geneva: League of Nations.

———— (1942). *The Network of World Trade, A Companion Volume to* Europe's Trade. Princeton and Geneva: League of Nations.

Leahy, William Daniel (1950). *I Was There.* New York: Wittesby House.

Lebergott, Stanley (1957). "Annual Estimates of Unemployment in the United States, 1900–1954." In *The Measurement and Behavior of Unemployment.* New York: National Bureau of Economic Research.

———— (1980). "The Return to U.S. Imperialism, 1890–1929." *Journal of Economic History* 60, no. 2, pp. 229–252.

Lebow, Richard Ned (1981). *Between Peace and War: The Nature of International Crises.* Baltimore: Johns Hopkins University Press.

Lebra, Joyce C., ed. (1979). *Japan's Greater East Asia Co-Prosperity Sphere in World War II.* London: Oxford University Press.

Leca, Dominique (1979). *La Rupture de 1940.* Paris: Fayrad.

Lederer, Ivo J., ed. (1962). *Russian Foreign Policy.* New Haven: Yale University Press.

Leigh, Michael (1976). *Mobilizing Current Public Opinion and American Foreign Policy, 1937–1947.* Westport: Greenwood Press.

Leontief, Wassily W. (1941, 1951, 1977). *The Structure of the American Economy, 1919–1939: An Empirical Application of Equilibrium Analysis.* New York and White Plains: Sharpe.

Lerche, C. O. (1965). *The Cold War and After.* Englewood Cliffs: Prentice-Hall.

Leuchtenburg, William E. (1957). *The Perils of Prosperity, 1914–1932.* Chicago: University of Chicago Press.

———— (1963). *Franklin D. Roosevelt and the New Deal, 1932–1940.* New York: Harper & Row.

———— (1983). *In the Shadow of FDR, from Harry Truman to Ronald Reagan.* Ithaca: Cornell University Press.

Leverette, William E., Jr., and Shi, David E. (1982). "Herbert Agar and Free America. A Jeffersonian Alternative to the New Deal." *American Studies* 16, no. 2, pp. 189–206.

Levering, Ralph B. (1976). *American Opinion and the Russian Alliance, 1939–1945.* Chapel Hill: University of North Carolina Press.

—— (1978). *The Public and American Foreign Policy 1918–1978.* New York: Morrow.

Levin, Gordon N., Jr. (1968). *Woodrow Wilson and World Politics: America's Response to War and Revolution.* New York: Oxford University Press.

Lewis, Arthur W. (1978). *Growth and Fluctuations, 1870–1913.* London: Allen and Unwin.

Lewis, Cleona (1938). *America's Stake in International Investments.* Washington: Brookings.

Liddell Hart, Basil H. (1970). *History of the Second World War.* London: Corselle.

Lieuwen, Edwin (1960). *Arms and Politics in Latin America.* New York: Praeger.

Lindbergh, Anne Morrow (1934). "Flying Around the North Atlantic." *National Geographic* 66, no. 3.

Lindbergh, Charles A. (1970). *The Wartime Journals of C. A. Lindbergh.* New York: Harcourt Brace Jovanovich.

—— (1977). *Autobiography of Values.* New York: Harcourt Brace Jovanovich.

Lindblom, Charles E. (1977). *Politics and Markets: The World's Political-Economic Systems.* New York: Basic Books.

Lingeman, R. (1970). *Don't You Know There's a War On? Oral History of the Home Front in USA.* New York.

Link, Arthur S. (1947, 1956). *Wilson: The Road to the White House* (1947). *Wilson: The New Freedom* (1956). Princeton: Princeton University Press.

—— (1954, 1963). *Woodrow Wilson and the Progressive Era; 1910–1917.* New York: Harper & Row.

—— (1957). *Wilson the Diplomatist.* New York: Harper & Row.

—— (1960). *Wilson: The Struggle for Neutrality.* Princeton: Princeton University Press.

Lippmann, Walter, ed. (1932). *The United States in World Affairs, 1931.* New York: Harper & Bros.

—— (1943). *United States Foreign Policy, Shield of the Republic.* Boston: Little, Brown.

—— (1944). *United States War Aims.* Boston: Little, Brown (Italian ed.: *Gli scopi di guerra degli Stati Uniti.* Turin: Einaudi, 1946).

Liska, George (1962). *Nations in Alliance.* Baltimore: Johns Hopkins University Press.

—— (1977). *Quest for Equilibrium: America and the Balance of Power on Land and Sea.* Baltimore: Johns Hopkins University Press.

—— (1978). *Career of Empire: America and Imperial Expansion over Land and Sea.* Baltimore: Johns Hopkins University Press.

—— (1980). *Russia and World Order: Strategic Choices and the Laws of Power in History.* Baltimore: Johns Hopkins University Press.

—— (1982). *Russia and the Road to Appeasement: Cycles of East-West Conflict in War and Peace.* Baltimore: Johns Hopkins University Press.

Little, Douglas (1985). *Malevolent Neutrality.* Ithaca: Cornell University Press.

Little, Robert D. (1964). *Organism Strategic Planning, 1945–1950: The National System and the Air Force.* Washington.

Lottman, Herbert R. (1984). *Pétain.* Paris: Seuil.

Louis, Henriette (1980). "Réactions américaines à la défaite française de 1940: Témoinages et documents." *Revue d'histoire de la deuxième guerre mondiale* 30, no. 119, pp. 1–16.

Louis, William Roger (1978). *Imperialism at Bay: The United States and the Decolonization of the British Empire, 1941–1945.* New York: Oxford University Press.

Loveland, William Allen (1979). "Deliverance from Dictatorship, American Diplomacy Towards France During the 1940s." Rutgers University (Ph.D. dissertation).

Lowe, C. J., and Marzari, F. (1975). *Italian Foreign Policy, 1870–1940.* London: Routledge and Kegan Paul.

Lubell, Samuel (1952). *The Future of American Politics.* New York.

Luce, Henry R. (1941). *American Century.* New York.

Ludwell, D. (1930). *America Conquers Britain: A Record of Economic War.* New York: Knopf.

Lukacs, J. (1961). *History of the Cold War.* Garden City: Doubleday.

Lundestad, Geir (1979). *The American Non-Policy Towards Eastern Europe, 1943–1947: Universalism in an Area of Essential Interest to the United States.* New York: Columbia University Press.

Lutz, Lorena S., and Lutz, Ralph Hasswell, eds. (1983). *Organization of American Relief in Europe, 1918–1919.* Stanford: Stanford University Press.

McCagg, William O. (1979). *Stalin Embattled, 1943–48.* Detroit: Wayne State University Press.

McCamy, L. James (1950). *The Administration of American Foreign Affairs.* New York: Knopf.

McClellan, David S. (1976). *Dean Acheson: The State Department Years.* New York: Dodd, Mead.

McClellan, David S., and Woodhouse, Charles E. (1960). "The Business Elite and Foreign Policy." *Western Political Quarterly* 13 (March), pp. 172–190.

MacCormack, John (1940). *America's Problem.* New York: Viking.

McCormick, Thomas J. (1967). *China Market: America's Quest for Informal Empire.* Chicago: Quadrangle Books.

McCoy, Donald R. (1973). *Coming of Age: The United States during the 1920s and the 1930s.* Harmondsworth: Penguin Books.

McCullogh, David (1977). *The Path Between the Seas: The Creation of the Panama Canal, 1870–1914.* New York: Simon & Schuster.

MacDonald, C. A. (1981). *The United States, Britain and Appeasement, 1936–1939.* New York: St. Martin's Press.

McDonald, I. S. (1974). *Anglo-American Relations Since the Second World War.* Newton Abbott.

McKee, Delbert L. (1977). *Chinese Exclusion Versus the Open Door Policy, 1900–1906: Clashes over China Policy in the Roosevelt Era.* Detroit: Wayne State University Press.

McNeill, Hardy William (1953). *America, Britain and Russia: Their Cooperation and Conflict, 1941–1946.* New York: Oxford University Press.

Machlup, Fritz (1977). *A History of Thought on Economic Integration.* New York: Columbia University Press.

Mackinder, Sir Halford (1919, 1942). *Democratic Ideals and Reality.* New York: Norton.

Macreddy, John A. (1924). "The Non-Stop Flight Across America." *National Geographic* 46, no. 1.

Madden, J. T., Nadler, M., and Sauvain, H. C. (1937). *America's Experience As a Creditor Nation.* Englewood Cliffs: Prentice-Hall.

Magdoff, Harry (1969). *The Age of Imperialism: The Economics of U.S. Foreign Policy.* New York: Monthly Review Press.

Mahan, Alfred Thayer (1890, 1957). *The Influence of Sea Power upon History, 1660–1783.* New York: Hill and Wang.

———— (1897, 1970). *The Interest of America in Seapower, Present and Future.* Boston: Little, Brown.

Maier, Charles S. (1970). "Revisionism and the Interpretation of Cold War Origins." *Perspectives in American History* 4.

———— (1975). *Recasting Bourgeois Europe.* Princeton: Princeton University Press (Italian ed.: *La rifondazione dell'Europa borghese: Francia, Germania e Italia nel decennio successivo alla prima guerra mondiale.* Bari: De Donato, 1979).

———— (1981). "The Two Post-War Eras and the Conditions for Stability in 20th Century Western Europe." *American Historical Review,* April 1981, pp. 327–52

Maiskij, Ivan (1960). *Guerra di diplomazia, Memorie in un ambasciatore sovietico 1939–1945.* Rome: Editori Riuniti.

Manchester, William (1974, 1978). *The Glory and the Dream: A Narrative History of America 1932–1972.* Boston: Little, Brown.

———— (1978). *American Caesar: Douglas MacArthur 1880–1964.* Boston: Little, Brown.

Markel, Lester, ed. (1946). *Public Opinion and Foreign Policy.* New York: Harper & Bros.

Marks, Frederick, III (1979). *Velvet on Iron: The Diplomacy of Theodore Roosevelt.* Lincoln: University of Nebraska Press.

Marris, Robin, and Mueller, Dennis C. (1980). "The Corporation Competition, and the invisible Hand." *Journal of Economic Literature* 18, no. 1, pp. 32–63.

Marshall, Charles Buston (1968). *The Limits of Foreign Policy.* Baltimore: Johns Hopkins University Press.

Martin, James J. (1964). *American Liberalism and World Politics, 1931–1941: Liberalism's Press and Spokesmen on the Road Back to War Between Mukden and Pearl Harbor.* 2 vols. New York: Devin-Adair.

Martin, Laurence, ed. (1979). *Strategic Thought in the Nuclear Age.* London: Heinemann.

Mason, Edward S., and Asher, Robert E. (1973). *The World Bank Since Bretton Woods.* Washington: Brookings.

Mason, Timothy W. (1977). *Sozialpolitik im Dritten Reich, Arbeiterklasse und Volksgemeinschaft.* Opladen: Westdeutsches Verlag (Italian ed.: *La politica sociale del Terzo Reich.* Bari: De Donato, 1980).

Mastny, Vojtech (1979). *Russia's Road to the Cold War, Diplomacy, Warfare and the Politics of Communism, 1941–1945.* New York: Columbia University Press.

Matloff, Maurice (1965). "The American Approach to War, 1918–1945." In M. Howard, ed. *The Theory and Practice of War.* London: Cassell.

Matloff, Maurice, and Snell, Edwin M. (1953, 1959). *US Army in World War II: Strategic Planning for Coalition Warfare.* Vol. 1, *1941–42;* Vol. 2, *1943–1944.* Washington: USGPO.

May, Ernest R. (1955). "The Development of Political-Military Consultation in the United States." *Political Science Quarterly* 70, no. 2, pp. 161–180.

——— (1959). *The World War and American Isolation, 1914–1917.* Cambridge: Harvard University Press.

——— (1961). *Imperial Democracy.* New York: Harcourt, Brace and World.

——— (1963). "The Alliance for Progress in Perspective." *Foreign Affairs* 41 (July).

——— (1968). *American Imperialism, A Speculative Essay.* New York: Atheneum.

——— (1973). *"Lessons" of the Past, The Use and Misuse of History in American Foreign Policy.* New York: Oxford University Press.

——— (1983). "Writing Contemporary International History." San Francisco (typescript).

May, Henry F. (1959). *The End of American Innocence: The First Years of Our Own Time, 1912–1917.* New York: Knopf.

Mayer, Arno J. (1959). *Wilson vs. Lenin: Political Origins of the New Diplomacy, 1917–1918.* New Haven: Yale University Press.

——— (1968). *The Politics and Diplomacy of Peacekeeping, Containment and Counter-revolution at Versailles, 1918–1919.* London: Weidenfeld & Nicolson.

——— (1981). *The Persistence of the Old Regime.* New York: Pantheon.

Maynes, Charles W., Yankelovich, Daniel, and Cohen, Richard L. (1976). *U.S. Foreign Policy, Principles for Defining the National Interest.* Washington: Carnegie Endowment for International Peace.

Mee, Charles L. (1975). *Meeting at Potsdam.* New York: Evans.

——— (1984). *The Marshall Plan: The Launching of the Pax Americana.* New York: Simon & Schuster.

Meikle, Jeffrey L. (1979). *Twentieth Century Limited, Industrial Design in America 1925–1939.* Philadelphia: Temple University Press.

Melandri, Pierre (1980). "L'apprentissage du leadership occidental. Les Etats-Unis et le monde, 1941–1949." *Relations Internationales,* no. 22 (Summer).

Mendershausen, Horst (1941). *The Economics of War.* New York: Prentice-Hall.

Mensch, Gerhard (1975). *Das Technologische Patt.* Frankfurt/M: Umschau Verlag (British ed.: *Stalemate in Technology: Innovations Overcome the Depression.* Cambridge: Ballinger, 1979).

Merk, Frederick (1963). *Manifest Destiny and Mission in American History.* New York: Vintage Books.

Michel, Bernard (1977). *Histoire économique et sociale du monde*. Vol. 2, tome 5. Paris: Colin Armand (Italian ed.: "Le tecniche economiche di guerra: l'esempio tedesco." In Pierre Leon, ed. *Storia economica e sociale del mondo*. Bari: Laterza).

Michel, Henri (1968). *La Seconde guerre mondiale*. Paris: Presses Universitaires de France.

_____ (1970). *La guerre de l'ombre, La Resistance en Europe*. Paris: Grasset (Italian ed.: *La guerra dell'ombra*. Milan: Mursia, 1973).

Migone, Gian Giacomo (1974). "Le origini dell'egemonia americana in Europa." *Rivista di Storia Contemporanea*, no. 4.

_____ (1980). *Gli Stati Uniti e il Fascismo: Alle origini dell'egemonia americana in Italia*. Milan: Feltrinelli.

Miller, Francis Pickens, and Hill, Helen (1930). *The Giant of the Western World: America and Europe in a North Atlantic Civilization*. New York: Morrow.

Miller, James Edward (1984). "Strategia della stabilizzazione. Gli Stati Uniti e l'Italia: 1917–1950." *Storia Contemporanea* 15, no. 4, pp. 745–780.

Miller, James G. (1978). *Living Systems*. New York: McGraw-Hill.

Millis, Walter (1935). *The Road to War*. Boston: Houghton Mifflin.

Millis, Walter, and Auffield, E. S. (1951). *The Forrestal Diaries*. New York: Viking.

Milward, Alan S. (1965). *The German Economy at War*. London: Milton Press.

_____ (1970). *The New Order and the French Economy*. London: Oxford University Press.

_____ (1977). *War, Economy and Society, 1939–1945*. Berkeley: University of California Press.

Ministero della Difesa (Italian Ministry of Defense), Stato Maggiore Esercito (1973). *Bollettini di guerra del Comando Supremo, 1940–1943*. Rome: SME, Ufficio Storico.

Minniti, Fortunato (1973). "Aspetti della politica fascista degli armamenti dal 1935 al 1943." In R. De Felice, ed. *L'Italia fra tedeschi e alleati*. Bologna: Il Mulino.

Morgan, Wayne H. (1965). *America's Road to Empire: The War with Spain and Overseas Expansion*. New York: Wiley.

Morgenstern, George (1947). *Pearl Harbor: The Story of the Secret War*. New York.

Morgenthau, Hans J. (1948). *Politics Among Nations: The Struggle for Power and Peace*. New York: Knopf.

_____ (1969). *A New Foreign Policy for the United States*. New York: Praeger.

Morgenthau, Henry, Jr. (1965). *Diary: China*. 2 vols. Washington.

Morison, Elting E. (1960). *Turmoil and Tradition: A Study of the Life and Times of Henry L. Stimson*. Boston: Houghton Mifflin.

Morison, Samuel Eliot (1947–1975). *History of United States Naval Operations in World War II*. 15 vols. Boston: Little, Brown.

_____ (1948a). "Did Roosevelt Start the War? History Through a Beard." *Atlantic Monthly* 182, no. 2.

_____ (1948b). *Strategy and Compromise*. Boston: Little, Brown.

_____ (1963). *The Two-Ocean War: A Short History of the United States Navy in the Second World War*. Boston: Little, Brown.

Morley, James William, ed. (1980). *The Fateful Choice: Japan's Advance into Southeast Asia, 1939–1941*. New York: Columbia University Press.

Morsel, Henri (1977). "Guerra economica ed economia di guerra." In P. Leon, ed. *Storia economica e sociale del mondo*. Bari.

Morton, Louis (1959). "War Orange: Evolution of a Strategy." *World Politics*, January 1959.

——— (1962). *Strategy and Command: The First Two Years*. Washington: USGPO.

Mosely, Philip E. (1940). "Iceland and Greenland: An American Problem." *Foreign Affairs* 18, no. 4, pp. 742–747.

Mosley, Leonard (1978). *Dulles, A Biography of Eleonor, Allen, John Foster Dulles and their Family*. New York: Dell.

——— (1982). *Marshall. Hero of Our Times*. New York: Hearst Books.

Mossé, Robert (1953). "La mobilisation économique aux Etats-Unis pendant la Seconde guerre mondiale." *Revue d'histoire de la Deuxième Guerre Mondiale*, October 1953.

Moulton, Harold G., and Pasvolsky, Leo (1932). *War Debts and World Prosperity*. Washington: Brookings.

Mounting, Roger (1984). "Lend-Lease and the Soviet War Effort." *Journal of Contemporary History* 19, no. 3, pp. 492–510.

Mowry, G. E. (1962). *The Era of Theodore Roosevelt*. New York: Harper & Row.

Muir, Ramsay (1933). *The Interdependent World and Its Problems*. Boston: Houghton Mifflin.

Mundt, Karl E., Berle, A. A., Worys, John M., and Eaton, Charles A. (1943). "Extension of Lend-Lease Act." Hearings Before Committee on Foreign Affairs, House of Representatives, 78th Congress, 1st Session. Washington: USGPO.

Murphy, Robert D. (1965). *Diplomat Among Warriors*. Garden City: Doubleday (Italian ed.: *Un diplomatico in prima linea*. Milan: Mondadori, 1967).

Murphy, Thomas P. (1971). *Science, Geopolitics and Federal Spending*. Lexington: Heath.

Murray, Williamson (1983). *Strategy for Defeat: The Luftwaffe, 1933–1945*. Washington: Air University, USGPO.

——— (1984). *The Change in the European Balance of Power, 1938–1939*. Princeton: Princeton University Press.

Namikawa, Ryo (1982). "Overseas Broadcasting by Japan during World War II and after." Bellagio Conference, April 5–9, 24 pp. (typescript).

National Security Congress (1916). "Proceedings of the National Security Congress Under the Auspices of the National Security League, Washington, 20–22 January, 1916." New York: National Security League.

National Security Council (1947–1953). *List of NSC Papers* (Oct. 15, 1947–Dec. 30, 1953). Modern Military Record Branch. Washington: National Archives.

National Security League (1917). "What It Is and Why, What It Has Done and Is Doing: A National Defense Catechism for the Busy Man or Woman." New York: The League.

Nearing, Scott, and Freeman, Joseph (1925, 1966). *Dollar Diplomacy: A Study in American Imperialism*. New York: Monthly Review Press (Italian ed.: Bari: Dedalo Libri, 1975).

Nelson, Donald M. (1946). *Arsenal of Democracy*. New York: Harcourt, Brace.

Nelson, Otto L. (1946). *National Security and the General Staff*. New York: Infantry Journal Press.

Néré, Jacques (1955). "Points de vue sur l'économie de guerre aux Etats-Unis." *Revue d'histoire de la deuxième guerre mondiale*, January.

Neumann, Franz (1942). *Behemoth: The Structure and Practice of National Socialism*. New York: Oxford University Press (Italian ed., introd. by E. Collotti: *Behemot*. Milan: Feltrinelli, 1977).

Neumann, William L. (1952). "F. D. Roosevelt, a Disciple of Admiral Mahan." *U.S. Naval Institute Proceedings*, July.

_____ (1965). *After Victory: Churchill, Roosevelt, Stalin and the Making of the Peace*. New York.

Nevins, Alan (1950). *The New Deal and World Affairs, 1933–1945*. New Haven: Yale University Press.

Newman, William J. (1968). *The Balance of Power in the Interwar Years, 1919–1939*. New York: Random House.

Nicholson, Harold (1923). *Peacemaking 1919*. New York: Harcourt, Brace and World.

Niebuhr, Reinhold (1947). *Moral Man and Immoral Society*. New York: Scribner's.

_____ (1952). *The Irony of American History*. New York: Scribner's.

_____ (1953). *Christian Realism and Political Problems*. New York: Scribner's.

Ninkovitch, Frank A. (1981). *The Diplomacy of Ideas: U.S. Foreign Policy and Cultural Relations, 1938–1950*. Cambridge: Cambridge University Press.

Nixon, Edgar, ed. (1969). *Franklin D. Roosevelt and Foreign Affairs, Jan. 1933–Jan. 1937*. Cambridge: Harvard University Press.

Noble, David F. (1977). *America by Design: Science, Technology and the Rise of Corporate Capitalism*. New York: Knopf.

North, Douglas (1962). "International Capital Movements in Historical Perspective." In Raymond F. Mikesell, ed. *U.S. Private and Government Investment Abroad*. Eugene: University of Oregon Books.

Notter, Harley A. (1949). *Postwar Foreign Policy Preparation, 1939–1945*. Washington: USGPO.

Nouailhat, Yves-Henri (1980). "Les Américains ont-ils été isolationnistes entre les deux guerres mondiales?" *Relations Internationales*, no. 22 (Summer 1980), pp. 125–140.

Nübel, Otto (1980). *Die Amerikanische Reparationspolitik gegenuber Deutschland, 1941–1945*. Frankfurt: A. Metzner Verlag.

Nuechterlein, Donald E. (1973). *United States National Interest in a Changing World*. Lexington: University Press of Kentucky.

_____ (1979). "The Concept of 'National Interest': A Time for New Approaches." *Orbis* 23, no. 1, pp. 73–92.

Nutter, G. Warren, and Einhorn, Henry Adler (1969). *Enterprise Monopoly in the United States, 1899–1958*. New York: Columbia University Press.

Nye, Joseph S., Jr., ed. (1984). *The Making of America's Soviet Policy*. New Haven: Yale University Press.

O'Connor, Raymond G. (1971). *Diplomacy for Victory: FDR and Unconditional Surrender*. New York.

Office of the Chief of Military History (1964). *U.S. Army in World War II*. Subseries: *Special Studies on Civil Affairs*. Henry L. Coles and Albert K. Neinboy, eds. *Soldiers Become Governors!* Washington: USGPO.

 (various years). *United States Army in World War II:* (1) *Chief of Staff: Prewar Plans and Preparations;* (2) *Washington Command Post: The Operation Division;* (3) *Strategic Planning for Coalition Warfare,* 2 vols. (a) *1941–1942,* (b) *1943–1944;* (4) *Global Logistic and Strategy,* 2 vols. (a) *1940–1943,* (b) *1943–1945;* (5) *The Army and Economic Mobilization;* (6) *The Army and Industrial Manpower.* Washington, USGPO.

 (various years). *United States Army in World War II:* (1) *The War Department;* (2) *The Army Air Force;* (3) *The Army Ground Forces;* (4) *The Army Service Forces;* (5) *The Western Hemisphere;* (6) *The War in the Pacific;* (7) *The Mediterranean;* (8) *The European Theater of Operations;* (9) *The Middle East Theater;* (10) *The China-Burma Theater;* (11) *The Technical Services;* (12) *Special Studies;* (13) *Pictorial Records.* Washington: USGPO

Offner, Arnold A. (1969). *American Appeasement: U.S. Foreign Policy and Germany, 1933–1938.* Cambridge: The Belknap Press of Harvard University Press.

 (1975). *The Origins of the Second World War: American Foreign Policy and World Politics, 1917–1941.* New York: Holt, Rinehart and Winston.

Organski, A.F.K., and Kugler, Jacek (1980). *The War Ledger.* Chicago: University of Chicago Press.

Ortona, Egidio (1984). *Anni d'Europa: la ricostruzione, 1944–1951.* Bologna: Il Mulino.

Ory, Pascal, ed. (1977). *La France Allemande (1933–1945): Paroles du collaborationisme français.* Paris: Gallimard.

Osgood, Robert E. (1953). *Ideals and Self-Interest in America's Foreign Relations: The Great Transformation of the Twentieth Century.* Chicago: University of Chicago Press.

 (1971). *Alliances and American Foreign Policy.* Baltimore: Johns Hopkins University Press.

Overy, R. J. (1980). "Hitler and Air Strategy." *Journal of Contemporary History* 15, no. 3, pp. 405–422.

Page, Benjamin I., and Shapiro, Robert Y. (1982). "Changes in American Policy Preferences." *Public Opinion Quarterly* 46, pp. 24–42.

Panebianco, Angelo (1977). "La politica estera italiana. Un modello interpretativo." *Il Mulino* 26, no. 254, pp. 845–879.

Parrini, Carl P. (1969). *Heir to Empire: United States Economic Diplomacy, 1916–1923.* Pittsburgh: University of Pittsburgh Press.

Pasquino, Gianfranco (1969). "Tradizione e scienza nello studio della politicainternazionale." *Il Politico* 34, no. 3 (September).

 (1980). "Fattori di destabilizzazione nella politica estera USA." *Il Mulino* 29, no. 269 (May-June).

Passigli, Stefano, ed. (1971). *Potere ed lites politiche.* Bologna: Il Mulino.

Pastorelli, Pietro (1967). "L'esaurimento dell'iniziativa dell'Asse," Part 1: "L'estensione del conflitto (June–December 1941)." *Annuario di Politica Internazionale (1939–1945)* 6, tomo 2, parte 1. Milan: ISPI.

 (1973). "La politica estera fascista dalla fine del conflitto etiopico alla seconda guerra mondiale." In R. De Felice, ed. *L'Italia fra tedeschi e alleati.* Bologna: Il Mulino.

Paterson, Thomas G. (1969). "The Abortive American Loan to Russia and the Origins of the Cold War, 1943–1946." *Journal of American History* 56, no. 1.
———, ed. (1970). *The Origins of the Cold War.* Lexington, Mass.: Lexington Books.
———, ed. (1971). *Cold War Critics.* Chicago: Quadrangle Books.
——— (1973). *Soviet-American Confrontation: Postwar Reconstruction and the Origins of the Cold War.* Baltimore: Johns Hopkins University Press.
——— (1979). *On Every Front: The Making of the Cold War.* New York: Norton.
Paxton, Frederic L. (1939). *America at War, 1917–1918.* Boston.
——— (1948). *American Democracy and the World War: Postwar Years: Back to Normalcy, 1918–1923.* Berkeley: University of California Press.
Paxton, Robert O. (1972). *Vichy France: Old Guard and New Order, 1940–1944* (French ed.: *La France de Vichy.* Paris: Seuil, 1973).
Pedroncini, Guy (1948). "La stratégie française et l'Italie à la veille de la seconde guerre mondiale." In J. B. Duroselle and E. Serra, eds. *Italia e Francia, 1939–45,* vol. 1. Milan: F. Angeli, pp. 212–227.
Peillard, Léonce (1974). *La bataille de l'Atlantique.* Paris: Robert Laffont (Italian ed.: *La battaglia dell'Atlantico.* Milan: Mondadori, 1976).
Pells, Richard H (1973). *Radical Visions and American Dreams: Culture and Social Thought in the Depression Years.* New York: Harper & Row.
——— (1985). *The Liberal Mind in a Conservative Age: American Intellectuals in the 1940s and 1950s.* New York: Harper & Row.
Pentzlin, Heinz (1980). *Hjalmar Schach: Leben und Werken einer umstrittenen Persönlichkeit.* Berlin: Ullstein Verlag.
Perkins, Dexter (1941, 1955). *Hands Off: A History of the Monroe Doctrine.* Boston: Little, Brown (Italian ed.: *Storia della dottrina di Monroe.* Bologna: Il Mulino, 1955).
Perlmutter, Amos, and Bennett, Valerie Plane (1980). *The Political Influence of the Military: A Comparative Reader.* New Haven: Yale University Press.
Perrett, Geoffrey (1973). *Days of Sadness, Years of Triumph: The American People, 1939–1945.* New York: Coward, McCann and Geoghegan.
Petersen, Jens (1973a). "La politica estera del fascismo come problema storiografico." In R. De Felice, ed. *L'Italia fra Tedeschi e Alleati.* Bologna: Il Mulino, pp. 11–56.
——— (1973b). *Hitler-Mussolini: Die Entstehung der Achse Berlin-Rom 1933–1936.* Tübingen: Max Niemeyer Verlag (Italian ed.: *Hilter e Mussolini, la difficile alleanza.* Bari: Laterza, 1975).
Peterson, Edward N. (1978). *The American Occupation of Germany: Retreat to Victory.* Detroit: Wayne State University Press.
Peterson, H. C., and Fite, Gilbert C. (1957). *Opponents of War, 1917–1918.* Madison: University of Wisconsin Press.
Petitot, Jean (1977). "Centrato/Acentrato." In *Enciclopedia,* vol. 2. Turin: Einaudi, pp. 894–954.
——— (1980). "Per un nuovo criticismo." *L'uomo, un segno* 4, no. 2-3, p. 15.
Petzina, D. (1968). *Autarkiepolitik im Dritten Reich: Der nationalsozialistiche Vierjahresplan.* Stuttgart: Deutsche Verlags-Anstalt.

Phillips, William (1952). *Ventures in Diplomacy.* Boston.

Pieri, Piero, and Rochat, Giorgio (1974). *Badoglio.* Turin: Utet.

Pithon, Rémy (1982). "An Attempt at Propaganda Through Film in France, July 1939–June 1940." Bellagio Conference, April 5–9, 17 pp. (typescript).

Playfair, I.S.O. (1954, 1956). *The Mediterranean and Middle East.* 2 vols. London: HMSO.

Plesur, M. (1971). *America's Outward Thrust: Approaches to Foreign Affairs, 1865–1890.* De Kalb: Northern Illinois University Press.

Plischke, Elmer (1950, 1961, 1967). *Conduct of American Diplomacy.* Princeton: Van Nostrand.

Pogue, Forrent C. (1966, 1973). *George C. Marshall.* Vol. 1, *Ordeal and Hope, 1939–42;* Vol. 2, *Organizer of Victory, 1943–45.* New York: Viking.

Polenberg, Richard, ed. (1968). *America at War: The Home Front, 1941–1945.* Englewood Cliffs: Prentice-Hall.

———— (1972). *War and Society: The United States, 1941–1945.* Philadelphia: Lippincott.

———— (1980). *One Nation Divisible: Class, Race, Ethnicity in the United States Since 1938.* Harmondsworth: Penguin.

Polonsky, Antony, ed. (1976). *The Great Powers and the Polish Question, 1941–45: A Documentary Study in Cold War Origins.* London: Orbis.

Pool, James, and Pool, Suzanne (1978). *Who Financed Hitler? The Secret Funding of Hitler's Rise to Power, 1919–39.* London: MacDonald and Jane's.

Porter, Susan Benson (1979). "Palace of Consumption and Machine for Selling: The American Department Store 1880–1940." *Radical History Review,* no. 21 (Fall), pp. 199–224.

Portinaro, Pier Paolo (1982). "Nel tramonto dell'Occidente: la geopolitica." *Comunità* 36, no. 184, pp. 1–43.

Prange, Gordon W. (1981). *At Dawn We Slept: The Untold Story of Pearl Harbor.* New York: McGraw-Hill.

Pratt, Fletcher (1939). *Sea Power and Today's War.* New York.

Pratt, Julius W. (1964). *The American Secretaries of State and their Diplomacy.* Vols. 12 and 13, *Cordell Hull.* New York.

Prothro, James W. (1954). *The Dollar Decade: Business Ideas in the 1920's.* Baton Rouge: Louisiana State University Press.

Puleston, W. D. (1941). *The Armed Forces of the Pacific: A Comparison of the Military and Naval Power of the United States and Japan.* New Haven: Yale University Press.

Putnam, Robert D. (1976). *The Comparative Study of Political Elite.* Englewood Cliffs: Prentice-Hall.

Putz, Karl Heinz (1975). "Strukturen amerikanischer Aussenpolitik." Freie Universität, Berlin (dissertation).

Quartarara, Giorgio (1942). *La futura pace.* Milan: Bocca.

Quartaro, Rosaria (1980). *Roma tra Londra e Berlino, la politica estera fascista dal 1930 al 1940.* Rome: Bonacci.

Radice, E. A. (1977). "Economic Developments in Eastern Europe Under German Hegemony." In Martin McCauley, ed. *Communist Power in Europe, 1944–1949.* London: Macmillan.

Radosh, Ronald (1975, 1978). *Prophets on the Right: Profiles of Conservative Critics of American Globalism.* New York: Simon & Schuster.

Ragionieri, Ernesto (1968). "Dalla 'Grande Alleanze' alla 'guerra fredda.'" *Critica Marxista* 6, no. 2 (March-April), pp. 8–27.

Range, W. (1959). *Franklin D. Roosevelt's World Order.* Athens: University of Georgia Press.

Rapaport, Anatol (1971). *The Big Two: Soviet-American Perception of Foreign Policy.* New York.

Rapking, David P., Thompson, William R., and Cristopherson, John A. (1979). "Bipolarity and Bipolarization in the Cold War Era: Conceptualization, Measurement and Validation." *Journal of Conflict Resolution* 23, no. 2, pp. 261–295.

Rappard, William E. (1930). *United Europe.* New Haven: Yale University Press.

Rauche, Basil (1950). *Roosevelt: From Munich to Pearl Harbor.* New York.

Rearden, Steven L. (1984). *History of the Office of the Secretary of Defense.* Vol. 1, *The Formative Years, 1947–50.* Washington: USGPO.

Reitzel, William (1948). *The Mediterranean: Its Role in American Foreign Policy.* New York: Harcourt, Brace.

Renouvin, Pierre (1951). "La politique des emprunts etrangers aux Etats-Unis de 1914 à 1917." *Annales,* July-September.

Resis, Albert (1978). "The Churchill-Stalin Secret Percentages Agreement on the Balkans." *American Historical Review* 83, no. 2.

Reynolds, David (1982). *The Creation of the Anglo-American Alliance, 1937–1941.* Chapel Hill: University of North Carolina Press.

Rich, Norman (1973). *Hitler's War Aims.* 2 vols. New York: Norton.

Richardon, G. L. (1972). "Cold War Revisionism: A Critic." *World Politics,* July, pp. 579–621.

Rieselbach, Leroy N. (1966). *The Roots of Isolationism: Congressional Voting and Presidential Leadership in Foreign Policy.* New York: Bobbs-Merrill.

Riker, William H. (1962). *The Theory of Political Coalitions.* New Haven: Yale University Press.

Ritter, Gerhard (1954, 1960, 1964, 1968). *Staatskunst und Kriegshandwerk. Das Probleme des "Militarismus" in Deutschland.* Vols. 1, 2, and 3. Munich: R. Oldenbang Verlag.

Robertson, Esmonde M. (1963). *Hitler's Pre-War Policy and Military Plan, 1933–1939.* London: Longman.

———, ed. (1971). *The Origins of the Second World War: Historical Interpretations.* London: Macmillan.

——— (1977). *Mussolini As Empire-Builder.* London: Macmillan (Italian ed.: *Mussolini fondatore dell'impero.* Bari: Laterza, 1979).

Roosevelt, Elliot, ed. (1950). *FDR: His Personal Letters, 1928–1945.* New York: Duell, Sloan and Pearce.

Roosevelt, Franklin D. (1928). "Our Foreign Policy: A Democratic View." *Foreign Affairs* 6 (July), pp. 573–93.

——— (1932–1945). *Complete Presidential Press Conferences of Franklin D. Roosevelt.* Vols. 13–18. New York: Da Capo Press.

_____ (1941–1950). *The Public Papers of Franklin D. Roosevelt, 1937–1941.* Washington: USGPO.

_____ (1943). Address Delivered by President Roosevelt at Chicago. October 5, 1937. In Department of State. *Peace and War: U.S. Foreign Policy 1931–1941.* Washington: USGPO.

Roosevelt, Franklin D., and Churchill, W. (1975). *Their Secret Wartime Correspondence.* London: HMSO.

Roosevelt, James, with Libby, Bill (1975). *My Parents: A Differing View.* Chicago: Playboy Press.

Roosevelt, Kermit (1976). *War Report of the OSS.* New York: Walter.

Roosevelt, Theodore (1910–1961). *The New Nationalism.* Introduction by William Leuchtenburg. Englewood Cliffs: Prentice-Hall.

Rose, Lisle A. (1973a). *After Yalta: America and the Origins of the Cold War.* New York: Scribner's.

_____ (1973b). *The Coming of the American Age, 1945–1946.* Vol. 1, *Dubious Victory. The United States and the End of World War II.* Kent: Kent State University Press.

Rosecrance, Richard N. (1963). *Action and Reaction in World Politics.* Boston: Little, Brown.

_____ (1980). "Deterrence and Vulnerability in the Pre-Nuclear Era." In C. Bertram, ed. *The Future of Strategic Deterrence.* Part 1. Adelphi Paper no. 160, pp. 24–31. London: International Institute of Strategic Studies.

_____ (1986). *The Rise of the Trading State.* New York: Basic Books.

Rosenau, James N. (1961). *The Scientific Study of Foreign Policy.* New York: Free Press.

_____ (1963). *National Leadership and Foreign Policy.* Princeton: Princeton University Press.

_____, ed. (1967a). *Domestic Sources of Foreign Policy.* New York: Free Press.

_____ (1967b). *Public Opinion and Foreign Policy.* New York: Free Press.

_____ (1968). "National Interest." In *International Encyclopedia of the Social Sciences,* vol. 11. New York: Free Press.

_____, ed. (1969). *International Politics and Foreign Policy.* New York: Macmillan.

_____ (1980). *The Study of Global Interdependence.* London: Pinter.

Rosenberg, Douglas H. (1973). "Arms and the American Way: The Ideological Dimension of Military Growth." In B. Russett and A. Stepan. *Military Force and American Society.* New York: Harper & Row.

Rosenberg, Nathan (1979). "Technological Interdependence in the American Economy." *Technology and Culture* 20, no. 1.

Rosenman, Samuel, ed. (1938, 1950). *The Public Papers and Addresses of Franklin Delano Roosevelt.* 13 vols. New York.

_____ (1952). *Working with Roosevelt.* London.

Rosenman, Samuel and Dorothy (1976). *Presidential Style: Some Giants and a Pygmy in the White House.* New York: Harper & Row.

Rosenstiehl, Pierre (1979). "Labirinto." In *Enciclopedia,* vol. 8. Turin: Einaudi, pp. 3–30.

Roskill, Stephen (1977). *Churchill and the Admirals.* New York: Morrow.

Rostan, N. M. (1952). *British War Production.* London: HMSO.

Rostow, Walt W. (1978). *The World Economy.* Austin: University of Texas Press.

Rothbard, Murray N. (1978). *America's Great Depression.* San Francisco: Cato Institute.

Rowland, B. M., ed. (1976). *Balance of Power or Hegemony: The Interwar Monetary System.* New York: New York University Press.

Royal Institute of International Affairs (1951). *Documents on International Affairs 1939-1946.* Vol. 2, *Hitler's Europe.* London: Oxford University Press.

———— (1954). *The Economic Structure of Hitler's Europe.* London: Oxford University Press.

Ruge, Freidrich (1956). *Der Seekrieg.* Annapolis: Naval Academy Press.

Ruhl, Jorg Klaus (1980). "L'alliance à distance: les relations économiques germano-espagnoles de 1936 à 1945." *Revue d'histoire de la deuxième guerre mondiale.* 30, no. 118, pp. 69–102.

Rupp, Leila J. (1978). *Mobilizing Women for War: German and American Propaganda, 1939-1945.* Princeton: Princeton University Press.

Russell, Ruth B. (1958a). *A History of the United Nations Charter: The Role of the United States, 1940-1945.* Washington: Brookings.

————, ed. (1958b). *The Charter of the United Nations.* Washington: Brookings.

———— (1968). *The United Nations and United States Security Policy.* Washington: Brookings.

Russett, Bruce M. (1972). *No Clear and Present Danger: A Skeptical View of the U.S. Entry into World War II.* New York.

Russett, Bruce M., and Hanson, Elizabeth C. (1975). *Interest and Ideology: The Foreign Policy Beliefs of American Businessmen.* San Francisco: Freeman.

Russett, Bruce M., and Stepan, Alfred, eds. (1973). *Military Force and American Society.* New York: Harper & Row.

Ryan, Henry B. (1979). "A New Look at Churchill's 'Iron Curtain' Speech." *Historical Journal* 22, no. 4, pp. 895–920.

Salisbury, Frederic R. (1951). *Design for War: A Study of Secret Power Politics, 1937-1941.* New York.

Salisbury, R. H. (1970). *Interest Groups in American Politics.* New York: Harper & Row.

Saly, Pierre (1980). "La Politique Française des grands travaux, 1929–1939, fut-elle keynesienne?" *Revue Economique* 31, no. 4 (July), pp. 706–742.

Sander, Alfred D. (1972). "Truman and the National Security Council: 1945–1947." *Journal of American History* 59 (September), pp. 369–388.

Santoro, Carlo Maria (1958). "La guerra civile di Spagna nei documenti diplomatici tedeschi." University of Rome (dissertation).

———— (1978a). "Appunti sul passaggio di fase." In *Crisi del sapere e nuova razionalità.* Bari: De Donato, pp. 183–227.

————, ed. (1978b). *Gli Stati Uniti e l'ordine mondiale.* Rome: Editori Riuniti.

———— (1980). "Modello economico a New Deal." *Problemi della Transizione,* no. 3, 1980.

———— (1981). "Bipolarismo e diffusione di potenza." *Politica Internazionale* 9, no. 4-5.

———— (1982). "Interdipendenza e relazioni internazionali: l'analisi concettuale." *Rivista Italiana di Scienza Politica* 12, no. 3.

———— (1984a). *Lo stile dell'aquila, Studi di politica estera americana.* Milan: Franco Angeli.

———— (1984b). "Il sistema di guerra: Teoria e strategia del sistema internazionale bipolare." *Il Mulino,* no. 294 (July-August), pp. 622–660.

———— (1984c). "Politica e guerra nel pensiero di Raymond Aron." *Politica Internazionale* 12, no. 7 (July 1984).

———— (1985). "The Tranquillized Fifties: Rise to Globalism." Asaia Conference, October (paper).

———— (1988a). *Il sistema di guerra.* Milan: Angeli

———— (1988b). *L'Italia e il Mediterraneo.* Milan: Angeli.

Sartori, Giovanni (1971). "La politica comparata: promesse e problemi." *Rivista Italiana di Scienza Politica* 1, no. 1, pp. 43ff.

Sassoon, Joseph, ed. (1981). *L'interdipendenza nel sistema internazionale.* Milan: Feltrinelli.

Sauvy, Alfred (1978). *La vie économique des Français de 1939 à 1945.* Paris: Flammarion.

Sbrega, John H. (1983). *Anglo-American Relations and Colonialism in East Asia, 1941–1945.* New York: Garland.

Schacht, Hjalmar (1937). "Germany's Colonial Demands." *Foreign Affairs* 15.

———— (1966). *Magie des Geldes.* Düsseldorf: Econ. Verlag (Italian ed.: *La Magia del denaro.* Rome: Il Borghese, 1968).

Schaffer, Ronald (1980). "American Military Ethics in World War II: The Bombing of German Civilians." *Journal of American History* 67, no. 2.

Schaller, Michael (1979). *The US Crusade in China: 1938–1945.* New York: Columbia University Press.

Schelling, Thomas C. (1960). *The Strategy of Conflict.* New York: Oxford University Press.

Schlesinger, Arthur F., Jr. (1957–1965). *The Age of Roosevelt.* 3 vols. (Italian ed.: *L'Età di Roosevelt.* Bologna: Il Mulino).

———— (1967). "Origins of the Cold War." *Foreign Affairs* 46, no. 3.

———— (1979). "The Cold War Revisited." *New York Review of Books,* October 25.

———— (1983). "Franklin D. Roosevelt and Europe" (typescript).

Schramm, P. E., ed. (1961–1965). *OKW: Kriegstagebuch des Oberkommandos der Werhrmacht.* 4 vols. Frankfurt/M.

Schroeder, P. M. (1958). *The Axis Alliance and Japanese-American Relations.* Ithaca: Cornell University Press.

Schrüder, H. J. (1970). *Deutschland und die Vereinigte Staaten.* Wiesbaden.

Schulzinger, Robert D. (1975). *The Making of the Diplomatic Mind, 1980–1931.* Middletown: Wesleyan University Press.

———— (1984). *The Wise Men of Foreign Affairs: The History of the Council on Foreign Relations.* New York: Columbia University Press.

Schünemann, Friedrich (1943). *Der USA Imperialismus von Heute.* (Italian ed.: Bari: Dedalo, 1980).

Schweitzer, Arthur (1964). *Big Business in the Third Reich.* Bloomington: Indiana University Press.

Scitovsky, T., Shaw, E., and Tarshis, L. (1951). *Mobilizing Resources for War.* New York.

Seldes, George (1934). *Iron, Blood and Profits: An Exposure of the World Wide Munitions Racket.* New York and London.

Shepardson, Whitney H. (1937–1941). *The United States in World Affairs: An Account of American Foreign Relations.* 5 vols. New York: Harper & Bros.

_____ (1942). *The Interest of the United States As a World Power.* Claremont.

Sherry, Michael S. (1977). *Planning for the Next War: American Plans for Postwar Defense, 1941–45.* New Haven: Yale University Press.

Sherwin, Martin J. (1969). "The Atomic Bomb As History: An Essay Review." *Wisconsin Magazine of History,* Winter 1969–1970.

_____ (1973a). "The Atomic Bomb and the Origins of the Cold War." *American Historical Review* 78, no. 4.

_____ (1973b). *A World Destroyed: The Atomic Bomb and the Grand Alliance.* New York: Vintage.

Sherwood, Robert E. (1948). *Roosevelt and Hopkins: An Intimate History.* New York: Harper & Bros.

Shindler, Colin (1979). *Hollywood Goes to War: Films and American Society, 1939–1952.* Boston: Routledge and Kegan Paul.

Shirer, William L. (1969). *The Collapse of the Third Republic: An Inquiry into the Fall of France in 1940.* New York: Simon & Schuster.

_____ (1984). *The Nightmare Years, 1930–1940.* Boston: Little, Brown.

Shotwell, James T. (1942). "Organizations Working in the Field of Post-War Reconstruction." *Bulletin of the Commission to Study the Organization of Peace* 2, no. 3-4.

_____ (1944). *The Great Decision.* New York: Macmillan.

_____ (1961). *The Autobiography of James T. Shotwell.* Indianapolis: Indiana University Press.

Shoup, Laurence H., and Minter, William (1977). *Imperial Brain Trust: The Council on Foreign Relations and United States Foreign Policy.* New York: Monthly Review Press.

Silbey, Joel H., Bogue, Allan G., and Flanigan, William H., eds. (1980). *The History of American Electoral Behavior.* Princeton: Princeton University Press.

Silk, Leonard, and Silk, Mark (1980). *The American Establishment.* New York: Basic Books.

Siracusa, J. M. (1973). *New Left Diplomatic History and Historians: The American Revisionists.* Port Washington, N.Y.: Kennikat.

Skaggs, Jianny A. (1975). *An Interpretative History of the American Economy.* Columbus: Grid.

Small, Malgin (1980). *Was War Necessary? National Security and US Entry into War.* London: Sage.

Smith, Arthur L. (1978). *Churchill's German Army: Wartime Strategy and Cold War Politics 1943–47.* London: Sage.

Smith, Bradley F. (1983). *The Shadow Warrior: OSS and the Origin of the CIA.* New York: André Deutsch.

Smith, Gaddis (1965). *American Diplomacy During the Second World War, 1941–45.* New York: Wiley.

———— (1972a). *The United States and the Origins of the Cold War.* New York.

———— (1972b). *Dean Acheson.* New York: Cooper Square.

Smith, Geoffrey S. (1973). *To Save a Nation: American Counter Subversives, New Deal and the Coming of World War II.* New York: Basic Books.

Smith, Malcolm (1980). "A Matter of Faith: British Strategic Air Doctrine Before 1939." *Journal of Contemporary History* 15, no. 3, pp. 423–442.

Smith, Perry McCoy (1970). *The Air Force Plans for Peace, 1943–1945.* Baltimore: Johns Hopkins University Press.

Smith, R. Elberton (1959). *The United States Army in World War II: The Army and Economic Mobilization.* Washington: USGPO.

Smith, R. Harris (1972). *OSS: The Secret History of America's First Central Intelligence Agency.* Berkeley: University of California Press.

Smith, Theresa Clair (1980). "Arms Race Instability and War." *Journal of Conflict Resolution* 24, no. 2, pp. 253–284.

Snell, John L. (1962). "The Cold War: Four Contemporary Appraisals." *American Historical Review,* October 1962.

———— (1963). *Illusion and Necessity: The Diplomacy of Global War, 1939–1945.* Boston.

Snow, Donald (1981). *Nuclear Strategy in a Dynamic World.* University: University of Alabama Press.

Snyder, Glenn H. (1984). "The Security Dilemma in Alliance Politics." *World Politics* 36, n. 4, pp. 461–495.

Snyder, Glenn H., and Diesing, Paul (1977). *Conflict Among Nations: Bargaining, Decision-Making and System Structure in International Crises.* Princeton: Princeton University Press.

Snyder, Richard C., Bruck, H. W., and Sapin, Burton (1962). *Foreign Policy Decision-Making: An Approach to the Study of International Politics.* New York: Free Press.

Sobel, Robert (1977). *The International Monetary System 1945–1976: An Insider's View.* New York: Harper & Row.

Somers, H. M. (1950). *Presidential Agency: The Office of War Mobilization and Reconversion.* Cambridge: Harvard University Press.

Sorlin, Pierre (1982). "Propaganda Struggles: The French Case." Bellagio Conference, April 5–9, 20 pp. (typescript).

Soule, George (1947). *Prosperity Decade: From War to Depression, 1917–1929.* New York.

Southard, F. E. (1931). *American Industry in Europe.* Boston: Houghton Mifflin.

Spector, Ronald H. (1984). *Eagle Against the Sun.* New York: Viking.

Speer, Albert (1969). *Erinnerungen.* Frankfurt/M: Verlag Ullstein (Italian ed.: *Memorie del Terzo Reich.* Milan: Mondadori, 1971).

———— (1975). *Spandauer Tagebucher.* Frankfurt/M.: Propyläen Verlag (Italian ed.: *Diari segreti di Spandau.* Milan: Mondadori, 1976).

———— (1981). *Infiltration.* New York: Macmillan.

Speier, Hans (1941). "Magic Geography." *Social Research,* September, pp. 310–330.

———— (1943). "Ludendorff: The German Concept of Total War." In E. D. Earle, ed. *Makers of Modern Strategy*. Princeton: Princeton University Press, pp. 306–322.

Spiro, Herbert J. (1968). "Totalitarianism." In *International Encyclopedia of the Social Sciences*, vol. 16, pp. 106–113. New York: Free Press.

Sprout, Harold and Margaret (1963). "Retreat from World Power: Processes and Consequences of Readjustment." *World Politcs* 15, no. 4.

Spykman, Nicholas J. (1942, 1970). *America's Strategy in World Politics: The United States and the Balance of Power*. Hamden: Archon.

———— (1944). *The Geography of the Peace*. New York: Harcourt, Brace.

Staley, Eugene (1937). *Raw Materials in Peace and War*. New York.

Stalin, Churchill, Roosevelt, Attlee, Truman (1953). *Perepiska predsedatelia sovieta ministrov Sssr s presidentami Ssa i Premier ministrami veliko britanii vo vremia velikoi octecestremos 1941–1945*. gg., Mosca, 1953 (Italian ed.: *Carteggio 1941–1945*. Rome: Editori Riuniti, 1957).

Stato Maggiore Esercito, Ufficio storico (1982). *L'esercito italiano alla vigilia della 2a guerra mondiale*. Rome: SME.

Stead, Peter (1981). "Hollywood's Message for the World: The British Response in the Nineteen Thirties." *Historical Journal of Film, Radio and Television* 1, no. 1, pp. 19–32.

Steel, Ronald (1967). *Pax Americana*. New York: Viking.

———— (1980). *Walter Lippmann and the American Century*. Boston: Little, Brown.

Steele, Richard W. (1970). "Preparing the Public for War: Efforts to Establish a National Propaganda Agency, 1940–1941." *American Historical Review* 75 (October), pp. 1640–1653.

———— (1973). *The First Offensive 1942: Roosevelt, Marshall and Making of American Strategy*. Bloomington: Indiana University Press.

———— (1984). "The Great Debate, the Media and Coming of the War, 1940–1941." *Journal of American History* 71, no. 1, pp. 69–92.

Stefansson, Vilhjalmus (1939a). *Iceland, the First American Republic*. New York.

———— (1939b). "The American Far North." *Foreign Affairs* 17, no. 2, pp. 508–523.

Steindl, Josef (1952, 1976). *Maturity and Stagnation in American Capitalism*. New York: Monthly Review Press.

Stettinius, Edward R., Jr. (1944). *Lend-Lease: Weapon for Victory*. New York.

———— (1949). *Roosevelt and Russians: The Yalta Conference*. Garden City: Doubleday.

Stevenson, David (1979). "French War Aims and the American Challenge, 1914–1918." *Historical Journal* 22, no. 4, pp. 877–894.

Stewart, J. D. (1958). *British Pressure Groups*. Oxford: Clarendon Press.

Stewart, William J., ed. (1974). *The Era of Franklin D. Roosevelt*. New York.

Stimson, Henry L., and Bundy, McGeorge (1948). *On Active Service in Peace and War*. New York: Harper.

Stoddard, L. Lethrop (1961). "The Danish West Indies." *Review of Reviews* 54 (September).

Stoessinger, John C. (1961, 1969). *The Might of Nations: World Politics in Our Time*. New York: Random House.

———— (1979). *Crusaders and Pragmatists: Makers of Modern American Foreign Policy.* New York: Norton.

Stoff, Michael B. (1980). *Oil, War and American Security: The Search for a National Policy on Foreign Oil.* New Haven: Yale University Press.

Strausz-Hupé, Robert (1942, 1972). *Geopolitics, the Stuggle for Space and Power.* New York: Arno.

———— (1945). *The Balance of Tomorrow.* New York: Putnam.

Streit, Clarence K. (1938). *Union Now: A Proposal for a Federal Union of the Democracies of the North Atlantic.* New York: Harper & Bros.

Stromberg, Roland N. (1953). "American Business and Approach of War, 1935–1941." *Journal of Economic History* 13, no. 1, pp. 58–78.

Stuart, Graham H. (1949). *The Department of State: A History of Its Organization, Procedure and Personnel.* New York: Macmillan.

Sulzberger, Cyrus L. (1969). *A Long Row of Candles: Memoirs and Diaries, 1934–1954.* New York: Macmillan.

Sundquist, James L. (1973, 1983). *Dynamics of the Party System.* Washington: Brookings.

Swanberg, W. A. (1972). *Luce and His Empire.* New York: Scribner's.

Taichiro, Mitani (1973). "Changes in Japan's International Position and the Response of Japanese Intellectuals: Trends in Japanese Studies of Japan's Foreign Relations, 1931–1941." In D. Borg and S. Okamoto. *Pearl Harbor As History.* New York: Columbia University Press.

Tansill, Charles C. (1932). *The Purchase of the Danish West Indies.* Baltimore: Johns Hopkins University Press.

———— (1938). *America Goes to War.* Boston: Little Brown.

———— (1952). *Back Door to War: The Roosevelt Foreign Policy, 1933–1941.* Chicago: Regnery.

Taylor, A.J.P. (1961). *The Origins of the Second World War.* London: Hamish Hamilton.

Taylor, Philip M. (1981). "Techniques of Persuasion: Basic Ground Rules of British Propaganda During the Second World War." *Historical Journal of Film, Radio, and Television* 1, no. 2, pp. 57–65.

———— (1982). "Propaganda in International Politics, 1919–39." Bellagio Conference, April 5–9, 26 pp. (typescript).

Taylor, Telford (1979). *Munich: The Price of Peace.* Vintage Books.

Terkel, Studs (1971). *Hard Times: An Oral History of the Great Depression.* New York: Avon.

———— (1984). *The Good War: An Oral History of World War Two.* New York: Pantheon.

Terraine, John (1985). *The Right of Line: The RAF in the European War, 1939–45.* London: Hodder & Stoughton.

Testi, Arnaldo, ed. (1984). *L'età progressista negli Stati Uniti.* Bologna: Il Mulino.

Thomas, Daniel H., and Case, Lynn M., eds. (1959, 1975). *The New Guide to the Diplomatic Archives of Western Europe.* Philadelphia: University of Pennsylvania Press.

Thomas, Gordon, and Morgan-Witts, Max (1979). *The Day the Bubble Burst: A Social History of the Wall Street Crash.* London: Hamish Hamilton.

Thomas, J. N. (1974). *The Institute of Pacific Relations*. Seattle.

Thompson, James C., Jr., Stanley, Peter W., and Perry, John C. (1981). *Sentimental Imperialists: The American Experience in East Asia*. New York: Harper & Row.

Thompson, Kenneth W. (1968). "Collective Security." In *International Encyclopedia of the Social Sciences*, vol. 2. New York: Free Press.

Thorne, Christopher (1972). *The Limits of Foreign Policy: The West, the League and the Far Eastern Crisis of 1931–1933*. London: Hamish Hamilton.

—— (1976). "The Indochina Issue Between Britain and United States, 1942–1945." *Pacific Historical Review*, February.

—— (1978). *Allies of a Kind: The United States, Britain and the War against Japan, 1941–1945*. Oxford: Oxford University Press.

Till, Geoffrey (1982, 1984). *Maritime Strategy and the Nuclear Age*. London: Macmillan.

Togo, Shigenori (1956). *The Cause of Japan*. New York: Simon & Schuster.

Tompkins, C. D. (1970). *Senator Arthur H. Vandenberg: The Evolution of a Modern Republican, 1884–1945*. Ann Arbor: University of Michigan Press.

Toniatti, Roberto (1983). *Costituzione e direzione della politica estera negli Stati Uniti d'America*. Milan: Giuffrè.

Toscano, Mario (1963). *Pagine di storia diplomatica contemporanea*. Vol. 2, *Origini e vicende della seconda guerra mondiale*. Milan: Giuffrè.

Tournoux, Raymond (1980). *Pétain et la France. La seconde guerre mondiale*. Paris: Plon.

Toynbee, Arnold J. (1961). *America and the World Revolution*. London: Oxford University Press.

—— (1962). *The Economy of the Western Hemisphere*. London: Oxford University Press.

Trani, E. P. (1976). "Woodrow Wilson and the Decision to Intervene in Russia: A Reconsideration." *Journal of Modern History*, no. 3.

Trask, D. F. (1961). *The United States and the Supreme War Council: American War Aims and Interallied Strategy*. Middletown: Wesleyan University Press.

Trefousse, Hans L. (1951). *Germany and American Neutrality, 1939–1941*. New York.

Trevor-Roper, Hugh (1960). "Hitlers Kriegziele." *Vierteiljahrsheft für Zeitgeschichte*, April 1960.

Triska, Jan F., ed. (1986). *Dominant Powers and Subordinate States*. Durham: Duke University Press.

Truman, Harry S. (1955, 1956). *Memoirs*. Vol. 1, *Years of Decision*; Vol. 2, *Years of Trial and Hope*. Garden City: Doubleday.

Tuchman, Barbara W. (1970). *Stilwell and the American Experience in China, 1911–1945*. New York: Macmillan.

Tucker, Robert W. (1971). *The Radical Left and American Foreign Policy*. Baltimore: Johns Hopkins University Press.

—— (1973). *De l'Isolationisme Américain, Menace ou espoir?* Paris: Calman-Levy.

Tufte, Edward R. (1978). *Political Control of the Economy*. Princeton: Princeton University Press.

Tugwell, Rexford G. (1957). *The Democratic Roosevelt.* Garden City: Doubleday.
———— (1968). *The Brain Trust.* New York: Viking.
Turner, Frederick J. (1893). *The Significance of the Frontier in American History.* (Italian ed.: *La frontiera nella storia americana.* Bologna: Il Mulino, 1968).
Tusa, Ann, and Tusa, John (1983). *The Nuremberg Trials.* London: Macmillan.
U.S. Bureau of the Census (1976). *Historical Statistics of the United States, Colonial Times to 1970.* Washington: USGPO.
U.S. Congress (1945). Special Committee on Post-War Economic Policy and Planning. *Economic Policy and Planning: Economic Problems of the Transition Period.* 78th Congress, 2nd Session, and 79th Congress, 1st Session. Washington: USGPO.
———— (1946). *Pearl Harbor Attack.* Hearings on Investigation of the Pearl Harbor Attack. Washington: USGPO.
———— (1950). *A Decade of American Foreign Policy: Basic Documents, 1941–49.* Washington: USGPO.
————, House of Representatives (1944). *Postwar Economic Policy and Planning.* Hearings before the Special Subcommittee on Post-War Economic Policy, 78th Congress, 2nd Session. Washington: USGPO.
————, Senate (1945). Committee on Naval Affairs. *Unification of the War and Navy Departments and Postwar Organization for National Security.* Report to the Hon. James Forrestal, Secretary of the Navy, 79th Congress, 1st Session, 1945 (Eberstadt Report).
U.S. Department of Commerce, Bureau of Economic Analysis (1975). *The National Income and Product Accounts of the United States, 1929–1973.* Washington: USGPO.
U.S. Department of State (1934–1946). *Commercial Policy Series 1934–1946.* Washington: USGPO.
———— (1942). *Peace and War: United States Foreign Policy, 1931–1941.* Washington: USGPO.
———— (1946). *Report to the President on the Results of the San Francisco Conference.* Washington: USGPO.
———— (1949). *United States Relations with China, 1944–1949.* Washington: USGPO.
———— (1955). *Foreign Relations of the United States. The Conferences at Malta and Yalta 1945.* Washington: USGPO.
———— (1957). *Documents on German Foreign Policy.* 10 vols. Series D. Washington: USGPO.
———— (1960). *Foreign Relations of the United States (FRUS). The Conference of Berlin (the Potsdam Conference).*
———— (1961). *Foreign Relations of the United States (FRUS). The Conference at Cairo and Teheran 1943.* Washington: USGPO.
———— (various years). *Diplomatic Documents, Record Group (USDD, RG).* National Archives, Washington.
———— (various years). *Foreign Relations of the United States (FRUS).* Washington: USGPO.
U.S. Government (1935). *Munitions Industry.* Final Report of the Chairman of the U.S. War Industries Board to the President of the United States. Washington: USGPO.

U.S. National Resources Planning Board (1941). *After Defense, What?* Washington: USGPO.

U.S. State Department (1943). *Peace and War: United States Foreign Policy, 1931–1941.* Washington: USGPO

U.S. Strategic Bombing Survey (1945). "The Effects of Strategic Bombing on the German War Economy" (mimeograph).

Ulam, Adam B. (1968). *Expansion and Coexistence: The History of Soviet Foreign Policy, 1917–1967.* New York: Praeger.

Uldricks, Teddy J. (1980). *Diplomacy and Ideology: The Origins of Soviet Foreign Relations, 1917–1930.* London: Sage.

Unger, I. (1967). "The 'New Left' and American History: Some Recent Trends in U.S. Historiography." *American Historical Review,* July, pp. 1237–1263.

United Nations (1949). *International Capital Movement During the Inter-War Period.* Lake Success: United Nations.

———, Department of Economic Affairs (1953). *Economic Survey of Europe Since the War: A Reappraisal of Problems and Prospects.* Geneva: United Nations.

USDD, RG: See U.S. Department of State (various years). Diplomatic Documents, Record Group (USDD, RG).

Utley, Jonathan G. (1985). *Going to War with Japan, 1937–1941.* Knoxville: University of Tennessee Press.

Van Alstyne, Richard W. (1944). *American Diplomacy in Action.* Stanford: Stanford University Press.

——— (1952). *American Crisis Diplomacy: The Quest for Collective Security, 1918–1952.* Stanford: Stanford University Press.

——— (1965). *The Rise of American Empire.* Chicago: Quadrangle Books.

——— (1970). *Genesis of American Nationalism.* Waltham: Blaisdell.

Van der Beugel, Ernst H. (1966). *From Marshall Aid to Atlantic Partnership.* Amsterdam: Elsevier.

Vandenberg, Arthur H., Jr. (1952). *The Private Papers of Senator Vandenberg.* Boston.

Van Dormael, Armand (1978). *Bretton Woods: Birth of a Monetary System.* London: Macmillan.

Varga, Evgenij (1934). *Die Grosse Krise und ihre politischen Folgen.* Moscow-Leningrad.

Vaudagna, Maurizio (1981a). *Corporativismo e New Deal.* Turin: Rosenberg & Sellier.

———, ed. (1981b). *Il New Deal.* Bologna: Il Mulino.

Vevier, C. (1960). "American Continentalism: An Idea of Expansion, 1845–1910." *American Historical Review,* January 1960.

Vié, Michel (1980). "Points de vue sur la politique extérieur du Japon entre les deux guerres." *Relations Internationales,* no. 22 (Summer).

Vietor, Richard H.K. (1980). "Planning and Building the British Bomber Force, 1934–1939." *Business History Review* 54, pp. 35–62.

Virilio, Paul (1976). *Essai sur l'insécurité du territoire.* Paris: Stock.

Von Ludendorff, Erich (1935). *Der Totale Krieg.* Munich.

Wagenfuhr, R. (1963). *Die deutsche Industrie in Kriege, 1939–1945.* Berlin.

Walker, R., and Curry, G. (1965). *The American Secretaries of State and Their Diplomacy*, vols. 14 and 15. New York.

Wallace, Henry (1942). *The Century of the Common Man*. New York: Harcourt, Brace and World.

Wallace, William (1975). *The Foreign Policy Process in Britain*. London: Royal Institute of International Affairs.

Walton, R. J. (1976). *Henry Wallace, Harry Truman and the Cold War*. New York: Viking.

Waltz, Kenneth N. (1954). *Man, the State and War: A Theorical Analysis*. New York: Columbia University Press.

—— (1964). *Foreign Policy and Democratic Politics: The American and British Experience*. Boston: Little, Brown.

—— (1979). *Theory of International Politics*. Reading: Addison-Wesley.

Walzer, Michael (1977). *Just and Unjust Wars: A Moral Argument with Historical Illustrations*. New York: Basic Books.

Ware, Edith E., ed. (1934). *The Study of International Relations in the United States. Survey for 1934*. New York: Columbia University Press.

Warner, Edward (1943). "Douhet, Mitchell, Seversky: Theories of Airfare." In E. M. Earle, ed. *Makers of Modern Strategy*. Princeton: Princeton University Press, pp. 485–503.

Washington Quarterly (1984). "Forging Bipartisanship."

Watson, Mark S. (1950). *U.S. Army in World War II: Chief of Staff, Prewar Plans and Preparations*. Washington: USGPO.

Watt, D. C. (1977). "American Anti-Colonial Policies and the End of European Colonial Empires." In A. D. Den Hollander, ed. *Contagious Conflict*. Leiden.

Webb, Steven B. (1980). "Tariffs, Cartels, Technology and Growth in the German Steel Industry." *Journal of Economic History* 40, no. 2, pp. 309–330.

Wehle, Louis B. (1953). *Hidden Threats of History: Wilson Through Roosevelt*. New York.

Weigert, Hans W. (1942). *Generals and Geographers*. New York: Oxford University Press.

Weigley, Russell F. (1967). *History of the United States Army*. New York: Macmillan.

—— (1973). *The American Way of War: A History of U.S. Military Strategy and Policy*. Bloomington: Indiana University Press.

Weil, Martin (1978). *A Pretty Good Club: The Founding Fathers of the U.S. Foreign Service*. New York: Norton.

Weinberg, A. K. (1935). *Manifest Destiny: A Study of Nationalist Expansion in American History*. Baltimore: Johns Hopkins University Press.

—— (1940). "The Historical Meaning in the American Doctrine of Isolation." *American Political Science Review* 34, pp. 539–547.

Weinberg, Gerhard L. (1964). "Hitler's Image of the United States." *American Historical Review* 69, pp. 1006–1021.

—— (1981). *The Foreign Policy of Hitler's Germany*. Chicago: University of Chicago Press.

Welch, David (1982). "Nazi Propaganda in Wartime Newsreels." Bellagio Conference, April 5–9, 23 pp. (typescript).

Welles, Sumner (1944). *The Time for Decision.* New York: Harper & Bros.
———— (1946). *Where Are We Heading?* New York: Harper & Bros (Italian ed.: *Dove andremo a finire?* Milan: Garzanti, 1974).
———— (1951). *Seven Decisions That Shaped History.* New York: Harper & Bros.
Werth, Alexander (1964). *Russia at War, 1941–45.* London: Dutton Press (Italian ed.: *La Russia in guerra, 1941–45.* Milan: Mondadori, 1966).
———— (1971). *Russia: The Post-War Years.* London: Robert Hale (Italian ed. *L'Unione Sovietica nel dopoguerra, 1945–48.* Turin: Einaudi, 1973).
Westcott, Allan, ed. (1947). *American Sea Power Since 1775.* Chicago: Lippincott.
Westerfield, H. B. (1955). *Foreign Policy and Party Politics.* New Haven: Yale University Press.
Wheeler, G. E. (1963). *Prelude to Pearl Harbor.* Columbia: University of Missouri Press.
Wheeler Bennet, John W. (1963). *Munich: Prologue to Tragedy.* London: Macmillan.
Whitaker, Arthur P. (1951). "From Dollar Diplomacy to the Good Neighbor Policy." *Inter-American Economic Affairs* 4, no. 4.
White, Donald Wallace (1979). "The American Century: The History of an Idea, 1941–1971." New York University (Ph.D. dissertation).
White, G. Edward (1968). *The Eastern Establishment and Western Experience.* New Haven: Yale University Press.
White, Thomas H., ed. (1948). *The Stilwell Papers.* New York.
White, William Allen (1946). *The Autobiography of William Allen White.* New York.
Whittlesey, Derwent (1942). *German Strategy of World Conquest.* New York: Holt and Rinehart.
Wight, Martin (1946, 1978). *Power Politics.* London: Penguin.
Wilkins, Mira (1970). *The Emergence of Multinational Enterprise: American Business Abroad from the Colonial Era to 1914.* Cambridge: Harvard University Press.
———— (1973). *The Maturing of Multinational Enterprise, American Business Abroad from 1914 to 1970.* Cambridge: Harvard University Press.
Wilkins, Robert P. (1957). "Middle Western Isolationism: A Re-examination." *North Dakota Quarterly,* no. 25, pp. 69–76.
Williams, William Appleman (1952, 1972a). *The Tragedy of American Diplomacy.* New York: Delta Books.
————, ed. (1956, 1972b). *The Shaping of American Diplomacy.* 2 vols. Chicago: Rand McNally.
———— (1959). *The Tragedy of American Diplomacy.* New York: World Publishing.
———— (1969). *The Roots of the Modern American Empire.* New York: Vintage Books.
————, ed. (1972c). *From Colony to Empire: Essays in the History of American Foreign Relations.* New York: Wiley.
———— (1980). *Empires As a Way of Life: An Essay on the Causes and Character of America's Present Predicament Along with a Few Thoughts About an Alternative.* New York: Oxford University Press.
Williamson, Jeffrey G. (1974). *Late Nineteenth-Century American Development: A General Equilibrium History.* London: Cambridge University Press.

Willkie, Wendell (1943). *One World.* New York: Simon & Schuster.

Wilmot, Chester (1952). *The Struggle for Europe.* New York.

Wilson, Hugh R. (1941). *Diplomat Between the Wars.* New York.

Wilson, Joan H. (1971). *American Business and Foreign Policy, 1920–1923.* Lexington: University Press of Kentucky.

⸻ (1974). *Ideology and Economics: U.S. Relations With the Soviet Union, 1918–1923.* Missoula: University of Montana Press.

⸻ (1975). *Herbert Hoover: Forgotten Progressive.* Boston: Little, Brown.

Wilson, Theodore A. (1969). *The First Summit: Roosevelt and Churchill at Placentia Bay 1941.* Boston.

Wiltz, John E. (1963). *In Search of Peace: The Senate Munitions Enquiry, 1934–1936.* Baton Rouge: Louisiana State University Press.

⸻ (1968). *From Isolation to War, 1931–1941.* New York: Crowell.

Wohl, Robert (1979). *The Generation of 1914.* Cambridge: Harvard University Press.

Wohlstetter, Roberta (1962). *Pearl Harbor: Warning and Decision.* Stanford: Stanford University Press.

Wolfers, Arnold (1952). *Discord and Collaboration.* Baltimore: Johns Hopkins University Press.

Wood, Bruce (1961). *The Making of the Good Neighbor Policy.* New York: Columbia University Press.

Wood, Junius B. (1930). "Flying the World's Longest Air Mail Route." *National Geographic* 57, no. 3.

Woodrow Wilson Foundation, The National Planning Association (1955, 1968). *The Political Economy of American Foreign Policy: The Concepts, Strategy and Limits.* New York: Rinehart and Winston.

Woodward, L. (1970, 1976). *British Foreign Policy in the Second World War.* 5 vols. London: HMSO.

Wootton, Graham (1970). *Interest-Groups.* Englewood Cliffs: Prentice-Hall.

Wright, Gordon (1968). *The Ordeal of Total War, 1939–1945.* New York.

Wright, Quincy (1940). "The Transfer of Destroyers to Great Britain." *American Journal of International Law* 34, pp. 680–689.

⸻ (1942a). "Repeal of Neutrality Act." *American Journal of International Law* 36, pp. 8–23.

⸻ (1942b, 1964). *A Study of War.* Chicago: University of Chicago Press.

Wriston, Henry M. (1943). *Challenge to Freedom.* New York: Harper & Bros.

Yergin, Daniel (1977). *Shattered Peace: The Origins of the Cold War and the National Security State.* Boston: Houghton Mifflin.

York, Herbert F., and Greb, Allen G. (1977). "Military Research and Development, A Post-War History." *Bulletin of the Atomic Scientists*, January, pp. 13–26.

Young, Eugene J. (1936). *Powerful America: Our Place in Re-Arming the World.* New York: Stokes.

Young, Robert J. (1979). *In Command of France: French Foreign Policy and Military Planning, 1933–1940.* Cambridge: Harvard University Press.

_____ (1981). "French Military Intelligence and Nazi Germany, 1938–39." 53 pp. (paper).

Zaleski, Eugene (1980). *Stalinist Planning for Economic Growth, 1933–1952.* London: Macmillan.

Zeitzer, Glen (1981). "A Place for All: Recent Trends in American Peace History Writing." *American Studies International* 19, no. 3-4, pp. 49–57.

About the Book
and Author

In this significant study of U.S. foreign policy, Carlo Maria Santoro traces the origin and implementation of the key principles that guided U.S. actions in the postwar world. The author argues that the period of U.S. neutrality at the beginning of World War II was crucial in developing the concepts of interdependence and national security that remain integral to U.S. foreign policy today. The heart of the book is Santoro's detailed case study of the Council on Foreign Relations' War and Peace Studies project, which was a major source of the theories that have shaped policy-making.

Informed by the author's European perspective and sweeping grasp of the literature, the book presents a rich and complex analysis of competing schools of thought and methodological approaches to the making of U.S. foreign policy.

Carlo Maria Santoro is professor of international relations at the University of Milan and codirector of the Istituto per gli Studi di Politica Internazionale, Milan. He was visiting professor at Brown University and the School for Advanced International Studies at The Johns Hopkins University and an associate at the Center for International Affairs at Harvard University. Dr. Santoro has written extensively on American foreign and security policy, theories of international relations, and Italian foreign policy decision-making.

Index